CHINESE INDUSTRIAL ESPIONAGE

This new book is the first full account, inside or outside government, of China's efforts to acquire foreign technology.

Based on primary sources and meticulously researched, the book lays bare China's efforts to prosper technologically through others' achievements. For decades, China has operated an elaborate system to spot foreign technologies, acquire them by all conceivable means, and convert them into weapons and competitive goods – without compensating the owners. The director of the US National Security Agency recently called it "the greatest transfer of wealth in history."

Written by two of America's leading government analysts and an expert on Chinese cyber networks, this book describes these transfer processes comprehensively and in detail, providing the breadth and depth missing in other works. Drawing upon previously unexploited Chinese language sources, the authors begin by placing the new research within historical context, before examining the People's Republic of China's policy support for economic espionage, clandestine technology transfers, theft through cyberspace and its impact on the future of the US.

This book will be of much interest to students of Chinese politics, Asian security studies, US defense, US foreign policy and IR in general.

William C. Hannas has an MA from the University of Chicago in Chinese and a PhD from the University of Pennsylvania in Asian languages. He served with the US Navy and Joint Special Operations Command, taught at Georgetown University, and holds a senior executive position in a component of the US federal government. Hannas is author of *Asia's Orthographic Dilemma* (1997) and *The Writing on the Wall: How Asian Orthography Curbs Creativity* (2003).

James Mulvenon is Vice-President of Defense Group, Inc.'s Intelligence Division and Director of DGI's Center for Intelligence Research and Analysis. Trained as a Chinese linguist, he is a leading expert on Chinese cyber issues, and has published widely on Chinese military affairs, party-army relations, C4ISR, and nuclear weapons doctrine and organizations. He has a PhD in political science from the University of California, Los Angeles, and is author of *Soldiers of Fortune* (2000).

Anna B. Puglisi has MA and MS degrees in public affairs and environmental science, has worked in research and technical infrastructure, and now holds a senior analyst position in a component of the US federal government. Ms. Puglisi studied at the Princeton in Beijing Chinese language school and was a visiting scholar in Nankai University's Department of Economics, where she studied China's S&T policies, infrastructure development, and university reforms.

Asian Security Studies

Series Editors: Sumit Ganguly, *Indiana University, Bloomington,* Andrew Scobell, *Research and Development (RAND) Corporation, Santa Monica* and Joseph Chinyong Liow, *Nanyang Technological University, Singapore.*

Few regions of the world are fraught with as many security questions as Asia. Within this region it is possible to study great power rivalries, irredentist conflicts, nuclear and ballistic missile proliferation, secessionist movements, ethnoreligious conflicts and inter-state wars. This book series publishes the best possible scholarship on the security issues affecting the region, and includes detailed empirical studies, theoretically oriented case studies and policy-relevant analyses as well as more general works.

China and International Institutions
Alternate paths to global power
Marc Lanteigne

China's Rising Sea Power
The PLA Navy's Submarine Challenge
Peter Howarth

If China Attacks Taiwan
Military strategy, politics and economics
Edited by Steve Tsang

Chinese Civil-Military Relations
The transformation of the People's Liberation Army
Edited by Nan Li

The Chinese Army Today
Tradition and transformation for the 21st Century
Dennis J. Blasko

CHINESE INDUSTRIAL ESPIONAGE

Technology acquisition and military modernization

*William C. Hannas, James Mulvenon
and Anna B. Puglisi*

Routledge
Taylor & Francis Group

LONDON AND NEW YORK

First published 2013
by Routledge
2 Park Square, Milton Park, Abingdon, Oxon OX14 4RN

Simultaneously published in the USA and Canada
by Routledge
711 Third Avenue, New York, NY 10017

Routledge is an imprint of the Taylor & Francis Group, an informa business

British Library Cataloguing in Publication Data
A catalogue record for this book is available from the British Library

Library of Congress Cataloging-in-Publication Data
    Hannas, Wm. C., 1946–
    Chinese industrial espionage :
    technology acquisition and military modernisation /
    William C. Hannas, James Mulvenon, and Anna B. Puglisi.
    p. cm.—(Asian security studies)
    Includes bibliographical references and index.
    ISBN 978–0–415–82141–4 (hardback)—
    ISBN 978–0–415–82142–1 (pbk.)—
    ISBN 978–0–203–63017–4 (e-book)
    1. Business intelligence—China. 2. Business intelligence—United States.
    3. Technology transfer—China. 4. Technology transfer—United States.
    I. Mulvenon, James C., 1970– II. Puglisi, Anna B. III. Title.
    HD38.7.H363 2013
    338.6—dc23
    2012044273

ISBN13: 978–0–415–82141–4 (hbk)
ISBN13: 978–0–415–82142–1 (pbk)
ISBN13: 978–0–203–63017–4 (ebk)

Typeset in Baskerville
by Swales & Willis Ltd, Exeter, Devon

CONTENTS

ILLUSTRATIONS

Figure

Tables

ABBREVIATIONS

Acronym	Term
2PLA	PLA's Military Intelligence Department (Second Department)
211 Program	国家 211 工程项目 (National Project 211 Program)
3PLA	PLA's SIGINT organization (Third Department)
863 Program	国家高技术研究发展计划 (National High-Tech Development Plan)
973 Program	国家重点基础研究发展规划 (National Basic Research Program of China)
985 Program	国家985 重点建设项目 (National Development Program of Key Disciplines)
ACP	Association of Chinese Professionals
ACSE	Association of Chinese Scientists and Engineers
ACSEJ	Association of Chinese Scientists and Engineers in Japan
AD Reports	Armed Services Technical Information Agency Document
BDS	Beijing Document Service
CAE	Chinese Academy of Engineering
CAEP	Chinese Academy of Engineering Physics
CAIEP	China Association for the International Exchange of Personnel
CALIS	China Academic Library and Information System
CANS	CAST Network Society
CAPST	Chinese Association of Professionals in Science and Technology
CAS	Chinese Academy of Sciences
CAS-TAF	Chinese American Science and Technology Advancement Foundation
CASB	Chinese Association for Science and Business
CASEJ	Chinese Association of Scientists and Engineers in Japan

CASPA	Chinese American Semiconductor Professional Association
CAST	China Association for Science and Technology
CCP	Chinese Communist Party
CDSTIC	China Defense Science and Technology Information Center
CETIN	China Engineering and Technology Information Network
CFIUS	(US) Committee on Foreign Investment in the United States
CIE	Chinese Institute of Engineers
CNA	Computer Network Attack
CNE	Computer Network Exploitation
CNIS	China National Institute of Standardization
CNO	Computer Network Operations
COEA	China Overseas Exchange Association
CONUS	Continental United States
COSSP	China Overseas Students and Scholars Pioneer
COSTIND	Commission on Science and Technology Industry for National Defense
CSA	Chinese Scholars Association
CSIS	Canadian Security Intelligence Service
CSPA	Chinese Student Protection Act
CSSA	Chinese Students and Scholars Association
CSSTI	China Society for Scientific and Technical Information
CYBERCOM	(US) Cyber Command (USCYBERCOM)
DHS	(US) Department of Homeland Security
DOD	(US) Department of Defense
DOE	(US) Department of Energy
ECM	Electronic Countermeasures
FACPSU	Federation of Associations of Chinese Professionals in Southern USA
FBI	(US) Federal Bureau of Investigation
FDI	Foreign Direct Investment
GAO	(US) Government Accountability Office
GDP	Gross Domestic Product
GIG	(US) Global Information Grid
HUMINT	Human Intelligence
HYSTA	Hua Yuan Science and Technology Association
IAPCM	Institute of Applied Physics and Computational Mathematics
ICBM	Intercontinental Ballistic Missile
IEC	International Electrotechnical Commission
IFCSS	Independent Federation of Chinese Students and Scholars
IO	Information Operations
IOSS	Interagency OPSEC Support Staff
IP	Intellectual Property
IPR	Intellectual Property Rights
ISO	International Organization for Standardization

ISP	Internet Service Provider
ISTIC	Institute of Science and Technical Information of China
ITER	Tokamak Consortium
MII	Ministry of Information Industry
MIIT	Ministry of Industry and Information Technology
MLP	Medium and Long Term Plan for S&T Development
MNC	Multinational Company
MNE	Multinational Enterprise
MOA	Ministry of Agriculture
MOC	Ministry of Commerce
MOE	Ministry of Education
MOF	Ministry of Finance
MOFTEC	Ministry of Foreign Trade and Economic Cooperation
MOP	Ministry of Personnel
MOST	Ministry of Science and Technology
MSS	Ministry of State Security
NACAST	North America Chinese Association of Science and Technology
NACSA	Northern America Chinese Clean-tech and Semiconductor Association
NAIEC	North American Chinese Scholars International Exchange Center
NASA	National Aeronautics and Space Administration
NCIX	(US) Office of the National Counterintelligence Executive
NDRC	National Development and Reform Commission
NETL	National Engineering and Technology Library
NGO	Non-Governmental Organization
NIM	National Institute of Metrology
NIPRNET	Unclassified but Sensitive Internet Protocol (IP) Router Network
NISS	National Internet-based Science and Technology Information Service System
NLS	National Library of Standards
NNSF	National Natural Science Foundation
NSA	(US) National Security Agency
NSF	(US) National Science Foundation
NSFC	Natural Science Foundation of China
NSL	National Science Library
NSTL	National Science and Technology Library
NTIS	(US) National Technical Information Service
NTTC	National Technology Transfer Centers
NUAA	Nanjing University of Aeronautics and Astronautics
OCAO	Overseas Chinese Affairs Office
OCEPA	Overseas Chinese Entrepreneurs and Professionals Association
OCPAN	Overseas Chinese Professional Association Cooperation Network
OCS	Overseas Chinese Scholars

OECD	Organization for Economic Co-operation and Development
OIG	(US) Office of the Inspector General
OPSEC	Operations Security
OSINT	Open Source Intelligence
PACOM	(US) Pacific Command
PGP	Pretty Good Privacy
PLA	People's Liberation Army
PRC	People's Republic of China
PRO	Public Research Organizations
PRS	Permanent Resident Status
R&D	Research and Development
RAND	Research And Development Corporation
RMB	Renminbi
S&ED	Strategic and Economic Dialogue
S&T	Science and Technology
SAC	Standardization Administration of China
SAFEA	State Administration of Foreign Experts Affairs
SAPA	Sino-American Pharmaceutical Professionals Association
SATEC	Sino-American Technology and Engineering Conference
SCEA	Silicon Valley Chinese Engineers Association
SCIC	Society of Competitive Intelligence of China
SCOBA	Silicon Valley Overseas Chinese Business Association
SEVIS	Student and Exchange Visitor Information System
SIGINT	Signals Intelligence
SIPO	State Intellectual Property Office
SOF	Special Operations Forces
SSD	Strategic Security Dialouge
SSTC	State Science and Technology Commission
STAN	Structure Analysis Statistics
SVCACA	Silicon Valley Chinese American Computer Association
SVSTA	Silicon Valley Science and Technology Association
UCAPO	Union of Chinese American Professional Organization
UCTID	Center for US-China Technology Innovation and Development
USSR	Union of Soviet Socialist Republics
US	United States
WOFE	Wholly Owned Foreign Enterprise
WTO	World Trade Organization

ACKNOWLEDGMENTS

No one can undertake a project such as this without the support and inspiration of others. We wish to personally thank the following people for their contributions to our knowledge and for their help in creating this book.

To our many Chinese friends who over the years shared their culture, lives, and language with us, and opened a world of understanding not available through other means. For their courage and generosity in opening up to foreigners – may they one day enjoy the same freedoms that we do.

To our mentors Bob S, whose counsel was indispensible; Victor M, who taught scholarship and integrity; and Janice H, who encouraged new ways to think about things. It is through their teaching, encouragement, and support that we have grown professionally.

To Peter M and Matt B, for sharing materials and intense discussions that formed some core arguments of this book; to friends in the FBI on the front lines of this fight, especially Pete M, Charles L, Tom B, Sean K, Ben E, Dave B, Elic C, Mike D, Ted E, Christine G, Laura D, and Mike M; and to current and former practitioners elsewhere – Mike D, Peggy C, Randy B, John S, Steve H, Roger U, Nigel I, Ben B, Fred N, and many others who cannot be named because they are still in close quarters combat.

Most importantly to our spouses, Jennifer, Mary, and Don for their patience and love during the years of work and travel that fed into the book. And finally to our daughters, Tiffany, Kate, Ellie, and Siena, this book is our small attempt to provide you with a more secure future.

INTRODUCTION

This book is about how a third world country used the technology of the world's greatest power to dominate it economically and – perhaps – strategically as well.

Suppose someone told you in 1970 – when China was torn apart by civil war, the Soviet Union was furiously building nuclear weapons, and the United States had the strongest economy on earth – that within four decades there would be no Soviet Union, that America would be mired in debt and endless recession, and that China would be the world's economic superpower.

Suppose that person also claimed China would:

- have a $30 billion trade surplus with the US
- hold more than $1 trillion of our treasury debt
- build a million cars more than the US in a year
- outpace the US in domestic computer sales.

In addition, Chinese exports to America would be manufactured goods of increasing technical sophistication, while the top US export to China would be, literally, scrap and rubbish.

Suppose he then told you that China would achieve this role reversal with minimal investment in basic science, through a technology transfer apparatus that worked – mostly off the books – to suck in foreign proprietary achievements, while the world stood by and did nothing.

If this story were a novel it could not be marketed, even as science fiction.

One decade ago we would not have believed it ourselves. Like most Americans, we were aware of China's economic progress and of complaints that this progress relied in part on prior Western art. So what? This is the globalized twenty-first century. We patent products, they build them and pay royalties, the world moves on. Let the music industry worry about pirated CDs.

The point is that China was not – and is not – paying, and the "piracy" issue barely scratches the surface. Indeed, one could argue that our obsession with counterfeiting distracts us from the real threat from China, namely its ability to latch onto high technology created abroad, and apply it to real products – without compensating its owners.

This brings us to the heart of the matter. While giving due credit to the Chinese people for their ability to produce, China could not have engineered this transformation, nor sustained its progress today, without cheap and unrestricted access to other countries' technology.

By this we do not mean "business competitive intelligence" or the habits of other nations that supplement their own research with informal technology acquisitions. We are talking here of an elaborate, comprehensive system for spotting foreign technologies, acquiring them by every means imaginable, and converting them into weapons and competitive goods. There is nothing like it anywhere else in the world.[1] The system is enormous, befitting a nation of 1.3 billion, and operates on a scale that dwarfs China's own legitimate S&T enterprise. Very little of it is secret. The projects are laid out in policy documents, discussed in the media, and implemented through venues whose general features are open to inspection. While traditional espionage plays a role, it is relatively minor.

This is little appreciated outside China. While China's rise is chronicled everywhere, studies linking this rise to China's appropriation of foreign technology and talent are few – a curious fact given the attention paid in the West to tracking China's growth, and the resources China lavishes on the practices we describe. We trust the reader will see the logic of our argument as it unfolds.

The book begins with a review of China's early technology acquisition efforts, from its nineteenth-century attempt to "import what is useful and keep China's essence" (体用 or *ti-yong*) to post-1949 Soviet collaboration. Chapter 2 describes China's large and mostly unknown open-source collection network – ironically one of the country's few examples of genuine innovation. In Chapter 3 we discuss the phenomenon of foreign R&D in China, especially the rise of the now-ubiquitous multinational R&D laboratory.

Chapter 4 on PRC technology outreach organizations and Chapter 5 on Sino-American advocacy groups are complementary, depicting two halves of a well-managed whole. The latter will be the book's least favored chapter as it strikes close to home for many, but we present the facts as they are, as described by those involved. Chapter 6 focuses on Chinese students in the United States, particularly their critical role in postgraduate hard science programs, and assesses the potential implications for deemed exports and counter-intelligence.

In Chapter 7 we dissect the original Chinese policy documents governing the establishment and evolution of these transfer mechanisms and let the official record speak for itself. There is a thin line between stealing secrets and informal technology transfer, and China pursues the latter to the limit. In Chapters 8 and 9 we show where China exceeds that limit by clandestine procurement and through cyberspace.

Chapter 10 discusses transfer mechanisms not explored in the book's main body and suggests reasons why China chose this back door approach to development. In the Conclusion we propose steps which the United States and other countries can take to shield themselves.

The authors claim no expertise in counter-intelligence. Our backgrounds are science, private sector research, and academia with a common focus on foreign S&T. We were led down this path by the nature of Chinese science itself. If we add anything novel, it stems from our ability to read Chinese sources in the vernacular, not from privileged access that we have deliberately eschewed.

That said, we do not live in a vacuum. The authors are acutely aware that professionals in law enforcement, defense, intelligence, and commerce are frustrated by a lack of resources to protect our intellectual property, because the threat is not appreciated at all levels of government, and because government alone cannot deal with it. Hence the book has two purposes:

1. To alert decision-makers to the gravity of the China technology transfer problem so that means are provided to address it.
2. To raise awareness of the threat nationally, since no amount of formal intervention will matter if the owners of technology do not act on their own to protect it.

One caveat: we have no stake in embellishing the magnitude of this problem. Our bias is to *downplay* the matter to maintain credibility and avoid alienating responsible people. The truth is that China's program to relieve the world of its high technology is so excessive, and the evidence for it so overwhelming, that portraying it fully would convey the same paranoia which China exhibits.

A word of caution: indignation seldom leads to solutions. Railing at China for "stealing" is unlikely to have much effect. By the same token, we have read many statements in PRC media that point to a "responsibility" (义务) for Chinese the world over to transfer foreign technology by any means possible to atone for injustices. We prefer that people on both sides adopt cooler approaches.

Given our topic and the emotions that it generates, we are obliged to disclaim any connection between this book and persons or organizations with which we are or have been associated. The study was an independent labor of love and does not necessarily reflect the attitudes or equities of our employers past and present.

Note

1 Since 2000, when the US National Counterintelligence Executive (NCIX) started naming foreign countries in its unclassified annual report to Congress, China has ranked at the top and is the only country to have received its own dedicated issue. It is so skewed that the NCIX has considered publishing two annual reports: one for China, another for the rest of the world. National Counterintelligence Executive, *Foreign Economic and Industrial Espionage*, www.ncix.gov/publications/reports.

1

CHINA'S HISTORY OF RELYING ON WESTERN TECHNOLOGY

> In the 21st Century, if a particular country fails to be in the lead in science and technology, it will be difficult for it to maintain its economic activities and international standing.
>
> *Qian Xuesen (*钱学森*)*[1]

Despite early advances in technology, modern China[2] has struggled to regain its technical prowess in the midst of political upheavals, outside interventions, civil war, and bad policies. In the late Qing to early Republican era, Chinese leaders began efforts to import technology and send promising students abroad to "learn from the West."[3] Many of these students came back to lead aspects of China's development and reform, and many in the later waves went on to play critical roles in China's nuclear, space, and missile programs.[4] The concept that best captures the focus of the earlier phase, put forth in 1878 by Zhang Zhidong (张之洞) in his essay *Quan Xue Pian* (劝学篇, "Exhortation to Study"), is the principle of *ti-yong* or "keep China's style of learning to maintain societal *essence* and adopt western learning for practical *use*." While much has changed since the late 1800s, this formula of using skills learned from the West to make China strong has colored not only the post-Qing period but survives to this day, as it is a focus of China's 2006 to 2020 Plan for S&T development and the foundation for much of what this book is about.

Although not stated as such, the founding leaders of the People's Republic of China did not reject the *ti-yong* concept. China's post-1949 development, for example, depended critically on Soviet aid, scholars, and designs. Reforms to its S&T infrastructure during this period reflected Beijing's closer ties to the Soviet Union and emphasized central funding, a centralized academy, and five-year plans. The subsequent Soviet "betrayal" in the late 1950s and early 1960s substantially shaped the way in which foreign support was to be sought, as many in

Beijing blame the Soviets for their setbacks, despite the upheavals brought about by their own disastrous policy choices. None of these upheavals had as profound an impact on China's development – or lack thereof – as the Cultural Revolution (1966–1976), which brought science and technology to a halt, with the exception of a few military programs such as nuclear weapons and missiles. This last and most grandiose of Mao's "struggles" closed the universities and left China in technological shambles to compete with the West at its zenith of development. This "lost decade" as it is called[5] is still felt today as China tries to rebuild its university system and import Western-trained talent to re-create its scientific infrastructure.

This chapter provides the historical context for our discussion of China's technology transfer practices. We will show that while each time period is unique, with its own set of challenges, a common factor throughout has been the importance of foreign technology in China's strategic vision, implemented in large part by students and scholars, who use the skills, knowledge, and goodwill afforded them while abroad to bring foreign technology "back" and transform China's universities, companies, and defense industries into direct competitors of the United States.

"Self-strengthening" and reaching out towards the West[6]

Defeated by a technologically superior West in the Opium Wars (1842, 1860) and, far worse, by a Japan that had learned from these same Western powers (1895), China embarked on a cautious path to engage the West, not to become a full member of the world community but as a way to protect itself from further humiliation.[7] This engagement was characterized by a quest to "save" China through science. Because the focus of China's exam system was on literary and classical texts, there was no venue – and no incentive – in the traditional system for Chinese students to study modern science and technology. Any exposure to science took place at missionary schools set up by foreigners throughout the country which, while lambasted as vanguards of imperialism, played a transformative role in the evolution of Chinese attitudes toward education.[8]

During this period, the efficacy of the exam system was questioned and its role in holding back the development of modern science debated. The exam system was eventually abolished in 1905. However, while the promotion of "Western" science and educational reform continued, there remained an ingrained belief in Chinese *cultural* superiority and that the two – science and culture – could be put into separate bins.[9] John Fairbank, the great historian of China, perhaps described it best as China's leaders of the time clinging to the idea that the country could "leap half-way into modernization," using Western science and technology to support traditional Chinese society.[10] The same idea is evidenced in PRC science and technology policy literature even today.

This dualist approach was captured by Zhang Zhidong in the term *tǐ-yòng* (simplified Chinese: 体用, traditional Chinese: 體用), a concept framed during the reform era at the end of the Qing Dynasty (1644–1912). The term is made up of two Chinese morphemes: tǐ, meaning "essence", and yòng, meaning "practical use." It came to describe a method of self-strengthening whereby China would maintain its own style of learning to keep the "essence" of society, while at the same time using Western learning for "practical application" in developing its infrastructure and economy.[11] While probably not the original intent, China's own press today often describes the adoption of foreign systems, technologies, or ideas as being "X with Chinese characteristics" (中国特色某某) which retains the core notion of cultural separateness.

Another outcome of the debate was the formation of the Chinese Educational Mission in 1872, which altogether sent 120 students aged 12–15 to the United States to study.[12] They were placed with local families, with some attending prep schools to learn English before attending universities. Their "mission" was to learn Western science and engineering, in the hope that some would attend the US Military Academy at West Point, then return to China and pass on the knowledge and skills they acquired.[13] By 1881, changes in both China and the US[14] – including the passing of the Chinese Exclusion Act – prompted the Qing government to discontinue the program and the students returned home, many without having graduated. By some accounts, the reason for the change of heart was concern that the students were "losing touch with the Chinese culture and becoming completely westernized."[15]

Despite the important knowledge they acquired while studying overseas, upon return to China these students were excluded from higher level official positions and their loyalty was questioned.[16] Their experience forecast the fate of returnees in more recent times, who complained initially of being shunned by establishment colleagues. Professionalism eventually spoke for itself and many veterans of the mission went on to contribute to China's development. Their numbers included the first presidents of Qinghua and Tianjin universities, the first Prime Minister of the Republic of China and 17 naval officers. Some 13 of the group served in other diplomatic positions and 14 were chief engineers or managers on the railroads.[17]

Benefiting from Western support during a period of transition

In terms of our topic, we identify the period from the fall of the Qing Dynasty (1912) through the warlord era (1916–1927), the Republican era (1927–1937), war with Japan (1937–1945), and the founding of the People's Republic in 1949, as a time of transition. While we acknowledge the differences in the periods and their associated upheavals, academic activities during these years consistently reveal the same quest for foreign knowledge and the same drive for access to Western technology.

In 1909, some three decades after the China Educational Mission had ended, a second wave of Chinese students arrived in the US, supported by scholarships established by the Boxer Indemnity Program (Table 1.1).[18] America's Open Door Policy, which sought to prevent rival nations from carving out spheres of exclusive influence in China, had laid the foundation for the project, with Congress author-izing $12 million owed the US for damages during the Boxer Rebellion to fund Chinese education.[19] The money was earmarked specifically for study abroad and to establish the Qinghua School (later Qinghua University, a leading technical institution).[20] Negotiations over the agreement strangely resemble Sino–US nego-tiations today, with due concern for sovereignty and fairness, and wording to make it appear that both sides "won." As one study put it:

> In the final agreement, the plan made no reference to remission: the United States did not appear coercive, nor China subjugated.[21]

A sticking point was the conflicting views over what the project was to accomplish, with the US wanting Chinese students to absorb Christian culture, while China wanted US know-how.[22] The debate is characterized by T.K. Chu as follows:

> [T]he cultural basis for sending students to America to study was to protect its institutionalized Confucianism. With the technical know-how of building strong battleships and powerful cannons, China could ward off aggressions and hence encroachment on its cultural traditions.

If you substitute "democracy" for "Christianity" one could argue that this debate presaged the current dispute over the importance and usefulness of Chinese stu-dents in the United States, where proponents of more robust S&T collaboration

TABLE 1.1 Accomplishments of Students who Participated in the China Educational Mission or Boxer Indemnity Program

Name	Program	Place of Study	Accomplishments
Qian Xuesen (钱学森)[23]	Boxer	CalTech, MIT	Father of China's rocket program, early proponent of open source data mining
Tang Guo'an (唐国安)[24]	CEM	Philips Exeter and Yale	First president of Qinghua University
Cai Shaoji (蔡绍基)[25]	CEM	Yale	First president of Tianjin University
Tang Shaoyi (唐绍仪)[26]	CEM	Yale	First president of Shandong University and ROC (1912–49) cabinet minister
Jiang Tingfu (蔣廷黻)[27]	Boxer	Columbia	Head of Qinghua History Department, diplomat
Chen Hengzhe (陈衡哲)[28]	Boxer	Vassar and University of Chicago	Beijing University
Guo Bingwen (郭秉文)[29]	Boxer	Wooster/Columbia	Transformed Nanjing University

For an in-depth look at Qian Xuesen, who became a key figure in China's missile development pro-gram, see Iris Chang, *Thread of the Silkworm*, Basic Books, 1995.

expound on how living in the US will make Chinese scholars more democratic and open, and thus supportive of US policies. Similarly, one can argue that today, as in the past, China continues to view Western education pragmatically as a means to acquire what it needs, and still frets about the added baggage of political reform.

China not only benefited from students and scholars studying abroad, but also from foreigners coming to China to help rebuild its moribund university system, so that China was eventually able to train its own students. Although China's modern universities were established indigenously in the late 1800s – Tianjin in 1895, Shanghai Jiaotong in 1896, Zhejiang in 1897, and Peking (Beijing) in 1898[30] – interactions with leading international universities helped to build modern curricula. Two such relationships in particular highlight the role of Western and Western-trained scholars in the development of Chinese universities.

The first is China's relationship with Columbia University, and with Paul Monroe in particular, who received an honorary degree from Beijing University in 1913. Monroe contributed to the development of modern curricula in China and worked with several Chinese students – including Guo Bingwen (郭秉文), Tao Xingzhi (陶行知), Chen Heqin (陈鹤琴), Jiang Menglin (蒋梦麟), and Zhang Boling (张伯苓) – who became leaders in Chinese education.[31] The second is the history of Qinghua University, which was established as mentioned above by the Boxer Indemnity Fund. Qinghua's (also Tsing Hua) instructors were recruited from the United States and its students were taught both "Chinese traditional culture and western knowledge."[32] The university continues that tradition today as it is on the leading edge of hiring foreign deans and professors, and incorporating Western-inspired changes to its curriculum and programs.[33]

As is the case today, the United States was not the only foreign destination for Chinese students. Many studied in Europe and returned to make significant contributions to China. Key among them were Beijing University chancellor Cai Yuanpei (蔡元培), who studied in Germany, several top experts who worked on the nuclear program and had spent time in France, and early leaders of the Chinese Communist Party, such as Deng Xiaoping and Zhou Enlai.

During the period after the Chinese Educational Mission and before the Boxer Indemnity Program had begun, very few Chinese students went to the US, as their preferred destination was Japan. The first such group arrived in Japan in 1896,[34] with the number expanding rapidly through the early 1900s. It is estimated that by 1906 Japan was host to almost 12,000 Chinese students.[35] Wang Xiaochu of Beijing University parsed the trend into five distinct periods as follows:[36]

1. 1896–1911   Study in Japan takes off.
2. 1912–1930   Chinese students in Japan develop a political sense.
3. 1931–1945   Tortuous period caused by the Sino–Japanese War.
4. 1946–1976   Depressed numbers coming from Communist China.
5. 1977–present   Restoration and high tide.

This characterization ignores the large number of Taiwanese who not only studied in Japan but were educated under the Japanese system in their native province during Japan's occupation (1895–1945). Many Chinese scholars believe that the early wave of students who returned to China from Japan had a major influence on China's military modernization,[37] as many studied military subjects there. Notable Chinese leaders who studied in Japan are Sun Yat-sen, Lu Xun, and Zhou Enlai.

Founding of the PRC – a move toward the USSR

While the founding of the People's Republic of China in 1949 seemed to entail a dramatic shift in China's S&T development policies – and in some ways it did – Beijing continued to look abroad for the means to build its technological capabilities. As part of Mao Zedong's "lean to one side" (一边倒) policy of moving China closer to the Soviet Union,[38] China established a centralized or "Soviet" S&T infrastructure.[39] This model placed the center of gravity for research in institutes associated with the country's Academy of Sciences[40] and de-emphasized research at universities. The idea was to create a pipeline through which developments from the institutes would flow into industry and, subsequently, to the economy or military.[41] Applied science was emphasized over basic science, inhibiting what little progress China made during the first half of the century in establishing modern universities.[42] From the early 1950s on, a premium was placed on heavy industry – concrete and tangible products – with non-experts awarded leadership positions both at the institutes and the leading universities, which had been the recipients of new ideas in previous decades.

China benefited enormously from the influx of Soviet scientists and engineers who came to set up and run the new institutes and industries, including strategic programs in nuclear weapons.[43] As in previous decades, China sent students abroad, but the number sent to the Soviet Union was unprecedented. In all, some 38,000 Chinese went to the Soviet Union for training and study.[44] Most were technical workers from priority industries, but there were also students, teachers and scholars. Included are China's former Presidents Hu Jintao (胡锦涛) and Jiang Zemin (江泽民), and former Premier Li Peng (李鹏).

China's first Five-year Plan (1953–1957) depended heavily on Soviet aid with some 156 major industrial projects in mining, power generation, and other heavy industries supported.[45] These transfers were facilitated by 11,000 Soviet scientific and technical personnel working in China at the height of Sino–Soviet cooperation. The majority were in heavy industries such as steel.[46] A Joint Sino–Soviet Commission for Cooperation in Science and Technology was formed that ran from 1954 until 1963 and put together over 100 major scientific projects. China was so dependent on the Soviet Union for its scientific base that a draft of the Chinese Academy of Sciences' 12-year plan for development in 1956 was sent to the Soviet Academy of Sciences for review.

Perhaps the most important area of support was the nuclear weapons program. In September 1956 the Sino–Soviet agreement on aid to the nuclear industry was signed in Moscow as part of the 12-year plan for S&T development.[47] The agreement provided technicians, blueprints, training, and support for uranium enrichment facilities and the industrial infrastructure needed to build a nuclear weapons program. In addition to Soviet support, the key scientists who worked on the program, namely Qian Sanqiang (钱三强) and Yang Chengzong (楊承宗), were both trained in France and used their experience as a force multiplier for the early developments. Nie Rongzhen (聂荣臻), Director of China's Science and Technology Commission and the man who ran the early nuclear weapons program, had studied in Belgium prior to the revolution. Nie credited the Soviets with providing prototypes for other military systems as well, including guided missiles, aircraft, and the technical data to support their production.[48]

Soviet abandonment and the Cultural Revolution

By the fall of 1960, all Soviet experts and advisors had been recalled from China, taking with them the know-how and technology needed to propel China's development. The progress made over the first decade of the People's Republic came to a halt both as a consequence of the Soviet withdrawal and the cumulative indigenous policy disasters that followed. In 1958 Mao launched the "Great Leap Forward" (大跃进), a fairy-tale scheme to expedite development by placing more emphasis on "red" than expert.[49] Among its outlandish goals was an aspiration to surpass the United Kingdom in steel production in three years. The "experiment" ended two years later, with predictable results – not to mention one of the greatest famines in world history.

Perhaps the one policy that had the worst impact on China's fledgling S&T programs was "walking on two legs" (两条腿走路),[50] a reference to Mao's plan to simultaneously develop both agriculture and industry, which in practice meant de-emphasizing everything but heavy industry. A corollary was the idea that anyone could do science. Unqualified workers were encouraged – sometimes under the Russian technicians' noses – to "improve" Soviet blueprints and prototypes. This had a lasting effect, especially in areas where China lacked returned experts such as heavy aircraft and engines, but less of an impact in those areas where domestic experts had experience, such as missile development and nuclear weapons.[51]

Mao's encore was the "Great Cultural Revolution" (文化大革命, 1966–1976), which threw the country into political turmoil, affecting the support and management of key strategic programs. The Cultural Revolution destroyed the nascent infrastructure that had grown, in fits and starts, since 1949.[52] Universities were closed or became sites of armed conflict. Experts or anyone with Western experience were "sent down" (下放) to the countryside and a whole generation of Chinese had its educational opportunities taken away or delayed.[53] China also recalled its overseas scholars and did not send students abroad again until 1978.

To understand how devastating the Cultural Revolution was to Chinese S&T development, one need only look at the events at Qinghua University. Established through the Boxer Indemnity Fund, by the late 1960s the university had evolved into a successful place of higher learning with many of its faculty having received an overseas education and enrolling only students with the highest credentials. By contrast, after closing entirely during the first part of the Cultural Revolution, Qinghua reopened in 1970 to enroll a class of "worker, peasant, soldier students."[54] The students arrived on campus with little formal education and on the recommendation of their political chain of command.[55] Scholarship and academic achievement were waived. Similar follies took place at universities across the country.[56]

Beijing later claimed that the Soviet pull-out, caused in part by tensions between Soviet leader Nikita Khrushchev and Mao, led to the cancellation of 34 major contracts and 257 other technical projects. While this "betrayal" undoubtedly contributed to China's lack of progress, the role of China's own policies in the breakdown can hardly be discounted.

A work in progress: rebuilding after the Cultural Revolution

Sending out the students to foreign countries was never for China a matter of cultural exchange. The goal is to make China a strong country—a fact which the overseas students must face.

Qian Ning[57]

If importing Western know-how had been a consistent goal before the Cultural Revolution, the devastation wrought by it strengthened the need to acquire technology by any means. The post-revolution period also broke with the non-specialist focus that Mao had championed. That the "red over expert" theme wasn't working became poignantly apparent in China's humiliating military defeat by Vietnam in 1979, a watershed event that drove home the desperateness of China's situation to its new leadership. China had already begun to appreciate that in addition to rebuilding institutions such as research institutes and universities, it also had to rebuild its human capital. This is best characterized by efforts that started in 1978 to restore ranks and titles, re-establish professional societies, and recognize technical achievement.[58] Early negotiations with the US science advisor included the first post-Mao requests China made to send students to the US.[59]

In 1978, the "Four Modernizations" (四个现代化) were adopted by the National People's Congress some 15 years after they had first been proposed. The reforms aimed at making China a world power by the twenty-first century through investment in agriculture, industry, S&T, and national defense. While vague, it constituted an initial developmental plan that went beyond the heavy industry, capital-intensive focus of the Sino–Soviet days to establish a broader set of advances for a new class of professionals to execute. China enjoyed two advantages in its efforts to rebuild. First, unencumbered by existing plans and infrastructure – there were none – it could lay out a new foundation for growth that was supported by new technologies. Second, in the most striking change of heart of the century, the same China that had relied on Soviet support to counter the US in the

1950s could position itself to benefit from America's Cold War concerns by renewing its technological links and educational exchanges with the United States.

In the post-Mao era, foreign know-how was seen as a catalyst to jump-start China's quest for capable military systems and industries, and to build capacity for the future. The first wave of post-CR students to go abroad tended to reflect this approach as well. They were older than even their American advisors, and sought overwhelmingly to study some aspect of technology or hard science.

China's embrace of science and technology crystallized in its adoption of the National High-Tech R&D Program (国家高技术研究发展计划), also known as the 863 Program.[60] Implemented in 1986, the program was personally endorsed by Deng Xiaoping and was designed to "meet new global challenges and competition."[61] Described accurately as China's "Sputnik" moment and "new technical revolution" (新技术革命),[62] the program is focused on biology, spaceflight, IT, lasers, automation, energy, new materials, and oceanography – each a key element in China's plan to develop world-class capabilities. The government's role was and continues to be macro-control and support.[63] Specific projects within the program are determined by a committee of experts, who look to international research developments to set priorities; Chinese research, however, is typically more applied. Launched by China's Ministry of Science and Technology (MOST), the program impacts all sectors of the country's science and technology enterprise and is tied closely to defense projects. A ceremony held in 2001 to celebrate the achievements of the 863 Program was hosted jointly by the MOST and the PLA General Armaments Department, chief developer of military technology systems.[64] That same year the program was re-evaluated *with the help of foreign experts* and widened to support China's competitiveness in international markets.

China has several other centrally directed programs focused on improving different aspects of the S&T infrastructure. They include the "Torch Program" (火炬计划) for creating high-tech commercial industries; the 973 Program (国家重点基础研究发展规划) for basic research; the 985 (国家985重点建设项目) and 211 Programs (国家211工程项目) aimed at university reform; and countless programs for attracting Western-trained scholars "back" to China, which are discussed in detail in Chapter 7. Each of these programs looks to foreign collaboration and technologies to cover key gaps, and each reaches out to Western-trained experts for support, both by returning to China and by "serving in place."[65]

Perhaps in no other document can we see how the past and the future merge than in China's *Medium and Long Term Plan for S&T Development, 2006–2020* (中长期科技发展规划, 2006–2020). This S&T blueprint lays out a development strategy that is still reliant on returnees,[66] still reliant on foreign collaboration, and adds a new dynamic of using the R&D laboratories of international companies that have flocked to China as another medium through which it can acquire the skills needed for China to move forward. This latter development is explored in detail in Chapter 3. The MLP, more than previous plans, demonstrates how far China has come since opening its doors in the late 1970s as it focuses as much on the process of science as it does on the specific topic areas it seeks to develop.[67]

One aspect of China's S&T development which we have not yet discussed is the difference between its ability to access foreign technology and to assimilate it. In the early days of the PRC, as best demonstrated by the failures of the Sino–Soviet cooperative period, China was at such a low level of technological development that it could not assimilate all that it acquired from the Soviet Union and needed Soviet experts to drive development to serve as the intellectual leaders for the projects. Today, however, as highlighted by scientific indicators such as patents and publications in Western journals,[68] it is evident that China's efforts over the past three decades have yielded gains in many fields, including a taste for science itself, and the technology and know-how acquired from abroad has a much more fertile place to grow roots.

Legacy of the ti-yong period still felt today

China's approach to technology development is both strategic and pragmatic, reflecting the evolution of early ideas of self-sufficiency into a far broader acceptance of the need for foreign technology to meet strategic goals – without losing sight of the original imperative to build things indigenously. This dichotomy, namely to seek Western technology while continuing to search for a distinctly Chinese way, confounds Western scholars and policy-makers, since we often think of the question in black or white terms – innovation vs. acquisition, and creativity vs. copying. In fact, a more nuanced view of what is happening in Chinese S&T is necessary to grasp the impact these developments will have on competitiveness.

What we see when we look at China's early period and subsequent decades of S&T development is a desire to meet, by whatever means are necessary, the strategic goals of the time – whatever they may be – while at the same time building a system that can eventually self-perpetuate and be self-sufficient. The image of a China forging a unique path that suits its needs at a given time is put forth by Nathan Sivin in his description of post-Mao science, noting that "China has gradually since 1949, by fits and by starts, invented policies towards education and science that reflect its own priorities rather than the expectations of other nations."[69] Simplifying the picture as one of total dependence on Western technology or – worse – China's "maturation" into a fair and sharing player in the world S&T arena misrepresents the threat its hybrid approach poses to the West.

The one feature that has been a central tenet of Chinese development from the late Republican to early Qing era through to today is the active role of the government in facilitating China's "catch-up" to ensure that China benefits from its interactions with the West and also to set the terms of those interactions to achieve goals determined by the state. Chinese students are sent out to learn with a purpose, and its business and S&T collaborations are a zero-sum game, with the goal being China "winning" and meeting its strategic goals. While Beijing has not always been successful in this endeavor, especially during the decades of political chaos, the efforts that will be outlined in subsequent chapters illustrate a government with a plan and the political will to use whatever means are necessary

(以多种方式) to acquire the "seed corn" of innovation and technology, as a means to catch up and eventually lead.

The following chapters examine each aspect of China's foreign technology acquisition efforts and how these aspects have evolved over time, reflecting China's developmental level, international status, and potential for access. Beijing's approach today is similar to its historic approach, differing only in the number of tools in the toolkit it can use to its advantage. Its methods of acquisition are holistic and comprehensive, using students, businesses, and overseas organizations as part of a complex web that on the surface appears to blend with international norms, but on further examination reveals the true agenda: one-sided technology acquisition, and an approach to the international community of science that is opaque. We begin by examining one of the least-known elements of this web: China's exploitation of open-source materials.

Notes

1 Qian Xuesen (1911–2009) benefited from the Boxer Indemnity Fund. He was later sent back to China under suspicion of spying during the McCarthy era and became a key figure in China's missile development program. For an in-depth look at his life see I. Chang, *Thread of the Silkworm*, New York: Basic Books, 1995.

2 Modern China refers to the 1909 to current time period. J.D. Spence, *The Search for Modern China*, New York: Norton, 1999, pp. 225–226.

3 For an overview of US–China educational exchanges from the 1800s to the founding of the PRC, see D.M. Lampton, *A Relationship Restored*, Washington, DC: National Academies Press, 1986, pp. 16–20.

4 "Returned Students and HEP Research in China," Institute of High Energy Physics, October 10, 2002, www.ihep.ac.cn/english/r.s.&hep/index.htm. According to the Institute for High Energy Physics, "It can be said that the development of high energy physics in China is inseparable from the returned students."

5 Scholars refer to this period as the lost decade in which an entire generation lost out on educational opportunities, and their absence currently affects Chinese academic "bench-strength" to this day.

6 For the purposes of this project, we look at a small snapshot of Chinese history, from the late 1800s to the present day. We focus here on the period when China fell behind the West in areas with direct applications to military and technological development. The time period of "self-strengthening" referred to here is from 1860 to 1900.

7 Edwin Pak-wah Leung, "China's Decision to Send Students to the West," *Asian Profile* 16 (1998), pp. 391–400, p. 392, pp. 399–400.

8 For additional information on engineering education in this time period see Junqiu Wang, Nathan McNeill, and, Sensen Li, "Growing Pains: Chinese Engineering Education in the late Qing Dynasty," 2010 ASEE Annual Conference and Expo.

9 This is mentioned here not to evoke the issue of how Chinese students are viewed in the US today or Chinese nationalism and ethnocentric views, but to highlight the concerns and suspicions in China at the time.

10 John King Fairbank, *The United States and China*, 4th edn, Cambridge, MA: Harvard University Press, 1983, pp. 173–176.

11 Spence, *The Search for Modern China*, pp. 225–226.

12 *The New York Times*, "The Chinese Educational Mission," August 18, 1873.

13 Jin Baicheng, "Early Educational Mission", *China Daily*, April 22, 2004, www.chinadaily.com.cn/english/doc/2004-04/22/content_325340.htm.

14 T.K. Chu, "150 Years of Chinese Students in America," *Harvard China Review*, Spring 2004, pp. 7–26.

15 Jin, "Early Educational Mission."

16 Stacy Bieler, *Patriots or Traitors? A History of American-Educated Chinese Students*, Armonk, NY: ME Sharpe, 2004, p.12.

17 Thomas E. LaFargue, *China's First Hunger: Education Mission Students in the United States, 1872–1881*, Pullman: Washington State University Press, pp. 77–78, pp. 107–108.

18 Bieler, *Patriots or Traitors?*

19 China's "Righteous Harmony Movement" (義和團运动) known in the West as the "Boxer Rebellion" was a popular reaction to the foreign presence in China and received ad-hoc support from the Qing government. The uprising culminated in the siege of foreigners in Beijing's Legation Quarter in June 1900, their emancipation by an eight-nation military force some two months later, and fines imposed on China, known subsequently as the Boxer Indemnity.

20 "History of Tsinghua," University of Tsinghua, 2001, www.tsinghua.edu.cn/publish/then/5779/index.html.

21 Chu, "150 years of Chinese Students in America."

22 Ibid.

23 For an in-depth look at Qian Xuesen, who became a key figure in China's missile development program, see Chang, *Thread of the Silkworm*.

24 Jin, "Early Educational Mission."

25 Ibid.

26 Ibid.

27 Bieler, *Patriots or Traitors?*

28 Ibid.

29 Ibid.

30 See "Tsinghua University," China Education Center Ltd., 2012, www.chinaeducenter.com/en/university/tsinghua.php; "Beijing University," China Internet Information Center, 2012, www.china.org.cn/english/features/beijing/31059.htm; "Introduction to Zhejiang University," Zhejiang University, 2012, www.zju.edu.cn/english/redir.php?catalog_id=235, "Shanghai Jiao Tong University," China Education Center Ltd., 2012, www.chinaeducenter.com/en/university/sjtu.php.

31 Bieler, *Patriots or Traitors?*

32 Ping Kuang and Ian Marshall, "Internationalisation of Chinese Higher Education: Application of Knowledge Management to Analysis of Tsinghua University," *Journal of Knowledge Management Practice* 11, no. 1, March 2010.

33 For more information on reforms at Tsinghua University see "Welcome to Tsinghua University," Tsinghua University, www.at0086.com/TsinghuaU/; Li Yuhong and Yin Qi, "Tsinghua's Foreign Academic Connection," *China Daily*, April 16, 2011, www.chinadaily.com.cn/opinion/2011-04/16/content_12336800.htm; Hao Xin and Dennis Normile, "Gunning for the Ivy League," *Science* 319, no. 5860, January 11, 2008; and Kuang and Marshall, "Internationalisation of Chinese Higher Education."

34 Linqing Yao, "The Chinese Overseas Students: An Overview of the Flows Change," Australian Population Society Biennial Conference, September 2004, www.apa.org.au/upload/2004-6C_Yao.pdf.

35 Chu, "150 years of Chinese Students in America."

36 Wang Xiaochu, "Retrospect and Revelation of the 110-year History of Chinese Returned Students in Japan," April 2004, Chinese National Knowledge Infrastructure, SUN:XZSB.0.2006-04-00.

37 Yang Dongming and Ji Changhe, "Talking about the Students Studying in Japan and China's Modernization," January 2001, Chinese National Knowledge Infrastructure, ISSN:1006-1975.0.2005-01-016; and WANG Jian-hua, "On the Relation between Japan and Modernization of Military Education in Late Qing Dynasty," May 2004, Chinese National Knowledge Institute, CNKI:SUN:AFSX.0.2004-05-009.

38 "Formulation of Foreign Policy of New China on the Eve of its Birth," Ministry of

Public Affairs of the People's Republic of China, November 17, 2000, www.fmprc.gov.cn/eng/ziliao/3602/3604/t18057.htm.

39 Richard P. Suttmeier, *Research and Revolution: Science Policy and Societal Change in China*, Lexington, MA: Lexington Books, 1974.

40 The Chinese Academy of Science was established in 1949: Chinese Academy of Science, October 25, 2012, www.cas.ac.cn/.

41 Richard P. Suttmeier, "New Directions in Chinese Science and Technology," in John Major, ed., *China Briefing*, Boulder, CO: Westview Press, 1986, pp. 91–102.

42 We refer to modern universities as those that offer both a robust teaching and research environment, which is very different from the Soviet system.

43 John Lewis and Litai Xue, *China Builds the Bomb*, Palo Alto, CA: Stanford University Press, 1988.

44 "A Country Study: China," The Library of Congress Country Studies, August 24, 2012, http://lcweb2.loc.gov/frd/cs/cntoc.html.

45 Ibid.

46 Ibid.

47 Lewis and Xue, *China Builds the Bomb*, p. 51.

48 Ibid.

49 Mao Zedong, "On the People's Democratic Dictatorship 30 June 1949," *Mao Zedong xuanji (Selected Works of Mao Zedong)*, Beijing: The People's Press, 1965.

50 Lewis and Xue, *China Builds the Bomb*.

51 Ibid.

52 Charles P. Ridley, *China's Scientific Policies: Implications for International Cooperation*, Washington, DC: American Enterprise Institute, October 1976.

53 Xin Meng and R.G. Gregory, "The Impact of Interrupted Education on Subsequent Educational Attainment: A Cost of the Chinese Cultural Revolution, Economic and Cultural Change," *Economic Development and Cultural Change* 50, no.4, July 2002, pp. 935–959 and "Front Matter," *The China Quarterly* 95, 1983, pp. f1–f6.

54 He Chongling, *Qinghua Daxue jiushi nian (Qinghua University ninety years)*, Beijing: Tsinghua University Press, 2001.

55 Ibid.

56 "History of Tsinghua," University of Tsinghua.

57 Qian Ning (钱宁). 留学美国 (*Studying in America*). Nanjing: Jiangsu Wenyi Chubanshe, 1996.

58 Leo A. Orleans, ed., *Science in Contemporary China*, Palo Alto, CA: Stanford University Press, 1980, p.39.

59 Chu, "150 years of Chinese Students in America."

60 The plan was jointly proposed by four Chinese scientists: Wang Daheng (王大珩), Wang Ganchang (王淦昌), Yang Jiachi (杨嘉墀), and Chen Fangyun (陈芳允), to accelerate China's high-tech development. "National High-tech R&D Program (863 Program)," Ministry of Science and Technology of the People's Republic of China, www.most.gov.cn/eng/programmes1/200610/t20061009_36225.htm.

61 www.863.gov.cn/.

62 Evan Osno. "Green Giant: Beijing's Crash Program for Clean Energy," *The New Yorker*, December 21, 2009, www.newyorker.com/reporting/2009/12/21/091221fa_fact_osnos.

63 "National Programs for Science and Technology," Chinese Government's Official Web Portal, 2012, www.gov.cn/english/2006-02/09/content_184156.htm.

64 Du Minghua, "863 Hi-Tech Program Blueprinting China's Future," January 1, 2001, www.edu.cn/achievement_1509/20060323/t20060323_4403.shtml.

65 Chinese government policy documents at www.china.org.cn/english/scitech/34496.htm, www.most.cn/eng/ and Cao Cong, Richard Suttmeier, and Denis Fred Simon, "China's 15-Year Science and Technology Plan," *Physics Today* 59, no. 12, December 2006, pp. 38–43.

66 "New Policies to be Issued to Lure Overseas Students Home," *People's Daily*, July 29, 2000; "China Allotted 200 Million Yuan for Students Returned from Overseas," *People's Daily*, January 22, 2002, http://english.people.com.cn/200201/22/eng20020122_89125. shtml. The funds have gone to 4,000 students who returned to China permanently and 3,000 who came back on a short-term basis, 中国留学人材信息网--回国指南 (Chinese Study Abroad Talent Information Network–Return to China Guide), www. chinatalents.gov.cn/hgzn/index02.htm.
67 Cao et al., "China's 15-y Science and Technology Plan."
68 James McGregor, "China's Drive for Indigenous Innovation: A Web of Industrial Policies," Washington, DC: US Chamber of Commerce, July 2010.
69 Nathan Sivin, "Science in China's Past," *Science in Contemporary China*, ed. Leo Orleans, Palo Alto, CA: Stanford University Press, 1980.

2

CHINA'S USE OF OPEN SOURCES

During the 1950s, when the PRC government was being consolidated, China's modernization depended critically on three props: Soviet aid, overseas scholars, and foreign scientific literature. There is a tendency today in China to downplay the importance of these non-Chinese elements and to stress indigenous contributions. While no one denies the role of early Soviet support, its termination in the late 1950s is said to have forced China down an independent path to scientific advancement.[1] Betrayed by Russia and denied free access to the world's technology, China relied on its own legacy of creative genius.

The difficulty here lies in how one interprets "indigenous." As shown in the previous chapter, the scientists who ran China's laboratories and technology programs were precisely those people who had studied abroad. Although Chinese in one sense, the knowledge they brought "back" with them was entirely foreign. Also overlooked is the degree to which China counted, and still counts, on openly available foreign information to jump-start innovation and short-cut the R&D cycle. Whereas all science begins with prior art, in China the systematic use of foreign sources to promote S&T development has been elevated literally to an "information/intelligence science" (*qingbaoxue* 情报学).

This chapter traces the growth of this open-source exploitation system. In the first section we examine early PRC institutions and practices. In the second section we take a closer look at the inner workings of China's "*qingbao*" (情报, intelligence/ information) network through an unusual book written by two architects of the system – a disclosure not likely to be repeated. In the third section we describe the system's present structure and its leading organization: the Institute of Scientific and Technical Information of China. Other first-tier open-source organizations are scrutinized in the fourth section: Beijing Document Service, China Defense S&T Information Center, Patent Documentation Library, and National Library of Standards. In the chapter's final section we examine some subsidiary organizations that contribute to the national open-source effort.

Building a national S&T open-source system

Chinese who specialize in foreign S&T exploitation date the emergence of a national open-source "intelligence/information" system from 1956.[2] In August of that year, the PRC State Council promulgated a "1956–1967 Long-term Plan for the Development of Science and Technology," which included as article 57 the following statement:

> The responsibility of S&T intelligence work is to report the most recent accomplishments and trends in domestic and foreign science in all types of important scientific and technological fields so that scientific, technological, economic and higher education departments get timely access to the information and materials needed to facilitate the absorption of modern scientific and technological accomplishments, reduce time and manpower, avoid duplication of work, and promote the development of science and technology in China.[3]

In keeping with the plan, S&T information offices (科技情报所) appeared that same year to support China's armaments industry, along with a new Scientific Information Institute (科学情报研究所) under the Chinese Academy of Sciences.[4] By late 1957, the Institute was researching how to match foreign science and technology information with China's concrete needs. In 1958, it was reconstituted as the Institute of Scientific and Technical Information of China (中国科学技术情报研究所, ISTIC), the "first and central element of the national system"[5] and China's foremost facility for acquiring, processing, and distributing foreign S&T materials.[6]

Also in 1958, a Chinese University of Science and Technology Information (中国科学技术情报大学) was established, the world's only known example, with departments of S&T information, translation and library science. Like ISTIC, it was focused on foreign materials.[7] The year also saw the first of a series of "National S&T Information Work Meetings." Delegates to the meeting produced five documents defining the goals and methods of China's S&T open-source system, including instructions on how to strengthen S&T information work, a list of principles and techniques, a proposed structure for a national S&T intelligence network, secrecy rules, and training requirements for "information workers."[8]

These calculated efforts to put the exploitation of foreign information on a rational footing contrasted with the chaos overtaking the country during its "Great Leap Forward" (1958–1960). While peasants were melting down their farm tools in backyard steel furnaces, the State Science and Technology Commission, predecessor to the Ministry of Science and Technology, in 1959 created an S&T Information Office (科技情报局) to coordinate S&T "information work" nationally. In

December the first specialized journal on S&T information appeared, along with a magazine devoted to methods of searching English-language periodicals.[9] ISTIC established a Chongqing branch in the heart of China's military R&D district to translate foreign technical documents, which by 1966 had reached several hundred thousand items.[10]

Meanwhile, a second National S&T Information Work Meeting in 1961 wrote guidelines for "national S&T document registration, search and retrieval" including three sets of regulations for foreign S&T documents, foreign S&T translations, and foreign S&T materials brought back by personnel going abroad. A third meeting in 1963 set out goals to 1972, defined responsibilities of S&T information organizations within the State Council's technical ministries, and provided another set of rules for information units at both provincial and local level.

By the mid-1960s, most ministries, state committees, provinces, municipalities, large firms, research institutes, and universities had their own S&T information organizations linked by networks for exchange that crossed regional and even national boundaries – a fully elaborated S&T information system and service network to support China's technical development. By 1966, a decade after it started, the system had garnered and was making available to end users 11,000 different foreign S&T periodicals; half a million foreign research reports, government publications, conference proceedings and academic theses; over five million foreign patents from 20-odd countries; more than 200,000 standards from 40 foreign countries; several hundred thousand foreign product samples; and had S&T document exchange links with more than 50 countries.[11]

The goal of China's S&T information system during this early period was to "size up" developments abroad so as to "improve China's ability to do scientific research, copy things (仿制) and make products," according to Chen Zeqian and Bai Xianyang, who studied the system's evolution. Its aim, in their words, was to "reflect comprehensively, accurately, and in a timely manner" the trends and developments in foreign S&T. "Intelligence/information work" (情报 工作) – China's term for systematically tapping foreign and domestic information – was the "main process for thoroughly understanding international S&T developments."[12]

This "information work" was limited at first to finding and translating foreign publications into Chinese but, as was noted above, this developed quickly into an end-to-end system with multiple layers of redundancy. As Miao Qihao, former director of ISTIC's Shanghai branch, stated:

> A unique feature of the Chinese *qingbao* system is that from its very outset, it has combined an intelligence function with conventional information activity.[13]

In other words, the system was targeted not at S&T information per se but at specific types of information useful primarily to the defense industry, graded by feedback loops and metrics. By the early 1960s, it was providing critical support to

China's nuclear weapons research, satellite launches, and the mainframe comput-ers used for military development.[14]

Data on the workings of the *qingbao* system for 1966 to 1975 are scant; those Chinese who comment on it lament the lack of progress, here and elsewhere, dur-ing the so-called Cultural Revolution.[15] National S&T Information Work Meet-ings did not reconvene until 1975 – a 12-year hiatus – and it was not until 1977 that the enterprise got back on track with the release by the State Science and Technology Commission of an S&T development plan that prescribed updated responsibilities for the S&T information system.[16]

This plan departed from past practice by mandating the use of advanced tech-nology for the acquisition and distribution of S&T materials, thus closing the circle: China would use foreign technology to improve its ability to exploit foreign tech-nology. The following year, 1978, was marked by three significant developments:

1. The China Society for Scientific and Technical Information (中国科学技术情报学会)—a professional group of S&T information workers founded in 1964 but dormant during the Cultural Revolution – convened its first meet-ing. The group renewed its commitment to "broadly collect foreign scientific and technical information materials through all types of venues." Units at all levels resumed their gathering of foreign S&T materials.[17]
2. ISTIC enrolled its first group of graduate students in "S&T information" (科技情报), followed by Beijing University, Wuhan University, and other top colleges. Analogies outside China to this new academic discipline would be "library science" or, to stretch things, "scientometrics" albeit limited to S&T topics and focused on foreign materials. Essentially this was a graduate degree in exploiting foreign scientific literature.
3. The Beijing Document Service (北京文献服务处), a key provider of foreign military S&T information, was founded by COSTIND's S&T Intel-ligence Bureau and the Beijing Science and Technology Association (北京市科技协会).

Another milestone was the Fifth National S&T Information Work Meeting in 1980, where a decision was made to tie intelligence work closely to economic con-struction and S&T development and to "broadly exploit" (广辟) novel informa-tion sources. This newer period is characterized by Chen and Bai as one of "inte-grated research and policy support" with greater "processing" of information, closer coordination with key national projects and their specific technologies, and an emphasis on solving "knotty" problems in research and production.[18] At this juncture, China's open source system had become, in all respects, a component of its all-source intelligence network targeting specific technologies for particular customers.

In 1982, the China Society for Scientific and Technical Information held its first policy seminar and issued recommendations, exercising its function as a "mass organization" that translates state doctrine to collectors and marshals their compliance. Two years later, a sixth S&T information work meeting created guidelines for computer search and retrieval, document indexing, format standardization, and professional training. The SSTC re-established its defunct S&T Information Office for national oversight; ISTIC began conducting directed searches for customers in support of technical programs; and the first databases and automatic abstract compilers began operating.[19]

By 1985 there were 412 major S&T intelligence institutes nationwide, including 35 attached to the State Council's technical ministries, 33 at the provincial and municipal levels, and 344 local institutes employing more than 25,000 people.[20] Miao Qihao, the Shanghai ISTIC Director, adds to that figure some 3,000 "basic cells" in grassroots units such as companies and labs for a total of 60,000 workers engaged full time by 1985 in data processing (investigating, collecting, sifting, analyzing, synthesizing, and repackaging data "in response to specific requirements"), database mining, benchmarking, and "reverse engineering."[21]

The proliferation of units engaged in S&T information work led to efforts by oversight bodies to reorganize the network. In a notice dated January 1989, the Science Commission stated:

> Up to now China's S&T information system has been in possession of a large volume of S&T documents that have had an important role in advancing the country's economy and S&T development. However, it is still far from adequate and many problems remain. We have not been able to form an effective system of document resource support. It lacks unified organization and its distribution is irrational. Some areas [of China] have a surplus of documents with duplication and underutilization, while other areas do not have enough. We are not reporting adequately on the content of our holdings, indexing is incomplete, and we lack national and local registries of publications. Most of the document handling and storage is done by hand. There are a limited number of document databases and a rational division of labor between different systems across networks cannot be carried out. And we are not spending enough on document acquisition.[22]

The Commission laid out three general requirements for: a comprehensive solution in which the particular natures and responsibilities of individual components are clarified and made to supplement one another; horizontal integration of the main organizations; and different levels for the nationwide system, including state, specialized ministries and departments, and local levels.

It went on to specify the five "main national level organizations" as follows (Chinese names are those given in the 1989 document):

1. *Institute of Scientific and Technical Information of China* (中国科技情报所).[23] "This is the national comprehensive S&T information center primarily responsible for collecting and storing documents on engineering technology, management science, and high technology."

2. *Chinese Academy of Sciences National Science Library* (中国科学院文献情报中心). "This is the national natural sciences information center primarily responsible for collecting and storing documents on mathematics, physics, chemistry, astronomy, geography, biology, hyphenated disciplines, and high technology."

3. *COSTIND S&T Intelligence Bureau* (国防科学技术工业委员会科技情报研究所). "This is the national military S&T information center primarily responsible for collecting and storing documents on military technology, engineering, weapons, and equipment."[24]

4. *China Patent Office Documentation Library* (中国专利局文献馆).[25] "This is the national patents document center, responsible for collecting and storing documents such as patent manuals, patent announcements, and patent category indices."

5. *State Bureau of Technical Supervision Standards Information Center* (国家技术监督局标准情报中心).[26] "This is the national standards document center responsible for collecting and storing documents on international standards, regional standards, national standards, standards for particular industries, and corporate standards."

These first-tier (一级) units were collectively tasked with the "basic collating and distributing of the original foreign language documents in their holdings that the foreign magnetic tape services bring in." A second tier (二级) was made up of two "levels": (1) "S&T information centers in the State Council's [technical] departments and committees that collect and store documents closely related to their own specialties," and (2) local S&T information organizations "at the provincial and municipal region level, and at the local city and county level. The scope of their document collection is determined by their [own] economic and S&T planning."[27]

A second major reorganization occurred in June 2000 when the State Council established the National Science and Technology Library (国家科技图书文献中心), "a virtual S&T document information service organization"[28] that subsumed ISTIC, the National Science Library, and three other technical libraries, completing the transition of China's open-source intelligence system to one that is primarily library-based. Other proposals addressed modernization and professionalization of the system's cadre:[29]

• To the traditional tasks of publishing and translation were added "aggregation and analysis of intelligence and information" (情报信息综合分析), software research, timely service, and an emphasis on end user consultation.

• China began looking at new methods for "collecting, transmitting, and managing foreign languages, text, voice, images, tables and data."

• An earlier requirement for entry into the "intelligence corps" (情报队伍) to be "good in one area" (一技之长), such as a technical discipline or foreign language, was no longer considered adequate. The modern open-source worker had to bring to the job IT skills, management savvy, and an academic background.

- Open-source workers were also asked to play a larger role in the intelligence process, becoming a "think-tank" (思想库) for the party and government by providing top leaders with information and playing a direct role in the policy-making process (出谋划策).
- "Security consciousness" (安全意识) also came to be a factor.

Although some reductions were made in the number of institutes and personnel, this was a consequence of greater automation, particularly web-based services. The role of open source itself continued to grow. According to Science Ministry statistics, by 2005 there were 15,782 people working in 353 S&T information institutes, down from some 20,000 people in 433 institutes in 1995.[30] Despite this absolute decline, the figures *increased* relative to the number of people and institutes engaged in real R&D: from 8.36 S&T information institutes per 100 R&D institutes in 1997 to 11.95 per 100 in 2005. The corresponding figures for personnel were 3.14 S&T information workers per 100 R&D personnel in 1997 and 5.62 per 100 in 2005.[31]

The same was true of budgets. According to ISTIC's Chen Jiugeng, the annual funding increase from 1997 through 2005 for S&T information institutes exceeded the growth of state expenditure on R&D, absolutely and per capita.[32] It is hard to see how investment like this supports China's stated goal of becoming a scientifically "creative nation" (创新型国家), except in the restricted sense of "creatively" adapting other countries' creations.

Chen provides the statistics in Table 2.1 on the combined holdings of the 353 institutes in 2005, which gives a sense of the operation's scale.

More statistics: in 2005 the number of networks used to host and distribute S&T information among the 353 institutes was 50,534, servicing 27 million "users" (用户, not requests). Chinese who accessed *overseas* networks through the institutes to obtain foreign S&T materials directly numbered slightly over one million.[33]

These are impressive numbers, which is not surprising since the *qingbao* system is largely library-based. Or is it library-based because that is the only way to manage a system this big? The key facts, however, that distinguish it from "libraries" as commonly understood are: (1) the Chinese system is run by intelligence experts working for the government, (2) in concert with end users, and (3) to short-cut R&D by leaning on foreign models. As Chen and Bai note,

TABLE 2.1 Combined Holdings of Chinese S&T Information Institutes

Foreign conference papers	1.2 million
Foreign S&T reports	1.8 million
Foreign periodicals	270,000
Microfilmed products	9.8 million
Audio-visual products	330,000
Titles and abstracts in databases	4.722 billion records
Full text documents in databases	644 million records

Through more than 50 years of development, the scope and scale of China's S&T information enterprise has continuously expanded. It has supported and advised the selection and research of comprehensive, forward-looking, and strategic key issues of the greatest concern to leaders and management at all levels, providing solutions for technology breakthroughs and management and policy decisions.[34]

S&T innovation in China is driven by foreign developments, tracked through open sources. Solutions to technical problems are culled from a knowledge base of prior art, freeing Chinese resources for commercialization and production. While this approach to innovation – the "early adapter" – is hardly unique, what differs with the Chinese system is its scale, and the degree to which it characterizes the entire R&D enterprise. In the following section we look more closely at how the system works in practice.

The view from China's "Spy Guide"

In 1991, two years after the State Science and Technology Commission reorganized China's open-source intelligence system into its modern form, a remarkable book appeared describing the system's goals, methodology, and targets. Entitled *Sources and Methods of Obtaining National Defense Science and Technology Intelligence* (国防科技情报源及获取技术), the book is a comprehensive account of China's foreign military open-source collection, comprehensive enough to prompt one reviewer to call it "China's Spy Guide."[35] Since the book deals with one intelligence venue only – open source – the nickname is overkill. But its characterization of open source as an element of PRC espionage is spot on.

Sources and Methods is based on materials compiled by authors Huo Zhongwen (霍忠文) and Wang Zongxiao (王宗孝) for a graduate course at the China Defense Science and Technology Information Center (CDSTIC), one of the five national open-source intelligence organizations that emerged from the 1989 regrouping. Although they do not acknowledge it, the authors likely played a key role in the overall system's evolution. Many recommendations that appear in the 1991 book parallel the 1989 document on which the reorganization was based. If you allow for preparation and time-to-publication, it is likely that drafts of this 361-page volume predate the SSTC edict. As its authors state, the impetus for "a rational overall arrangement of national defense S&T document resources was begun by COSTIND's S&T Intelligence Bureau in 1986" (i.e., Huo and Wang's home unit), and spread to "each respective intelligence organization."[36]

It is also worth speculating on how a book like this saw the light of day. One reason may be that it was not as big an anomaly in China as it seemed to be in the West. When Bruce Gilley drew attention to the book a decade after its release, materials on this topic were still available in Chinese. Huo and Wang admit their debt to "papers and books written by many of our domestic colleagues" and their bibliography contains a good sample.[37] Thus the only real secret was the West's failure to notice it. Another reason for the book's release may be that the publishers took its thesis for granted. The use of foreign models to guide S&T development is so pervasive in China that no one imagined any comeback.

Huo and Wang begin their book by noting that the volume and variety of S&T information now available require changes in the way in which it is sought and managed. The old ways of operating could not deal with the explosion in foreign sources. These prior practices included: (1) gathering data and waiting for customers to use it; (2) judging quality from the amount of information collected; (3) focusing on written documents only; (4) considering one's own collection in isolation; (5) hiring staff simply because they know a foreign language; and (6) spending without planning.[38]

The new paradigm, which the authors helped put into practice, involves: (1) targeted collection; (2) metrics based on customer feedback; (3) collecting all types of media and making it available in database form; (4) treating collection as a science governed by systems theory; (5) hiring staff with IT skills who can adapt to consumer demand; and (6) planning before spending.[39]

Intelligence to the authors is a "science" and much of the book is spent explicating its theoretical basis as a prelude to their practical recommendations.[40] Collection, the basis for intelligence, is not simply a task but a complex social activity with continuous dialog among all of its elements. The emphasis must always be on consumer needs and helping consumers understand these needs, based in part on what is *available* for exploitation. In China, part of the collector's role is to inform consumers about what is realistically possible based on what may be found.[41]

So what does China collect? Huo and Wang provide a summary:

> S&T periodicals, conference records, S&T reports, government publications, academic degree treatises, S&T books, standards, product samples, patent documents, and others (such as newspapers, technical archives, and drawings).

Verbal information, an area of intelligence not normally associated with open source and usually gathered by a country's clandestine services, is prized by the authors for its timeliness and accuracy. It is more current than written records. You get it instantaneously instead of two years after the lab experiments were conducted.[42] It is also easier to collect:

> The party presenting a lecture or the two parties in a discussion are lecturing or having a dialogue within the bounds of a determined topic, and obtaining intelligence from a colleague who is studying the same topic is clearly more suited to one's needs and much more convenient than searching through the relevant sections scattered in hundreds or thousands of documents. Secondly, because the feedback in verbal exchanges is rapid, when there is something you don't understand, you can ask about it and clear it up, and when you find some new intelligence leads, you can pursue them.[43]

The authors categorize foreign sources by how they are obtained: scanning type, tracking type, surveillance type, topical collection, and complete set collection, access to which is described in terms of an elaborate search theory. The efficiency of collection is assessed then by "numerical probability values," such as:

> the probability of collecting the needed information within the period of time stipulated by the consumer; the mathematical expectation of the amount of the needed information that will be collected within the period of time stipulated by the consumer; and the mathematical expectation of the amount of time required to collect the needed information, etc.[44]

They go on to propose a collection taxonomy based on media type, the level of processing, technical nature of the content, its field of application, transmission means, user demands, time constraints, level of expectation (the information's predictability), whether the sources are "internal" (Chinese) or "external" (foreign), specialized or synthesized, organized or diffuse, the level of compression, accuracy of content, and the probability of its existing at all.[45] Everything is tagged and binned. Nothing is overlooked. Source evaluation is based on an indexing scheme that takes into account reliability, suitability, timeliness, availability, cost, and ease of decoding. A number of formulas are proposed to quantify these evaluations.[46]

An entire chapter (6) is given to explaining transmission channels for information – what to do with it after you get it – for example, serial, centralized, ring, bilateral, and mutual, each having its own advantages or drawbacks for passing information from collectors to user. Other characteristics such as time, capacity, susceptibility to interference and, of course, security are also discussed.

The technical nature of S&T materials, the sophisticated requirements of consumers, and the rigors of "scientific" collection demand a professional cadre of open-source specialists working constantly "according to fixed collection policies." By the authors' count these workers populate some "4,000 intelligence organizations throughout all of China."[47] This figure roughly matches the ISTIC officials' estimates (cited above) for the mid-1980s of 412 major S&T intelligence institutes, another 3,000 basic cells, and an undisclosed number of S&T novelty search centers.

To clarify their topics, Huo and Wang give examples of real sources they have used. They acknowledge the Lockheed Corporation with its "Dialog database" online dissemination system.[48] They also describe the AD reports sold by the US National Technical Information Service (NTIS). US military standards are highly valued:

> The US Naval Printing and Publishing Center sells them in book form, while the American National Standards Institute sells them both in book and film form. The US Information Processing Service Corp. sells them in cassette film form, while the Global Engineering Documents company in the United States can output a section or sections of the military standards data in book form, depending on the user's specific requirements.[49]

PRC open-source collectors are enjoined to learn the "information output periods" of foreign sources and to scrutinize publication schedules, especially plans to declassify secret materials. One such case involved a *Nuclear Weapons Data Handbook* published in the United States:

> The first volume was published in January 1984, and while it was originally determined that the next one published would be volume three, the publication plan was again adjusted so that they issued volume two in April 1987. There are some S&T personnel who are anxiously waiting to read this series.[50]

Under "Response time to user needs" we find:

> Take for example when you want to buy a publication of the US Congress that has already been issued openly. Buying it through an information source like the China National Publications Import and Export Corporation takes about one year before you receive it. Buying it overseas through an information source such as an institution with an overseas office generally takes about two to three months before you get it. However, using the express collection method of a certain document company, in general you will get the material in two to three weeks.[51]

In describing "characteristics of national defense intelligence sources" the authors explain (with examples drawn from NASA, RAND, and NTIS) that the data are often classified. However:

> A common saying has it that there are no walls that completely block the wind, nor is absolute secrecy achievable, and invariably there will be numerous open situations in which things are revealed, either in a tangible or intangible form. By picking here and there among the vast amount of public materials and accumulating information a drop at a time, often it is possible to basically reveal the outlines of some secret intelligence, and this is particularly true in the case of the Western countries.[52]

Sometimes collectors get lucky thanks to careless declassification decisions, one of which led to the release of a top-secret DOE report on thermonuclear weapons. In the authors' words, "It was like finding a rare treasure."[53] Huo and Wang cite another example of US mistakes that bring cheer to their workday:

> From 1971 to 1976, the US Department of Energy conducted declassification reviews of a large amount of classified material, covering a total of 2.8 million items, of which 1.5 million were declassified. At the Los Alamos National Laboratory, they reviewed a total of 388,000 documents in 33 days, so each reviewer had to review around 1,000 documents a day, about

two a minute. The pace of the reviews was startling, and resulted in a large number of errors — around five percent – that is, some 19,400 documents were mistakenly declassified, and of these there were at least eight highly secret items regarding thermonuclear weapons, which ended up being open material that could be browsed freely by outside visitors.[54]

They conclude:

> This incident tells us that, on the one hand, absolute secrecy is not attainable, while on the other hand, there is a random element involved in the discovery of secret intelligence sources, and to turn this randomness into inevitability, it is necessary that there be those who monitor some sectors and areas with regularity and vigilance.[55]

Reference works published by foreign countries on their open-source holdings are used by Chinese intelligence officers as a short cut to identify materials. Other such indices are compiled locally in China (e.g., *Searching Foreign Science and Technology Documents and Materials* by ISTIC,[56] and *Basic Knowledge About Chemical Literature* by Yang Shanji and Yang Jingran, (1981):

> This book focuses on introducing chemistry and chemical engineering materials that are commonly seen in foreign countries, including periodicals, conference proceedings, scientific and technical reports, patents, abstracts, summaries, book series and collections, dictionaries, and various large reference works. The book has 12 chapters in all, which are, in order: Overview of Books and Literature; Periodicals – An Important Information Source; Document Search Tools; Scope and Application of the Index of the US Chemical Abstracts; Summaries, Collections, S&T Reports and Academic Degree Treatises; Patents and Searching Them; Dictionaries, Handbooks, Physics Tables and Spectral Data; Organic Chemistry Reference Books; Inorganic Analysis, Chemical Engineering, and Materials Reference Works; S&T Literature Retrieval Services; Development Trends in Chemical Information Retrieval; and Books and Materials.[57]

In a section entitled "Typical National Defense Intelligence Sources and Materials" Huo and Wang list several US sources. Congressional publications, particularly those by committees on national defense and appropriations, are analyzed in detail. The authors say that these sources yield data on:

- The US military's view and estimate of the world situation.
- The research and development plan for American weapons and equipment, as well as the objectives and rationale for the Americans' development of various kinds of strategic weapons, conventional weapons, and C³I.
- The status of American investment in the development of weapons and equipment.

- The status of scientific research, testing, and evaluation of American weapons and equipment.[58]

They also make use of the Congressional Information Service, through which "you can find on your own all the Congressional publications and statistical information you need," especially "AD reports" (Armed Services Technical Information Agency Document), which are described accurately as "scientific research reports on research projects funded or assisted financially by the US Department of Defense."[59] Moreover:

> The content of AD reports touches upon every area of national defense S&T, such as aviation, space technology, guided missile technology, nuclear technology, ordnance, military science, electricity and electronic engineering, communications research, etc. Therefore we can say that AD reports are a major source of intelligence on national defense S&T work.[60]

Huo and Wang show detailed knowledge of AD reports' declassification procedures, their numbering schema, the organizational histories of US agencies producing and distributing the reports, and their distribution schedules. Besides CDSTIC itself, ISTIC's main Shanghai and Sichuan branches, and the Beijing Document Service, all have complete sets.[61]

The book describes everything a collector needs to know about NTIS: what materials it makes available from whom, in what formats, its structure and customer base.[62] NASA reports are described in eight pages of detail. The American Institute of Aeronautics and Astronautics gets five pages. DOE reports get another five pages; their value is described as follows:

> DOE reports include a large number which are concerned with research into nuclear energy, and which involve dual military–civilian uses. Examples are reactors of various types (including those used on ships); nuclear power systems used in space; research, development, testing, and production of nuclear weapons; laser nuclear fusion technology; isotope separation technology; production and control of nuclear material; nuclear material safety issues; personnel security issues; secret information security issues; export control issues; nuclear weapons control issues; nuclear power stations, etc. This portion of the reports continually gets a great deal of attention from those engaged in national defense S&T work in various countries, and it is a source of intelligence with great value.[63]

PRC collectors are given 13 pages of advice on how to exploit US military standards, which:

> can be used for reference in formulating one's own standards. Referring to them can yield an understanding and a grasp of the level of technology and

developmental trends in US military industrial products. It can improve the
level of one's own research and design, promote the technical transformation of industrial enterprises, accelerate innovation and upgrade to new gen-
erations of products, improve operations and management, expand foreign
trade and exports, and increase economic efficiency.[64]

The authors go through a list of open sources with military applications in the US
and Britain, including publications of governments and private think-tanks, specialized books, periodicals, and conference papers. The last are described in detail
according to type, format, organizations publishing them, their intelligence value,
and problems collecting and exploiting them.[65] On the subject of S&T periodicals
we learn:

> As an intelligence source, they are the first choice of rank-and-file S&T
> personnel as well as intelligence researchers. According to estimates,
> S&T personnel and intelligence workers obtain 60 percent and 80 percent,
> respectively, of their S&T intelligence from periodicals.[66]

According to the authors, in 1985 CDSTIC subscribed to 1,022 of these foreign-
language periodicals. Some 45 of the top 56 foreign journals (measured by use)
were from the US and Britain. Of the top 60 (measured by their value to China),
53 were US and British journals.[67]

Huo and Wang go on to describe the IBM-based "strategic intelligence database system" used by CDSTIC in the 1980s to process all of these data:

> The strategic intelligence resource database system was designed to meet
> the needs of the China National Defense S&T Data Center's intelligence
> researchers in their strategic research on weapons facilities development,
> and the needs of information collection operators in developing strategic
> information resources. Its purpose is to help intelligence researchers find
> the information they need for their own research subjects as quickly as pos-
> sible; and to help information collectors to study, understand and master
> the circumstances, special features and publication rules of foreign strategic
> information resources.[68]

There are sub-databases with information on foreign "organization names,
addresses, cable and telephone numbers, histories of changes and developments,
nature of missions, distinguishing features, leadership organizations, financial circumstances, primary activities, publications and databases." A sub-system on foreign persons contains:

> given names and surnames, gender, biographical notes, work and home
> addresses, occupations, achievements, writings, range of primary activities,
> recent work circumstances, and whether they have visited China. It can

display or print out all information according to name and whatever the database contains according to special subject category numbers, and the circumstances of all persons engaged in any special activity.[69]

So China's open-source collectors not only provide information on foreign technology, they also serve up profiles of foreign organizations and persons with access to this information, for use by other PRC intelligence services.

Huo and Wang make a few other points that bear on our present study. They support our own observation that open-source intelligence in China is library-based. In their words: "Information work is a spin-off of library science. It has benefited significantly from library science. Methods such as indexing and abstracting are very successful because they are the foundation of library science."[70]

They also confirm in a roundabout way that Chinese researchers are expected to look first at foreign projects before starting their own projects. In a passage on "obstacles" to the use of foreign information, Huo and Wang note that there are people in China who do not believe copying, benchmarking, and reverse engineering are the right way to do science:

> In principle, the advance and development of science and technology are the true desire in achieving China's economic vitality. In reality, this has not been universally accepted by society. There are many important people in society who consider intelligence and information work to have a "supplemental" status and function in China's economic construction.[71]

In other words, there are Chinese scientists who prefer to do their own research and we suspect many of them ended up emigrating abroad. This does not mean they do not benefit China nonetheless, as we demonstrate in later chapters.

Finally, after several tortuous pages discussing the meaning of *qingbao* and the differences between "information" and "intelligence," the authors come clean with an innocuous admission that "There are similarities between what we refer to as 'information' and what the foreign intelligence community refers to as intelligence work."[72]

We examine these nuances toward the end of this chapter. Meanwhile, thanks are due to Huo and Wang for a wonderfully detailed snapshot of one part of China's open-source intelligence system as it looked three decades ago. And for all their complaints about its inadequacies, it is – on an international scale – a model then and now of how open-source intelligence should be done. In the remainder of this chapter we look at how the system is constituted today.

ISTIC and the structure of open source in China

China's apparatus for exploiting foreign science is complex and redundant, as one would expect of a system in use for half a century. The country's size, the paramount role of mimicry in its S&T development, and bureaucratic inertia make this proliferation of organizations inevitable. That said, there is a logic to its "design" that invites admiration.

There are five distinct levels of "S&T information organizations" in China today, including a dozen or so national organizations (depending on how they are counted); another 89 attached to technical ministries and State Council committees; 303 S&T information bodies at the provincial and municipal levels; about 3,600 information offices in company units ("basic cells"); and some 400 websites nationwide for exchanging S&T information. These figures have remained roughly constant for two decades, although the number of websites continues to grow.

Another taxonomy divides these organizations by type, including:

> (1) Professional S&T information management organizations. (2) Comprehensive and specialized S&T information enterprises. (3) Local and specialized S&T information networks. There are also (4) document centers engaged in important S&T information activities, S&T libraries, and universities and training centers that offer majors in information [management], along with state, collective and privately run S&T information organizations. Finally, there are (5) society-based resources engaged in information activities, such as personnel involved in information [gathering] as an adjunct to their regular jobs, retired S&T personnel, and translators. Types 1–4 are main components of the "national S&T information system" and type 5s are supplementary resources.[73]

No matter how you slice it, there is a huge number of organizations and people in China today that collect, analyze, and communicate foreign S&T information to state, military, and corporate consumers. Our focus for the rest of this chapter is on the national bodies, which are:

1. The National Science and Technology Library (国家科技图书文献中心, NSTL), a virtual organization formed in 2000 that encompasses four major "libraries" including ISTIC.
2. China Defense Science and Technology Information Center (中国国防科技信息中心), i.e., Huo and Wang's organization, of which the Beijing Document Service (北京文献服务处) is a part.
3. Patent Documentation Library (专利文献馆) and its adjunct China Patent Information Center (中国专利信息中心).
4. National Library of Standards (国家标准馆), part of the China National Institute of Standardization (中国标准化研究院).

The NSTL has four divisions for basic science, engineering, agriculture, and health. They are:

1. The Chinese Academy of Sciences' National Science Library (中国科学院文献情报中心).

2. National Engineering and Technology Library (国家工程技术(数字)图书馆, NETL), which like NSTL is a virtual organization.
3. Library of the Chinese Academy of Agricultural Science (中国农业科学院图书馆).
4. Library of the Chinese Academy of Medical Sciences (中国医学科学院图书馆).

The China National Institute of Standardization and the National Institute of Metrology (中国计量科学研究院) are credited on NSTL's website as joint sponsors but are functionally independent and treated separately here.

Drilling down further, the NETL itself comprises four major components:

1. The Institute of Scientific and Technical Information of China (ISTIC, 中国科学技术信息研究所).
2. China Machine Industry Information Institute (机械工业信息研究院).
3. China Metallurgical Information and Standardization Research Institute (冶金工业信息标准研究院).
4. China National Chemical Information Center (中国化工信息中心).

These institutes are depicted in Figure 2.1. We omit a few supporting organizations that are discussed toward the end of this chapter.

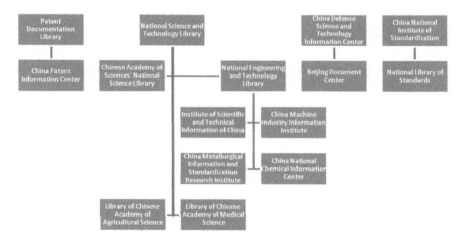

FIGURE 2.1 China's Foreign S&T OSINT Organizations

The National Science and Technology Library, one of the four top-tier elements, was created by China's State Council in June 2000 as "the authoritative Chinese repository and service center for S&T document information and resources."[74] A virtual organization, it has no holdings of its own. Its purpose is to direct and coordinate the activities of member libraries. The NSTL's main responsibilities are:

to exercise overall planning and coordination, collect in a more integrated way domestic and foreign document and information resources, draft data processing standards and norms, build S&T document databases, utilize modern networking technology, provide multi-level services, promote the joint creation and sharing of S&T document and information resources, organize in depth development of S&T document and information resources and their digitized application, and expand cooperation and exchange between China and the world.[75]

Member libraries manage their own operations according to guidelines laid down by the NSTL board, which is made up of scientists, open-source specialists, and library representatives. Actual leadership is vested in the Ministry of Science and Technology.[76]

NSTL also runs a comprehensive distribution network called the "National Internet-based Science and Technology Information Service System" (NISS) that makes the holdings of member libraries available to the public round the clock. As of 2004, its online retrieval services offered access to some 26 million items, including 4.9 million foreign journals; 1.8 million foreign S&T conference papers; some 900,000 foreign dissertations, reports and standards; and about 11 million foreign patents. Subscribers get navigational support for "important science and technology websites from all over the world."[77]

Beyond its own (vertical) hierarchy, NSTL has resource-sharing agreements with the horizontal components of the system – CDSTIC and the patents and standards libraries – along with major PRC libraries outside the defined system, including the National Library of China, the China Academic Library and Information System (CALIS),[78] and the Shanghai Library – a merger of the former Shanghai Library and Shanghai S&T Information Institute (上海科学技术情报研究所), one of many such composite S&T information organizations in China that were consolidated over the past two decades.[79]

As illustrated in Figure 2.1, NSTL's four member libraries are the National Science Library, the National Engineering and Technology Library, and libraries for agriculture and medicine. The latter two are not within the scope of the present study, while the former two are central to it.

The National Science Library, also known as the Library of the Chinese Academy of Sciences and the CAS Document Information Center (中国科学院文献情报中心),[80] is managed by a board of trustees appointed by the CAS. It has a main library in Beijing, with branches in Shanghai, Wuhan, Lanzhou, and Chengdu;[81] 120 document information offices at R&D institutes throughout China; smaller collections attached to factories, schools, and publishing houses; and some two dozen specialized information networks.[82]

The NSL regards itself as NSTL's "key member" and the "national reserve library for natural sciences and high tech literature."[83] Some 70 percent of its holdings are in the fields of mathematics, physics, chemistry, astronomy, geology, biology, electronics, computers, semiconductors, and nuclear energy.[84] In his 2006

study Chen Jiugeng called NSL and its branches China's "basic science information resources system" and credited it with 6.3 million books, 21.8 million issues of
periodicals, and 13.4 million "other types of documents" in natural science, basic
science, and new and high technology.[85] NSL itself claims:

> a collection of about 11.5 million items. In recent years it acquired or devel-
> oped more than 30 databases, covering over 5,000 foreign science, technol-
> ogy and medicine full text journals, 11,000 Chinese full text journals, 80,000
> foreign theses and dissertations, 180,000 e-books, and an increasing number
> of full text proceedings and reference books, all accessible from 89 CAS
> institutes over 24 cities across China. NSL provides an interlibrary loan sys-
> tem connecting every CAS institute, and connecting to NSTL and major
> academic libraries, delivering documents within two working days from a
> pool of more than 20,000 foreign journals.[86]

NSL branch libraries serve regional needs. The library in Lanzhou, a backwater
notable for its proximity to China's nuclear weapons industry, collects "special
document information" and conducts "deep-level studies" for local research institutes. It has some 50,000 visitors annually and fields more than 100,000 queries
a year from its 1.7 million document holdings. Its specialties include chemistry,
chemical engineering, nuclear science, applied mathematics, and computer science. Unspecified "strategic information research" (战略情报研究) is also done
by the branch on demand.[87]

The engineering counterpart within NSTL to the National Science Library is
the National Engineering and Technology Library (NETL), an umbrella organization for the China Machine Industry Information Institute,[88] China Metallurgical
Information and Standardization Research Institute,[89] China National Chemical
Information Center,[90] and those offices within the Institute of Scientific and Technical Information of China concerned with engineering. Chen credited the NETL
in 2006 with more than 7,000 types of foreign-language periodicals and with
providing online access to some two million foreign and domestic documents.[91]

NETL's aggregated holdings are in electronics, automation, computers and
networks, materials science, environmental science, aerospace, biotech, energy,
transportation, architecture, hydraulics, and other engineering fields in general.
Beyond its five million books, the library has been adding some 4,200 foreign-
language S&T periodicals annually, covering all the world's key engineering technology journals. It also holds over 100,000 foreign conference proceedings and
114,000 foreign academic theses. Its collection of nearly two million US government S&T reports is augmented annually by 20,000.[92]

This brings us to ISTIC. As we noted earlier in the chapter, the Institute
of Scientific and Technical Information of China was established in 1958 and
grew to become China's premier organization for gathering and disseminating
foreign technical information in fields that have a direct impact on PRC S&T
development. While part of the NETL framework, and a component *within* the

national S&T information infrastructure, ISTIC is NETL's largest member, predates it by decades, and is responsible for developing it. The reality of the relationship is depicted on ISTIC's website, where NETL's name appears *under* ISTIC's logo.[93]

ISTIC in fact views itself as "the center for managing and providing services in the field of S&T information for the entire country" and as "exercising leadership over and serving as a model for the entire country's S&T information system."[94] ISTIC at present has 850 employees in seven functional divisions and six "public-good" departments. It owns three corporations including the digital S&T document provider Wanfangdata. Its business areas are data research and analysis in support of government decision-making; S&T information services; research, development and propagation of new technologies and service platforms; fostering talent in the field of S&T information; and media publication services."[95] More specifically, ISTIC:

> processes and reports on domestic and foreign S&T publications including documents, translations, reference works, reports, and research; builds domestic and foreign document databases that conform to China's needs and circumstances; does research and analysis on domestic and foreign S&T sources that pertain to China's national economic and S&T issues; reports on domestic and foreign S&T achievements and trends; performs strategic information services for [government] policy making departments; provides in a planned fashion specialized information services for the nation's many priority science research programs; does research on information science, policy, management, service, methods and research; and develops international cooperation and exchange in S&T information work.[96]

ISTIC's "service center" has two sections for "searches" and "special services." The first is an online facility for searching full text, abstracts, TOCs, and web resources within five media categories including print, AV, web-based (e.g., ISI Derwent Innovations Index, ProQuest Science Journals, LexisNexis), "other" web media (e.g., Lawrence Erlbaum Online Journals), and CDs. Print media offerings include "western language conference proceedings, western language periodicals, foreign language S&T reports, Chinese language conference proceedings, and a Chinese language academic theses database." The last three categories – web through CDs – provide access to 110 sources, only *three* of which are Chinese; the remaining 107 are foreign.[97] Under "special services" ISTIC:

> obtains and delivers for registered clients original documents from its own and outside (馆外) holdings; verifies the originality of S&T content for customers setting up research programs; appraises S&T achievements, does evaluations, and applies for patents; offers document research services and advice to central Party, government, and military leadership organizations, to state key lab production units, and to clients at large; verifies the recorded

content and citations of papers and works publicly available through Chinese and foreign search engines; arranges proxy searches and loans of resources in domestic and foreign libraries and information organizations; and performs other personalized services.[98]

The Institute does more than collect and provide science and technology materials to domestic customers. It actively supports state R&D projects through "comprehensive, policy-driven strategic research" on the latest worldwide S&T achievements and trends for leading government departments.[99] Here is an example from ISTIC Director He Defang, in a celebratory article he wrote for the industry trade journal *Zhongguo Xinxi Daobao*:

> According to He, ISTIC over the course of three years provided a Beijing design bureau working on a maglev train documents in English, French, Japanese, German and Russian from which they "found answers that solved many key problems in their R&D" and reduced the time needed for experimentation. Decisions were made by "seeking truth from facts" (foreign facts). By using foreign resources, China's researchers reduced their costs by 40–50% and their time by 60–70%. Thanks to ISTIC, China can "stand on the shoulders of giants" to reduce the risks of innovation. By studying trends in worldwide S&T, he continued, China can distinguish hot areas of research from "empty" pursuits, and get a grip on competitors' technologies and patent strategies.[100]

ISTIC's Chongqing branch was established in 1960, in the heartland of China's high-tech military industrial region. Its responsibilities, according to a Chinese wiki source, are to collect materials on new technology and practical technology of benefit to China's southwest; edit, translate and publish periodicals with S&T information; create databases for documents on energy, computer and information technology, and for facts on S&T developments in the former Soviet Union and Eastern European countries; compile an index of foreign S&T periodicals in the southwest region; provide search services; perform research assigned by the state; provide information consulting and fixed topic services; and organize training in information work.[101]

The branch holds 310,000 books; 15,000 foreign language S&T journals; some 7 million patent records; 190,000 documents on standards; 64,000 product user manuals; and 28,000 technical manuals.[102] Following ISTIC's launch of its commercial venture Wanfangdata, the Chongqing branch in 1993 transformed its former Database Research Center into the for-profit digital S&T service provider CQVIP (重庆维普资讯).[103] There are ISTIC knock-offs in all PRC provinces and major cities that use the suffix of ISTIC's old (科技情报研究所) or new (科技信息研究所) names. This arrangement is unique to China; we know of nothing similar elsewhere.

Other top-tier S&T information providers

Three major organizations outside the NSTL system support China's access to foreign S&T information. They are the China Defense Science and Technology Information Center (中国国防科技信息中心, CDSTIC), the Patent Documentation Library (专利文献馆), and the National Library of Standards (国家标准馆). Each is important in its own way.

CDSTIC, previously the Commission on Science and Technology Industry for National Defense (国防科学技术工业委员会, COSTIND)[104] S&T Intelligence Bureau (情报研究所), is focused on foreign defense-related science and technology information. Being a military technical intelligence unit, openly available information is sparse, although we were acquainted with its workings by Huo and Wang. The Center's functions and relationship to other S&T units were outlined in a 1984 document entitled "Regulations on National Defense Science and Technology Information Work":

> The national defense S&T intelligence work system is made up of the following components: the Commission on Science and Technology Industry for National Defense (abbreviated below as COSTIND); each defense industry ministry (including the Ministry of Electronics Industry, the China State Shipbuilding Corporation, etc.); the PLA's General Staff Department and General Logistics Department; related departments from each branch of the military services; organizations responsible for S&T intelligence work within the national defense S&T industry offices of each province, autonomous region, and municipality directly under the central government; national defense S&T intelligence professional working units at each level; local national defense S&T intelligence service centers; and the defense S&T intelligence network.[105]

The proliferation of military S&T intelligence units at each level is notable. The document goes on to name CDSTIC's predecessor as the main unit within this network.

> COSTIND's S&T Intelligence Bureau is the integrated center for national defense S&T intelligence. Each of the national defense industry departments' S&T intelligence bureaus is an S&T intelligence center within the system. The S&T intelligence offices directly subordinate to related departments and bureaus in the General Staff Dept., General Logistics Dept., and each branch of military service should gradually develop into S&T intelligence centers within the system.[106]

Article 9 outlines the military S&T centers' duties.

> Each of the national defense S&T intelligence centers have the following responsibilities: collect, organize, and make available domestic and foreign

S&T materials needed by the system; take responsibility for managing the systems' series of S&T intelligence reports and organizing S&T intelligence exchanges; carry out analytic work and provide intelligence for policymaking and scientific research and production; write reports; research S&T intelligence theory, methods, and the application of modernized techniques; and provide guidance to the system's units.[107]

Another section emphasizes the importance of S&T intelligence work to defense.

> Collection of S&T materials is the foundation for the defense S&T intelligence enterprise. Each department must actively, systematically and on a priority basis collect and utilize relevant domestic and foreign national defense S&T intelligence materials, including AV material and materials from professional and academic conferences. Scientific management of the materials is needed along with an integrated indexing system. Duplication should be avoided by sharing between units.[108]

Foreign copyright owners will no doubt appreciate that advice. Other notable provisions are requirements for national defense S&T intelligence units to invite subject matter experts in the relevant disciplines "on leave or retired" to participate in their S&T intelligence work (Article 24) and for annual increases in the defense S&T budget (Article 26).

A more recent source on CDSTIC lists similar tasks, such as building information resources, developing and using S&T information, managing the information, training individuals in the field of S&T information, integrating information organizations, providing policy consultations on weapons and equipment modernization, and safeguarding S&T information. The Center has supported China's nuclear weapons, ballistic missile and satellite programs (两弹一星), *Yinhe* (Galaxy) military supercomputer, and 863 program with its library of 38 million articles and 80-odd databases holding over four terabytes of information gleaned from American, Japanese, Russian, and British publications, military reports and standards.[109]

Tied closely to CDSTIC is the Beijing Document Service (北京文献服务处, BDS), founded in 1978 with cooperation from the Beijing Science and Technology Association (北京科技协会). CDSTIC provides most of BDS's funding and is also its heaviest user. In addition to its own document holdings, BDS is the network administrator and service center for COSTIND's China Engineering and Technology Information Network (CETIN), a one-stop shop for foreign military technology information.

For example, CETIN provides a hotlink to a "(sub)network on foreign quality and reliability information" (国外质量与可靠性信息网) that gives detailed information on standards, test results, and maintenance issues of foreign (mostly American) military equipment.[110] Another link leads to "foreign military engineering and equipment" (外军工程装备),[111] while a third labeled "C³I" takes you to "electronic countermeasures" (电子对抗).[112] One can do full text searches or look for particular military technologies, such as mine detection, camouflage, and bridging devices.

CETIN periodically highlights foreign military technologies of interest. On January 11, 2010 the site featured Northrop Grumman's AN/ALQ-162 countermeasures set. Several other American ECM devices were described in great detail. There was a "pictorial description of the American national missile defense system" (美国国家导弹防御系统图解) and a side bar with links to 41 "specialized areas" such as radar and radar countermeasures, laser weapons, computer warfare, network centric warfare, stealth and anti-stealth technology, and GPS systems, all in the Chinese language and all focused on foreign – especially American – systems.

As valuable as information on existing foreign equipment is to China's technology planners, equally important are the insights gained from foreign patent exploitation. Although China did not enact its own patent law until 1985, it was busy exploiting foreign patents some 30 years before that. Indeed, according to a 2005 article celebrating 50 years of patent work, China's S&T workers early on adopted the mottoes "Scientific research work cannot be separated from the support of foreign patent literature" (科研工作离不开外国专利文献的支持) and "Patent literature is a treasure trove for science and technology" (专利文献是科学技术的宝库).[113]

Recognizing these facts, the CAS National Science Library set up a Patents Section (专利组) in 1956 and started gathering foreign patents literature for use by China's S&T workers. In 1965, ISTIC set up a Patents Library (专利馆), which took over the NSL Patents Section's holdings and "began continuously expanding the scope of its foreign patents literature collection, turning patents literature into the main source of China's S&T information." The S&T information offices that were springing up all over China at that time also gathered foreign patents literature and made it available to local patrons.[114]

In 1980, the China Patents Office (中国专利局) was formed, which the following year took over ISTIC's Patents Library and renamed it the Patent Documentation Library (专利文献馆). It retained this name after the Patents Office was reborn in 1998 as the State Intellectual Property Office (国家知识产权局, SIPO) and is now China's largest and most complete repository and service center for patent documents and information.

The Patents Library provides "multi-faceted, multi-level, multi-channel" patent document and information services, including collecting, reading, consulting, searching, and training. Patrons begin work in the reception hall, where they register, consult with library staff, and learn how to use the search facilities. The patent search room has 70 computer terminals that customers use free of charge. Half of them search the library's holdings and the other half are linked to international patent databases. The stacks hold 3,760 shelves of patent specifications from 28 countries. The Library also offers consignment services, including patent reproduction, searching, and analytic services delivered personally or by mail, phone, fax, email or online.[115] SIPO in addition operates 47 local patent information centers across the country.

Finding space for its massive holdings has been a problem, as the following comments suggest:

> Workers at the Patents Library have been overworked trying to manage the truckloads (一车车) of foreign patent specifications that arrive. Their biggest headache was finding room for it all. Today the paper documents have been largely replaced by CDs and computers. Although the number of customers has grown, most people access the library's services remotely. Library workers spend less time finding and copying documents and more time helping customers analyze the patents, spot trends, and find loopholes to avoid patent fees, for example, by researching how a product's patent is treated by other countries.[116]

Challenges caused by volume led to the establishment of an "Automated Work Division" (自动化工作部) within the Library and in 1993 to a separate China Patent Information Center (中国专利信息中心) also subordinate to SIPO. The new center is charged with building SIPO's automated systems; processing, disseminating, searching and providing consultancy services for patents and other IPR information; "exhibiting, mediating, developing, implementing, using patented technology and organizing test production of patented products"; and information engineering and related services. It has offices for searching and consulting, translation and information processing.[117] Some 140 technical staff members are on call.[118]

Just as patents provide China's S&T cadre critical insight into foreign technology, so do foreign technical standards offer short cuts to development. The National Library of Standards (国家标准馆), which collects foreign technical standards and supports development of China's own, was established in 1963. Prior to that, its functions were carried out by a Library of Standards within ISTIC. In 1978, it became part of a new Institute for Standardization and Integration (标准化综合研究所) within the Office of National Standards (国家标准局) and in 1989 it was put under the State Bureau of Technical Supervision's (国家技术监督局) Standards Information Center (标准情报中心). In 1999, its functions were transferred to the China Center for Standards Research (中国标准研究中心), which was reborn in 2003 as the China National Institute of Standardization (中国标准化研究院, CNIS), the present parent of NLS.[119]

The Library supports research by the Standardization Administration of China (国家标准化管理委员会, SAC) established in 2001 to exercise "unified management, supervision and overall coordination of standardization work."[120] NLS's parent body CNIS is affiliated, in turn, with the General Administration of Quality Supervision, Inspection and Quarantine of the PRC (国家质量监督检验检疫总局). CNIS has overall control of foreign standards research, as suggested by the following:

The main responsibilities of CNIS are to conduct *all-round, strategic, and comprehensive research of standardization during the development process of economy and society*, to research and develop comprehensive fundamental standards, as well as to provide authoritative standards information services.[121]

SAC, on the other hand, is China's public face to the international standards community and is tasked to:

> represent China in the International Organization for Standardization (ISO), International Electrotechnical Commission (IEC) and other international and regional standardization organizations; organize the activities of the Chinese National Committee for ISO and IEC; organize domestic sectors and local areas to participate in international or regional activities on standardization; sign and implement international cooperation agreements in standardization, and examine, approve and implement international cooperation and exchange projects on standardization.[122]

Information on foreign and domestic technical standards is provided over the China Standards Service Network (中国标准服务网), owned jointly by NLS and a National Standards Document Sharing Service Platform (国家标准文献共享服务平台).[123] The "platform" was built by CNIS to collect, edit, and publish information on standards, facilitate standards research, provide full text delivery of standards documents, and perform other online services, such as consulting, training, and translation. Some 1.3 million titles are available.[124]

Other organizations are also involved in exploiting foreign standards. A directory posted to the "measurement forum" (计量论坛) website[125] lists names and contact information of offices that provide information on particular categories of standards. Many of the offices are inside the technical ministries (shipbuilding, aviation industry, etc.), including the *Ministry of Electronics' Fourth Institute for Standardization, which handles "US national military standards."*[126]

Foreign standards are also scrutinized by China's National Institute of Metrology (中国计量科学研究院), which like CNIS is subordinate to the General Administration of Quality Supervision, Inspection and Quarantine. The value of foreign technical standards to national development is acknowledged by the Institute:

> NIM participates actively in international and regional key and supplementary comparisons to ensure our national standards' equivalence and their traceability to the SI, and provides the country with a very important technical basis for her involvement in international trade and economic globalization.[127]

NIM sits at the top of the standards chain ensuring that the tools and processes used to model foreign specifications are up to the task, so that "Chinese" products work and are marketable internationally. A key purpose of the Institute's new campus that opened in 2009 is to attract "elite" scientists for "global collaboration" to "serve national strategies."[128] In China, foreign experts help design processes that ensure foreign technology is faithfully copied.

The professionalization of open-source intelligence

Chinese exploitation of foreign open-source S&T information is an all-consuming, systematic endeavor aimed at accelerating China's scientific development. Transforming open-source S&T information into useful intelligence is pursued not just to keep tabs on foreign threats, as is done by western services, but to circumvent the cost and risk of indigenous research. Another distinguishing characteristic of Chinese open-source operations – beyond the scale itself – is the diversity of venues through which information is gathered, from scanning technical literature to analyzing patents, reverse engineering product samples, and capturing conversations at scientific meetings. Nothing is overlooked.

In intelligence circles the term "open source" connotes information obtained for fee or free without violating legal statutes. But there is a huge difference between what is needed to openly *monitor* foreign technical programs and the apparatus needed to covertly *model* foreign R&D as the basis for one's own development. Not only does China invest far more effort in open-source collection than other countries, the "back-end" components – analysis, customer interaction, and feedback to collectors – also play a much larger part, as befits a nation whose progress depends more on adaptation than innovation.

This qualitative distinction between the roles of open-source intelligence in the PRC and in other countries is also apparent in the professionalization of China's S&T open-source cadre. Whereas western services typically regard open source as a poor cousin to "real" (clandestine or technical) intelligence, China staffs its OSINT[129] organizations with top-line career personnel, backed by an industrial organization with its own trade journals. We know of no other nation where open-source intelligence enjoys this level of support.

As noted above, the China Society for Scientific and Technical Information – the state-backed professional body for open-source S&T workers – emerged in 1964 as an "academic and non-profit institution" to promote open-source S&T exploitation.[130] All of China's national S&T information organizations are corporate members. CSSTI has branches in every province and major city of China as well as 11 committees to represent technical and other disciplines.[131]

CSSTI's tasks are to promote open-source intelligence research, provide consulting and other services "to meet various information requirements of the nation," strengthen links between the S&T intelligence network's central and local units and between the organizations and their individual members, and acknowledge outstanding personal achievements in S&T intelligence – in essence to create a "home" for China's S&T information workers.[132] Information on open-source S&T tradecraft is shared at annual meetings and through its periodical publications: the *Journal of the China Society for Scientific and Technical Information* (情报学报) and the *China Information Review* (中国信息导报).

Organizationally, CSSTI is a component of the China Association for Science and Technology (中国科学技术协会, CAST), an alleged NGO that plays a major role in facilitating foreign S&T technology transfers (see Chapter 5). CSSTI's headquarters are located within ISTIC's building at 15 Fuxing Road in Beijing. The Society is chaired by a Party figure from the science ministry but is run by ISTIC's incumbent director. Board members include representatives from ISTIC, ISTIC's quasi-independent Shanghai chapter, the National Science and Technology Library, the Academy of Machine Information (机械信息研究院), and the Department of Electronic Information (电子信息部) within the PLA's General Armament Department (总装备部).[133]

CSSTI also manages the Society of Competitive Intelligence of China (中国竞争情报研究会), one of its 11 disciplinary committees (竞争情报分会). SCIC claims 400 corporate and more than 800 individual members from among "China's 20,000-plus intelligence research and information consulting personnel."[134] "Competitive intelligence" organizations worldwide typically focus on business intelligence in general. In China the emphasis is on S&T intelligence as indicated by SCIC's subordination to two S&T organizations (CSSTI and CAST).

Formed in 1995, SCIC studies the theory and practice of competitive intelligence, popularizes its techniques, offers consulting services, helps companies gain competitive advantages, cooperates and exchanges information with other professionals worldwide, and protects the legal interests of competitive intelligence professionals.[135] It holds annual meetings, training sessions, and has its own journal, *Competitive Intelligence* (竞争情报). Beyond its connections within China, SCIC "has established a long-term partner relationship of cooperation and exchange with America's Society of Competitive Intelligence Professionals."[136]

We conclude this chapter on Chinese open-source "information/intelligence" (*qíngbào* 情报) with a few words on the etymology of this italicized term, which is problematic not only for translators but for Chinese as well, who are aware of its different connotations in translation. "Information" has neutral or positive associations, while "intelligence" to those outside the field conjures up a negative cloak-and-dagger image. We have resisted the impulse to color our readers' perception by using one term or the other in translation and rely wherever possible on China's own English usage, for nomenclature especially.

The problem with *qingbao* (Japanese: *jōhō*) is this: not only does the Chinese term cover multiple English words but the Chinese themselves use it inconsistently. It is not simply a case of polysemy (e.g., "intelligence" in English, the distinct meanings for which Chinese have no trouble sorting out). The *concept* denoted by *qingbao* is broad enough to encompass both "intelligence" and "information." And if you focus on the basic meaning, without its emotive nuances, there is not much difference between the two, from a layperson's view especially.

As a result, use of the term *qingbao* varied for decades in China's intelligence community. According to Cheng Jixi, professor at the Beijing Science and Technology University, in the mid-1950s China built a "system for collecting, translating, and studying foreign S&T materials," i.e., the apparatus we described above.

Needing a name for it, China translated the Russian word for "information" with Chinese "*qingbao*," which was used in China to depict the full range of activities from clandestine collection (espionage) to straightforward open-source monitoring to one's particular knowledge of events.[137] By the 1970s, however, China had also adapted the word "*xinxi*" (信息) to translate the English word "information." So "information" ended up with two Chinese words that were used interchangeably.

Some Chinese open-source workers saw *qingbao* as a subset of *xinxi* meaning "processed or distilled information" and believed *qingbao* should be used exclusively for "intelligence".[138] Huo and Wang adopted this position and their usage eventually became the norm. Interestingly, it also parallels how western services treat the two terms today. In Huo and Wang's words:

> There are currently a considerable number of people who appreciate the fact that, even though information is the primary source and basic vector for intelligence, information nevertheless is not intelligence. One must go through a catalyzing and activating process in order to extract intelligence from information.[139]

More exactly:

> Information is knowledge put into material form or symbols. Intelligence is knowledge needed to solve specific problems that has been extracted from information. Information is the source from which intelligence is extracted.[140]

As such, "information" (*xinxi* 信息) is the target of open source collection and "intelligence" (*qingbao* 情报) is its output:

> The primary task of collection work within the broader modern S&T intelligence setup is to collect information that serves as an intelligence source, and to provide raw knowledge for intelligence analysis and synthesis work.[141]

More recently, ISTIC's Chen Jiugeng affirmed Huo and Wang's distinction, but added an important nuance:

> "*Qingbao*" (intelligence) is a special class of "*xinxi*" (information) used to keep secrets that pertain to national security, social stability, and business competition. "*Qingbao*" includes both "original" (源) and "processed" (加工) "information" (信息). And processed information does not necessarily become "intelligence"—that depends on one's goal and intended use.[142]

That is, "information" becomes "intelligence" depending on who uses it for what. Another factor governing choice is psychological impact, which played a role in the State Science and Technology Commission's 1992 decision to change ISTIC's and other S&T agencies' names from "*qingbao*" to "*xinxi*" despite the nature of these organizations. As Chen put it:

Eliminating the sensitivity and suspicion that the public – especially in Taiwan, Hong Kong, and among overseas Chinese – has toward the old practice of calling publicly shared and used S&T information "S&T intelligence" will help expedite the spread of knowledge, technology exchanges and foreign cooperation.

The nuance is important. It matters to China's foreign supporters whether they simply share "information" with the PRC or support that state's "intelligence" efforts. Similarly, whether foreign firms with research labs in China are "cooperating" or "betraying" their own nation's interests depends on which end of the stick you hold. In the following chapter we address the issue of foreign high-tech investment in China and its implications for the transacting partners.

Notes

1 John Lewis and Litai Xue, *China Builds the Bomb*, Palo Alto, CA: Stanford University Press, 1988, pp. 223–224.
2 Guan Jialin (关家麟) and Zhang Chao (张超), "我国科技信息事业发展的回顾与展望" ("Review and Outlook for Scientific and Technological Information Undertaking of China"), 情报科学 (*Qingbao Kexue*), 25, no. 1, January 2007, p. 2; Chen Zeqian (陈则谦) and Bai Xianyang (白献阳), "我国科技信息事业发展的轨迹" ("The Locus of Development for China's S&T Information Enterprise"), 现代情报 (*Xiandai Qingbao*), December 2007, p. 12.
3 "1956–1967年科学技术发展远景规划" ("1956–1967 Long-term Plan for the Development of Science and Technology"). www.cdstm.cn/?action-viewnews-itemid-14784-page-1.
4 Guan and Zhang, "Review and Outlook for Scientific and Technological Information Undertaking of China."
5 Miao Qihao, "Technologial and Industrial Intelligence in China: Development, Transition and Perspectives." In Prescott and Gibbons, eds, *Global Perspectives on Competitive Intelligence*, Alexandria, VA: Society of Competitive Intelligence Professionals, 1993.
6 ISTIC's Chinese name was changed again in 1992 from 中国科学技术情报研究所 to 中国科学技术信息研究所. The rationale for the shift from 情报 (*qingbao*, intelligence/information) to 信息 (*xinxi*, information) is discussed later in the chapter.
7 Guan and Zhang, "Review and Outlook for Scientific and Technological Information Undertaking of China." In 1959, the university became a department within the University of Science and Technology of China (中国科学技术大学).
8 Ibid.
9 The magazine was entitled 科技情报工作讲义 ("Instructional Materials on S&T Information Work").
10 Guan and Zhang, "Review and Outlook for Scientific and Technological Information Undertaking of China."
11 Ibid.
12 Chen and Bai, "The Locus of Development for China's S&T Information Enterprise."
13 Miao Qihao, 1993, p. 51.
14 Guan and Zhang, "Review and Outlook for Scientific and Technological Information Undertaking of China" and Chen and Bai, "The Locus of Development for China's S&T Information Enterprise."
15 Guan and Zhang, "Review and Outlook for Scientific and Technological Information Undertaking of China."

16 1978–1985 年全国科学技术发展规划 (Regulations on National S&T Development 1978–1985). State Science and Technology Commission, 1977.
17 Guan and Zhang, "Review and Outlook for Scientific and Technological Information Undertaking of China."
18 Chen and Bai, "The Locus of Development for China's S&T Information Enterprise."
19 Guan and Zhang, "Review and Outlook for Scientific and Technological Information Undertaking of China." The authors claim that half of the 1,038 databases operated by China's 64 state-level ministries and committees, and 27 provinces and autonomous regions, from the early 1980s to mid-1990s were S&T information databases.
20 Chen Jiugeng, "Actual Strength of S&T Information Service System in China," *China Information Review*, no. 10, 2006, pp. 17–22.
21 Qihao Miao, 1993, pp. 49–53. There was also a large (but indeterminate) number of S&T novelty searching centers (查新咨询中心) throughout China to guide technical projects by foreign literature retrieval; see Guan and Zhang, "Review and Outlook for Scientific and Technological Information Undertaking of China."
22 Paraphrase of SSTC document "关于调整和加强全国科技情报系统文献工作的意见" ("Opinions on Restructuring and Strengthening National S&T Information System Document Work"), January 1989.
23 The expansion is: 中国科学技术情报研究所. ISTIC is now called 中国科学技术信息研究所; its English name remains unchanged.
24 The S&T Intelligence Bureau is now the China Defense Science and Technology Information Center (中国国防科技信息中心). COSTIND expands to "Commission on Science and Technology Industry for National Defense." Further down in the notice the Science Commission assigns coverage of US government AD and NASA documents to this unit. "AD" means "<u>A</u>rmed Services Technical Information Agency <u>D</u>ocument."
25 Now called the Patent Documentation Library (专利文献馆) and the China Patent Information Center (中国专利信息中心), both part of the State Intellectual Property Office (国家知识产权局).
26 Now the China National Institute of Standardization, National Library of Standards (中国标准化研究院国家标准馆).
27 "关于调整和加强全国科技情报系统文献工作的意见" ("Opinions on Restructuring and Strengthening National S&T Information System Document Work"), January 1989. Huo and Wang's description of the three levels and their respective functions matches the SSTC prescription. See Huo Zhongwen and Wang Zongxiao, *Sources and Methods of Obtaining National Defense Science and Technology Intelligence*, Beijing: Kexue Jishu Wenxuan Publishing Company, 1991.
28 www.nstl.gov.cn/index.html.
29 Xia Chengyu (夏承禹), "科技情报部门领导在新形势下的新角色" ("A New Role for Leaders of S&T Information Departments under the New Circumstances"), in 科技进步与对策 (Science & Technology Progress and Policy), 2001.1, pp. 104–105. Guan and Zhang also date the third (modern) phase of the system's development from 2001. See Guan and Zhang, "Review and Outlook for Scientific and Technological Information Undertaking of China."
30 MOST statistics cited by Chen, "Actual Strength of S&T Information Service System in China." Chen states the figures do not include institutes within the Aviation Industry Corp, China State Shipbuilding Corp, China National Nuclear Corp, China North Industries Group Corp, and other companies working on sensitive projects not suitable for public disclosure.
31 Ibid.
32 Ibid.
33 Ibid.
34 Chen and Bai, "The Locus of Development for China's S&T Information Enterprise."

35 Bruce Gilley, "China's Spy Guide: A Chinese Espionage Manual Details the Means by Which Beijing Gathers Technology and Weapons Secrets from the United States," *Far Eastern Economic Review*, December 23, 1999, p. 14. See also Huo and Wang, *Sources and Methods of Obtaining National Defense Science and Technology Intelligence*. An English-language translation by the US government completed in 2000 and verified by the present authors has been posted to <www.fas.org/irp/world/china/docs/sources.html>.

36 Huo and Wang, *Sources and Methods of Obtaining National Defense Science and Technology Intelligence*, p. 32. All citations refer to pagination in the translation.

37 Ibid. p. 5.

38 Ibid. p. 7.

39 Ibid. p. 8.

40 The authors' efforts to treat their topic scientifically sometimes border on banal. For example, on page 151 we learn that "Intelligence consumer studies refer to studies of the consumers of intelligence." In the same spirit, the authors launch into an explanation of human needs that begins with Maslow's hierarchy and ends with references to "Bradford's Law of Grade Distribution" and "Zipf's 'Least Effort' Principle."

41 "Research on consumer demand for intelligence is the basis for information collection and is one of the key research areas in collection science. Without consumer demand, collection loses its significance. . . . The difficulty with research on consumer demand lies in the fact that hardly any consumers are skillful or adept at communicating their real needs." Ibid. p. 14.

42 Ibid. p. 68.

43 Ibid. p. 69.

44 Ibid. p. 19.

45 Ibid. pp. 42–44.

46 Ibid. pp. 57–58.

47 Ibid. p. 24.

48 Ibid. p. 72.

49 Ibid. p. 75.

50 Ibid.

51 Ibid. p. 78.

52 Ibid. p. 81.

53 Ibid.

54 Ibid. p. 82.

55 Ibid.

56 Cited in ibid. p. 85.

57 Ibid. p. 85.

58 Ibid. pp. 88–89.

59 Ibid. pp. 90–91.

60 Ibid. p. 93.

61 Ibid. p. 95.

62 Ibid. pp. 98–99.

63 Ibid. pp. 108–118.

64 Ibid. p. 120.

65 Ibid. p. 147.

66 Ibid. p. 182.

67 Ibid. pp. 184–185.

68 Ibid. p. 221.

69 Ibid. p. 224.

70 Ibid. p. 228.

71 Ibid. p. 53.

72 Ibid. p. 230.

73 "国家科学技术情报发展政策" ("National Science and Technology Information Development Policy"), State Science and Technology Commission, January 1992. Accessed at: www.srstc.gov.cn.

74 "Home Page," National Science and Technology Library, www.nstl.gov.cn/index.html.
75 Ibid.
76 Liansheng Meng and Yan Quan Liu, "The Present and Future of China's National Science and Technology Library: A New Paradigm of Sci-tech Information Resource Sharing," *New Library World* 106, no. 7 (2005), 343–351.
77 Ibid.
78 CALIS is sponsored by the Ministry of Education for the entire range of academic disciplines. It has centers at seven regional locations, plus a "Northeast Regional National Defense Document Information Service Center" (东北地区国防文献信息服务中心). Established in 1998, the system promotes joint acquisitions and sharing through a digital network. Some 500 libraries participate (www.calis.edu.cn/calisnew).
79 Chen, "Actual Strength of S&T Information Service System in China."
80 CAS Document Information Center (中国科学院文献情报中心) was its name from 1985 to 2006.
81 Tracing their name changes through time can be challenging. The Lanzhou Branch Library, founded in 1955 as the "LCAS Lanzhou Library" (中国科学院图书馆兰州分馆), was renamed in 1957 the "CAS Northwest Branch Library" (中国科学院西北分院图书馆), and renamed again in 1959 the "CAS Lanzhou Branch Library" (中国科学院兰州分院图书馆). During the Cultural Revolution it was known as the "CAS Gansu Provincial Library" (中国科学院甘肃省图书馆). In 1973 it was renamed the "CAS Lanzhou Library" (中国科学院兰州图书馆), and in 1987 redesignated as the "CAS Lanzhou Documentation and Information Center" (中国科学院兰州文献情报中心) while continuing to use its former name the "CAS Lanzhou Library." In 1997 it became the "CAS Scientific Information Center for Resources and Environment" (中国科学院资源环境科学信息中心) while retaining "CAS Lanzhou Library." Today its website (www.llas.ac.cn) sports three names: CAS National Science Library, Lanzhou Branch Library (中国科学院国家科学图书馆兰州分馆), and the legacy names CAS Scientific Information Center for Resources and Environment, and Gansu Province S&T Library (甘肃省科技图书馆).
82 www.hudong.com/wiki/中国科学院文献情报中心 and Chen, "Actual Strength of S&T Information Service System in China."
83 www.las.ac.cn.
84 www.hudong.com/wiki/中国科学院文献情报中心.
85 Chen, "Actual Strength of S&T Information Service System in China."
86 www.las.ac.cn.
87 Ibid.
88 www.gmachineinfo.com.
89 www.cmisi.com.cn.
90 www.cncic.gov.cn.
91 Chen, "Actual Strength of S&T Information Service System in China."
92 www.istic.ac.cn.
93 Chinese normally order relationships from superordinate (on the top or left) to subordinate (toward the bottom or right).
94 www.istic.ac.cn.
95 Ibid.
96 www.chinabaike.com.
97 www.istic.ac.cn.
98 Ibid.
99 www.chinabaike.com.
100 He Defang, "As for Indigenous Innovation, Information Should Go Ahead of Rest," *China Information Review*, no. 10, 2006, pp. 12–13.
101 *www.hudong.com/wiki/*中国科学技术信息研究.
102 Ibid.

103 www.cqvip.com.
104 In 2008, COSTIND became the State Administration for Science, Technology and Industry for National Defense (国家国防科技工业局) and part of the newly formed Ministry of Industry and Information Technology.
105 国防科学技术情报工作条例 (*Regulations on National Defense Science and Technology Information Work*), PRC State Council, July 1984.
106 Ibid. Article 8.
107 Ibid. Article 9.
108 Ibid. Article 13.
109 home.cetin.net.cn, accessed May 2006 and January 2010.
110 home.cetin.net.cn/storage/cetin2/QRMS/index.htm.
111 home.cetin.net.cn/storage/cetin2/xw/indexgcb/indexgcb.htm.
112 home.cetin.net.cn/storage/cetin2/xw/xxz/xxz.htm.
113 Wu Xuanzhou (吴泉洲), "50 Years of Patent Documents" ("专利文献50年"), in *Zhongguo Faming yu Zhuanli*, April 2005, qkzz.net/Announce/Announce.asp?BoardID=13200&ID=120156.
114 Ibid.
115 www.sipo.gov.cn/sipo2008/wxfw/.../t20080416_381338.html.
116 Wu "50 Years of Patent Documents."
117 www.cnpat.com.cn.
118 www.sipo.gov.cn/sipo_English/news/official/200904/t20090417_453529.html.
119 Chronology reconstructed from information posted to baike.baidu.com/view/2473995.html and *www.zjj315.gov.cn/b25.asp. NLS is also called the* National Standards Document Center (国家标准文献中心).
120 *www.sac.gov.cn.*
121 www.cnis.gov.cn. Our italics. The terms are standard euphemisms for foreign collection.
122 Paraphrase of information on *www.sac.gov.cn.*
123 www.cei.gov.cn/homepage/gov/zgbzqbzx.htm.
124 www.cssn.net.cn.
125 www.gfjl.org.
126 *www.gfjl.org/thread-14428-1-1.html.* The information was reportedly posted on November 19, 2007 and was accessible as late as January 2010.
127 www.nim.ac.cn.
128 Ibid.
129 OSINT (Open Source INTelligence).
130 edu.istic.ac.cn.
131 Ibid.
132 www.cssti.org.cn (defunct as of November 21, 2009).
133 Ibid.
134 www.scic.org.cn.
135 Ibid.
136 Ibid.
137 Cheng Jixi (成冀西), "关于情报改信息的再思考" ("Rethinking the Change of 'Qingbao' to 'Xinxi'") in 大学图书情报学刊 (*Journal of Academic Library and Information Science*), 1998.2.
138 Ibid.
139 Huo and Wang, *Sources and Methods of Obtaining National Defense Science and Technology Intelligence*, p. 10.
140 Ibid.
141 Ibid. p. 12.
142 Chen Jiugeng (陈久庚), "关于情报和信息" in 情报杂志 (*Journal of Intelligence*) 19.1, January 2000.

3

TRADE FOR TECHNOLOGY

This chapter analyzes the phenomenon of foreign R&D in China, and assesses its implications for foreign technology transfer. The main arguments are four-fold:

1. The Chinese economy is undergoing a fundamental transformation from an export-processing economy assembling foreign technology to a globalized economy producing indigenous innovation.
2. The past decade has witnessed a dramatic increase in the number of foreign R&D labs in China.
3. There are multiple reasons for the growth in foreign R&D labs in China, including (a) governmental regulation and laws encouraging the establishment of the labs, (b) desire by MNCs to globalize their innovation cycle and tap expertise and resources around the world, including relatively cheap pools like in China, and (c) MNCs seeking to improve their penetration of the China market by adapting their products better to local markets.
4. The presence of foreign R&D labs in China presents a potential national security problem, due to the possible transfer of foreign technology, know-how, and expertise.

Fundamental transformation: from export-processing zone to globalized economy

The growth of the Chinese economy since reform began in 1978 has been one of the fastest and largest accumulations of national wealth in world history. As reform enters its fourth decade, however, Beijing is attempting to fundamentally transform the Chinese economy from export-led to consumption-based growth, reflecting the maturing affluence of the Chinese consumer base and a desire to shift the center of gravity from foreign multinational companies to domestic firms. The reason for this desire is clearly explained by Auerswald and Branscomb:

> [U]nless an economy enjoys success at every stage of the process – from invention, through innovation and economic disruption, to growth – it may lead the world in research but the final economic returns will flow to others.[1]

A key requirement for this transformation is the creation of an innovation base in China, including both basic and applied research and development. Over the past ten years, the Beijing government has dramatically increased expenditures on R&D, rising 0.6 percent to 1.6 percent of GDP from 1999 to 2011.[2] While the PRC government is unlikely to meet its publicly articulated goal of reaching 2 percent of GDP by 2015, it has revised the future goal to 2.5 percent of GDP by 2020.[3]

Behind the spending, China has also significantly altered the distribution of R&D monies and the structure of R&D organizations within the country. As Liu and Lundin show,

> Currently around two-thirds of the total R&D is conducted by enterprises in the business sector, compared to less than 30% in the beginning of 1990s. It demonstrates an impressive structural shift from an innovation system dominated by research institutes to an enterprise-centered innovation system during the past two decades. This change is driven by a combination of the restructuring of research institutes, the expansion of the higher education sector and the strengthening of the innovation capacity of enterprises. The ambition underlying this systematic change is to establish an innovation system, in which market mechanisms encourage applied R&D activities and stimulate rapid commercialization of R&D results in the business sector, while the basic and strategic R&D capacity building will be conducted in the research institutes and the higher education sector, with long-term government support.[4]

China is also producing a large number of researchers to staff these research units, ranking second in the world after the United States and ahead of Japan in number of researchers over the past decade.[5]

It is clear, however, that the Beijing government has concluded that its efforts to date have not been sufficient to create the required levels of innovation to compete independently in the global economy. First, spending levels on R&D are still well below that of the United States and Japan, which in 2011 spent 2.8 percent and 3.5 percent of GDP, respectively.[6] Within the umbrella of R&D spending, funding for basic research dropped from 6 percent of total research expenditure in 2006[7] to 4.7 percent in 2009,[8] compared with USA at 19 percent in 2009[9] and Japan at 13.7 percent in 2008.[10] In terms of dollars, China's total spending on R&D includes RMB27 billion (US$398 million) on basic research, RMB73 billion (US$10.7 billion) on applied research and RMB400 million (US$70.6 billion) on experimental research and development.[11] But the problem is not simply money, but major structural impediments to a national innovation system. Serger and Widman describe at least seven major problems: (1) low level of investment in basic research, (2) low level of investment in high-tech sectors, (3) underdeveloped service sector, (4) inadequate protection of IPR, (5) underdeveloped financial and capital sectors to fund innovation, (6) high levels of academic corruption, and (7) over-focus on hard sciences versus soft sciences and lack of exchanges between hard and soft sciences.[12] Perhaps the most important impediment, however, is that the national economy is still far too dependent on foreign technology, expertise, and know-how. Indeed, as Kate Walsh argues, an underlying theme of Chinese S&T reform is that "the PRC continues to need foreign technology and R&D investment but must make better use of these inputs or fall prey to foreign exploitation with innovative indigenous capacity to show for it."[13] As a result, 83 percent of China's high-tech exports in 2009 were products from foreign companies.[14]

Despite China's historical aversion to foreign dependence, it should be noted that China's innovation strategy is being implemented in an environment of increasingly globalized research and development, driven primarily by multi-national enterprises.[15] As a UN report concludes,

> [T]he increase of foreign R&D activities reveals a fundamental shift in the international economic geography, in which both knowledge generation and exploitation are becoming increasingly internationalized, and even mobile, and with developing countries actively competing for knowledge resources such as corporate R&D activities and highly skilled labor.[16]

For example, since 2004, around 75 percent of the growth in R&D workers employed by US-based multinational companies has been abroad.[17] According to the Chinese Ministry of Commerce, foreign companies increased their share of total R&D expenditure in large and mid-sized manufacturing from 19.7 percent in 2002 to 27.2 percent in 2008, and hold 29 percent of all invention patents in China.[18] Despite this relative dominance of R&D by foreign firms in China, there is strong evidence to suggest that MNCs are not providing a great deal of technology. Widman and Serger conclude from the data that "R&D intensity is twice as high among domestic firms than FDI firms, which suggests that FDI firms are making very cautious R&D efforts and many R&D activities are still home-based."[19] Moreover, "although domestic firms are rapidly strengthening their R&D inputs, FDI firms in China are still outperforming their Chinese competitors, in many qualitative aspects, in terms of both economic performance in general, as well as R&D output in particular."

Of course, it was in China's interests in the early decades of reform to attract as much foreign technology and know-how to China as possible. From Beijing's perspective, there are at least four major reasons to seek R&D-oriented FDI: (1) to increase domestic participation in knowledge creation, accumulation and diffusion; (2) to increase domestic technological capacity; (3) to acquire foreign technologies; and (4) to generate training that benefits domestic industrial development and spur innovation by domestic industries competing with foreign players. The OECD succinctly describes the phases:

> S&T industrial parks, university science parks and technology business incubators were started under the Torch program as new infrastructures to encourage industry–science relationships, and spin-offs from public research organizations (PROs) started to fill the gap; (Phase Two) The maturing of this embryonic system was accelerated in the 1990s through the combined effect of continued international opening (e.g., accession to the World Trade Organization [WTO] in 2001), improvement of corporate governance and key framework conditions for innovation (e.g., protection of intellectual property rights [IPR]), as well as further reforms of the university and public research sectors; (Phase Three) By the turn of the century, a combination of experimental national policies in special zones, bottom-up initiatives supported by regional and local authorities, and top-down systemic reforms had given birth to what could be considered an NIS under construction, in the image of the entire Chinese economy.[20]

While foreign dominance of R&D may have been helpful in the early phases of Chinese economic development, government plans and official statements strongly suggest that Beijing is no longer satisfied with the situation. The 2006 OECD study on Chinese innovation makes Beijing's costs–benefits case well:

> FDI projects and the operations of foreign-invested firms have also helped to improve China's access to advanced technologies, to management practices and to a wide range of skills. Foreign-invested firms have therefore served as a major channel of technology imports. At the same time, they have located aspects of an increasingly fragmented manufacturing process in China, but have performed little technological innovation or product design in the country. Core technologies mostly remain controlled by the foreign partners in joint ventures or by company headquarters abroad. Generally speaking, foreign-invested companies are less R&D-intensive than domestic firms, although this is not specific to China. Overall, this has contributed to a perception that technology transfer to China and related spillovers to the domestic economy have not met expectations. Current patterns of specialization, a lack of absorptive capacities in Chinese firms and shortcomings in framework conditions, such as a lack of effective intellectual property rights (IPR) protection may have limited the amount of spillovers.[21]

As a result the Chinese government over the past ten years has undertaken a strategy "revitalizing the nation through science, technology and innovation,"[22] with a particular focus on "independent innovation."[23] A series of major policy documents since 1995 has sought to build the foundation for domestic innovation.[24]

At the same time, the government has also sought to "source knowledge" from abroad, putting in place incentives to send Chinese students abroad for education and experience and then attract them back to China,[25] and encouraging Chinese enterprises to engage in mergers and acquisitions and gain access to knowledge through overseas R&D and design labs.[26] In particular, China now has internationally recognized centers of excellence, especially in IT and electronics, materials, nanotech, and life sciences.[27] R&D expenditure by these types of high-tech industries tripled in just five years: from RMB 22.2 billion in 2003 to RMB 65.5 billion in 2008, growing at an average annual rate of 24.1 percent. Electronics and telecommunications accounted for 61.5 percent of all high-tech expenditure on R&D in 2008.[28] Evidence of early payoffs from this strategy may also be seen in Chinese authorship of articles in peer-reviewed international science journals, rising from thirteenth place in 1994 to 1998 to second place in 2011, and poised to overtake the United States in 2013.[29] There has also been a significant rise in Chinese patent applications, which increased 33.4 percent from 2010 to 2011.[30] Domestic invention patents surpassed foreign-owned invention patents for the first time in 2011, comprising 50.1 percent of the total (342,466), with 49.9 percent being foreign-owned (341,697).[31] Despite these impressive figures, the R&D intensity of high-tech industry in China remains much lower than that of developed countries. In 2008, the ratio of R&D expenditure to the value of gross industrial output of high-tech industries was just 1.15 percent in China. This was much lower than the 2006 ratio for the US (16.41%), the UK (11.04%), Japan (10.64%), Germany (8.34%) or the Republic of Korea (5.98%), according to the 2008 databases of the Organization for Economic Co-operation and Development (OECD) on Structural Analysis Statistics (STAN) and Analytical Business Enterprise Research and Development (2009).

More recently, the Chinese government has undertaken a strategic policy push for "indigenous innovation." Since 2006, James McGregor and others have highlighted "Chinese policies and initiatives aimed at building 'national champion' companies through subsidies and preferential policies while using China's market power to appropriate foreign technology, tweak it and create Chinese 'indigenous innovations' that will come back at us globally."[32] While the 2006 *Mid- to Long-Range S&T Plan* and other policy documents are examined in detail later in this chapter, Chinese government documents clearly highlight the potential value of encouraging the introduction of foreign R&D labs to China, especially as a platform for technology transfer to kick-start indigenous innovation. The remainder of this chapter tracks the rise of these labs, analyzes the institutional and policy means by which Beijing encourages their establishment, and assesses the potential national security implications of their activities in China.

The rise of the foreign R&D lab

One of the most striking recent phenomena in China's economic revolution has been the proliferation of foreign research and development (R&D) labs. In the

1980s and 1990s, foreign enterprises were almost single-mindedly focused on production and trade. The small number of R&D efforts consisted primarily of product development and adaptation to the local market.[33] However, since the late 1990s, as China became the world's workshop, there has also been a dramatic increase in the number of multinational company (MNC) R&D labs,[34] though most are still focused on applications of technology rather than pure R&D.[35] While there were only an estimated 30 labs in China in 2000,[36] official government numbers show that the number of labs reportedly grew to 600 in June 2004,[37] 750 in 2006,[38] 1,160 in 2007, and 1,200 in March 2010.[39] As of the end of 2009, 465 of these R&D centers were established as independent legal entities with approval of the Ministry of Commerce. These centers have a total investment amounting to US$12.8 billion and registered capital of US$7.4 billion.[40]

Companies with known R&D labs span the spectrum of foreign MNCs in China, from the largest Fortune 100 firm to smaller concerns. Among the most prominent MNCs with R&D centers are Microsoft, IBM, Motorola, Siemens, Nortel, GE, GM, Volkswagen, and Honda.[41] These R&D centers are not evenly divided across the Chinese economic spectrum, but concentrated in certain sectors:

> Foreign R&D organizations established by multinational firms (MNEs) are highly concentrated in the information and communication technology (ICT) industries (including software, telecommunication, semiconductors and other IT products) but equipment and components, biotechnology and drugs as well as automotive industries also attract a significant amount of foreign R&D investment.[42]

Other sectors with disproportionate participation by foreign R&D centers include electronic and telecommunications equipment manufacture, transport equipment manufacture, medicine production, and the chemical industry.[43]

Not surprisingly, these foreign R&D centers are largely clustered in a small number of cities in China, including Beijing, Shanghai, Guangdong, Shenzhen, and Tianjin.[44] In Beijing, one can find R&D labs run by ABB, Agilent Technologies, Alcatel Lucent, DoCoMo, Ericsson, France Telecom, Fujitsu, Google, Hewlett Packard, IBM, Infineon, Intel, Matsushita/Panasonic, Microsoft, Motorola, NEC, Nokia, Nortel, Novo Nordisk, Novozymes, P&G, Ricoh, Samsung, Siemens, and Sony Ericsson. Shanghai possesses a similarly impressive roster of R&D centers, including labs started by Alcatel Lucent, AMD, Astra Zeneca, Ciba Spec. Chemicals, Cisco Systems, Coca Cola, Dell, Dupont, Electrolux, Eli Lily, Ericsson, General Electric, General Motors, GSK, Hewlett Packard, Honeywell, Intel, Microsoft, Motorola, Omron, Philips, Ricoh, Roche, Rohm and Haas, Samsung, Siemens, Sony, Toray, and Unilever.[45]

Why these cities? First, they are a comfortable locale for foreigners, given their large expatriate populations and the presence of many foreign companies. Indeed, some analysts have criticized the overabundance of R&D centers in these metropoli, arguing that the clustering may be stifling the exploitation of innovation in second- and third-tier cities in China. In terms of the available Chinese workforce, these cities also all share similar demographic and socio-economic characteristics, such as relative affluence, higher than average education levels, advanced communications infrastructure, and major universities. In other words, a perfect environment for fostering innovation.

There are at least three common ways for foreign firms to establish R&D operations in China. The first is to start a wholly independent R&D lab. In the early days of the Chinese economic reforms, a wholly owned foreign enterprise (WOFE) was not an option, but is now possible thanks to Beijing's accession to the World Trade Organization on December 11, 2001.[46] A high-tech WOFE requires start-up capital of at least RMB100,000–500,000, but has the advantage of providing the best chance of protecting a company's intellectual property (IP) and technology secrets, since it does not need to expose the IP to a Chinese partner. The second is to set up an R&D unit within a branch of an existing Chinese company as a joint venture opportunity. The third is to conduct cooperative R&D with a Chinese university or research institute.[47] In the latter two cases, the devil is in the details with respect to percentage shares of ownership, sophistication of transferred technology and equipment, participation of technical experts from each side, the role of graduate students, negotiated length of time before the venture reverts to Chinese control, and division of the financial remuneration from any technology applications.

Reasons for the growth of foreign R&D labs

On the face of it, there are many clear barriers to entry and disincentives for foreign companies seeking to do R&D in China. A 2006 OECD study listed at least eight, though there could be more: (1) overcapacity and "unknown" consumers (especially in the automotive industry); (2) lack of experienced/qualified specialists (especially in the automotive and biomedical industries); (3) weakness of institutional infrastructure, e.g., China's known problems with protecting intellectual property rights (IPR); (4) uncertainty regarding the objectivity and impartiality of the Chinese legal system; (5) extremely intensive competition among Chinese players; (6) high employee turnover, especially in the private sector; (7) a realization that establishing R&D facilities simply for "window dressing" no longer works; and (8) the abolishment of some preferential policies.[48] In addition to these, there are at least three other barriers. First, often the volume of new products is insufficient to achieve economies of scale, due to either overcapacity (e.g., automotive industry) or competition (e.g., telecoms industry). Second, there is a lack of local experienced or qualified specialists in certain sectors. Third, the technology and R&D gap between foreign and domestic firms may give foreign firms the opportunities to capture some "high-end" markets in the short run, but the possibility for long-term strategic partnership with domestic firms is still limited.

So, given these barriers, why do foreign companies still seek to conduct R&D in China?

There are three interlocking reasons, including (1) governmental regulation and laws encouraging the establishment of the labs, (2) desire by MNCs to globalize their innovation cycle and tap expertise and resources around the world, including relatively cheap, skilled, and well-trained pools of R&D personnel in China, and (3) desire by MNCs to improve their penetration of the China market by adapting their products better to local markets.[49]

Reason 1 ("Pull"): Governmental regulation and laws encouraging the establishment of foreign R&D labs

After 30 years of rapid economic development, Beijing is implementing long-range industrial plans designed to transition the Chinese economy from export processing of foreign innovation to indigenous innovation. The plans are driven in part by a belief that China's current economic structure is limited by reliance on foreign technology. As State Councilor Liu Yandong told an internal audience:

> The majority of the market is controlled by foreign companies, most core technology relies on imports, [and] the situation is extremely grave as we are further pressured by developed countries who use blockades and technology controls – if we are not able to solve these problems we will forever be under the control of others.[50]

The success of China's indigenous innovation plans is predicated, in part, on accelerated technology transfer from foreign companies and research centers, leveraged by the competition for access to the Chinese market. The Chinese government has so far actively encouraged and promoted foreign corporate R&D in China, viewing it as a way to upgrade domestic technology and skills by importing, and ideally internalizing, foreign know-how.[51] By 2015, the plan calls for China's overall reliance on foreign technology to drop to 30 percent from its 2006 level of 60 percent.

Government organizations

At the national level, the Chinese government shares responsibility for identification, recruitment, and exploitation of foreign science and technology across a wide range of inter-agency coordination groups, ministries, and industrial policy commissions. At the highest level, the Leading Group on Science, Technology and Education, until recently headed by Premier Wen Jiabao, is a permanent Politburo-level coordination mechanism across both Party and government organs. From the loins of this organization sprang an ad hoc Leading Small Group for the Development of a National Mid- to Long-Term Science and Technology Development Plan in 2003, which eventually produced the *Outline for National Medium to Long-Term Science and Technology Development*, described in detail below. The State Council Steering Group for Science, Technology and Education is a top-level government coordination mechanism, which meets two to four times a year to deal with strategic issues. A number of ministerial level agencies – the National Development and Reform Commission (NDRC),[52] the Chinese Academy of Sciences (CAS), the Chinese Academy of Engineering (CAE), sectoral line ministries such as the Ministry of Industry and Information Technology (MIIT)[53] and the Ministry of Agriculture (MOA), and the National Natural Science Foundation of China (NSFC)[54] – play a direct role in designing and implementing S&T and innovation policies. A number of other ministerial agencies, notably the Ministry of Finance (MOF), the various state banks (e.g., China Development Bank), the Export-Import Bank of China, and the Ministry of Commerce (MOC) have significant influence on financing S&T innovation policies and implementation, while others, such as the Ministry of Personnel (MOP), the Ministry of Education, and the State IP Office (SIPO), also exert an important influence on human capital issues such as attracting returning scientists.[55] Within these ministries, some key departments may be identified:

- *Ministry of Science and Technology's Department of High and New Technology Development and Industrialization*[56] is responsible for formulating plans and policies for the development and industrialization of high and new technologies in related fields, organizing the implementation of the National High Technology Research and Development Program, National Key Technologies R&D Program, and other S&T programs, guiding the construction of state-level hi-tech industrial development zones, facilitating the construction of a technology service system for hi-tech industrialization, and drawing up policies for the promotion of technology market development. Subordinate divisions include General Affairs and Planning, Energy and Transportation, Information and Space, Advanced Manufacturing and Automation, Materials, and Industry Development.
- *Ministry of Science and Technology's Department of Basic Research*[57] is responsible for formulating plans and policies on national basic research, organizing the implementation of the National Program on Basic Research Projects and key science research programs, mapping out plans for the building of key science projects, organizing the construction of state laboratories, state key laboratories, and state field science observation bases, and facilitating the infrastructure for S&T research. Subordinate divisions include General Affairs and Basic Research, Bases Administration, and Major Projects Administration.
- *Ministry of Science and Technology's Department of Development Planning*[58] organizes the formulation of S&T development blueprints and annual plans, puts forward suggestions on fund allocation for national S&T programs, and coordinates the implementation of the programs. It works with related agencies in giving advice to the building of national S&T platforms and major innovation bases, stimulates regional S&T advancement, and serves in the administration of S&T projects and achievements appraisal, as well as the administration of S&T statistics. Subordinate divisions include General Affairs and Planning,

Planning and Coordination, High Technology Research and Development, Key Technologies Research and Development, Facilities and Infrastructure, Regional Technology Development, and Evaluation and Statistics.

- *Ministry of Science and Technology's Department of Policy, Regulations and Reform (Office for Building Innovation System)*[59] is responsible for drafting plans and policies to enhance rural development through S&T, organizing the implementation of a hi-tech R&D plan, S&T supporting plan and policy-guiding S&T plan in related fields, promoting rural S&T progress, guiding the application and demonstration of key S&T achievements, and leading the development of agricultural science parks. Subordinate divisions include General Affairs and Policy Study, Regulations and IPR, Institutional Reform (Division of Science and Technology Personnel Management), and Science and Technology Outreach.
- *National Development and Reform Commission's High-Tech Industrialization Department*[60] "organizes and coordinates the relevant international cooperation and international exchanges."
- *Ministry of Industry and Information's Science and Technology Department* "organizes, formulates and implements regulations, policies and standards for high-tech industries involving biomedicine, new materials, aviation, aerospace, and information technology."[61]
- *Ministry of Foreign Trade and Commerce's Mechanical, Electronic, and High-Tech Industry Department* "organizes and promotes mechanical, electronic, and high-tech foreign trade exchanges and cooperation with enterprises."[62]

Industrial plans, policies, and regulations

"China encourages multinationals to establish R&D centers in China."
— Chinese President Hu Jintao at the national science and technology conference in early 2006[63]

Since the late 1970s, relevant Chinese government organs have published plans, regulations, and policies encouraging the transfer of technology through the establishment of joint R&D labs. The most important and far-reaching of these plans is the *Medium and Long Term Plan for S&T Development, 2006–2020* (2006–2010中长期科技发展规划) (MLP), published in 2006 by the Ministry of Science and Technology. The MLP describes itself as the "grand blueprint of science and technology development" to bring about the "great renaissance of the Chinese nation." The MLP "is part of the government's effort to shift China's current growth model to a more sustainable one, seeks to make innovation the driver of future economic growth, and emphasizes the building up of an indigenous innovation capability."[64] The overarching goal is to make China an "innovation-oriented" society by the year 2020 and over the longer term to transform China into one of the world's leading "innovation economies," emphasizing the need to develop capabilities for "indigenous" or "home-grown innovation."[65] Specifically, the MLP outlines three strategic objectives: (1) building an innovation-based economy by fostering indigenous innovation capability; (2) fostering an enterprise-centered technology innovation system and enhancing the innovation capabilities of Chinese firms; and (3) achieving major breakthroughs in targeted strategic areas of technological development and basic research.[66] If achieved, China's leaders believe that the country will never again be dependent on foreign technology. As Premier Wen Jiabao said in 2009 when launching the "indigenous innovation" regulations: "Only by using the power of science and technology will China be able to produce the immeasurable ability to allow nobody to stop our advance forward."

To achieve these goals, the MLP must overcome significant structural challenges. The OECD assesses that China must undergo a

> change from an uncoordinated, piecemeal style of S&T policy making to a coordinated whole-of-government policy approach; from policies targeted at promoting R&D activities to policies for creating an innovation-friendly framework; and from one-size-fits-all policy measures to fine-tuned and differentiated policy measures tailored to delivering more sophisticated support for policy needs.[67]

At the outset of the period covered by the plan, the MLP is clear that foreign technology and know-how will play a key role in jump-starting indigenous innovation, and that the government must pursue national industrial policies designed to obtain and exploit this foreign information. The MLP defines "indigenous innovation" as "enhancing original innovation through co-innovation and re-innovation based on the assimilation of imported technologies." Indeed, the MLP rejects the importation of foreign technology without a clear plan to convert it into Chinese technology: "One should clearly be aware that the importation of technologies without emphasizing the assimilation, absorption and re-innovation is bound to weaken the nation's indigenous research and development capacity." These bald assertions lead some foreign analysts to conclude that the MLP is a "blueprint for technology theft on a scale the world has never seen before."[68]

The document acknowledges that foreign technology played a key role in the early years of the Chinese economic reform period, allowing China to "improve the level of industrial technology, enhance innovation capacity, [and] promote economic and social development."[69] Yet another period of acquiring foreign technology and know-how is perceived as critical for China to eventually wean itself from this reliance on foreign technology and know-how, transitioning to indigenous innovation. In a section entitled "The Expansion of International and Regional Scientific and Technological Cooperation and Exchanges," the plan calls for the strengthening of "national capability of independent innovation." To achieve this goal,

> we must make full use of favorable conditions for opening up and expanding various forms of international and regional scientific and technological cooperation and exchanges.[70]

Specifically, the document calls for government units and enterprises "to encourage scientific research institutes, universities and overseas research and development institutions to establish joint laboratories or research and development centers . . . [and] to encourage multinational companies to set up research and development institutions."[71] In addition, the document calls for institutions to:

- "further encourage multinational companies to establish R&D institutions in China to improve China's overall research and development level";
- "encourage transnational corporations and domestic research institutions, schools, enterprises [to] expand R&D cooperation";
- "encourage foreign investment and technological achievements in R&D centers in China for industrial production";
- "encourage foreign investment enterprises . . . and private enterprises to transfer technology";
- "encourage and guide enterprises and multinational companies or developed countries with advanced technology enterprises to establish a strategic alliance to participate in the technical R&D activities by transnational corporations"; and
- "encourage domestic enterprises and foreign-invested enterprises to develop technology supporting, high-tech research and development to accelerate the process of internationalization."[72]

Reading between the lines, the policies also encourage companies, whether domestic or foreign, to engage in R&D in China to boost domestically owned intellectual property (IP).[73]

Why would foreign companies participate in this wholesale transfer of innovation, particularly when it is designed to facilitate domestic innovation presumably at the expense of multinational companies? Serger and Widman point out the obvious: "The bait is the large Chinese market."[74] But to further sweeten the pot, foreign companies are given incentives to set up manufacturing in China and transfer technological knowledge to Chinese partner companies. As an example, foreign automotive firms seeking to sell in China face high import duties, leading them to pursue joint-venture manufacturing relationships. The energy sector is under pressure to transfer technology in exchange for commissions. Telecom companies have been encouraged to move production and increasingly R&D to China. Local procurement is encouraged by offering significant tax rebates, among other things.[75] In addition to the traditional fear of technology dependence, this mindset explains why the government seeks a 30 percent reduction of reliance on foreign technology in 15 years' time, down from the current assessment of 60 percent.[76]

Following the promulgation of the MLP in 2006, the Chinese government has issued a series of implementation documents:

- The February 2006 "Medium and Long Term Plan for S&T Development, 2006–2020" detailing preferences for domestic goods and service providers.
- A September 2006 tax bureau "Circular on Preferential Tax Policies for Innovation Enterprises" offered a two-year exemption from enterprise income tax.
- The December 2006 "Administrative Measures on the Accreditation of National Indigenous Innovation Products" outlined the plans for creating national indigenous innovation product catalogs.
- The May 2007 "Measures for Administration of Government Procurement Budgets for Indigenous Innovation Products" warned government at all levels to develop specific indigenous innovation procurement plans or they would lose procurement funds.
- Also, in May 2007, "Measures for Assessment of Government Procurement of Indigenous Innovation Products" lowered government procurement supplier qualification standards for companies doing indigenous innovation.
- In December 2007, the MOF issued "Measures for the Administration of Government Procurement of Imported Products" which directed that approval by a board of experts is necessary for government entities to purchase imported goods. It called for favoring foreign suppliers that provide the domestic industry with technology transfers and training services.
- A January 2008 "Enterprise Income Tax Law" offered a preferential rate of 15 percent to high-tech enterprises designated by the government as indigenous innovation companies because they developed and owned their intellectual property.[77]

Perhaps the most important of these is the National Indigenous Innovation Products Accreditation Program (Notice 618) (国家自主创新产品认定管理办法 --实行), more commonly known as the "indigenous innovation" regulation. The Program implements the "Measures for the Administration of the Accreditation of National Indigenous Innovation Products," issued in November 2006. The key elements of the regulation, jointly issued in November 2009 by the Ministry of Science and Technology (MOST), the National Development and Reform Commission (NDRC), and the Ministry of Finance, include (1) a mandate for an accredited catalog of products given priority in government procurement; (2) requirement that the products contain domestically owned intellectual property rights, and that the applicant's use, disposal, and improvements of the intellectual property involved in the underlying product must not be subject to foreign restrictions and any trademark used must be registered in China first and must not be restricted by related foreign brands; and (3) an initial focus on six high- and new-technology fields including computers and application equipment; communications products; modern office equipment; software; new energy and new energy devices; and high-efficiency and energy-saving products.

The issuance of the indigenous innovation regulations has roused a strong reaction from foreign business and trade associations. In a December 2009 letter to Wan Gang (Minister of Science and Technology), Xie Xuren (Minister of

Finance), and Zhang Ping (Chairman of the National Development and Reform Commission), more than 30 foreign organizations asserted:

> the criteria of Notice 618 diverge markedly from global practices and include unique requirements that the product's intellectual property be developed and owned in China, and that any trademarks be originally registered in China. By contrast, quality, performance and value are given only a minimal role. China and the international community have a common interest in ensuring robust protection of intellectual property rights as we forge a closer economic agenda. China's new criteria fail to recognize the truly collaborative, cross-border and global nature of R&D that produces innovation and that few if any products are developed in a single national territory. Establishing local intellectual property ownership as a market access condition would run counter to free and open trade and to fostering collaborative innovation.[78]

As a result of this outcry, China's indigenous innovation regulations became the subject of dialogue between senior government officials at the Sino–US Strategic & Economic Dialogue in spring 2010.

Reason 2: MNCs seeking to improve their penetration of the China market by adapting their products better to local markets

According to research by Quan Xiaohong, MNC R&D labs in developing countries are established primarily for the purpose of image building, *local* adaptation, supporting *local* manufacturing subsidiaries, and, at most, product development for *local* markets.[79] This is in line with the widely held belief that "R&D follows production."[80] Evan Thorpe concurs, arguing that the original impetus for MNC investments in R&D in China was localization of existing products for the China market, and points out that "most of the handful of R&D centers that conduct basic research did not begin to do so until they had already established strong product development functions."[81]

One way of categorizing these activities is provided by Quan's field study and survey on MNC R&D labs in China, which identified four types of R&D activities in those labs: "old product for local market"; "new product development for local market"; "new product development for global market"; and "research".[82] These first two represent the early phases of foreign R&D in China. MNCs' branch R&D labs of this type focus on relatively low innovative activities such as local adaptation of imported products, technical support for local sales, and production support. No effort is put into developing new products in the emerging market, only product adaptation. Many companies like Microsoft, SAP, and Nokia were engaged in this type of activity when they entered China.[83] In "new product development for local market," MNC R&D labs in host developing countries begin to explore the local market through identifying and meeting local needs from the beginning of product development. MNCs often start new product development after they get familiar with local market conditions.[84] The later phases, "new product development for global market" and "research," are advanced stages of development.

Evan Thorpe offers two additional functions for local R&D work. The first is information technology support, customer service, and after-sales services. As Thorpe writes,

> These types of services are especially important for companies that deliver complex products that require technical support. As Chinese companies expand, they buy large orders of sophisticated industrial goods more frequently and, as a result, often require plentiful, high-quality support provided by a large and able staff.

The second function is supply chain base support. Thorpe argues that "proximity to suppliers and other partners means that companies can address matters locally and immediately. Locating complementary functions near each other can reduce costs or even provide tax exemptions depending on local taxation requirements." The final benefit of in-country R&D is "proximity to customer base," whereby "locating R&D centers close to the customer base allows companies to respond more quickly to local demands for new or adapted products."[85]

Reason 3: Desire by MNCs to globalize their innovation cycle and tap expertise and resources around the world

While the original impetus for moving basic R&D abroad was product localization, many MNCs now see foreign locales as a source or perhaps even a center of innovation.[86] At the strategic level, Western MNCs have sought to globalize their R&D enterprise for multiple reasons. Some want to take advantage of cheap native labor to perform basic R&D work, while retaining core innovation at home. Others have decided to go "all-in" and move their global R&D centers offshore, hoping to benefit not only from lower costs but also to tap into pools of local innovation. As Serger argues, these two modes together are changing the global R&D game, as "transition and developing countries are becoming increasingly important sources <u>and</u> drivers of innovation (demanding and supplying new innovative solutions) [emphasis added]."[87]

In particular, many outside analysts view China as an attractive innovation hub. Serger and Widman argue that "China's rise as an important knowledge base and large domestic market will make it an increasingly strong contender for R&D."[88] Moreover, they assert that "China will rapidly gain ground in knowledge-intensive sectors, and it may become a world leader in some fields of R&D."[89] Denis Fred Simon, a specialist in Chinese science and technology, remarked in the *New York Times* that "the Chinese are going to become sources of innovation . . . they will find themselves enmeshed in global R&D more and more."[90]

But why are companies increasingly choosing to locate their innovation in China as against other countries?[91] Is it solely a response to Chinese government pressure? As discussed earlier in the chapter, Beijing's policies certainly have a large impact on the business environment, distorting the level playing field and creating perverse incentives for technology transfer. Yet global firms also appear to be shifting innovation to China of their own accord. According to Kate Walsh, companies have undergone a key shift, where the dominant rationale for establishing R&D in China has changed from catering to Chinese governments' requirement to one stressing internal corporate interests.[92]

As a result of these shifts, China is increasingly becoming a magnet for innovation centers. Speaking in 2004, Max von Zedtwitz, a professor at Tsinghua University, claimed that "within five years, China could overtake UK, Germany and Japan as a base for corporate research, leaving it second only to the US."[93] According to a global survey by the Economist Intelligence Unit in September 2004, which interviewed 104 senior executives (with 37 percent from US-based companies, 34 percent from European companies, and 16 percent from Asia-based companies), China was identified as the top R&D location by 39 percent of respondents, followed closely by the US, India and then the UK. Multinationals have increased their investment in R&D centers in China by a large margin as the market there becomes more important in their global business strategy. Some global business giants, such as GE, Philips, Motorola, and Siemens, invest tens of millions of US dollars in R&D centers in China, the Ministry of Commerce said.[94] Dr. Li Wanlin, senior vice-president of Siemens (China) Telecommunication Ltd., said that the establishment of Siemens China R&D centers is a vitally important strategy for the German company's future development.[95]

But what is the real form of this innovation and R&D work? Is it largely a PR exercise to ameliorate Chinese government edicts, or is there genuine innovation occurring? As always, the picture is complicated, with a wide range of activities subsumed under the term "research and development." According to *Xinhua*, some centers (Microsoft, Nokia, Bell-Alcatel, and Panasonic) only conduct basic R&D work.[96] At the same time, some R&D centers have become the global R&D centers for MNCs.[97] Quan noted that her 2004 survey of MNC R&D labs in information technology industries in Beijing found that these labs are not just providing technical support, product localization, or product development for the local market; rather, they are developing products for the global market.[98]

Building on the typology discussed in the previous section, Quan distinguishes between "new product development for global market," and "research" activities.[99] The former includes product development conducted in MNC R&D branches in developing countries not only for the host local market, but also for the "developed country" market and/or other emerging markets (mostly developing countries). This type of R&D activity marks a change in business strategy by MNCs, indicating an emphasis on exploration of global R&D labor.[100] The latter R&D activities, by contrast, are identified as "research" activities. According to the OECD definition of R&D, research further includes basic research and applied research: "basic research is experimental or theoretical work undertaken primarily to acquire new knowledge of the underlying foundations of phenomena and observable facts, without any particular application or use in view."[101] Applied research, by contrast, "is also original investigation undertaken in order to acquire new knowledge. It is, however, directed primarily towards a specific practical aim or objective."[102] Companies and analysts have also identified exemplar cases of this latter type in China. For example, Nokia moved core R&D for its handset operating system to its Beijing R&D center.[103] By 2010, 5 percent of R&D engineers in China designed 40 percent of worldwide Nokia phones.[104] Microsoft's research center in China is as productive in terms of papers and patents as any other Microsoft R&D center in the world.[105] For General Electric, its "ultra-compact medical imaging technology" was developed in Beijing, which it claims pioneered the concept of "reverse innovation." Finally, ABB has located its worldwide robotics R&D and HQ in Shanghai since 2005.

Of course, it is far too didactic to expect Quan's typology to be so clearly delineated in an actual research center. As she writes,

> It is not unusual to observe all three types of R&D activities within one MNC R&D lab. It appears in some instances that MNC R&D labs are likely to focus on Type I activities upon entering the Chinese market. For example, R&D activities of the SAP Lab in Beijing have evolved from Type I to Type II then to Type III over these years.[106]

Depending on your point of view, one key facilitator or bottleneck for the evolution of innovation centers in China is people. Not surprisingly, Quan found in survey data that "availability of R&D personnel" was the most important location incentive for MNC R&D labs in China.[107] Quan elaborates,

> Availability of R&D personnel is very essential for MNC R&D labs in China. One major function of these R&D labs is product development for the global market as stated earlier, and the labs usually provide some small modules to contribute to the overall R&D task. As a result, the R&D work conducted in the labs in China is less technologically sophisticated than work done in developed countries. What MNC R&D labs need in the host developing countries is essentially a rich pool of low-cost, but considerably quality R&D labor. While market information can be crucial for local market-oriented R&D activities, the need for R&D labor pool is pervasive for all R&D lab activities in China.[108]

Looking at official numbers, it would appear that high-quality personnel should not be a problem in China. According to the US National Science Foundation's China Office, an estimated 3.2 million people were involved in China's R&D activities in 2009, the largest number in the world.[109] The number of scientists and engineers more than doubled between 2000 and 2008 to 1.59 million.[110] It is easy to deceive with raw numbers, however, especially given the size of China's overall population. Indeed, the density of researchers in China remains lower than that of developed countries, even if China is rapidly closing the gap. In 2007, there were

1,071 researchers per million population in China, compared to 5,573 in Japan, 4,663 in the USA (2006), 3,532 in Germany, and 4,181 in the UK.[111]

Of course, numbers do not tell us anything about quality. One MNC R&D lab manager proudly presented that in 2006 they hired 100 good-quality engineers out of an application pool of 10,000.[112] But for most MNCs, what Chinese employees lack in quality they make up for with their low labor costs. According to the vice-president of the SAP lab, "there are very creative software developers in China. Although there are also good software developers in Germany, they are too expensive."[113] Quan writes,

> While supply is abundant and quality is good, these scientists and engineers are very inexpensive in China compared to many other countries. For example, in Beijing, the average monthly salary of a design engineer in a state-owned firm in IT industries ranges from 3,000 RMB (~ US $380) to 5,000 RMB (~ US $650). In private firms, the salary can be 50% to 60% higher. Multinational corporations in Beijing usually provide a higher salary to attract the best people in the country to work for them. They offer approximately US$1,000 to US$2,000 as monthly wages to their employees (according to interviews with MNC R&D lab managers). This is still much lower than the pay of a US engineer for similar work. In Shanghai, the salary level is about the same as in Beijing. But in other cities in China, the salary is much lower. For instance, in Chengdu, the capital city of Sichuan province which has also attracted an increasing number of MNCs, MNCs pay about 50% less to engineers compared to those in Beijing.[114]

This attention to costs has only gotten more acute with the global economic downturn since 2008 and the margin pressures on various industries in both the global and the Chinese markets.

In addition to personnel, another key indicator of evolutionary success for foreign R&D centers is the nature of their partnerships in China.[115] One popular arrangement is to establish an R&D center at a Chinese university. Quan Xiaohong identifies multiple formats for an MNC–university relationship, including outsourcing, sponsored research, joint-lab model, internship, training, or donation.[116] Evan Thorpe outlines the advantages that come from pairing with a post-secondary educational institution:

> Partnerships with universities are valuable to companies' R&D potential. For IP and management reasons, these partnerships are usually contracted on a project-by-project basis, but a single project can generate momentum toward future cooperation. Because many universities have close ties to the government, these projects and relationships between experts and professionals can help lead to government procurement projects. Joint efforts in curriculum development, book publishing, and special programs are key ways through which universities and enterprises can strengthen ties and

promote innovation. Because university resources are limited, foreign companies often contribute training, equipment, and funding to the partnership projects. In addition to building relationships and local ties, companies can use these partnerships to educate potential employees and customers about their products and introduce new products to local markets. Companies should carefully evaluate university capabilities and determine which key academics are leaders in their fields and most suitable to help run cooperative R&D projects. Many top Chinese universities have faculty with significant experience in conducting research jointly with MNCs.[117]

Another popular arrangement is a joint venture (JV) with a commercial enterprise in the same industry. Thorpe again lays out the pros:

> A joint venture (JV) can allow the foreign partner to access the PRC partner's local talent and customer networks. Even wholly foreign-owned enterprises can conduct joint projects with local partners to gain access to local resources. In the current PRC operational climate, many tech companies and manufacturers of advanced products have expanding customer bases with changing needs.[118]

Yet it is the choice of these partnerships that often raises the first concerns about science and technology espionage in China. The following section explores the national security implications of the rise of the foreign R&D lab in China, especially the possible illicit transfer of foreign technology, know-how, and expertise.

Potential national security implications of foreign R&D labs

The evolution of foreign R&D labs in China remains controversial, raising fundamental structural questions for trade relations and national security. Does the rise in offshore investment and R&D in China have a profound and positive impact on China's technology development capabilities or does it necessarily weaken or threaten America's own technological strength and leadership?[119] Is industry right when it says offshoring of R&D is a necessary evil in an age of globalization in which the Chinese market plays an increasingly vital role?[120] Is there actually little cause for concern because of China's past failures to assimilate technology? Will the US stay ahead regardless because of superior innovation?[121] Or, as Kate Walsh has succinctly put it: "when do we need to worry?"[122]

A balanced assessment of foreign labs in China must acknowledge that, at least from the perspective of MNCs and policy-makers in China, the globalization of R&D is generally perceived as a positive development. The optimists argue: (1) R&D investments by FDI firms are an important step to further improve the "quality" of foreign investment in China as well as to promote the S&T development in the Chinese business sector; (2) the establishment of full-scale R&D centers engaged in partnerships with local research organizations fosters "brain circulation" of human resources; (3) the emerging global R&D network and improved domestic environment of advanced physical infrastructure and research networks attracts expatriate scientists back to China; (4) newly established R&D centers will bring new knowledge and new projects which will result in training for Chinese workers at the forefront of international industry; (5) the R&D centers will become the center of industry or sector clusters, and may attract more foreign players; and (6) MNCs may eventually decide to move their R&D headquarters to China.[123] As an overall assessment, Walsh sums up the "glass half full" view: "Given the more manageable, preferred form of wholly foreign-owned R&D investment in China and the beneficial effects possible in a global economy, the rewards from high-tech R&D investments in China appear at present to outweigh the potential risks to US interests."[124]

But the increasing legions of pessimists about the Chinese business environment and the overall dynamic of US–China trade relations counter: (1) the R&D activities of most foreign firms/labs are still predominantly development focused (rather than research focused) to support local business and customers; (2) the development carried out in China is to a large extent targeted at the Chinese market, with a few exceptions of worldwide mandates for certain products and technologies; (3) IP protections are still too primitive and local legal systems too unpredictable;[125] (4) the links between foreign-invested R&D firms and domestic firms and local R&D institutes are still weak; (5) domestic firms have limited absorptive capacity and continued weakness of human resources, as well as the limited labor mobility between foreign and domestic firms; and (6) the market entries of multinationals and increased concentration among a few large foreign firms have caused concerns of monopolistic power and decreased market competition. Some Chinese academics and policy-makers criticize foreign firms' presence and their behavior in China, claiming that they charge unduly high license fees for their patents, that they "crowd out" domestic firms in the market for highly skilled labor, and that they thwart technology transfer and knowledge spillovers.[126] Furthermore, foreign firms are seen as dominating standards and technology platforms, and reducing Chinese companies to the role of producers with low profit margins.[127] Finally, Sun and Wen identify internal structural impediments to bringing R&D to China and making it productive: (1) rising wages; (2) high mobility and turnover; (3) lack of experience among recent graduates; (4) limited creativity; and (5) cultural differences with their Western counterparts.[128]

Reading through the optimistic and pessimistic assessments, it is clear that R&D in China is not an unalloyed good or bad, and offers no easy Manichean outcome. Rather, there appear to be tremendous variations between sectors and within sectors, between different geographic locales, and between different levels of the system (national, provincial, local). Moreover, the policy and business environment is not static, but has changed over time. Walsh argues:

> it is important to note that the risks from . . . R&D collaboration with Chinese partners probably were highest under the joint R&D ventures formed during the mid- to late-1990s period of investment. These risks may have

lessened since due to the shift in many R&D investments to wholly foreign-owned enterprises. Due to WTO reforms, foreign investors are no longer required by law to work with Chinese partners on R&D or to establish R&D centers as a condition for market access (although this is still encouraged). Moreover, while both the joint venture and WFOE models involve a transfer of technological know-how to mostly locally hired staff, there is an important distinction between conducting R&D with a joint venture partner – who shares equally in any IPR resulting from R&D collaboration – and similar work conducted under the WFOE structure. In the latter case, the IPR remains solely that of the foreign investor, who now has greater recourse in the event of IPR infringements in China (and an option short of having to dissolve the venture entirely if serious concerns arise). Thus, much of the damage and the potential risk from this type of technology transfer might already have passed.[129]

Going forward, the risk can likely only be evaluated on a deal-by-deal basis, not at the macro-level, and the relative gain or harm is deeply dependent on the risk mitigation strategies implemented by the owners of the intellectual property. In other words, there is no "one-size-fits-all" critique of foreign R&D transfers in China, despite the ideological temptation to do so.

What are the types of policy responses that the US government could pursue to mitigate the possible loss of intellectual property and technological competitiveness to China? Kate Walsh offers two policy recommendations for the bilateral relationship, one near term and the other far term:

> In the near-term, the US "deemed export" rule should be amended to cover advanced foreign R&D investments and technology transfers outside the United States. Over the longer-term, the US export control system should be reformed to provide a means of monitoring global R&D and other newly emerging international business dynamics.[130]

On the latter point, the Obama White House has undertaken a series of initial steps to reform export controls, but the measures seem focused on consolidation of the technologies we seek to control and better coordination of the controls under a unified organization. Walsh's final recommendation is perhaps the most strategic and long term, and focuses attention on a neglected but critical determinant of the future strength of American competitiveness, our own R&D base and workforce:

> Although the United States benefits from a continued net inflow of R&D investment from around the world, US government funding for basic research and education should be increased in order to maintain the US lead in critical high-tech industries and innovation. This is crucial to ensuring the United States remains economically, technologically, and militarily competitive. Additionally, as foreign nationals working in US labs, universi-

ties, and high-tech companies become able to find similar work in their own economies due to globalization, the US government must invest more in grade school and secondary education, particularly in basic sciences, mathematics, and engineering, or risk falling behind.[131]

Notes

1 Philip E. Auerswald and Lewis Branscomb, "Research and Innovation in a Networked World," *Technology in Society* 30, 2008, pp. 339–347, p. 339.
2 Battelle, *2012 Global Funding Forecast*, December 2011, www.battelle.org/aboutus/rd/2012.pdf. Sylvia Schwaag Serger, "Research and Innovation as a Forward-Looking Policy Response to the Crisis? The Case of Asia," Presentation, June 26, 2009. See also Evan Thorpe, "Bringing R&D to China," *China Business Review* 35, no. 2, March to April 2008.
3 Thorpe, "Bringing R&D to China."
4 Xielin Liu and Nannan Lundin, "The National Innovation System of China in Transition: From Plan-Based to Market-Driven System," In *The New Asian Innovation Dynamics*, ed. Govindan Parayil and Anthony P. D'Costa, New York: Palgrave Macmillan, 2009. See also Sylvia Schwaag Serger, "Research and Innovation as a Forward-Looking Policy Response to the Crisis? The Case of Asia," Presentation, June 26, 2009.
5 Organisation for Economic Co-operation and Development, *OECD Reviews of Innovation Policy: China*, p. 23.
6 Battelle, *2012 Global Funding Forecast*.
7 2009 numbers found in Hao Xin, "China Hopes to Boost Basic Research as Overall R&D Spending Soars," *Science Insider*, November 24, 2010, http://news.sciencemag.org/scienceinsider/2010/11/china-hopes-to-boost-basic-research.html.
8 2006 numbers from OECD, *OECD Reviews of Innovation Policy: China*.
9 www.nsf.gov/statistics/seind12/c4/c4h.htm.
10 www.nsftokyo.org/rm10-02.pdf.
11 NSF China Office, "S&T Highlights: December 2010, January 2011," www.nsfbeijing.cn/download/China_S&T_Highlight_Dec2010_Jan2011.pdf.
12 Sylvia Schwaag Serger and Eric Widman, *Competition from China: Opportunities and Challenges for Sweden*, Stockholm: Swedish Institute for Growth Policy Studies, 2005.
13 Kathleen Walsh, "China R&D: A High-Tech Field of Dreams," in Yifei Sun, Maximilian von Zedtwitz, and Denis Fred Simon, eds, *Global R&D in China*, London: Routledge, 2009, pp.14–15.
14 http://r-center.grips.ac.jp/gallery/docs/11-05.pdf.
15 Rajneesh Narula and Antonello Zanfe, "Globalization of Innovation: The Role of Multinational Enterprises," in Jan Fagerberg, David C. Mowery, and Richard R. Nelson, eds, *The Oxford Handbook of Innovation*, New York: Oxford University Press, 2005.
16 United Nations Conference on Trade and Development, World Investment Report, 2005: *Transnational Corporations and the Internationalization of R&D, 2005*, www.unctad.org/Templates/webflyer.asp?docid=6087&intItemID=1397&lang=1&mode=downloads.
17 James R. Hagerty, "US Loses High-Tech Jobs as R&D Shifts Toward Asia," *The Wall Street Journal*, January 18, http://online.wsj.com/article/SB10001424052970204468004577167003809336394.html?mod=googlenews_wsj, citing a report by the National Science Board, a policymaking arm of the National Science Foundation.
18 Jianmin Jin, "Foreign Companies Accelerating R&D Activity in China," Fujitsu Research Institute, May 13, 2010, http://jp.fujitsu.com/group/fri/en/column/message/2010/2010-05-13.html.
19 Nannan Lundin and Sylvia Schwaag Serger, "Globalization of R&D and China:

Empirical Observations and Policy Implications," IFN Working Paper No. 710, Stockholm: Research Institute of Industrial Economics, 2007, p. 6.

20 OECD, *OECD Reviews of Innovation Policy: China.*
21 Ibid.
22 Serger, "Research and Innovation."
23 "China Vows to Become Nation of Innovation," *People's Daily Online*, November 25, 2005.
24 Strategy for National Reinvigorating through S&T and Education (1995), Strategy for Sustainable Development (1996), Strategy for National Reinvigorating through Talents (2002). See Serger, "Research and Innovation."
25 Serger, "Research and Innovation."
26 OECD, *OECD Reviews of Innovation Policy: China.*
27 Serger and Widman, *Competition from China.*
28 United Nations Education, Scientific, and Cultural Organization, *UNESCO Science Report 2010: The Current Status of Science Around the World*, http://unesdoc.unesco.org/images/0018/001899/189958e.pdf.
29 http://royalsociety.org/uploadedFiles/Royal_Society_Content/policy/publications/2011/4294976134.pdf.
30 www.thefiscaltimes.com/Articles/2012/03/05/China-Leads-Global-Patent-Growth.aspx#page1.
31 http://ip.people.com.cn/GB/152255/16803234.html.
32 James McGregor, "Time to Rethink US–China Trade Relations," *Washington Post*, May 19, 2010. See also James McGregor, "China's Drive for 'Indigenous Innovation': A Web of Industrial Policies", Washington, DC: US Chamber of Commerce, July 2010, www.uschamber.com/sites/default/files/reports/100728chinareport_0.pdf.
33 Lundin and Serger, "Globalization of R&D and China."
34 Quan Xiaohong, "MNCs Rush to Set Up R&D Labs in China: What is the Nature?" National University of Singapore, East Asia Institute. EAI Background Brief, No. 332, 2007.
35 "Multinationals Speed Up R&D Center Establishment in China," *Xinhua*, February 12, 2006.
36 Quan, "MNCs Rush to Set Up R&D Labs in China."
37 Ibid.
38 Ibid.
39 "China Home to 1,200 Foreign R&D Centers," *People's Daily*, March 16, 2010. For earlier numbers, see Evan Thorpe, "Bringing R&D to China," *China Business Review*, March to April 2008. Of course, it should be noted that there are a number of reasons why these numbers may be distorted: (1) R&D is strategic and sensitive and therefore not always disclosed, (2) some foreign R&D activities exist more on paper than in reality, (3) some non-R&D activities are miscategorized as R&D to fulfill requirements, and (4) Foreign R&D labs are also missing from official S&T statistics. See Oliver Gassman and Zheng Han, "Motivations and Barriers of Foreign R&D Activities in China," *R&D Management* 34, no. 4, September 2004, pp. 423–437; Quan Xiaohong, "MNC R&D Labs in China," Stanford Projects on Regions of Innovation and Entrepreneurship, Presentation, November 29, 2005; and Lundin and Serger, "Globalization of R&D and China," p. 6.
40 "China Home to 1,200 Foreign R&D Centers," *People's Daily.*
41 "Multinationals Speed Up R&D Center Establishment in China," *Xinhua.*
42 OECD, *OECD Reviews of Innovation Policy: China*, p. 32.
43 "Multinationals Speed Up R&D Center Establishment in China."
44 "China Home to 1,200 Foreign R&D Centers," *People's Daily*, March 16, 2010. See also OECD, *OECD Reviews of Innovation Policy: China*, p. 32, and "Multinationals Speed Up R&D Center Establishment in China."
45 Serger, "Research and Innovation."
46 Walsh, "China R&D: A High-Tech Field of Dreams," p. 14. For specific details about

China's accession to the WTO, see www.wto.int/english/thewto_e/countries_e/china_e.htm. For a general definition of WOFEs, see http://en.wikipedia.org/wiki/Wholly_Foreign_Owned_Enterprise. For details on how to set up a WOFE, see www.pathtochina.com/reg_wfoe.htm.

47 Maximilian von Zedtwitz, "Managing Foreign R&D Labs in China," *R&D Management* 34, No. 4, 2004, pp. 439–452.
48 OECD, *OECD Reviews of Innovation Policy: China*, p. 34.
49 Ibid., p. 34; Lundin and Serger, "Globalization of R&D and China," p. 6.
50 Quoted in McGregor, "China's Drive for 'Indigenous Innovation'," p. 17.
51 OECD, *OECD Reviews of Innovation Policy: China*, p. 34.
52 The NDRC is China's "macro policy planning powerhouse." See McGregor, "China's Drive for 'Indigenous Innovation'," p.11.
53 MIIT is responsible for creating and implementing China's high-level industrial policies, particularly in telecommunications, software, Internet, and electronics sectors.
54 Within the Chinese system, McGregor describes NSFC as a "champion of focusing on peer-reviewed basic and applied research." See McGregor, "China's Drive for 'Indigenous Innovation'," p.11.
55 OECD, *OECD Reviews of Innovation Policy: China*, p. 49.
56 www.most.gov.cn/zzjg/jgsz/jgszgxjsfzycyhs/index.htm.
57 www.most.gov.cn/zzjg/jgsz/jgszjcyjs/index.htm.
58 www.most.gov.cn/zzjg/jgsz/jgszfzjhs/index.htm.
59 www.most.gov.cn/zzjg/jgsz/jgszzcfgytzggs/index.htm.
60 http://gjss.ndrc.gov.cn/.
61 http://kjs.miit.gov.cn/.
62 http://cys.mofcom.gov.cn/aarticle/gywm/200203/20020300003730.html.
63 "Multinationals Speed Up R&D Center Establishment in China," *Xinhua*.
64 OECD, *OECD Reviews of Innovation Policy: China*, p. 46.
65 Ibid.
66 Ibid., p. 48.
67 Ibid., p. 46.
68 McGregor, "China's Drive for 'Indigenous Innovation'," p. 4.
69 www.most.gov.cn/ztzl/gjzctx/ptzcyjxh/200802/t20080225_59303.htm.
70 www.most.gov.cn/kjgh/.
71 www.most.gov.cn/kjgh/.
72 www.most.gov.cn/ztzl/gjzctx/ptzcyjxh/200802/t20080225_59303.htm.
73 Thorpe, "Bringing R&D to China."
74 Serger and Widman, *Competition from China*.
75 Ibid.
76 "关于鼓励技术引进和创新，促进转变外贸增长方式的若干意见" ("Various Opinions on Encouraging the Introduction of Technology and Innovation, and Promoting Changes in the Foreign Trade Growth Mode"), July 14, 2006. Accessed at www.most.gov.cn/ztzl/gjzctx/ptzcyjxh/200802/t20080225_59303.htm.
77 This list derived from McGregor, "China's Drive for 'Indigenous Innovation'," p. 19.
78 http://cbi.typepad.com/files/12-10-09-international-business-letter-on-indigenous-innovation-accreditation-policy.pdf.
79 Quan, "MNCs Rush to Set Up R&D Labs in China."
80 Serger and Widman, *Competition from China*.
81 Thorpe, "Bringing R&D to China."
82 Quan, "MNCs Rush to Set Up R&D Labs in China."
83 Ibid.
84 Ibid.
85 Thorpe, "Bringing R&D to China."
86 MNC R&D labs also quickly realize that setting up a lab for pure image-building purpose is costly.
87 Serger, "Research and Innovation."

88 Serger and Widman, *Competition with China.*
89 Ibid.
90 Chris Buckley, "Let a Thousand Ideas Flower: China is a New Hotbed of Research," *New York Times*, November 13, 2004, www.nytimes.com/2004/09/13/technology/13china.html?_r=0.
91 For more research on location incentives for MNCs' R&D abroad, see Prasada Reddy, *Globalization of Corporate R&D: Implications for Innovation in Host Countries*, New York: Routledge, 2000; Oliver Gassmann and Max von Zedtwitz, "Organization of Industrial R&D on a Global Scale," *R&D Management* 28, no. 3, 1998, pp. 147–161; Christopher A. Bartlett and Sumantra Ghoshal, *Managing across Borders: The Transnational Solution*, 2nd edn, Boston, MA: Harvard Business School Press, 1998; Jack N. Behrman and William A. Fischer, "Overseas R&D Activities of Transnational Companies," *The International Executive* 22, no. 3, Fall 1980, pp. 15–17; Robert Pearce, "Decentralised R&D and Strategic Competitiveness: Globalized Approaches to Generation and Use of Technology in Multinational Enterprises," *Research Policy* 28, nos 2–3, March 1999, pp. 157–178; and Lars Hakanson and Robert Nobel, "Determinants of foreign R&D in Swedish Multinationals," *Research Policy* 22, nos 5–6, November 1993, pp. 397–411.
92 Walsh, "China R&D: A High-Tech Field of Dreams," p.16.
93 Buckley, "Let a Thousand Ideas Flower: China is a New Hotbed of Research."
94 "Multinationals Speed Up R&D Center Establishment in China," *China Daily.*
95 Ibid.
96 Ibid.
97 Ibid.
98 Quan, "MNC R&D Labs in China."
99 Quan Xiaohong, "Multinational Research and Development Labs in China: Local and Global Innovation," unpublished PhD Dissertation, University of California, Berkeley, 2005.
100 Quan, "Multinational Research and Development Labs in China."
101 Organisation for Economic Co-operation and Development, *Frascati Manual 2002*, OECD Publishing, 2002, pp. 240, 245.
102 Ibid.
103 Maximilian von Zedtwitz, "Managing Foreign R&D in China: Some Lessons," Presented at the "Asian Rise in ICT R&D Conference," Brussels, February 17, 2011.
104 Ibid.
105 Ibid.
106 Quan, "Multinational Research and Development Labs in China."
107 Quan, "MNC R&D Labs in China." Other important factors that attract MNC R&D labs to locate in China include "proximity to regional and local markets," "low cost of R&D," etc.
108 Quan, "MNCs Rush To Set Up R&D Labs in China."
109 NSF China Office, "S&T Highlights: December 2010, January 2011."
110 UNESCO, *UNESCO Science Report 2010.*
111 Ibid.
112 Quan, "MNCs Rush To Set Up R&D Labs in China."
113 Ibid.
114 Ibid.
115 For research on models of how MNCs organize and manage their global R&D network, see Bartlett and Ghoshal, *Managing across Borders*; Daniele Archibugi and Jonathan Michie, "The Globalization of Technology: A New Taxonomy," *Cambridge Journal of Economics* 19, no. 1, 1995, pp. 121–140; Mark C. Casson, "Modelling the Multinational Enterprise: A Research Agenda," *Millennium Journal of International Studies* 20, no. 2, 1991, pp. 271–285; J.W. Medcof, "A Taxonomy of Internationally Dispersed Technology Units and Its Application to Management Issues," *R&D Management* 27, no. 4, 1997, pp. 301–318; Ivo Zander, "How do you mean 'global'? An empirical

investigation of innovation networks in the multinational corporation," *Research Policy* 28, nos 2–3, March 1999, pp. 195–213; Gassmann and von Zedtwitz, "Organization of industrial R&D on a global scale"; Pearce, "Decentralised R&D and strategic competitiveness."

116 Quan, "MNC R&D Labs in China."
117 Thorpe, "Bringing R&D to China."
118 Ibid.
119 Michael Pillsbury, "China's Progress in Technological Competitiveness: The Need for a New Assessment," Report prepared for the US-China Economic and Security Review Commission, April 21, 2005.
120 Boston Consulting Group (BCG) and Knowledge at Wharton (KW), *China and the New Rules for Global Business*, China Report: Studies in Operations and Strategy, May 26, 2004.
121 George J. Gilboy, "The Myth Behind China's Miracle," *Foreign Affairs* 83, no. 4, July/ August 2004, pp. 33–48.
122 Walsh, "China R&D: A High-Tech Field of Dreams," p. 20.
123 Lundin and Serger, p. 6.
124 Walsh, "China R&D: A High-Tech Field of Dreams," p. 129.
125 Thorpe, "Bringing R&D to China."
126 Cheung K.Y., and Lin P., "Spillover Effects of FDI on Innovation in China: Evidence from the Provincial Data," *China Economic Review* 15, no. 1, 2004, pp. 25–44.
127 Lundin and Serger, "Globalization of R&D and China."
128 Yifei Sun and Ke Wen, "Country Relational Distance, Organizational Power, and R&D Managers: Understanding Environmental Challenges for Foreign R&D in China," in Yifei Sun, Maximilian von Zedtwitz, and Denis Fred Simon, eds, *Global R&D in China*, London: Routledge, 2009.
129 Walsh, "China R&D: A High-Tech Field of Dreams," pp. 128–129.
130 Ibid., p. xv.
131 Ibid.

4

PRC-BASED TECHNOLOGY TRANSFER ORGANIZATIONS

China's quest for foreign technology goes well beyond the modest efforts to supplement indigenous research that most countries pursue as a normal practice. Rather it is part of a deliberate, state-sponsored project to circumvent the costs of research, overcome cultural disadvantages, and "leapfrog" to the forefront by leveraging the creativity of other nations. This fact is evident in policy declarations, in the scale and variety of transfer operations, and in the number of organizations China devotes to foreign technology acquisition.

Sorting through the list of PRC institutes engaged in technology transfer is a daunting task. On the national level alone, more than a dozen organizations ensure that China has direct and indirect access to foreign technologies and to the scientists who develop them. This figure includes technical ministries focused on particular sectors and dedicated national offices that promote transfer in general. Exempted from the tally are clandestine services, open-source networks, mil-tech procurement offices, co-opted foreign groups and multinationals, whose roles are documented in other chapters.

Local venues complement the national organizations: incubation parks, returnee facilities, conventions for overseas Chinese scientists, liaison offices, and transfer centers that address technology "exchange" at the grass-roots level. Straddling the national and local levels are the sundry outreach groups, alleged non-governmental organizations (NGOs) ranging from technology transfer offices in hometown associations (同乡会) to sanitized fronts for state-sanctioned operations. This physical network is supported by a digital maze of recruitment websites subsidized by the PRC government.

Foreign "talent" recruitment offices

Among the many national-level organizations that support technology transfer, the Beijing-based State Administration of Foreign Experts Affairs (国家外国专家

局) stands out as the highest formal administrative unit, reporting directly to the PRC State Council. SAFEA's mission, according to its website, is to facilitate the "introduction of advanced technology and make Chinese industry more competitive internationally" by managing the recruitment of skilled persons from abroad and sending PRC citizens overseas for training.[1]

At the national level, SAFEA's direct involvement in recruiting is limited to high-value targets. Mostly it acts on a general, administrative plane to determine recruitment strategy, establish policy, oversee its implementation, provide funding, and monitor the activities of affiliated organizations, including a network of chapters in China's major provinces and cities. Its role is to "guide, coordinate, and organize national priority programs to recruit foreign specialists, augment the supervision of personnel sent abroad for training, assume responsibility for foreign liaison work to recruit skilled personnel, open recruitment channels, and build relationships with official foreign institutions and other organizations for skilled personnel exchanges and cooperation".[2]

SAFEA's functions are further described as "certifying the qualifications of and providing relevant services to social intermediary organizations in China and abroad" involved in attracting foreign specialists. It is also responsible for "building an information network for recruitment" and maintaining a "comprehensive database" of foreign resources. Its oversight function is affirmed in a director's message posted to the website, which states that the office annually investigates and certifies "all types of intermediary organizations involved in the international exchange of skilled personnel."[3] Some 80 overseas expert organizations and 73 domestic intermediaries have been accredited by SAFEA to date, which gives some idea of the scale of its operation (and of China's dependence on foreign technology).

Beyond accrediting other tech transfer organizations, SAFEA runs an "international skilled person exchange service system" that includes a network for matching available talent with PRC domestic programs and an annual "exchange fair" to attract foreign specialists with skills the PRC government deems to be important. SAFEA's success is reflected in statistics posted to its website that boast of 440,000 "foreign experts" working in China annually, a quarter of a million of whom are from western countries and Japan.[4]

Unlike other PRC technology transfer institutions that focus on overseas Chinese, SAFEA is more eclectic, drawing support from foreigners of all ethnicities.[5] Nor is its recruitment practice constrained necessarily by foreign espionage laws. On November 8, 2006, the FBI indicted Noshir Gowadia, a US citizen and former employee of Northrop Grumman, for divulging military secrets to China.[6] Gowadia reportedly arranged through a SAFEA rep to visit China "at least six times" between 2003 and 2005 to hand over stealth-related technology.[7]

This case is consistent with a recurring theme on SAFEA's website and in the Chinese tech transfer literature typically, namely encouragement to "use multiple types of recruitment channels" (以多种方式) to achieve the mission. One such posting to the site exhorts SAFEA to "make full use of contacts with governments, exchanges with sister cities, international economic and trade negotiations, international conferences, and like opportunities" to recruit foreign experts.[8] Other recommended venues – overseas provincial associations, alumni associations, international friends, academics and advisers with foreign citizenship, and "visiting scholars well disposed toward China" – betray the informal side of its agenda.

Two more themes that define SAFEA's operations characterize Chinese S&T transfer in general. First, there is no imperative to improve China's theoretical grasp of science and methodology. The focus is entirely on practical technologies. A typical posting to its site states China's need for "high level foreign specialists able to solve key technical problems" and commercialize existing technology. Priority must be given to "actual needs" and state-defined projects.[9] A second theme, emphasized in SAFEA's announcements, is China's need for foreign technology as a "short cut" to national development.

Complementing SAFEA's aim at foreign experts of all nationalities is the State Council's Overseas Chinese Affairs Office (国务院侨务办公室), which focuses on ethnic Chinese abroad. In keeping with PRC practice, the office defines "overseas Chinese" (华侨) in broad terms that include Chinese expatriates overseas, their dependants and relatives (侨眷); ethnic Chinese in foreign countries who may or may not have lived in China (华人); and Chinese who have "returned" (归华) to China (although they may never have been there before).[10]

OCAO's mandate to "protect the legitimate interests" of overseas Chinese is interpreted to mean providing them with opportunities to support the growth and prosperity of their ancestral country (祖国). Specifically, Article 4 of its charter authorizes OCAO to "investigate and study the introduction of overseas Chinese funds, technology, and skilled personnel." This function is localized in OCAO's Department 4 for Economics, Science and Technology, and is consistent with the office's mission to mobilize overseas Chinese to support the Beijing government's priorities.

Department 4's activities include sponsoring international business innovation and exchange forums, building liaison with overseas Chinese professional groups, and supporting high-tech innovation centers in China staffed by returnees. For example, in 2003 it sponsored week-long conferences in Shenyang, Xiamen, Wuhan, and Nanjing on establishing high-tech firms and exchanging S&T personnel aimed primarily at Chinese-Americans with advanced technical degrees.[11] The following year OCAO hosted conferences in Xi'an, Dalian, and other cities, billed as "Face-to-Face Meeting with Overseas Chinese Scholars," "Conference for Cooperation and Exchange between Overseas S&T Personnel and Chinese Enterprises," or "Overseas Chinese Enterprises S&T Innovation Cooperation and Exchange Conference."

In some cases, such as the above, OCAO's connection with the technology transfer event is overt. In other cases it works through the Chinese Overseas Exchange Association (中国海外交流学会), an alleged NGO that shares facilities and telephone lines with OCAO and whose Science and Technology Office is staffed by OCAO personnel. Like SAFEA, OCAO operates branches at the provincial and municipal levels to contact visiting overseas Chinese experts and support their involvement in local "innovation centers."

OCAO's Department 4 also maintains formal liaison with China advocacy groups abroad, many of which are technology oriented. A 2003 posting to the Chinese Overseas Exchange Association's website showed members of the US-based Association of Chinese Scientists and Engineers presenting an award to former Department 4 director Wu Hongqin. A year before, the director of the Association of Chinese Scientists and Engineers in France, a group made up of PhDs working in high-tech fields, met the Department 4 director in Beijing to pledge support for developing the "ancestral country."[12]

Finally, the two institutions – OCAO and its nominal NGO – sponsor annual "Discovery Trips to China for Eminent Young Overseas Chinese" (海外华裔青年杰出人士华夏行) aimed at "understanding China, enhancing friendship and seeking common development." An announcement for the 2008 event, which started in Beijing and ended a week later in Jinan, invited overseas Chinese active in "economy, science and technology" to fulfill their strong aspiration "to visit the hometown of Confucius" while engaging in informal discussions with OCAO leaders and local entrepreneurs.[13]

Another national organization involved heavily in foreign recruitment is the Ministry of Personnel (国家人事部).[14] The MOP has been running outreach projects to attract overseas Chinese experts since at least 1985, when it began a program of "Financial Support for Returned Scholars Involved in S&T Activities." The program now has five components to subsidize S&T projects, international exchanges, technology start-ups, priority state projects, and petty expenses.[15] There is also a "Subsidy Program for Overseas Chinese Scholars to Return to China for Short Periods to Work in Areas Outside the Educational System" and a separate pool of funds for returned scholars who work in China's western region.

Three of the MOP's 12 internal offices engage directly in some form of foreign technology transfer.[16] The "Specialized Technical Personnel Management Department" (专业技术人员管理司) handles personnel evaluation and other management tasks for specialists returning to China as permanent residents. It formulates policy toward overseas Chinese "returning to serve their country" and helps with logistics, expenses, and the paperwork needed to settle in. In addition, it formulates policy for technical specialists entering or leaving the country and for foreign institutes in China hiring key Chinese personnel. The department has an "Overseas Chinese Scholars and Returning Specialists Division" that gives policy support and service guarantees to returnees working in China.

A second office called the "Talented Persons Mobility and Development Department" (人才流动开发司) maintains an "access system" for foreign organizations to enter China's market for skilled personnel as part of its overall task of coordinating the flow of technical personnel within China. Finally there is an "International Exchange and Cooperation Department" (国际交流与合作司),

which runs cooperative personnel programs with foreign governments and international organizations; coordinates and organizes overseas training for state employees and specialized technical personnel; and manages the selection, sending, and coordination of international staff members.

Beyond these three internal offices, the MOP supervises nine subordinate units, one of which – an "Overseas Scholars and Experts Service Center" (留学人员与专家服务中心) – supports technology transfer by interacting with Chinese studying abroad. The center is an amalgamation of the MOP's former "Experts Service Center" and the "China Post-doctoral Science Foundation," which serves as the unit's name outside China. According to an item posted to the Fujian Overseas Scholars Association website,[17] the center is an "important part of China's integrated personnel resources development system" responsible for attracting skilled personnel to China and serving as an intermediary between "domestic employment units" and "overseas students, institutions of learning, and academic organizations."

Its external name notwithstanding, the center functions less as a facilitator for academic exchange and more as a scouting and placement office for PRC state labs and high-tech businesses. The scope of its activities is further apparent in its organization, which includes a Returning Overseas Personnel Service Office, a Service Division for Overseas Personnel Founding Businesses, a Post-doctoral Evaluation and Service Division, an Experts Service Division, an Information and Counseling Division, and a Training and Exchange Service Division – all aimed at matching foreign skills to China's domestic needs.[18]

Among the tasks it performs for overseas scholars returning to found businesses, the center handles "selection, subsidy cost, and evaluation of their S&T activities." It hosts a database of available overseas "talent." It also manages the Science Foundation's capital, oversees the country's "post-doctoral research stations" and "company post-doctoral research stations,"[19] and provides unspecified "intermediary services." By late 2002, there were 947 such units operating in China hosting more than 7,000 people.[20]

Information posted to the MOP website and to its outreach site "China Overseas Talent Network" (www.chinatalents.gov.cn) indicates that the MOP has spent more than RMB200 million in the past 15 years supporting the scientific and technological work of some 4,000 returned overseas scholars and subsidizing another 3,000 overseas Chinese scholars who "return for short periods of service." This latter group is described as "strongly patriotic" with "superior knowledge and far-flung academic connections."[21]

Examples of the foreign skills the MOP hopes to attract may be found on the China Talents website. In December 2005, there was a banner-type ad posted near the top of the site's home page with the headline "Beijing Institute of Applied Physics and Computational Mathematics Invites Talented Persons from All Walks of Life to Join the Alliance." This was followed by a description of the Institute's mission in general terms, its facilities, staffing, and the types of skills sought. Details on application and compensation were also provided.

For those unfamiliar with China's S&T infrastructure, the Institute of Applied

Physics and Computational Mathematics (IAPCM) is China's premier nuclear weapons modeling facility. According to information provided by the Federation of American Scientists (www.fas.org), the IAPCM "under the Chinese Academy of Science, conducts research on nuclear warhead design computations for the Chinese Academy of Engineering Physics (CAEP) in Mianyang, Sichuan." While IAPCM also engages in Nuclear Test Ban Treaty-related activities, the skills sought here – including condensed matter physics, fluid dynamics, and computational mathematics – are consistent with the Institute's primary mission of atomic weapons design.[22]

In plain language, the MOP was asking ethnic Chinese scientists living abroad to support its atomic weapons program. No clandestine service could ask for more. Also noteworthy was a statement requiring applicants to "cherish the socialist fatherland, support the leadership of the Chinese Communist Party, and submit to the needs of the country" – a reminder to applicants that they will undergo security vetting. References to the ancestral country (祖国) and the lack of an English version indicate that the ad was aimed at overseas Chinese.

The Ministry of Science and Technology

Given the extensive technology transfer activities engaged in by PRC state institutions in general, it is not surprising that China's Ministry of Science and Technology (国家科技部) also dedicates significant resources to acquiring foreign technology. Formerly known as the "State Science and Technology Commission," MOST became a full-fledged ministry in 1998 in recognition of the importance China's leaders place on technological development. The following lines from MOST's mission statement suggest the role foreign S&T is expected to play in the process:[23]

> [MOST will] research and formulate the guidelines and policies for China's international cooperation and exchange in science and technology; take charge of bilateral and multilateral governmental science and technology cooperation programs as well as programs related to relevant international organizations; guide the work of science and technology agencies posted abroad; take charge of the selection and administration of science and technology officials posted at Chinese embassies and consulates in foreign countries; manage the work of science and technology aid from foreign governments and international S&T organizations towards China.

MOST's collection posture abroad included some 135 declared "operational personnel" (工作人员) posted to overseas embassies and consulates at 60 places in 45 countries as of 1991 and it has grown since then.[24] This will be discussed in subsequent chapters that deal with China's S&T support structures within the United States and elsewhere. Domestically, MOST helped found more than 30 Pioneering Parks for Overseas Chinese Scholars (海外留学人员创业园) since 1995 at the National New and High Technology Development Zones (国家高新技术开发区)

and Innovation Service Centers for New and High Technology (高新技术创业服务中心) created to exploit ("incubate") S&T skills brought "back" to China by returnees. These parks are treated in detail in Chapter 8.

Our present focus will be on four internal or affiliated MOST organizations: the Department of International S&T Cooperation (国际科技合作司), the China Science and Technology Exchange Center (中国科学技术交流中心), the Shanghai Training Center (上海培训中心), and the Service Center for S&T Personnel Exchange and Development (科技人才交流开发服务中心). This last organization is run by the Institute of Scientific and Technical Information of China – China's main open-source S&T intelligence service – but is "directly subordinate to MOST's leadership," according to the MOST and ISTIC websites.[25]

MOST's Department of International S&T Cooperation has offices for planning, international liaison, and individual geographic regions, including an office for "North America, South America, and Oceania." Its specific responsibilities are:

> To study and deliberate programs, policies, and related regulations for international S&T cooperation; organize and implement bilateral and multilateral S&T cooperation plans between governments and related international organizations, and foreign activities such as official S&T cooperative agreements; examine and negotiate important civilian S&T cooperative exchange projects; organize and implement foreign governments' and international organizations' S&T aid to China and Chinese S&T aid abroad; guide the work of [Chinese] S&T institutions stationed abroad, maintain contact with foreign governments' and international organizations' S&T structures in China, as well as the S&T work of the Hong Kong and Macau special administrative regions and Taiwan.[26]

This sweeping mandate establishes MOST as China's leading body for official S&T exchanges worldwide, while formalizing its supervisory role in private interactions as well. In addition, the International S&T Cooperation Department has authority over 47 municipal and provincial "Science and Technology Commissions" or "Science and Technology Provincial Government Departments" (厅), whose missions are heavily biased toward acquiring foreign technology and expertise.

The Shanghai Commission's program is typical of these second-tier MOST organizations. Among its responsibilities are leadership of the city's high-tech industrial R&D districts, which are populated largely by foreign-invested firms and start-ups run by returned scholars; managing S&T foreign affairs and international S&T cooperation; participating in international S&T cooperative events; reviewing applications from foreign S&T personnel for cooperative ventures; "studying means to increase S&T investment through multiple channels and to optimize S&T resources" (code words for informal foreign tech transfer); and promoting "conversion of S&T results" (科技成果转化).[27]

This last function is discharged, in the Shanghai example, by a Shanghai New and High Technology [Achievements Conversion] Service Center (上海市高新

技术成果转化服务中心, the bracketed terms are omitted from its formal English title). The Center is commissioned by the Shanghai municipal committee (and ultimately by MOST) to evaluate technologies in terms of national policy and expedite their transfer to domestic firms.[28] A Chinese study of these transfer centers describes their function as "coordinating the R&D abilities of each company, research institute and university" in the locale so as to "convert advanced foreign technology into domestic innovative ability" in key areas where challenges are faced.[29] The study recommends "making technology transfer even more the core feature of our technology innovation."

What is evident from these examples is MOST's role across the entire transfer process: from policy formation to conversion of foreign know-how into equipment and capabilities. The other point that stands out is the value it places on American technology in particular. In a document entitled "An Outline of Sino–US Technology Cooperation," MOST asserts "anyone with eyes can see" that the United States is the most scientifically developed country in the world. The corollary offered a few lines later is "other countries undoubtedly can draw lessons from America's S&T policies, management structure, planning and investment, areas of key scientific research, and the successes that it has attained."[30]

Complementing MOST's International S&T Cooperation Department is its quasi-independent China Science and Technology Exchange Center. Founded in 1982, some 16 years before the S&T Ministry itself, the Center has an internal structure similar to the S&T Cooperation Department's and responsibilities that overlap. The chief difference is the persona it presents to the international community, the Center being nominally a people-to-people organization, which facilitates MOST's membership in international groups, such as the Tokamak consortium (ITER). The Center itself describes its role as "promoting cooperation in the fields of science and technology and economy between Chinese and foreign scientists."[31]

The Center's "main responsibilities are to take charge of foreign person-to-person science and technology exchanges and cooperation within the Science Ministry's purview and under the direction of nationally unified foreign policies, general and specific, including S&T exchanges with ethnic Chinese of foreign citizenship." In his introductory greeting on the website the Science Minister acknowledges the Center's important contributions "in opening venues for people-to-people international S&T exchange, expanding the stages for S&T exchange and cooperation, bringing in large amounts of advanced technology and intellectual resources, and training a large number of internationalized (国际化) S&T personnel."[32]

The Center manages foreign personnel exchanges in both directions. By August 2002, the most recent year for which statistics were posted, it claims to have "led in" (引进) some 4,376 foreign experts, mostly from the United States and Japan, to "shrink the gap" between Chinese and world technology. Meanwhile, it sends on average 11 teams of technical "trainees" abroad per annum. Ten such missions were listed in 1998, each with 20 to 30 people, targeted at the US, Europe, and Japan. Like its formal counterpart – the Department of International S&T Cooperation – the Center runs a network of 30 second-tier organizations at municipal and provincial levels called "foreign science and technology exchange centers" (对外科学技术交流中心) that focus on the people-to-people dimension of tech transfer.[33]

Two more offices – MOST's Shanghai Training Center and the Service Center for S&T Personnel Exchange and Development – also support the ministry's efforts to harvest foreign technology. The Training Center was set up under the Exchange Center's management in 1982 to train S&T "administrators", particularly those involved in overseas exchange missions and other types of "scientific and technological foreign affairs." The facility, a self-contained complex located within Shanghai's Zhangjiang Hi-tech Park, offers language instruction in English and Japanese alongside its curriculum in "S&T systems" management. Some 20,000 people trained there as of 2005.[34]

MOST's Service Center for S&T Personnel Exchange and Development was created in 1993 to keep track of the whereabouts and activities of China's "S&T talent," especially "mobile personnel" (流动人员), i.e., graduates, post-docs, and visiting scholars not permanently identified with a PRC institution. Through the use of databases, the Service Center maintains files on available personnel and brokers their distribution among research facilities and work units. It also provides unspecified "professional training" presumably in the exploitation of foreign S&T literature that its host organization – ISTIC – professionally gathers.[35]

Other national-level organizations

China's Ministry of Education (国家教育部), which sets policy for the country's primary through graduate schools, is focused to an extraordinary degree on sending Chinese students abroad and insuring the skills they acquire find their way "back" to China. These tasks are the particular responsibility of the "International Cooperation and Exchange Department" (国际合作与交流司), which manages the education system's overseas activities, including dealings with international bodies and foreign governments. The department makes policy and does overall planning for Chinese studying abroad and foreigners studying in China; manages the hiring of foreign professors; approves cooperative institutions and projects related to education; and guides the work done by education offices at Chinese ministries abroad.[36]

The MOE in addition works several incentive programs to expedite acquisition of foreign high technology. Among them is the "Spring Light" (春晖计划) program, which pays overseas Chinese scientists and engineers to "return for short periods of time and render services to the country" (短期回国服务) in key S&T areas, for compensation up to five times one's normal overseas salary.[37] The program has been in effect since 1996. Foreign technology gets transferred through seminars, cooperative exchanges, technical consultations with state-owned enterprises, and "other short-term activities that involve returning to China for service approved by the MOE or its offices (teams) in embassies (consulates) abroad."[38] Some 20,000 persons have passed through the program to date.[39]

The Changjiang Scholar Award Plan (长江学者奖励计划) began in 1998 and is aimed at creating professorships for returning scholars. There is a "China Scholarship Council" (国家留学基金管理委员会) affiliated with the MOE that provides financial assistance to students going abroad and to foreigners studying in China "for projects conducive to the development of China." Eleven ministries and national bodies are on the Council, including the Ministry of Public Security and eight organizations with links to China's tech transfer projects.[40] The MOE is also involved in an "R&D Start-up Fund for Overseas Scholars Returning to China" designed to cut down on the time needed for returnees to begin their "creative" R&D efforts. It organizes annual transfer conventions in Beijing and Guangdong. It also sponsors other, unspecified "projects to pass on technology" (传授技术项目) from abroad.[41]

In a note posted to the MOE website, Zhang Xiuqin, head of the International Cooperation and Exchange Department, describes another initiative – the "Three First-rates" (三个一流) plan to choose first-rate students and send them to first-rate universities abroad to study with first-rate professors. The plan sprang from a State Council "strategic initiative" in 2003 to upgrade the skills of Chinese S&T workers and attract highly talented overseas personnel to China. Previously PRC universities and research institutes sent students abroad to meet what Zhang called "short-term needs." The emphasis now is on long-term strategic goals. Zhang expressed confidence that China's economic growth will attract more students back, adding that those who stay abroad nevertheless "can do many other things for the country."[42]

Finally, according to a policy document posted to the MOE site,[43] the ministry is building a database on overseas Chinese scholars to match China's needs for specific technologies with the pool of overseas talent and to keep better tabs on its foreign-trained nationals from PRC embassies and consulates abroad. The ministry will also arrange for personnel from Chinese universities and labs to travel to countries with a high density of ethnic Chinese professionals such as the United States and – under MOE auspices – track them down (跟踪), discuss with them opportunities to support PRC high-tech projects, and find ways to enlist their support. It also intends to strengthen "connections with and leadership of overseas student academic organizations and associations" as a bridge to recruit persons of talent.[44]

The Chinese Academy of Sciences (中国科学院), founded in 1949, is an umbrella group for 108 scientific research institutes and more than 200 S&T enterprises. Its staff of 30,000-plus "research professionals, technicians, administrators and other permanent employees" is matched by an equally large number of "guest researchers, visiting scholars, post-doctorates, graduate students and other mobile staff."[45] The foreign component of CAS's membership is also supplemented by "international" scientists permanently elected to the body, and through the Academy's sponsorship of cooperative visits by scholars abroad. These visits numbered 29,530 in 1986 to 1990; 33,881 in 1991 to 1995;[46] and they now run to some 8,000 trips annually.[47]

CAS technology transfer programs resemble in content and name transfer programs run by other state equities, which sometimes trip over each other in their efforts to attract foreign talent.[48] For example, the CAS's "100 Persons Plan" (百人计划) aims to "draw in, select and nurture" leading scholars and technical personnel. Between 1994 and 2000 some 470 people were supported. Fewer than half were in China when the awards were made. Between 1994 and 1997 its annual cost was RMB 60 million; by 1998 the "100 Person Plan" was spending RMB 200 million on 120 people per annum, and during the Tenth Five-year Plan (2001–2005) its annual budget increased to RMB 300 million.[49]

The "China Youth Scholar Academic Forum" (中国青年学者学术讨论会) has been jointly administered by the CAS and Natural Science Foundation of China since 1991. Its goal is to "strengthen academic exchanges and contacts between young domestic scholars and Chinese scholars abroad" with emphasis on the latest R&D trends to "further the development of the ancestral country's science and technology."[50] Each year seven or eight events are organized. There are also a "Western Lights Plan" (西部之光计划), a "High-level Visiting Scholar Plan" (高级访问学者计划), a "CAS Preferential Support Fund for Returning to China to Work" (中科院择优支持回国工作基金), a "CAS Wang Kuancheng R&D Scholarship" (中科院王宽诚科研奖金), and a "Special Fund for Overseas Scholars to Return to China for Short Periods to Work and Lecture" (留学人员短期回国工作讲学专项基金) that CAS also runs with the NSFC. In addition, the Academy funds a group of "Expert Overseas Evaluators" (海外评审专家) and is building an Internet-based "overseas personnel management system."[51]

Supervising these projects is CAS's International Cooperation Bureau (国际合作局), whose responsibilities, according to the CAS website, are:

> To formulate CAS rules and regulations for international cooperation and academic exchanges; make annual plans aimed at academy-level international cooperation; conduct negotiations, signing ceremonies and the administration of CAS cooperative agreements with overseas partners; explore new channels for exchanges and cooperation with foreign organizations; and manage major international cooperative projects of CAS and its affiliates.[52]

The Bureau boasts over 700 cooperative agreements with 40 nations worldwide, including "joint investigations, joint ventures, joint laboratories, young scientist groups, workshops, training courses, bilateral and multi-lateral seminars."[53]

The Natural Science Foundation of China (国家自然科学基金委员会) partners with CAS on some projects but has its own "Bureau of International Cooperation" (国际合作局) that is independent of the CAS body.[54] According to its charter, the office is authorized to draw up cooperation and exchange projects, including those involving overseas students, arrange funding, and negotiate agreements with foreign governments. The NSFC's website lists 66 such agreements designed to "produce results (出成果) and persons of talent."[55]

Beyond programs run jointly with CAS and other bodies, the NSFC manages a "National Outstanding Youth Science Fund" (国家杰出青年科学基金), which by 1999 was spending 180 million Yuan annually or 20 percent of the foundation's budget. A second youth program started in 1998, called the "Young Overseas Scholars Cooperative Research Fund" (海外青年学者合作研究基金), underwrites foreign support for PRC projects in science. The program has a separate budget for Hong Kong. A Chinese language study of these NSFC programs credits them with building "a stable foundation in China for cooperative exchanges with overseas scholars and creating beneficial conditions for serving the country through use of the 'two bases' (两个基地) model."[56]

Documents posted to the NSFC site describe this "two bases" model as encouraging overseas Chinese scholars to remain abroad in their regular jobs but to return to China for short periods to work.[57] To qualify for subsidies under this formula, candidates must have a "permanent or relatively stable overseas work post, run their own [overseas] lab or research team, and have their own independent research budget." They must travel to China at least 30 days a year – either once or as accumulated over the year – and have clear and settled research projects with their domestic counterparts. A complementary NSFC plan drawn up in 2007 subsidizes efforts by "domestic research units" to attract foreign scientists to work in China for longer periods.[58]

Provincial and municipal organizations

As noted above, several of China's national-level technology transfer organizations control networks of local affiliates. Beijing's State Administration of Foreign Experts Affairs works through its public liaison organization and program executor – the China Association for the International Exchange of Personnel (中国国际人才交流协会) – to recruit foreign experts and send PRC citizens abroad. Its provincial and municipal offices, named after one or the other of these two parent groups, grew from 45 three years ago to their present number of 51. More will be said about CAIEP later under "private" outreach groups.

The Overseas Chinese Affairs Office, also discussed above, has 30 provincial-level offices that include four large municipalities[59] and another 63 local offices for other cities.[60] These latter offices belong nominally to OCAO's affiliated NGO – the Chinese Overseas Exchange Association (中国海外交流学会) – which, like CAIEP and its relationship to SAFEA, fronts for the OCAO. Most of these 93 local organizations have "economics and S&T" departments modeled on OCAO's "Department 4 for Economics, Science and Technology" to work technology transfers with overseas Chinese.

The Shanghai chapter of the OCAO, for example, promotes and facilitates "S&T exchanges and cooperation with overseas Chinese professional groups and individuals."[61] The chapter claims to have attracted some 4,000 overseas Chinese technical persons, who spawned more than 400 enterprises primarily in Shanghai's Zhangjiang Hi-tech Industrial Zone, winning praise from China's State Council for "drawing in intellect" from abroad. In 2006 the OCAO designated parts of the Zhangjiang zone priority support areas for returning Chinese founding businesses and conducting exchanges "of various types" (多种形式).[62]

The Science Ministry as well has regional offices throughout China under various rubrics depending on their affiliation with particular MOST departments. One such office – Shanghai's chapter of the International Science and Technology Cooperation Department – was described above. These MOST chapters are not reticent about describing their plans to use foreign persons and technology, both generally and for specific projects. A statement on the Beijing Municipal S&T Commission's website notes:

> Being fully aware of the globalization of S&T activities, BMSTC opens its arms to all the government institutions, enterprises and NGOs worldwide who are seeking opportunities for S&T cooperation, and, together with its affiliates, readily provides a full range of support and services.[63]

MOST and the regional offices of other national organizations work in tandem with local governments on projects to obtain foreign technology, and typically defray part of the costs incurred by municipalities, for example, in subsidizing the high-tech zones that cater to overseas specialists. City and provincial governments also work independently to attract foreign talent. In 2000, the city of Beijing created a so-called "green channel" (绿色通道)[64] to reward foreign specialists who set up shop locally. The city's Overseas Scholars Service Center (留学生服务中心), a part of its personnel department, has helped large numbers of returnees establish high-tech firms in Beijing's Haidian, Daxing and Konggang industrial parks.[65]

Other examples of local projects to attract foreign S&T personnel may be found in every major PRC province and city. Shanghai's Office of Personnel manages its own Overseas Scholars Service Center in the city's Pudong New District to provide a "full range" of incentives for Chinese specialists living abroad to work and set up businesses in Pudong, or to engage in "other forms of exchange and cooperation." Information posted to its website indicates that more than 7,000 returnees had set up some 800 businesses there by the end of 1994.[66] China's Xinhua News Agency noted that:

> The center mainly serves as an intermediary agency for recruiting students for S&T programs, employing students abroad, designing *an overseas project exchange information network*, holding international large recruiting business activities, and implementing international high-tech exchanges and trade standards [italics added].[67]

Guangzhou, for its part, has an "Overseas Scholars S&T Innovation Fund" (留学人员科技创业资金) that provides financial subsidies for returning scholars to "convert the results" (成果转化) of new and high technology brought in from abroad. Many recipients have set up local businesses with support from the Guangzhou Overseas Scholars Innovation Service Center (广州留学生创业服务中心).[68]

In addition, Guangzhou has been hosting since 2000 a "Convention of Overseas Scholars in Science and Technology" (中国留学人员广州科技交流会). Although billed as an annual event, this and other foreign-oriented high-tech fairs are semi-permanent features of Chinese cities and, in Shenzhen's case (see below), evolved into what one study called a "year round operating technology transfer center."[69] Planning begins well in advance of the formal event, which itself lasts several weeks. The events typically are supported by the local municipality and one or more national ministries.

The Guangzhou Convention, China's largest tech fair for overseas Chinese, has as its goal "bringing to China knowledge and technology obtained overseas and opening opportunities for overseas Chinese to establish high-tech enterprises in China."[70] Its inaugural event in December 2000 attracted 300 foreign participants, half of whom were from the United States, who brought technical specifications for 158 items.[71] The number of attendees has grown through the years, with the 2003 conference attracting 1,532 overseas Chinese affiliated with 16 foreign-based advocacy groups.[72] By 2004 some 2,200 "overseas Chinese scholars" (留学人员)[73] were gathering at Guangzhou's Pazhou convention center to meet 2,000 PRC "national and local delegates" from China's technical ministries, labs, universities, and high-tech parks to "exchange" technical products, skills, and services.[74]

Foreign participants, according to the website, are motivated to attend by the opportunity to market in China the knowledge, skills, and high-tech products they acquired and developed while abroad. Domestic institutions, for their part, bring to the Convention lists of skills and technologies sought by China. The conference provides the physical and electronic venues for the exchanges to take place. Wrap-ups of the event are posted on the Convention's website, including an account of the transactions, which in 2004 included such items as "digital signal processor design," "remote site surveillance cameras," and "manufacturing technology for super-high performance rare earth permanent magnets."[75] The slogan for 2008 "Open to the world, serving the whole nation" captures its one-way nature.

Unlike the Guangzhou event that seeks technologies owned or appropriated by individual overseas Chinese, Shenzhen's "High-tech Fair" (中国国际高新技术成果交易会) attracts international participants of all ethnicities and is company- rather than people-oriented. In operation since 1999, the fair is the largest, most influential, and "most richly pragmatic" (最富实效) S&T convention in China, offering "multi-level, multi-directional and specialized ancillary services for high-tech achievement transactions." The value of exchanges reaches into the billions of dollars.[76] It is co-sponsored by the Shenzhen city government and half a dozen national ministries, and run by Shenzhen's China Hi-Tech Transfer Center, one of many such transfer facilities in China.

There are also lesser events convened at intervals to attract foreign talent and technology, such as the "Overseas Chinese Scholars Business Founding Week" (创业周) held annually in major Chinese cities. Some insight into their workings is provided by Japanese professor Endo Homare, director of foreign programs at Tsukuba University, whose status as a China-born Japanese and history of support for PRC exchange programs has earned him privileged access to these conventions and their organizers.[77]

Endo describes one such transfer venue in Shenyang he attended in 2001 that attracted hundreds of overseas Chinese. Prior to the meeting, the event's municipal sponsors asked the region's major companies, research institutes, and labs to fill out "tender invitation forms for difficult problems" (难题招标表) that were posted online in advance of the gathering. OCS worldwide were asked to peruse the list and contact the lab or company in advance with their proposed solutions. By Endo's account, the list "went on and on for some 40 pages." Labs with the "difficult problems" reviewed their responses and chose the best solutions. Final terms were negotiated at the Convention.[78]

Endo cites by way of an example a request from a PRC nanotech company for "extremely specific and detailed knowledge of a technology." The request included an appeal: "Please lend us the latest advanced technology so we are not defeated in the post-WTO competition." Endo considered it "amazing" that a local government would appeal openly to the Chinese community worldwide for a "loan" of foreign technology, adding, "I suppose the Shenyang government did not consider the possibility that anyone besides Chinese would read it."[79]

At another such convention in Dalian sponsored by the Science, Education, Personnel, and Foreign Affairs ministries with support from the Liaoning provincial and Dalian municipal governments, some 7,000 locals turned up to greet 1,080 overseas Chinese scholars. Endo summarized the opening address:

> You have all taken advanced degrees abroad, are at the leading edge of science, and are acquainted with market economics. Many of you have your own companies and patents. You have international social networks and are deeply versed in all kinds of information (あらゆる情報に精通しています). Most importantly, you are deeply concerned with your ancestral country and bring a strong determination to contribute.

More encouragement followed, after which the facilitator importuned, "All of you, please, in whatever way you can, make good use of your inventions, research results, and experience to set up innovative enterprises in Liaoning." The ceremony, according to Endo, was conducted with great pomp: individual signatories who agreed in advance to contribute were escorted to the stage by "tall women in evening gowns."[80]

That done, the groups were bused off to signing ceremonies where these Chinese bearers of Western technology inked formal agreements with their PRC sponsors. Some 1,556 letters of intent were exchanged between the overseas Chinese and their PRC recipients, and 359 contracts were signed. Appeals to "patriotism" were thick. The event ended with the groups singing the PRC National Anthem, performed by the guests "with tears in their eyes."[81]

Technology transfer centers

Technologies obtained abroad must be converted into real equipment and products. In China, this process is played out through several venues: in high-tech development zones where tenets with a knowledge of foreign technology found businesses with government support; in face-to-face meetings between technology owners and Chinese company reps; in working-level meetings at international symposia; in debriefing rooms maintained by government tech transfer organizations; and at dedicated "transfer centers" all over the country.

Some three dozen major transfer centers and many more affiliated units were operating in China by early 2008. Several have branches overseas, including the Jiangsu International Technology Transfer Center with its office in the United States. The following account of their goals is given on the TT91 website, a "science and technology transfer information service provider" run by Shanghai's Zhonglin Science and Technology Transfer Co., Ltd.

> National Technology Transfer Centers are established to speed up technology transfer, encourage the use of advanced technology to rebuild traditional industry, hasten development of new and high tech industries in China, and optimize China's industrial structure. They do this by mobilizing the technologies of universities and labs, talented persons and other resources and linking up with priority industries and companies in a three-way alliance of businesses, universities and research institutes. Their major task is to pave the way for the development and expansion of openly available technology (共性技术), support the creation of technology centers within companies, and promote conversion and transfer of technologies held by higher education.[82]

This description fails to point out that nearly all these centers, alongside their domestic activities, engage in international tech transfer, as evidenced by information posted to their websites and as attested in the previously cited 2003 PRC study on China's tech transfer centers, which describes their mission to convert "advanced foreign technology" in areas where challenges are faced, such as information, electronic, chemical, biological, material, and manufacturing technologies.[83]

Shanghai alone has ten such transfer centers. There is the Shanghai New High Technology Service Center mentioned above run by the city's municipal committee with MOST support "to provide effective technology conversion services." The center offers one-stop shopping (一门式) for government and business customers alike. It studies foreign tech standards, maintains a cadre of evaluators, and manages matching funds used for products "*recreated* through the conversion process [emphasis added]."[84] A second Shanghai-MOST venture, the Shanghai Technology Transfer Exchange (上海技术交易所), supports "theoretical and practical" international transfer activities based on a technology bank of 10,000 projects.[85]

The Shanghai National Technology Transfer Center (上海分院国家技术转移中心), a part of the Chinese Academy of Sciences, was founded in 1950 and is the oldest and probably largest such organization in Shanghai with some 7,500 employees staffing 18 laboratories, nine "research" institutes, and half a dozen offices in nearby coastal cities. The institution claims many conversion successes in such high-tech fields as microelectronics, lasers, and nuclear technology.[86] Complementing the National Academy's efforts, the Shanghai Academy of Sciences has its own tech transfer center (上海科学院技术转移中心) that claims expertise in "dual-use" military technology and patents exploitation.[87]

Continuing our survey, the Shanghai-based East China (Huadong) University of Science and Technology (华东理工大学) operates a National Technology Transfer Center (国家技术转移中心), with an International Cooperation Office responsible for "bringing technology into the country." It focuses on transfers to PRC companies, "large ones in particular."[88] The Center claims to have cooperative links with 60 research institutes in the United States, Europe, and Japan.[89] A second university-affiliated National Technology Transfer Center at Jiaotong University puts small and medium-sized businesses in contact with technology providers at home and abroad, and "organizes international symposia in high-tech fields" for its constituents.[90]

Zhonglin Science and Technology Transfer Co. (中临技术转移有限公司) is a semi-private corporation in Shanghai providing technology transfer "solutions" (解决方案) for local firms, government and research institutes. The company includes returned overseas students and "professional associations of ethnic Chinese abroad" among those with which it has "good cooperative relations."[91] Another is Shanghai's Co-Way International Technology Transfer Co. (上海科威国际技术转移中心有限公司), run by a consortium of private, municipal, and academic interests. Co-Way's staff is made up almost entirely of technical persons who have studied abroad. The company researches foreign technology "trends" and brokers interactions between domestic firms and foreign technology providers in Europe and the United States.[92]

Rounding out the collection are two more entities: a China-Europe Technology Transfer Center (中欧技术转移中心) that has been operating since 1993,[93] and a hybrid organization called the Shanghai International Technology Transfer Network (上海国际技术转移协作网络), a web-based platform run by several of the above-mentioned units.[94] This pattern of technology transfer centers is duplicated in other major cities such as Beijing, Shenyang, Guangdong, Dalian, and Xi'an, and at the provincial level as well. They constitute one more component of China's multi-faceted effort to absorb foreign technology.

China's "non-official" transfer organizations

Foreign-based advocacy groups also play a key role in the transfer process. These groups are formed in the main by overseas Chinese to create business opportunities for themselves and to promote development of their ancestral country. As we shall see in the following chapter, foreign S&T advocacy groups interact directly with PRC state organs to achieve shared goals and there are cases where their members hold advisory posts in the Chinese government. In addition, Beijing promotes and monitors "people-to-people" transactions through a network of NGOs that insulates overseas specialists serving China as individuals or through advocacy groups from the potential risks of dealing openly with the PRC government.

Three such organizations were mentioned above in the context of their state counterparts. The China Science and Technology Exchange Center has overlapping responsibilities with MOST's International S&T Cooperation Department and replicates its internal structure. Two other alleged NGOs, the China Association for the International Exchange of Personnel (中国国际人才交流协会) and Chinese Overseas Exchange Association (中国海外交流学会), front respectively for the State Administration of Foreign Experts Affairs and the Overseas Chinese Affairs Office, and at one time shared offices, staff, and telephone lines.

According to a description posted to the China Internet Information Center,[95] CAIEP is a Beijing-based, non-official "government-sponsored" institution founded in 1985 to support the "international exchange of specialized technical and managerial personnel." CAIEP has chapters in 45 Chinese provinces and cities, and offices in ten countries including the United States. Its stated goal is to recruit foreign experts to work in China and send people abroad for technical training. Specifically,

> It invites experienced foreign specialists to China to solve technical and management problems for Chinese industry; invites foreign professors and scholars to Chinese universities and research institutes to lecture and engage in cooperative research; and sends Chinese technical personnel abroad to develop exchanges, receive training, and do research.[96]

Beyond efforts aimed at individuals, CAIEP "acts as a bridge to promote understanding, international cooperation, and skilled personnel exchanges between relevant organizations and groups in China and abroad" through cooperation with "more than 60 government institutions, social groups, research institutes, universities, and corporations worldwide."[97] Examples of macro-level recruitment initiatives include: a "Sino-US Symposium on Hi-Tech and Economic Development" held in Houston in 2002;[98] an "International Executive Council" co-sponsored with the US government to "provide volunteers with technical and management expertise to manufacturing and service companies in China";[99] and an "International Human Resources Forum" co-hosted by SAFEA, CAIEP, and China Services International (a division of CAIEP with offices in Beijing's Zhongguancun).[100]

The link between SAFEA and CAIEP is apparent in their co-hosting of national events, the co-appearance of representatives of the two organizations at foreign functions, the dual roles assigned to key employees, and in Internet citations that name CAIEP as being "under the direct guidance" of SAFEA.[101] Hence in practice there is no distinction to be made between cooperating with the one or the other. Foreigners entering SAFEA/CAIEP's technology transfer program are lodged at the large and modern Beijing Foreign Experts Building, and, if needed, are assigned CAIEP translators to support their exchanges with technical experts.[102]

Similarly, the Beijing-based China Overseas Exchange Association identifies itself as an NGO founded in 1990 to "interact extensively with overseas Chinese, ethnic Chinese abroad and their organizations, promote friendship, and develop cooperative exchanges."[103] It also encourages Sino–foreign exchanges in economics, trade, science, and technology. In structure and operation the group is hard to distinguish from its counterpart in the State Council.

COEA is managed by six vice-directors, each of whom holds a concurrent position in the Overseas Chinese Affairs Office, according to biographical data posted to its website. The organization's true status is also evident in the membership of its standing committee: most of the 79 members hold top posts in a related PRC state bureaucracy, such as the OCAO, the Overseas Chinese Affairs Committee of the National People's Congress, MOST, and the State Bureau of Foreign Experts. Like its official counterpart, COEA operates a Department for Economics, Science, and Technology headed by the same OCAO manager.

COEA's tech transfer function is located within that department's Science and Technology Office, which "is mainly responsible for rendering help and service to support cooperation and exchange between Chinese scientists and engineers at home and abroad." COEA claims many successes in "attracting funds, technology, and skilled personnel to China." It is also involved in "various kinds of cooperative talks on foreign business and technology" with backing from official PRC entities engaged in tech transfer.[104]

A fourth major "unofficial" group supporting technology transfer to China is the All-China Federation of Returned Overseas Chinese (中华全国归国华侨联合会) or Qiaolian (侨联), a "national NGO under the leadership of the Chinese Communist Party composed of returned overseas Chinese and their family members" which serves as "a bridge and a link connecting the party and government with the broad masses of returned Chinese, their family members, and Chinese compatriots abroad."[105] Qiaolian traces its origin to a "Yan'an Overseas Chinese Save the Country Federation" formed in 1940. In 1956 it gained formal status as a national organization.

A close association between Qiaolian and the State Council's Overseas Chinese Affairs Office is suggested by the co-appearance of members in delegations traveling to and from China and by the revolving-door relationship its leadership has with the OCAO. A Japanese source notes, "Although Qiaolian is an NGO, in the Chinese system it is a unit on the same formal ministerial level as OCAO (its officers correspond to Japanese cabinet members in rank)."[106] If there is any difference at all between Qiaolian and the OCAO (and its unofficial counterpart the COEA) it is the emphasis Qiaolian places on "returned Chinese" and their links to expatriates still abroad.

Another measure of Qiaolian's status is the number of its subordinate groups – some 11,000 at the regional and local levels. Its internal structure includes a Liaison Department, which gathers "real time information" on returned Chinese, and the expected Economics, Science and Technology Department chartered to "promote economic cooperation and scientific and technological exchange between Chinese compatriots abroad and China."[107] The success of its technology exchange mission is reflected in examples posted to its website and in Internet citations of Qiaolian's involvement in transfer forums.[108] Other types of exchanges include the group's sponsorship of a "Volunteer Corps of Outstanding Overseas Scholars in Service to China," whose members are chiefly from the United States.[109]

No list of China's tech transfer groups is complete without CAST – the China Association for Science and Technology (中国科学技术协会) – "the largest national non-governmental organization of scientific and technological workers in China," according to its website.[110] Although accredited as an NGO with the United Nations and other international bodies, CAST's status is betrayed by statements such as the following:

As the bridge linking the Chinese science and technology community with the Communist Party of China and the Chinese government, CAST is a constituent member of the Chinese People's Political Consultative Conference, where it joins the nation's political parties and other social groups in the state affairs of political consultation, policy-making and democratic supervision.[111]

CAST is run nominally by a National Committee, actually by a Secretariat of five members who make the executive decisions. Chief among them is Deng Nan, daughter of former CCP leader Deng Xiaoping, supported by four others with S&T and international backgrounds. One of them, Feng Changgen, is employed by the Chinese Academy of Engineering Physics (中国工程物理研究院), the Mianyang-based atomic weapons design facility, in its Laboratory for Shock Wave Physics and Detonation Physics Research.

CAST includes among its tasks – about 80 percent down the list in the spot typically reserved for key elements of a Chinese discourse – a requirement "to organize international science and technology exchanges, promote international cooperation, and develop friendly relations with the international scientific and technological community." This function is discharged by a Department of International Affairs and a "service center" called the "China Council for the Promotion of Applied Technology Exchange with Foreign Countries." In addition, CAST's nearly 200 member societies have bilateral agreements with 40 foreign organizations in 20 countries, with particular emphasis on the United States, Europe, and Japan.[112]

Other Chinese non-governmental organizations devoted to foreign tech transfer include the China Association for International Science and Technology Cooperation (中国国际科学技术合作协会), a national non-profit organization founded in 1992 under the science ministry with participation from CAST and other national groups, which acts as "an extension of and supplement to the government's foreign S&T work."[113] The Overseas Doctor of Philosophy Association (中华海外博士联合会), with a dozen chapters abroad including three in the United States, "complements and assists the State Council's departments, committees, and the various provinces and municipalities' beneficial activities to make the country prosper through science and technology."[114] It aims to focus the strength of Chinese scientists abroad to make China a "marvel" in world S&T.[115] Finally, the China Education Association for International Exchange (中国教育国际交流学会), with its technology-oriented agenda, serves as a "non-governmental network for Chinese international educational exchange."[116]

Recruiting and placement networks

Technology transfer is also achieved through web-based services or by organizations that exist mostly on the Internet. At the basic level they act as conduits of information to Diaspora Chinese with technical skills and as rallying points for government initiatives. At the other extreme are state-run websites for linking overseas experts with PRC projects.

An example of the former type is China Scholars Abroad (www.chisa.edu.cn). Established in December 1995, Chisa claims to be "China's first Internet-based news medium and nationwide, comprehensive website for overseas scholars." It is registered in Beijing and maintained by the editors of a paper journal with the same Chinese name – Shenzhou Xueren (神州学人) – although the electronic and paper publications have different content. China's Ministry of Education has supervisory control over both versions.[117]

Chisa offers online "news" about China aimed at mobilizing overseas Chinese support for government themes and programs. More particularly, it provides information on academic funding (including technology-oriented scholarship programs), study abroad, academic exchange programs, study in China (for those who read Chinese), job offers in the PRC, and government policy on overseas study and incentives for returning. There is detailed information on China's "pioneering parks" (创业园) and hotlinks to Chinese student associations worldwide.

A similar web-based service is the China Overseas Students and Scholars Pioneer (中国留学人员创业网站)[118] operated by the Chengdu Gaoxin Center of Technology Innovation (城都高新区技术创新服务中心).[119] Established in 2001, the site is supported by Chisa's editorial staff and its content is defined by MOST and MOE. Like Chisa, COSSP offers information on PRC business law and policies and keeps overseas Chinese apprised of opportunities to found tech-oriented businesses in China.

The World Overseas Chinese Professional Association Cooperation Network (全球华侨华人专业协会协作网) is an online almanac for technology transfer information run by OCAO's Department 4 for Economics, Science and Technology.[120] OCPAN provides data on job opportunities in China, transfer-related project funding, cooperative projects planned and under way, exchange conferences in China and abroad, state policy directives, and hotlinks to nearly 100 member (成员) organizations worldwide with news on their current activities.[121]

Online placement services also play an important role in bringing technical skills to China. An example is the China International Employment Net (中国国际人才网, chinajob.com.cn), run by SAFEA and its front organization CAIEP. Its purpose is to "utilize foreign resources to satisfy the needs of domestic employers for foreign talent."[122] Another example is China Human Resources (中华英才网, www.chinahr.com), "a talent finding and personnel resources management service for PRC and foreign companies." Founded in 1997, China HR has its headquarters in Beijing, 12 brick-and-mortar offices in China, and a "professional staff of over 1,000 persons." A partnership in 2005 with Monster Worldwide, Inc. allowed China HR to "enter an entirely new stage of international development."[123]

China's ministries operate several web-based services aimed at facilitating the movement of technical personnel to and from China. The MOE's China Education and Research Network (中国教育和科研计算机网), an online collaboration venue for PRC universities, has global links to the United States, Japan, and Europe. Its public site (www.edu.cn) offers an upbeat assessment of S&T developments in China, a calendar of international events, job announcements, funding opportunities, and hotlinks to PRC research institutes for the benefit of overseas specialists contemplating cooperative exchanges. Its introductory statement emphasizes the importance of "technology import" to China.[124]

The MOE also runs a Chinese Service Center for Scholarly Exchange (中国留学服务中心), a web-based service "to promote worldwide scholarly interaction, facilitate the movement of students to and from China, and help keep tabs on the whereabouts and activities of Chinese students overseas."[125] The Center, in turn, controls a Beijing Yinhong Technical Developing Consultant Center (北京吟虹国际教育咨询公司) engaged in international "talent hunting" and tech transfer. The latter claims as one of its goals "turning [China's overseas scholars] into a practical type of expert whose talents are used internationally."[126]

The China Overseas Talent Network (中国留学人才信息网, www.chinatalents.gov.cn), run by the MOP, traces its genesis to former Chinese President Jiang Zemin's call to "draw in foreign intellectual talent and encourage personnel studying abroad to return home to work or serve their ancestral country by appropriate means," according to the website. The site links ethnic Chinese experts abroad with the "overseas Chinese student work organizations in various regions and departments throughout China, its higher institutes of learning, Chinese R&D institutes, large and medium-sized companies, and overseas scholar pioneering parks." The website hosts information on policies and regulations, guidelines for returning students, an online form for persons requesting specific types of employment in China, a form for PRC work units seeking overseas talent, an employment "hotline," and a venue to help overseas Chinese market their high-tech projects in China.[127]

MOST, for its part, hosts a China International Science and Technology Cooperation website (中国国际科技合作网, www.cistc.net) that provides S&T news to the overseas community; a calendar of global cooperative events; information on patent laws, trademarks, S&T policy, and techno-park regulations; a positive account of Chinese history and culture for scientists planning travel to China; and information on how to get there.[128] Part of the site gives details on successful Sino–foreign technology projects, two recent ones being biosensors (Israel) and precision ion-deposition processes (Belgium).

Finally, the Overseas Chinese Entrepreneurs and Professionals Association (中国留学人员创业协会) is primarily a web-based organization (www.returnchina.org) devoted to promoting China's high-tech development. Founded in February 2002,[129] OCEPA claims 3,200 members worldwide and is chaired by a person living in Xi'an, China. Other leaders live at US and UK locations or claim dual residences, such as Silicon Valley and Hangzhou, or San Antonio and Dalian. The organization acknowledges the "guidance" (指导) it receives "from China's Ministry of Personnel and the San Francisco Consulate."[130]

OCEPA recruits overseas Chinese scholars "who studied and worked in Western countries and moved back to China" and others "who still work and live overseas but are interested in jobs, business opportunities, or conferences with airfare allowances in China." Its "purpose is to provide network and support opportunities in and out[side] China for business and academic exchanges." The website explains:

> We are also working closely with Science and Technology Parks, Technology and Business Incubators, government agencies and local governments, and venture capital firms [in China] to create a network to promote exchanges on business ideas, tips and information.

With representation both in China and abroad, OCEPA bridges the PRC "outreach organizations" specialized in technology transfer and the complementary US "advocacy groups" that we examine in the following chapter. While our account here of PRC tech transfer organizations is lengthy, we have no confidence that it is exhaustive. Entities expand, new ones appear, while others – including those run by technical ministries – stay mostly beneath the radar. Details about their transactions are often unavailable.

What emerges from the foregoing is an appreciation of China's efforts to gather foreign technology on a scale that outsiders cannot begin to fathom. By contrast, those on the inside managing these transfer projects take their acceptance for granted, as if they cannot imagine anyone objecting to their appropriating the world's technology, or that the developed world would notice. In the next chapter we explore how this apparatus links up with US groups, whose sympathy for China's goals allows these transfers to happen.

Notes

1 www.safea.gov.cn.
2 Ibid.
3 Ibid.
4 Ibid.
5 Photos posted to its site (2009), however, show a predominance of ethnic Chinese among the recruits. A comprehensive study in 2001 of China's use of overseas talent noted that "in recent years" SAFEA has expanded its target from non-ethnic Chinese to "the intellectual resources of ethnic Chinese experts abroad" (Liu and Shen, 2001).
6 Peter Boylan, "Isle man gave China stealth tech, feds say," *The Honolulu Advertiser*, November 9, 2006, http://the.honoluluadvertiser.com/article/2006/Nov/09/ln/FP611090349.html.
7 Mark A. Kellner, "China a 'Latent Threat, Potential Enemy': Expert," *Defense News Weekly*, December 4, 2006, www.defensenews.com/story.php?F=2389588&C=america.
8 www.safea.gov.cn.
9 Ibid.
10 www.gqb.gov.cn.
11 According to information posted to the New England Chinese Information & Network Association's website, www.necina.org.
12 www.asicef.org.
13 www.gqb.gov.cn/special/2008/1029/19.html.
14 The Ministry of Personnel was renamed "Ministry of Human Resources and Social Security" (人力资源和社会保障部) in 2008. Individual offices described in this chapter survived the transition.
15 According to information posted to its website, www.mop.gov.cn, in 2005.
16 Ibid.
17 www.forsa.org.cn, visited in 2005.
18 www.mop.gov.cn.
19 博士后科研流动站 and 企业博士后科研工作站, respectively. The former is sometimes rendered "centers for post-doctoral studies" and the latter is sometimes translated as "post-doctoral project work stations."
20 According to an interview with former Minister of Personnel Zhang Xuezhong posted to the website headhunting.job.365.net.
21 www.chinatalents.gov.cn.
22 A similar advertisement was posted to the recruitment page of the IAPCM's own website (www.iapcm.ac.cn, visited December 6, 2005) with some details on specific projects, many of which are weapons related. They include nonlinear evolution equations, infinite dimension dynamic systems, and under "computational mathematics" numerical solutions to nonlinear evolution equations, computational fluid dynamics, calculation methods for transport equations, numerical modeling of fluid dynamic instability, numerical modeling of explosions, and high-performance parallel computing.
23 www.most.gov.cn.
24 Liu Yun (刘云) and Shen Lin (沈林), "海外人才资源开发利用的现状及发展对策" ("The Current Situation and Countermoves on Development and Utilization of Overseas Chinese Experts Intellectual Resources") in 科研管理 (*Science Research Management*) 22, no. 4 (July 2001), pp. 115–125.
25 www.most.gov.cn, www.istic.ac.cn.
26 www.most.gov.cn.
27 www.stcsm.gov.cn.
28 www.hitec.net.cn.
29 Sun Lijun (孙理军) and Huang Huaye (黄花叶), "美日技术转移实践及其对我国技术转移中心的启示" ("US and Japanese Technology Transfer Practices and What

We Can Learn for Our Country's Technology Transfer Centers"), in 科技管理研究 (*Keji Guanli Yanjiu*), 2003.1, pp. 70–72.

30 www.most.gov.cn. The document goes on to describe the size of the USG's research budget, the particular sectors within which advanced research is carried out, what technologies are earmarked for funding, and which USG offices have roles in the nation's R&D effort. Its assessment of the Sino–US S&T relationship is mixed. It notes that cooperation is "comprehensive, multi-lateral, broad-based, widely partnered, done in key areas, and on a high level, as evidenced between governments, R&D institutes, companies, and the exchange of S&T personnel." At the same time, there are some "issues and inadequacies. In particular, non-S&T factors still commonly interfere with normal development of the two countries' S&T cooperation and exchange. Limitations that the United States puts on cooperation and trade with China in high technology have impeded broader and deeper Sino-US S&T cooperation."

31 www.cstec.org.cn.

32 Ibid.

33 Ibid.

34 www.most-training.org.

35 www.istic.ac.cn.

36 www.moe.edu.cn.

37 David Zwieg, Chung Siu Fung, and Donglin Han, "Redefining the Brain Drain: China's Diaspora Option," *Science, Technology & Society* 13, no. 1 (2008), pp. 1–33.

38 Liu and Shen, 2001.

39 www.huiguo.cn.xbpd/index.htm.

40 www.csc.edu.cn/gb.

41 Liu and Shen, 2001, p. 117.

42 According to Zhang, her office solved the problem of getting Chinese students into top-notch schools by negotiating 45 "cooperative project" agreements between the China Scholarship Council and famous foreign universities.

43 "MOE's Views on the Work of Further Strengthening the Introduction of Talented Overseas Scholars" (教育部关于进一步加强引进海外优秀留学人才工作的若干意见), March 2, 2007.

44 Ibid.

45 News item posted to the CAS website, viewed 29 February 2008.

46 Lian Yanhua (连燕华), "科学研究全球化发展评价" ("An Assessment of the Growth of Scientific Research Globalization"), in 科研管理 (*Science Research Management*), July 2000, pp. 1–14.

47 http://english.cas.ac.cn, visited February 28, 2008.

48 "The demarcation between the responsibilities of the Chinese Academy of Sciences and the State Science and Technology Commission [predecessor to MOST] in policy formulation and consultation is not always entirely clear, and there is a certain degree of ambiguity and contention in their dealings with each other" ("State Science and Technology Commission," Federation of American Scientists Space Policy Project, June 20, 1998), www.fas.org/spp/guide/china/agency/sstc.htm.

49 Liu and Shen, 2001.

50 Ibid.

51 Ibid.

52 www.cas.cn.

53 Ibid.

54 The NSFC Bureau's present director, Han Jianguo (韩建国), spent most of his earlier career in the CAS's Bureau of International Cooperation.

55 www.nsfc.gov.cn.

56 Liu and Shen, 2001, pp. 117–118.

57 www.nsfc.gov.cn.

58 Ibid.

59 www.gqb.gov.cn.

60 www.chinaqw.com.cn.

61 www.overseas.sh.cn.

62 qwb.sh.gov.cn.

63 www.bjkw.gov.cn.

64 Ibid. The program is authorized under "Certain Regulations by Beijing Municipality to Encourage Overseas Scholars to Come to Beijing, Found Businesses and Work" (北京市鼓励留学人员来京创业工作的若干规定).

65 Liu and Shen, 2001, p. 119.

66 www.pudongos.com.

67 Beijing Xinhua in English 1416 GMT, November 11, 2003.

68 科研管理 (*Science Research Management*), 2001.4a, p. 119.

69 Can Huang, Celeste Amorim, Mark Spinoglio, Borges Gouveia, and Augusto Medina, "Organization, programme and structure: an analysis of the Chinese innovation policy framework," *R&D Management* 34, no. 4 (2004), pp. 372–375.

70 www.ocs-gz.gov.cn.

71 Endo Homare, 中国がシリコンバレーとつながるとき (*When China Links Up with Silicon Valley*). Tokyo: Nikkei BP, 2001, p. 55.

72 www.ocs-gz.gov.cn.

73 Literally "personnel who have studied or are studying overseas." The translation "overseas Chinese scholars" is the standard translation used in China's English-language publications; "OCS" is the acronym used at the event and generally.

74 According to information posted to www.ocs-gz.gov.cn in March 2005.

75 Ibid.

76 www.chtf.com.

77 Endo, *When China Links Up with Silicon Valley*.

78 Ibid., pp. 208–209.

79 Ibid., pp. 210–212.

80 Ibid., p. 222.

81 Ibid., p. 238.

82 www.tt91.com/jishu.asp.

83 Sun Lijun (孙理军) and Huang Huaye (黄花叶), "美日技术转移实践及其对我国技术转移中心的启示" ("US and Japanese Technology Transfer Practices and What We Can Learn for Our Country's Technology Transfer Centers"), in 科技管理研究 (*Keji Guanli Yanjiu*), 1 (2003), p. 72.

84 www.hitec.net.cn/structure/aboutus/jgjj.

85 www.technology4sme.com.cn.

86 www.nttc.ac.cn and www.tt91.com/zhuanyi/zhuanyi004.htm.

87 www.tt91.com/zhuanyi/zhuanyi006.htm.

88 www.tt91.com/zhuanyi/zhuanyi001.htm.

89 nttc.ecust.edu.cn/org/org_list.asp.

90 www.tt91.com/zhuanyi/zhuanyi002.htm.

91 www.tt91.com/zhuanyi/zhuanyi015.htm.

92 www.tt91.com/zhuanyi/zhuanyi013.htm.

93 www.coatren.cn/memberabout/luqiangsppc.html.

94 www.sittnet.cn.

95 www.china.org.cn.

96 www.caiep.org.

97 Ibid.

98 www.chinajob.com.cn.

99 www.internationalexecutive.org.

100 www.chinajob.com.cn.

101 www.china.org.cn.

102 www.internationalexecutive.org.

103 According to COEA's Overseas Chinese Network (*Zhongguo Qiao Wang*) website www.chinaqw.com.cn.

104 Ibid.
105 www.chinaql.org.
106 www.melma.com.
107 www.chinaqw.com.
108 www.ccba.bc.ca.
109 www.bjql.org.cn. Qiaolian's leaders applauded them for coming to China "for research" and reminded them of their importance to China's S&T development.
110 www.cast.org.cn.
111 Ibid. CAST's constitution also affirms, "The China Association for Science & Technology (hereinafter referred to as CAST) is a mass organization of Chinese scientific and technological workers, and a bridge to link scientific and technological workers with the Communist Party of China and the Government."
112 Ibid.
113 www.caistc.com.
114 www.codpa.org.
115 www.acp-atlanta.org.
116 www.ceaie.edu.cn.
117 According to an undated posting on www.chinaedunews.com.cn, read in May 2008.
118 www.cossp.gov.cn.
119 www.cdibi.org.cn.
120 OCAO's role is not acknowledged on the site. Under "contact" information is listed Guo Wenwei (郭文伟), who also appears on the Chinese-American Association of Engineering's (中国留美工程学会) website with the same phone and an OCAO email extension (gqb.gov.cn). A reference on CAST-LA's site identifies Guo as an employee of OCAO's Department 4 (www.cast-la.org/archive/2008/02/GQB_Class.doc).
121 www.ocpan.org.
122 chinajob.com.cn.
123 www.chinahr.com.
124 www.edu.cn/introduction.
125 www.cscse.edu.cn.
126 使之成为国际通用的应用型人才   (www.cscse.edu.cn/publish/portal0/tab40/info15.htm).
127 www.chinatalents.gov.cn.
128 www.cistc.net.
129 OCEPA was originally the Association of Chinese Entrepreneurs and Scholars (中国留学人员回国创业协会) with a website at www.sinoaces.org and a Yahoo! group at sinoaces@yahoo.com.
130 www.returnchina.org.

5

US-BASED TECHNOLOGY TRANSFER ORGANIZATIONS

China's appetite for foreign technology is fed by a maze of organizations inside China and by a massive network of foreign-based venues. These foreign venues are managed in part by entities that report directly to the PRC government but in larger part by "non-political" expatriate groups, whose members' sympathy for China and ability to profit by ceding technology have made them China's de facto agents. The transfer mechanisms discussed in the preceding chapter could not operate without active support from these overseas organizations.

Although China's technology network is worldwide, this chapter focuses on the United States, which the PRC regards as its main technology "partner." We begin by examining five types of US-based venues – diplomatic offices, a facilitation company, an alleged NGO, an ethnic Chinese professional organization, and alumni associations – to demonstrate the variety of channels through which technology transfer happens. In the remainder of the chapter, we take a closer look at these Sino-American professional organizations. As is the case with PRC-based organizations, the number of groups in the US runs up quickly, so we will limit our survey to prominent organizations in three categories: Sino–US S&T associations, the California groups (as an example of geographic concentration), and groups focused on certain technology fields.

The commitment shared by these professional groups varies. Some are social networking associations formed chiefly to promote the careers and ethnic interests of their members. For them, technology transfer is a business opportunity, which their familiarity with Chinese culture positions them to exploit. Other groups regard handing China the latest American technology as an existential imperative and coordinate with their PRC counterparts to achieve this end while submitting to China's formal guidance. Still others have members who hold official PRC posts and sit on Chinese S&T advisory panels.

From US to China through "multiple channels"

China's diplomatic missions to the United States are focused to an extraordinary degree on transferring US technology, both directly by promoting tech-oriented business and "cooperative" relationships, and indirectly by leveraging their relationships with US-based China advocacy groups. A third dimension – support for clandestine operations – is documented in Chapter 8 on traditional Chinese espionage. Each of China's diplomatic offices in the US, including its embassy in Washington, DC, consulates in New York, Chicago, Houston, San Francisco and Los Angeles, and its UN mission, have well-staffed S&T offices (科技处 or 组) to support these transactions.

According to a description posted to an official Chinese S&T exchange network,

> The PRC embassy's S&T office utilizes all advantages associated with being on the front line of Sino–US S&T cooperation and makes full use of its resources at every quarter to raise the level of service it provides to China's domestic S&T plans in priority sectors and project development work, endeavoring to build an innovative nation.[1]

This description accurately captures the multi-faceted role played by the Washington embassy's S&T office in technology transfer.

The office helps plan national events, where agreements are made between the US and PRC governments for cooperation in science and technology, and plays a direct role in the negotiations leading to these agreements. Its staff meet with high-tech US companies, universities, and S&T consortia in the United States, the heads of which are typically ethnic Chinese who have demonstrated commitment to China's S&T development. It receives visitors from China's tech transfer organizations, briefs them on the local situation, and arranges meetings or tours at US companies and technology centers.

Reps from the PRC embassy and consular S&T offices meet, in turn, with the officers of US-based China advocacy groups to communicate policy decisions, appeal for expanded support, and acquaint them with opportunities for S&T investments and other types of exchanges that involve travel to China to support favored projects. They facilitate the paperwork for individuals planning PRC S&T ventures in China or "return" visits, track their involvement, and arrange for them to meet appropriate persons while in China. Picnics, annual celebrations, and business meetings held by Sino-American S&T advocacy groups usually have someone from the S&T office in attendance along with other personnel registered to the embassy or consulate.

Here is a typical example of how the embassy's mediation process works. In November 2006, its S&T counselor (科技参赞) and the head of the Washington, DC-based "Center for US-China Technology Innovation and Development" (UCTID, see below) presided over a seminar attended by four major DC area China advocacy groups – the UCTID, the Overseas Chinese-American Entrepreneurs Association (留美华人企业家协会), the CAST Network Society (a group within CAST-USA), and the China Society (中国协会) – at George Mason's Fairfax Innovation Center to introduce technology transfer projects plugged by a Shandong-based "information technology outsourcing" company.[2] Other participants included the embassy's S&T Ministerial Counselor Jin Ju,[3] another member of the S&T office who specializes in IT, and the owner of a large IT service company in the I-270 technology corridor.[4] Speeches given by embassy officials met with "enthusiastic response" and the event ended with an agreement to pursue transfer activities with the Shandong firm.[5]

The embassy's S&T office also sends delegations of personnel from US companies in particular technology sectors (e.g., pharmaceuticals, software) to China under formal and informal PRC state auspices to market their technology in China or engage in ventures that result in technology transfer. It also facilitates meetings for S&T delegations traveling from China. For example, in June 2006 a nine-person group from the PRC's Ministry of Science and Technology and several technical universities seeking automotive technology from the United States were greeted by S&T ministerial counselor Jin Ju and escorted by his subordinate, the embassy's S&T counselor, to various US sites.

Beyond the practical, hands-on support they render, China's S&T officers in the United States engage in public discourse to promote expanded US–China technology trade and rally sentiment against "obstacles" (障碍) the US government places in the way of "free scientific exchange."

For example, in 2002, the embassy's S&T counselor met a China science delegation headed by MOST that came to celebrate the opening of the University of Maryland's "Zhongguancun National Innovation Model Park" (or Z-park), China's first such facility abroad.[6] At a seminar to mark the event, the counselor complained about "political roadblocks" Congress puts in the way of technology exports to China. Two years later, the PRC counselor conveyed to a CAST-USA assembly his country's displeasure with technology export restrictions and "political pressure."[7]

S&T officers assigned to these diplomatic posts rotate regularly through other tech transfer jobs in China and abroad, bringing experience to the task. The director of the China Association for International Science and Technology Cooperation did a three-year stint as S&T counselor and S&T minister at the Washington embassy. His prior service included tours of PRC embassies in Europe. Addresses given at ceremonies to welcome incoming science counselors and honor the outgoing incumbent typically cite the officers' scientific background and diplomatic skills.

The role these officers play in technology acquisition may be gauged in part by their interactions with expatriate scientists. Serious efforts to involve Chinese scientists in the US in PRC S&T projects began in the mid-1990s, with the New York consulate's formation of an overseas experts committee (海外专家委员会) to "help overseas students realize their hopes of serving the country" and to "use the intellect of ethnic Chinese experts abroad to contribute planning and strategy for the enactment of important domestic scientific and technology programs."[8] By 1997 the consulate had:

> [M]obilized community organizations with a relatively [high] concentration of overseas ethnic Chinese experts, such as the Chinese Association for Science and Technology USA, the North American Chinese Association of Science and Technology, the Chinese Finance Society, the Chinese Association for Science and Business, the Association of Chinese Scientists and Engineers USA, and the Silicon Valley Chinese Engineers Association, and organized in the United States 100 high-level ethnic Chinese scholars in all fields to carry out investigations and research on the future direction of China's S&T development and on related policies, who submitted the four volume "Recommendations for the Development of Chinese Science and Technology" in which coalesced the wisdom of the ethnic Chinese scholars and their sincere thought to repay their native country.[9]

Included were eight topics covering the major high-tech disciplines marked for transfer. At the same time, "an effective model was sought for overseas scholars to serve their [native] country." In November of that year a MOST delegation:

> arrived in Canada and the United States and interviewed more than 120 ethnic Chinese scientists and the organizations to which they belong. These ethnic Chinese scientists offered their valuable opinions and recommendations on various levels such as developmental trends in worldwide basic research and on China's basic research development strategies, choice of priority areas, and international cooperation, planning and administration of basic research.[10]

Both sides agreed that China's practice of sending groups to solicit the opinions of Chinese scholars abroad on S&T policy issues was a positive development – a "scientific and democratic means of determining national policy." The US-based scholars "hoped through the combined efforts of those in China and abroad China would be able to regularize and systematize this kind of model and build a formal, normalized pathway and mechanism for exchanges with China's science policymakers."[11]

This pattern of cooperation with Sino-American S&T groups has continued through to the present. For example, in May 2007, the New York Consul-General reported to the annual CAST-USA gathering that China's policy of "bringing in, digesting, absorbing and recreating" (引进消化吸收再创新) foreign science and technology has made "continuous breakthroughs." The C-G asked the Chinese-American scientists there to continue "serving China through various means."[12] A delegation from the PRC's State Administration of Foreign Experts Affairs subsequently visited the consulate to express thanks for its support in recruiting S&T talent. Both sides reportedly "carried out deep discussions on recruitment efforts inside the US."[13]

Similar efforts are pursued at China's other diplomatic facilities in the US, which have carved out areas of responsibility throughout the 50 states and overseas territories. In April 2008, while US auto firms were fighting for their survival, the PRC's Chicago S&T counselor addressed the American Association of Chinese Scientists and Engineers in Detroit on China's need for advanced automotive technology. The head of a major PRC auto company was there helpfully to explain "opportunities and challenges facing China's automotive industry."[14] Ten months later at a Lunar New Year feast the counselor enjoined the same group "to make greater contributions to the stable and healthy development of Sino–US relations."

The power which China's diplomatic offices have over these US-registered S&T organizations is considerable, as indicated by the number of groups they can bring under their umbrella. In November 2007, the Los Angeles consul hosted a banquet for 30 representatives of 11 southern California S&T professional groups. He thanked them for their contributions to Sino–American S&T cooperation and exchange and expressed the consulate's desire to continue providing these groups with support.[15] Then, in May 2008, the LA consulate's S&T counselor gathered 220 members of local Chinese S&T groups for a meeting with a "policy advising and reporting group" sent by the PRC State Council's Overseas Chinese Affairs Office and MOST's Department of International S&T Cooperation, held at the OCAO's own conference center in LA. The OCAO group was led by Zhang Jianqing, head of the Department 4 technology transfer unit, who prior to this worked in the NYC consulate and Washington embassy. The S&T counselor described the attendees as people who live abroad but whose "hearts and minds belong to China" (心系祖国).[16] Dong Jianlong, another Department 4 officer formerly employed at the LA consulate, explained to the expatriate scientists "in detail" how to participate in China's S&T development.[17]

Consular S&T officers advise PRC delegations how to leverage relationships with these groups during their stay in the United States and they broker agreements between the visitors and US centers of technical excellence. They also maintain ties with the ethnic Chinese owners of high-tech companies. For example, in February 2009, a delegation from the San Francisco consulate called on a local biotech firm, where they were "warmly received" by the Chinese CEO and staff. Both sides exchanged views on China's biotech development and the support rendered by US-based experts.[18] News items posted to the LA and SF consulates' websites describe frequent visits by the S&T counselors to California high-tech companies.

These same websites offer a host of information to those contemplating technology ventures, including a summary of China's official S&T programs, an introduction to China's overall plan for international S&T cooperation, links to PRC S&T-oriented websites, Chinese S&T policy documents, information on China's high-tech zones, and useful contacts. There are news items posted on S&T

"exchange" events in China, and S&T "communiqués" (中国科技通讯) from PRC ministries and other official organizations announcing opportunities to support Chinese S&T projects, both general and specific. Most of this information is in Chinese. Readers are enjoined to "use multiple means to develop multi-channel, multi-layer, all-round international cooperation and exchange" and contribute research of a "practical nature" (可行性).[19]

Besides its diplomatic missions in the United States, the Chinese government facilitates tech transfer through other state organizations established directly on US soil. SAFEA's New York office is one example. Another is Triway Enterprise, Inc. (三立国际有限公司), an "external training institute" set up under SAFEA's auspices in Falls Church, VA with branches in Beijing and Nanjing. The company "since 1993 has been putting its energy into promoting bilateral exchange and cooperation between China and the US in the fields of S&T, culture, education and management with great success."[20] It claims to have an excellent reputation arranging travel to the US for "training and inspection" and in "international exchange services."

Triway also hosts "talented persons exchange conferences" for recruiters from Shanghai, Guangzhou, and elsewhere in China at venues in New York, DC, Chicago, the west coast, and Toronto. In 2008 Triway organized for a Changzhou delegation "talks and exchanges" with some 150 local Chinese scholars, overseas students, and professional persons in Los Angeles. The event was sponsored by Changzhou's municipal personnel office and by SAFEA. In 2009 it arranged a conference in New York City for a Guangdong headhunting team sent by the Ministry of Personnel and SAFEA, and it helped run CAST-USA's seventeenth annual meeting in Washington, DC. Triway boasts "a one-stop, fully-integrated solution" to technology transfer that includes handling "complex travel arrangements" and providing "top-quality translators."[21]

As a measure of the company's success, Triway was hired in October 2006 by the Shanghai Association for the International Exchange of Personnel (上海国际人才交流协会) – an alleged NGO and part of the China Association for the International Exchange of Personnel, which is a SAFEA front organization – to help establish a liaison office in Washington, DC. The office links up east coast Chinese S&T personnel with the appropriate units in Shanghai and has participated in meetings run by area Chinese professional groups.

Nominal "non-governmental" offices such as this provide PRC state and provincial units with direct access to US S&T talent while insulating the latter from the stigma of supporting a foreign state whose goals are often inimical to US interests. Besides its DC foothold, SAIEP has an office in Sunnyvale, CA as part of a worldwide network that includes Toronto, London, Paris, Hannover, Osaka, and Sydney. The west coast unit was established with help from the Silicon Valley Chinese Engineers Association (see below), the largest Chinese professional group in the valley, and is run by former SCEA director and president June Chu.[22] Shanghai's decision to locate an office in Silicon Valley is explained on the SAIEP website: "The US is the most developed country in the world. It has at the same time the highest population of top talent."[23]

SAIEP California's main partner, besides SCEA, is the Hua Yuan Science and Technology Association, another California Chinese-American group (see below).[24] Some idea of the scale of SAIEP's operation is evident in its "10,000 Overseas Scholars Convergence Program" (万名海外留学人才集聚工程),[25] which aims at raising the level of Shanghai's S&T talent and "breaking conceptual restraints on using overseas scholars." The program boasts "new methods" that involve analyzing the city's talent pool, determining its shortcomings, and using foreign experts to fill posts "at all levels of Party and government, institutes of higher learning, scientific research institutes, medical facilities, state-owned large and medium-sized businesses, and other associated facilities."[26]

Straddling the line between PRC organizations in the US and US-based China advocacy groups is the Chinese Association for Science and Technology, USA (中国留美科技协会), a "non-political" professional association founded in New York City in 1992, whose 11 chapters span 30 states. Although the organization does not claim direct affiliation with its PRC namesake, the China Association for Science and Technology (中国科技协会), CAST-USA lists CAST China as one of its two "partners" (the other is the MOE's China Education and Research Network).[27] The PRC connection is further spelled out in CAST-USA's charter, where it claims to "serve as a 'bridge' between the United States and China for both personnel and information exchanges, and for cooperation in science and technology, economics, trade and other areas."[28]

The organization goes on to list under its "activities" the following:

> To establish cooperative relations with American corporations, enterprises, institutions and organizations, to create favorable conditions and environment for cooperation between the American and Chinese people in seeking funds, market development, technology transfer and investment opportunities between the United States and China.[29]

A critical reader might ask why this "US" organization emphasizes a need for relations with US organizations. In apposition to what? We also note in the last phrase the penultimate position of "technology transfer," the preferred spot for key elements in a Chinese list and what CAST-USA is all about. Then there is the US organization's Chinese name, which differs from the PRC organization's name by two characters only – 留美 or "residing in America." But these are minor points, as a survey of CAST-USA's literature demonstrates its orientation and the beneficiary of its activities.

CAST-USA lists among its "advisors" current and former members of the Chinese Academy of Science and Chinese Academy of Engineering, the PRC's highest scientific bodies. Also named are former Minister of Science and Technology Zhu Lilan, members of China's National Natural Science Foundation, members of China's National People's Congress and National Committee of the Chinese People's Political Consultative Conference, and professors at PRC universities.[30] These advisors play active roles in the US organization's proceedings. For example, the CAS president led off the annual meeting in 2005 with an address entitled "Envoys of S&T Cooperation, Bridge for Sino–American Friendship." A specialist in systems control also from CAS addressed the same gathering with a tribute to Qian Xuesen – father of China's strategic missile force (see Chapter 1), outspoken advocate of US technology transfer and the beacon behind China's foreign S&T open source collection program–whom he noted used to study at nearby Cal Tech.[31]

Many CAST-USA members who live in the US occupy PRC positions. An example is Professor Chao Xiuli of the North Carolina chapter. Chao is tenured at Qinghua University and a member of CAS's International Research Team on Complex Systems. He has served as adjunct professor in the CAS Graduate School since 2002, at Dalian University of Technology, and as a distinguished professor at CAS's Academy of Mathematics and System Sciences.[32] He won the Outstanding Overseas Young Scientist Award from China's NNSF, another outstanding scientist award from CAS, and has participated directly in PRC national S&T planning.[33]

The usual complement of Chinese officials attends CAST-USA's business meetings and social events. PRC Consul General Zhong Jianhua opened CAST-USA's 2004 convention and ended it with a banquet at his residence. China S&T Counselor Li Wuqiang spoke at the 2007 national convention in New York and S&T Counselor Mao Zhongying began the regional NYC meeting in 2008. On Double Ten Day (October 10, a Chinese national holiday) in 2007, CAST-USA's New York chapter met under the S&T attaché's auspices with officials from China's Ministry of Science and Technology, OCAO's Department 4, and two Shanghai industrial groups to discuss founding S&T-oriented businesses in China.[34]

Besides interacting with PRC delegations to the United States, CAST-USA sends missions to China, such as an annual visit during "Returning Overseas Scholars Innovation Week," when the CAST-USA team meets with officials from MOST, academics from CAS and CAE, financial sponsors, and managers of China's "pioneering parks" to line up cooperative projects. CAST-USA also backed a 2008 "Return Visit to China," which met with an OCAO team in Wuhan for a series of activities aimed at "combining the technologies provided by overseas Chinese with local funding for mutual benefit." The group had "broad contacts and exchanges with relevant domestic units and personnel," and direct exchanges with OCAO and local government leaders.[35]

CAST-USA also plays a prominent role in the Guangzhou OCS tech transfer conventions. At the seventh annual event in 2004, CAST-USA sent a 50-person delegation, which brought to China "over 40 projects," more than any other foreign delegation.[36] While at the convention, it joined up with the PRC organizing committee to host the first "High-level Forum on a Strategy to Strengthen China through Knowledge" (中国知识强国战略高层论坛) and to pass a declaration of support for China's efforts to usher in high-tech industry. The proposal – conceived, drafted, and presented by CAST-USA – aimed at positioning China among the world's top seven countries in innovation by 2010. A report describing it began by affirming "competition between countries in the 21st century is a competition in knowledge."[37] The irony of helping China prevail in a competition against the country in which one lives seems to have gone unnoticed.

On top of its regional chapters CAST-USA has eight disciplinary subcommittees specializing in information engineering, networking, e-commerce, chemistry and chemical engineering, biology, medicine, finance, and law.[38] One of them is the "CAST Network Society" (网络学会) founded in 2000. The group organizes an annual Chinese-American Networking Symposium, alternately held in the US and China, where CAST experts give presentations, run panels, and engage their PRC counterparts in technical break-out sessions.[39] It has close ties with Beijing's Zhongguancun Science Park and the University of Maryland, which jointly sponsor the CANS event.

Chinese alumni associations are another venue which Beijing uses to promote its technology transfer agenda. Degree holders from Chinese colleges living abroad who belong to these associations are, from China's perspective, a self-selected talent pool with the knowledge and motivation to contribute to China's technical modernization. They also constitute a ready-made support base inside the host country with concentrations of personnel in high-tech corridors.

The Shanghai Jiaotong University Alumni Association, for example, has chapters in Houston, Michigan, North Carolina, Washington, DC, Boston, New York, Florida, New England, Pittsburg, and Texas.[40] The Nanjing University Alumni Association with some 200,000 US members has branches in Atlanta, Boston, Chicago, Dallas, Houston, Los Angeles, New York, North Carolina, and Philadelphia. Technology transfer masquerading as scientific exchanges is written into their bylaws and charters.[41] These "exchanges" typically take the form of the PRC government informing the alumni associations of China's technology needs, and the US-based alumni traveling to China to service those needs.

For example, in June 2007 the NUAA sent a US delegation to Nanjing under the provincial government's auspices to discuss technology transfer opportunities with PRC companies. Some 23 presentations, cleared with the host beforehand, were given by the delegation on finance, management, bio-pharmaceuticals, materials, software, and IT. Their presentations were made simultaneously in three "fully packed" conference rooms. During the seven-day event, the US-based alumni visited high-tech industrial parks in Nanjing, Changzhou, Wuxi, and Suzhou, which were "well prepared" for their arrival.[42]

In 2009, China's OCAO "formally commissioned" (正式委托) the NUAA to "convene" (召集) 40 Chinese-American experts in biotechnology, as part of a 100-person draft required by a new "Plan for Overseas Talented Persons to Render Service to China." The OCAO asked specifically for ethnic Chinese who had worked three years or longer overseas and could bring to China "practical items" developed with their own IPR. In a separate pitch for a project in Hainan, the OCAO asked the association to provide "high-level talented persons with academic attainments in the United States, definite business achievements, and specific ideas for cooperative ventures" in "medicine, electronics, management, finance, high-technology, computers and autos."[43]

Chinese alumni associations from both sides of the Taiwan Straits can put aside political differences for their common interests vis-à-vis the non-Chinese world. The Tsinghua Alumni Association of Northern California plays "a key role in the research, development and incubation of high-tech industry in both mainland China and Taiwan."[44] Another example is the Chiao-Tung University Alumni Association in America,[45] which enrolls alumni from all five Jiaotong universities, China and Taiwan alike.

Chinese-American S&T associations – general

Complementing the technology outreach organizations in China and PRC venues operating within the United States itself are well over 100 US-registered China advocacy groups that aim directly at technology transfer or achieve this as a consequence of their organizational structure. While some of these groups are open to professionals of any ethnicity, most are made up exclusively of overseas Chinese – US citizens, green card holders, H-1B visa workers, and graduate students – whose interests coincide with those of their ancestral country.

Although there is no a priori reason for Chinese-American S&T associations to identify with China, a sovereign foreign state, in practice this is nearly always so given the advantages that accrue to members who can overcome linguistic and other obstacles to provide their know-how to China. At the risk of belaboring the obvious, their common heritage predisposes them to focus on doing what they can do best. This internal dynamic is exploited by China, which courts these associations and steers their activities using a mix of psychological pressure, political control, and financial incentives. The Sino-US organizations in turn become credible through their interactions with China and the access they provide to their members.

Evidence of a China bias on the part of these S&T groups is found in their charters, activities, and web postings – which we shall explore below – and in the spirit that pervades their literature. For example, among the dozens of S&T associations examined by the authors, not one failed to solicit money for the 2008 Sichuan earthquake relief – a project that has nothing to do with S&T and everything to do with helping China. By contrast, nowhere did we find concern expressed about contributing technology to a foreign country whose position on issues is often antagonistic to that of the US. The assumption, when it is made at all, is what's good for China is good for everyone.

Let us look at these organizations in detail, beginning with the North American Chinese Scholars International Exchange Center (北美洲中国学人国际交流中心) in McLean, VA,[46] one of nine generic Sino-American S&T associations we will cover. According to its website, NAIEC is:

> an independent, non-profit institution registered in the United States and headquartered in suburban Washington DC. It is led by a group of Chinese-

American individuals who have earned doctorates in social sciences, biological sciences, information technologies, and management in the United States and have been highly successful in their respective fields. They have led Chinese-American professional and community organizations/institutions for years while maintaining broad ties both in the United States and in China.[47]

NAIEC achieved prominence during 2000 to 2002 through a series of "overseas Chinese scholar talented persons exchange meetings" held in DC and other US and Canadian cities. Supported by the PRC embassy in Washington, the meetings were joined by representatives from various Chinese provinces and cities and by overseas Chinese scholars and ethnic Chinese living abroad. The meetings were considered "enormous successes."[48] The first event organized in 2000 with help from the Union of Chinese American Professional Associations (see below) and alumni from technical universities was attended by some 70 PRC delegates and 750 US and Canadian OCS. A second session in 2001[49] was billed as giving Chinese scientists in the US a "historical opportunity" to support China's competitiveness as it entered the WTO.[50] Statistics for the 2001 event were 100 PRC and 2,450 resident attendees. The meetings "emphasized bridge-building and practical results." Some 20 percent of the projects discussed at the meeting were put into effect.[51]

By the third year these meetings had become "a famous platform and conveyor belt linking overseas Chinese scholars and the ancestral mainland." The October 2002 session attracted 73 US-based OSC expert *associations* and several PRC-based transfer organizations including the OCAO, the Jiangsu branch of SAFEA, and that province's personnel office. Delegates from 17 Jiangsu cities attended to conduct "project discussions on high-tech items."[52] For this event, NAIEC consulted a "database of talented personnel" to select US-based scholars whose skills matched the "concrete personnel needs . . . of PRC industrial firms and government institutes."[53] Selectees performed various "services" in China, including evaluating PRC state projects.[54]

Illustrating its close links with official PRC bodies, NAIEC was invited in 2003 by Zhejiang Province's Expert and Overseas Chinese Scholar Service Center, with backing from two offices in the Ministry of Personnel, to propose "technical cooperation and exchange projects." The group asked its US members to submit detailed forms describing their projects in advance so that appropriate PRC government units and companies could be lined up. Applicants who passed online screening were invited to China for "deeper discussions."[55] This requirement to have tech transfer ideas vetted in China beforehand has become *de rigueur* and was invoked by NAIEC again in 2008 in a solicitation for projects in China's coastal cities and western regions.[56]

NAIEC's partner in the annual DC "exchange" meetings is the Union of Chinese American Professional Organizations (美国大华府华人专业团体联合会), a non-profit group founded in 1998 that "coordinates 28 Chinese American professional organizations in the Washington area."[57] UCAPO's claimed following of 20,000 is based on the combined membership of these participating organizations; its own staff numbers about half a dozen. Most member groups are centered on particular technologies or professions with the balance made up of friendship associations and groups promoting politics and culture. Those with an S&T orientation are listed below.[58]

- CAST/DC Chapter (中国留美科技协会, 华盛顿分会)
- CAST/Network Society (旅美科技协会, 网络分会)
- Chinese American Entrepreneur Assoc.(美国华人创业者协会)
- Chinese Association of Pharmaceutical Scientists, USA (北美华人药物发展协会)
- Chinese Biopharmaceutical Association, USA (美国华人生物医药科技协会)
- National Society of Medical Scientists–Chinese-American Association (美国华裔医学科学家协会)
- North American China Overseas Transportation Association (中国旅美交通协会)
- Overseas Chinese-American Entrepreneurs Association at DC (留美华人企业家协会, 华盛顿分会)
- Pharmaceutics Association of Chinese-American Scientists (美国华人医药科学家协会)
- US-China Industry & Commerce Association (美中工商联合会)

The term "professional" is not used here loosely. Some 95 percent of the participating organizations' members have advanced degrees.[59] Many have become "the top experts in their fields or senior officials in government agencies."[60] UCAPO's role is to guide interaction between the groups, support their members' careers, lobby for PRC national interests ("promote understanding and cooperation between China and the US"), and improve relations between Chinese and "other ethnic groups" in the US.[61] The Shanghai chapter of the PRC State Council's Overseas Chinese Affairs Office, with which UCAPO is closely affiliated, states that one of UCAPO's purposes is to "integrate technology resources" between China and the US, and combine "the intellectual resources of US-based expert personages" with the "market resources" of China.[62]

UCAPO's member groups have sponsored "nearly 100 technological and trading delegations to visit China and participated in hi-tech fairs and professional forums and workshops."[63] These are in addition to projects carried out in the United States. According to the Shanghai OCAO, more than 100 UCAPO members "relocated their technological enterprises" to China. Updated information posted to the UCAPO site in 2009 puts that figure at 300.

A third major DC-area technology transfer organization is the Center for US-China Technology Innovation and Development (中美技术创新与发展中心), a "research and consulting company" founded in 2006 by River Doan (段渠), a

1990s immigrant to the US who managed high-tech projects in China for CAS and MOST. Dr. Doan now regards himself as "a friend of US-China governmental, academic and industrial communities involved in international technology transfer, innovation, and outsourcing."[64] His eight-person management team is staffed entirely by Chinese-Americans. They are assisted by an advisory committee of 12 people, including the PRC embassy's S&T counselor, deans of prominent PRC science and engineering universities, officers of Chinese technical conglomerates, a former MOST official, and four George Mason University professors.[65]

This core of officers acts through "a huge network of specialists" in China and the US to provide "integrative service" for technology transfer and talent exchange. These specialists:

> conduct research in emerging technologies and business opportunities, innovation methodology and development strategies; they conduct technology and innovation policy study; provide evaluation and risk analysis for technology investment; and provide assistance and training programs for emerging businesses and innovative start-ups.[66]

In plain terms, UCTID and its affiliates spot new US technology, find PRC customers for it, determine how to pass the technology to China in a cost-effective way, and help get the project off the ground. It works at both ends of the business, encouraging US-based Chinese entrepreneurs to market their technology in China and helping PRC state and corporate equities find foreign talent. To achieve this, UCTID networks with other Sino-American S&T groups such as CAST, the Overseas Chinese-American Entrepreneurs Association, and the Chinese Biopharmaceutical Association USA, directly or under consular auspices.

For elite customers UCTID offers membership in a "Summit Club" (高峰俱乐部) where one can meet successful "executives, officers, scholars, domain experts, and senior professionals" united by their "interest in international cooperation between the USA and China."[67]

New York City, besides being host to the founding CAST-USA chapter, is also home to the Chinese Association for Science and Business (美国国际华人科技工商协会), a Sino-American advocacy group founded in 1997. Current membership is about 1,000 according to CASB, or over 2,000 according to the Chinese consulate.[68] Although CASB emphasizes its "uniqueness," the organization typifies US-based Chinese S&T associations in most respects:

- it is made up entirely of Chinese with careers in S&T and management;
- it has members who hold top posts in business, government and academia;
- it supports its members' professional development;
- it promotes high-tech "exchanges" with China through a global network;
- it organizes and participates in tech transfer conferences in China;
- it sends delegations to China to engage in transfer-related activities;
- it co-sponsors conferences in the US with delegations from China;

- it maintains close ties with PRC diplomats stationed in the US;
- it works with local PRC governments to help OCS set up high-tech businesses.

Here is part of a recent posting to the CASB website, the essence of which may be found on any of the dozens of Sino-American tech transfer sites we examined.

> It is my great pleasure to report to you our CASB delegation's successful visit to Beijing and Tianjin in April [2009] in response to the Chinese Government's "Thousand Talents" program.
>
> CASB members were excited at the Chinese Government's announcement of the new program to hire 1,000 specialists from overseas, and they have responded enthusiastically. As many accomplished members intended to return to China together to serve the motherland under this program, we organized a delegation which visited Beijing and Tianjin from April 15 to 21. We received a very warm welcome and high-level reception.[69]

The posting went on to describe meetings with high PRC officials in the Chinese Academy of Engineering, the National Committee of the Chinese People's Political Consultative Conference, the OCAO, Tianjin's mayor, two Communist Party politburo members, MOST officials, and the heads of a high-tech industrial zone in Tianjin, to whom they presented their slate of projects.[70] A follow-up visit, presumably to discuss implementation, was being scheduled.

Not to be confused with CAST-USA (中国留美科技协会) described earlier in the chapter is the North America Chinese Association of Science and Technology (北美华人科技协会), a Chinese S&T advocacy group that grew out of Boston and now claims 3,000 members in 14 US chapters. NACAST was founded in 1993 by MIT's Liu Yaping (刘亚平) under the guidance (指导下) of China's State Science and Technology Commission (predecessor to MOST) and the Chinese consulate in New York.[71] Liu, a strong believer in the "mutual benefits" of Sino–US technical cooperation, reportedly "advocates relying on talented persons overseas to directly infuse the world's first-rate technology" into China.[72]

NACAST's stated goal is to promote and expedite Sino–US cooperation and exchange in S&T. To achieve this, it:

- serves as liaison between Chinese and US research facilities, universities, companies, and related institutions;
- arranges visits, lectures and *short periods of work* in China for members who have demonstrated success in their careers (emphasis added);
- helps PRC scholars and entrepreneurs come to America for training;
- builds regular channels for Sino–US two-way exchanges.[73]

More than 85 percent of NACAST's members have PhDs from top US universities and "have or are acquiring important technologies and management positions."[74] Its directors hail from research facilities at Bristol-Meyers, Chrysler, Exxon, Hughes, Lucent, Microsoft, Rockwell, Siemens, United Technologies, and Harvard, MIT, Stanford, and Yale universities. Each year NACAST's management organizes trips to China by overseas scholars from these and other US facilities to carry out exchanges and "perform services." According to the OCAO, the organization lobbies on China's behalf not just for technology transfer but for political matters as well.[75]

The southern states also have vigorous China S&T advocacy groups, beginning with Houston's Chinese Association of Professionals in Science and Technology (中国旅美专家协会), another non-profit, "non-political" group founded in the early 1990s. CAPST's generic missions are "to facilitate and promote scientific, cultural and economic exchanges between China and the United States" and support their members' career advancement through networking.[76] Its 500 members, chiefly scientists, engineers, and other professionals, "hold various important positions in private companies, universities and research institutions." Some have dual appointments at US and PRC technical universities. Members are split functionally into six divisions for computing, energy, chemistry, medicine, law, and business management.

CAPST works with PRC technology transfer organizations such as OCAO, SAFEA, and MOST to send specialists to China, receive delegations from China and organize technology "exchange" conferences in both countries. Here are examples of its PRC interactions:[77]

- In February 2008 CAST (China)'s International Department arrived in Houston to discuss with CAPST leaders its Overseas Knowledge Plan (海智计划). Launched in 2004, the Plan makes use of CAST's function as a bridge between China and overseas Chinese S&T groups to stimulate scientists and engineers abroad "to contribute their intellect and strength" to China's economic development and "scientific innovation."
- Three months later, CAPST hosted five PRC delegates, including the heads of OCAO's S&T Office and MOST's Department of International S&T Cooperation, for an "advisory readout of China's innovation policies." Among the topics discussed were how to "better utilize OCS' knowledge and intellectual property to serve China."

CAPST's liaisons with PRC diplomatic representatives in the US are commonplace. The reader is invited to examine CAPST's quarterly newsletter (专协通讯) for numerous examples. Here is one from the China Talents website:

- A North American OCS Exchange Meeting (北美留交会) opened in Houston in 2006 with support from CAPST, Chinese alumni groups, the consulate in Houston, and various PRC delegations that brought nearly 2,000 work opportunities. Many of the work units offered high salaries to attract the overseas talent to China. The meeting was "strongly coordinated" (有力配合) by the PRC embassy, enjoyed enthusiastic support from the PRC government at all levels, and had tremendous impact. The Houston C-G predicted China technology scouts would "return fully loaded" (满载而归) and, indeed, "several hundred high-tech projects" found their way to China.[78]

Every year the Houston C-G delivers the keynote speech at CAPST's annual meeting. The 2007 event, a typical affair, was also attended by the consulate's S&T team and by representatives from the China Council for the Promotion of Peaceful National Unification.[79] Consul Qiao Hong congratulated CAPST "for 15 years of accomplishments in bringing together local ethnic Chinese specialists and promoting Sino-US bilateral cooperation and exchanges in S&T, education, specialized technology and personnel." She thanked CAPST for acting as a bridge for Sino–US technical exchanges and for "dedication in serving China."[80]

In 1996 CAPST put together a Federation of Associations of Chinese Professionals in Southern USA (美南中国专家协会联合会), an umbrella organization representing 22 Sino-US advocacy groups in the south, including CAPST, which has become the Atlanta-based regional center for Sino-American professionals in 11 southern states. FACPSU claims thousands of members, including scientists, engineers, and other types of experts, 90 percent of whom have graduate degrees.

The Federation's goals are to foster interaction between members and "promote exchange and cooperation between overseas Chinese professional organizations and expert personnel in the southern region of the United States and China[81] in science and technology, economics, and culture, becoming a bridge for S&T cooperation between China and the US." It offers an "environment and opportunities" for members to participate in Sino–US S&T exchanges. Its advisory center, established in 2004, acts as an executive mechanism to further strengthen S&T cooperation and exchange with China. FACPSU demonstrates its legitimacy as a coordinating body by citing statements of approval from official PRC organizations, such as the following:

> Many PRC government and civilian organizations have fully approved of the FACPSU and established long-term, stable relationships with it, including CAST, OCAO, SAFEA, CAS, the National Natural Science Foundation, the Western Returned Scholars Association, MOST and other provincial and municipal departments, universities and colleges.[82]

A second major group – besides CAPST – under the FACPSU umbrella is the Association of Chinese Professionals (中华专业人士协会) in Atlanta. The ACP makes explicit in its charter an inference we drew earlier in this chapter about the motivation of Chinese-Americans who join these advocacy groups, namely the opportunity to benefit personally from their "natural connections with China."[83] Another interesting sideline is a reference by its president in 2007 to building a "talent database" for the group to act "as a professional exchange platform." Are the persons in the database all aware of this? Who paid for the project and to whom are the data given?

ACP consorts with the usual PRC players. In 2005 it organized a Sino-US S&T and talented persons study group under FACPSU auspices in cooperation with CAST (China) and the China Association for the International Exchange of Personnel (SAFEA's front group). In 2006, ACP hosted an S&T delegation sent by Sichuan provincial authorities and the regional OCAO aimed at "linking up the fruits of foreign new and high technology with domestic PRC companies and research institutes." In 2007 it sponsored trips to Returning Overseas Scholars Innovation Week in Beijing and the Guangdong Convention of Overseas Scholars. Its annual gathering in 2008 was joined by the Houston C-G and officers from CAIEP.[84]

In the Midwest, Sino-US talent is represented by the Association of Chinese Scientists and Engineers (留美中国科学家工程师专业人士协会), an organization that duplicates in all particulars the patterns noted for S&T advocacy groups above. ACSE was founded in 1992 by Chinese professionals as a non-political non-profit group headquartered in Chicago.[85] It now has 12 chapters throughout the US and another 12 affiliated professional societies.[86] Some 90 percent of its 1,500 members boast graduate degrees.[87] Its charter contains the usual statements about supporting its members' career development, promoting S&T "exchange" with China, and serving as a "bridge for cooperation between the two nations."

ACSE's China credentials are impeccable. Its honorary members include the vice-director of the National Political Consultative Conference, heads of the CAS and CAE, current State Council members, and a former MOST director. The Chicago consul and MOST officials often address its meetings. PRC president Jiang Zemin personally received ACSE international exchange and cooperation delegations to China in 1996 and 1998. Its members frequent the yearly Guangzhou exchange convention and Dalian's annual Innovation Week.[88]

A passage in the Chinese language section of its website describes the group's "China–US exchanges and activities in service to China" (为国服务):

> The association has established relations with the relevant PRC ministries and committees, CAS, CAE, and provincial and municipal entities in all places. It organizes biannual exchange visits to China, entertains Chinese S&T delegations to the United States, and facilitates visits of American companies, organizations and personnel to China.

ACSE has supported transfer initiatives in Suzhou Industrial Park, Xi'an Software Industrial Park, and the Changsha National Development Zone. Beyond the exchange activities organized by its central committee, "more than one hundred separate exchanges" have been carried out by individual subcommittees for technical disciplines.[89] ACSE's guiding assumption is that Chinese scientists everywhere "aim to cooperate with China, plan its development, and pay back their ancestral country. Promoting the common aspirations of the Chinese people has become the spirit of the ACSE."[90]

Chinese tech transfer groups in California

The largest concentration of China S&T advocacy groups in the United States is in California – particularly Silicon Valley – where high-tech enterprise has attracted some of the world's best minds. "The Valley" is ground for the most intense foreign tech-scavenging operations in the country – legal, illegal, and quasi-legal practices that fall just below the thresholds set by US law. While many countries exploit this resource, none matches China's efforts.

We focus in this section on ten such Sino–US organizations, beginning with the Silicon Valley Chinese Engineers Association (硅谷中国工程师协会), which with 6,000 members claims to be "the largest, the most prestigious and influential Chinese professional organization" in the US.[91] According to a listing in a Silicon Valley trade directory, the SCEA:

> is a non-profit professional organization formed mainly by the professionals in the Bay Area from mainland China with a mission to promote professionalism and entrepreneurship among members and to protect the members' professional and business interests. This is done through organizing a variety of professional activities and *establishing channels to allow members to engage in China's rapid economic development* [emphasis added].[92]

Examples of SCEA's other activities are provided by Bernard Wong in his book *The Chinese in Silicon Valley*:

> This organization has professional meetings, dance parties, sport events, annual meetings, and events to celebrate Thanksgiving and [PRC] National Day. When China was admitted to the WTO, the SCEA held an event to which officials of the Chinese Consulate were invited. It is concerned with promoting the professional interests of its members. In this role, the SCEA once filed a protest against NBC for misrepresenting the Olympics position of China, and it was a strong supporter of [accused nuclear spy] Wen Ho Lee.[93]

Descriptions of the group in Chinese media point directly to its role in technology transfer. A PRC listing of worldwide overseas Chinese organizations states: "Its goals are to increase and develop the exchange of information with China's engineers and other high level technical and university personnel through multiple channels and various activities and promote China's S&T development."[94] The Shanghai Qiaowu Bao explains that SCEA "endeavors wholeheartedly to establish channels of cooperation and exchange between high-tech regions of China and Silicon Valley" and organizes regular delegations to China and round-table conferences.[95] Events listed on the SCEA website support this characterization. They include hosting a "Xi'an Investment and Outsourcing Forum" with the Global Sourcing Alliance[96] and a PRC delegation to attract foreign talent and "convince Chinese entrepreneurs to set up Chongqing offices" both in 2008.[97]

SCEA's guiding light has been former board director and president June Chu, software engineer and founder in 2003 of Allrizon Communications, a Shanghai-based company. Chu studied at the University of Oklahoma and University of Michigan, was formerly employed by 3Com, and holds several PRC national S&T awards. In 2004 she became director of the west coast office of the Shanghai Association for the International Exchange of Personnel, a branch of the SAFEA front organization CAIEP (see above), with which SCEA has a "collaborative contract."[98]

Another high-profile California group is the Hua Yuan Science and Technology Association (华源科学技术协会) founded in 1999 by a group of Chinese graduate students, who "later rose to prominence as founders and leaders of billion dollar public companies."[99] HYSTA's members include co-founder of Yahoo Jerry Yang, Cisco's corporate VP Jack Xu, and Baidu's CEO Robin Li. China Netcom CEO Edward Tian and Lenovo president Yang Yuanqing are on its board.

In a classic case of self-fulfilling prophecy, HYSTA gives the following rationale for its technology link-ups with China: "If the last century was a time when China struggled to find its identity and its place in the world, the new millennium is an era when China returns to center stage."[100] The group has multiple links to China through which IT skills and entrepreneurship are channeled, including chapters in Beijing and Shanghai. As its website points out, "Hua Yuan, the first two words of HYSTA, means 'Chinese origin' and represents HYSTA's deep roots in China and with the Chinese government."[101]

Indeed, the organization has evolved well beyond a simple networking and technology exchange venue to a champion of political causes affecting China's economic growth and the ability of its overseas technocracy to profit thereby. Drawing an analogy with the Beijing Olympics, HYSTA pledges to "continue to go for the gold jumping through every hurdle placed before us," including overcoming "negative international media attention" toward China and "regulatory bodies such as the FDA [that] now scrutinize and criticize almost all of China's industries."[102]

HYSTA is linked with 20 alliance organizations and to other PRC advocacy groups through cross-memberships of its cadre. An example is the Asia–Silicon Valley Connection, whose director Vinnie Zhang sits on HYSTA's board and founded its Venture Capital Group – a "platform for members to exchange information, share knowledge and leverage resources."[103]

Zhang, a Shanghai native, holds a business degree from Berkeley. Her career has been spent making and brokering strategic investments in Asia in various technology fields.[104] The Asia–Silicon Valley Connection, Zhang's current venture, was created as "a forum for understanding and networking between Silicon Valley and Asia" and a vehicle for promoting the "natural links" between the two. Although California's expatriate experts "still have strong ties to Asia," they lack knowledge of business opportunities and suffer a dearth of "infrastructure" to bridge the gap. ASVC provides that infrastructure. The group claims it "is not race-based" even though seven of its eight board members have Chinese surnames.[105]

One organization that is intentionally race-based is the Chinese American Science and Technology Advancement Foundation (美華科技基金). CAS-TAF takes a different approach to bilateral S&T cooperation by focusing on the education of Chinese-Americans in the US and Chinese nationals in China or the US. Specifically, it assists "Chinese-American technical professionals" via seminars, continuing education, scholarships, and language training; "Chinese scholars enrolled in masters or doctoral programs in the United States"; and Chinese professors in China through intensive short-term training programs in the US. CAS-TAF acknowledges "collaborating with donors in the selection of educational assistance recipients."[106]

Beyond this, CAS-TAF supports Sino–US technology exchange by brokering cooperative ties between American and Chinese universities, "organizing visits between Chinese and American technology and industry leaders to facilitate business and technology ventures," and consulting with "Chinese agencies in developing technology and economic development zones," including projects in Jinan, Wuhan, and Chengdu.[107] The organization was on the short-list of invitees to a reception for China advocacy groups hosted by the PRC's Los Angeles consulate in 2007.[108]

The Silicon Valley Science and Technology Association (美国硅谷科技协会) is another PRC-oriented group that has gained prominence in the Valley. Founded in 1998 by Chinese specialists in IT and biomedical disciplines, it gives as its mission to:

> Promote China's economic reform and opening, promote prosperity for both China and the US through building channels for technological, commercial, and cultural exchange between the two countries.[109]

Related goals are: forging cooperative links between members and "business communities in China" and promoting "investment and technology exchange between the US and China,"[110] which includes providing information to PRC state-run transfer organizations.

For example, in 2003 SVSTA entertained a delegation from the Guangdong Overseas Chinese Affairs Office at its headquarters in Fremont. Some 20 reps from other California Chinese S&T professional organizations also attended. The OCAO leader thanked participants for their important contributions to the "scientific progress of humanity" and assured them of "long-term service" (长期服务) from the OCAO. SVSTA and the other groups then reported to the OCAO the "status" of their organizations and results of their exchange missions to China.[111]

In May 2005 it was SVSTA's turn to call on the Office. Director Fan Qun told his PRC hosts that although its members have lived in the US for a long time, they "are paying very close attention to China's development. . . . Every year SVSTA forms groups to bring painstakingly selected high-tech projects back [*sic*] to China for exchange and discussion." The Guangdong OCAO vice-director who met Fan said his organization would do "everything in its power" to support these overseas experts, emphasizing the "great importance of strengthening bilateral cooperation and exchange" given the fact that "many OCS and ethnic Chinese professionals in the US have their hands on (掌握) advanced science and technology."[112]

In October 2008 Fan led his tenth (!) SVSTA delegation to Shenzhen. According to a report by the Guangdong OCAO, these trips over the years have been responsible for introducing more than 100 high-tech projects to China, while affording SVSTA members a chance to "repay and return kindness to their ancestral country and hometowns." Fan wants Shenzhen to be another Silicon Valley and is helping to bring this about by making available to the PRC a database of "all Silicon Valley inventions, patents, and projects." He also wants China to put "technology transfer mechanisms" (技转换机制) in Europe.[113]

Of the many China S&T advocacy groups in California, the Silicon Valley Chinese Overseas Business Association (硅谷留美博士企业家协会) has some of the best links to the Chinese government (or is less reticent about claiming them). Established in 1999 as a result of trips made to China under the Spring Light program, SCOBA serves as "a bridge for exchange" between Silicon Valley and the PRC. Although its members are technical experts, many own high-tech businesses, hence its name. SCOBA describes its ties to China as follows:

> Some members serve as advisors to MOST, MII, MOFTEC, and provincial and municipal governments such as Beijing, Shanghai, Hunan, Liaoning, Dalian, etc. They assist and participate in planning and policymaking for the development of China's high-tech industry. Many members hold concurrent posts as professors and researchers in China's domestic universities and research institutes.[114]

These links are also apparent in the CVs of top members. Chairwoman Huang Jing (黄劲), a Berkeley engineering PhD and owner of San Jose's Anbow Corp., received China MOE funds for three consecutive years to return to China for cooperation. She has led "cooperation groups" to China, met leaders of the central government, and was awarded a professorship at the University of Electronic Science and Technology of China.[115]

Daniel Zhu is a Virginia Tech graduate, CEO of the Silicon Valley firm Zaptron, and serves on several official US boards and professional committees. At the same time, Zhu is a member of MOST's Foreign Experts Advisory Group, a senior researcher at Beijing University, a member of the Ministry of Information Industry's Expert Advisory Group, a technical advisor to Hunan's Office of Information Industry, editor of a PRC magazine (*Kexue Touzi* or Science Investment), and a "technical advisor to several high-tech PRC firms."[116]

Jack Peng, another top SCOBA officer, is a senior engineer at AMD in microprocessor design. He has headed delegations of technical experts to China, alone and in concert with the OCAO, and has held several prominent posts in US-based overseas Chinese organizations. In 1996 he accepted a MII invitation to lead a "lecture group" of experts in microelectronics to 24 places in China.[117] Peng described the importance of overseas Chinese scholars to China's development in an interview he gave to Japanese academic Endo Homare:

> I think if we quit America and went entirely back to China, China's development would halt. Even if it didn't halt, it would certainly have limitations. For us, America is the base that will allow China to develop. If we stay here, or at least some of us do, we can always be chasing after the latest high tech that advances day by day at a dazzling pace.[118]

Peng went on to claim:

> China regards those of us living overseas as essential. It extends a hand to us, encouraging us to make the results of our research blossom on Chinese soil. It also asks us for know-how to develop its market. Most of us serve as advisors to the Chinese government through the SCOBA organization.[119]

Finally:

> It's more advantageous to China for us to make our contributions living here. . . . Everyone has entered into a system of full-scale cooperation.[120]

Member Sam Liu, CEO of Silicon Valley's Newnex Technology and former director of the Chinese American Semiconductor Professional Association (see below), got his start as a dual major in nuclear physics and computer science at Colorado State University. He then did post-doc work for the US Department of Energy. Liu is frequently invited to lecture in China and has multiple connections with MOST, MOFTEC, and other state-level PRC organizations.[121] Liu told Endo:

> We are not only heartened that our country [i.e., China] is venturing forth as a matter of policy to bring its overseas intellectuals inside the China market, but we feel a sense of fulfillment brimming with pride. The strength of Chinese PhD entrepreneurs in America lies here. Those born in China and most familiar with that culture will bring the world's most advanced technology to China.[122]

SCOBA's aims are straightforward:

- To link up with Silicon Valley and overseas Chinese scholars.
- To exchange information on technology, products, markets, and personnel with domestic Chinese firms in the same line of business.
- To conduct all types of training and seminars for the Chinese government and domestic companies.
- To engage in cooperative research and development and joint training of personnel with Chinese universities and research institutes.
- To perform consulting services for high-tech Chinese domestic industries.
- To assist Chinese companies in developing international markets.

- To introduce overseas experts, knowledge, and venture capital to China.
- To develop high-tech products.
- To return to China to found and develop overseas scholar businesses and entrepreneurial parks.[123]

Four more organizations round out our survey of China's California advocacy groups. The Chinese American Professors and Professionals Network (美国华裔 教授专家网)[124] or "Scholars Net" was established in 1991 for "high-level" specialists, some 7,000 of whom are distributed "throughout China and the world but primarily the US." Its leading members are in California. The group organizes and participates in Sino–US tech exchange activities, sponsors technology transfer missions, sends delegations of experts to lecture in China, and mobilizes large numbers of Chinese in the US to attend the Guangzhou transfer convention. Scholars Update (即时通讯) is its online journal.[125]

Scholars Net provides a platform for "rapid exchange" of information among overseas Chinese scholars and a "bridge" between scholars inside and outside of China. Its members greet PRC scientists coming to the US, put them in touch with US experts, and arrange visits to appropriate US universities and R&D facilities. It provides information on lecture visits to China so that more OCS can "participate in cooperative planning." It also brokers meetings in China for members to "exhibit the latest technology and help start all types of scientific research programs."[126]

"Net" members are linked to high-level PRC universities and labs. The group claims "close relationships with PRC government departments and R&D institutes and *is often called on to convey information on important activities*" (emphasis added).[127] As part of its communicative function, its website posts announcements from outreach groups such as the Shanghai OCAO and the LA consulate. Photos of members with their PRC counterparts are posted to the site under the caption "What did they contribute?"[128]

The Chinese Scholars Association, Southern California (美国南加州华裔教 授学者协会) is another such scholarly group dedicated to the "development of science, technology and higher education and enhancement of Sino–American friendship and mutual understanding," terms the reader will recognize by now as euphemisms for technology transfer. Members attend the same Guangzhou tech transfer convention, the same dinners hosted by the LA Consul General and its S&T staff, and receive the same delegations from outreach groups like CAST. CSA missions to China have "carried out broad and deep exchanges" with PRC scholars and the OCAO, achieving "huge results." One such trip resulted in 19 project agreements with funding from MOST.[129]

The North American Chinese Semiconductor Association (北美中国半导体 协会) with some 4,000 members joins many of its sister organizations in claiming to be "one of the largest and most active Chinese professional organizations in the US." It shares the usual S&T advocacy group goals of networking, support for its members' careers, and "global" technology exchange (the Chinese version of its website has 中美交流 or "Sino–American exchange" instead).[130] Examples of its interactions include: hosting a 2008 China–US IT Forum with officials from Wuhan, sponsoring a delegation from Nanjing whose purpose "is to recruit and/ or interact with high-level overseas Chinese scholars and professionals," sending members on a familiarization visit to Zhongguancun science park, exchanging ideas with officials from Wuxi about "further technical cooperation," sharing "knowledge and experience" with officials from Suzhou, and a follow-up trip to Nanjing to discuss projects with "high ranking government officials."[131]

Finally, the Silicon Valley Chinese American Computer Association (美華電腦協會), as is evident in the traditional character forms used in its title, began as a Taiwanese group that broadened its allegiance as trade and business opportunities moved across the Straits. The group describes itself as "the oldest high-tech organization of its kind in Silicon Valley . . . comprised of hundreds of computer enterprises with thousands of employees and aggregate revenues in the billions of dollars."[132] Its history demonstrates the predicament in which tech transfer places the host country:

> In 1980, when the computer revolution was erupting in Silicon Valley, groups of Chinese science students brought computer technology back [*sic*] to Taiwan and began producing hardware to export back to the United States. Other groups of students many of whom are now members of the SVCACA seized the opportunity to import these products, assemble them into PC systems, and distribute them all throughout the United States.[133]

Technology created in the United States and used to produce computers in the US was "brought back" to Taiwan to make components repackaged for sale by Chinese students in the US.

> Today, much of Taiwan's computer manufacturing operations have been moved to Mainland China. Our Association's relations have shifted alongside this trend. Our Association was the first high-tech organization to visit China. Since that initial visit, we have sent delegations to China virtually every year, several times per year. Due to our constant level of activity, we have established strong relations with associations, science parks, civil servants, and politicians in China. We have also helped to coordinate many investment forums in the United States, featuring Chinese delegations.[134]

With offices in Beijing, Shenzhen, Hong Kong, and Taipei, SVCACA is on track to continue its mission of connecting Greater China with Silicon Valley.

Specialty groups and Taiwan-oriented S&T organizations

Space limitations preclude detailed treatment of many dozens of other China and Taiwan S&T advocacy groups, including those focused on particular technical disciplines and professions. We describe a sampling of them in the remainder of this chapter.

The Chinese American Semiconductor Professional Association (華美半導體協會) was founded in 1991 to become "the largest Chinese American semiconductor professional organization worldwide" (NACSA's claim notwithstanding).[135] Headquartered in Silicon Valley, CASPA has chapters in Austin, Dallas, Phoenix, and Portland and another five offices in Hsin Chu (Taiwan), Hong Kong, Shanghai, Beijing, and Singapore. Its 3,000 members host delegations from China and Taiwan and go there in return to participate in overseas exchange symposia and enjoy "face-to-face round-table meetings" with executives from China's high-tech parks.[136]

The Chinese Information and Networking Association (中华咨询网路协会) in Silicon Valley and its "sister organization" in New England "serve as a unique bridge for American and Far East technology companies to proactively exchange information, develop mutual understanding, and create business opportunities" in the field of computer networks.[137] The organization "plays a major role in introducing resources and opportunities from Asia to members who are interested in going back to Asia and China for their business and career opportunities." It, too, organizes delegations to China and hosts visiting expert groups from China, Hong Kong, and Taiwan.[138]

Looking at other technical professions, the National Society of Medical Scientists – Chinese American Association (美国华裔医学科学家协会) has as its goals a typical mix of advancing its members' livelihoods and supporting the PRC's technological development. The "activities" part of its website is littered with announcements about exchange programs, China investment and cooperation opportunities, programs for introducing technology and knowledge (引技引智), link-ups with PRC technology development projects and transfer organizations, visits to China and hosting PRC delegations to the US, as well as support for official PRC programs.[139]

The Sino-American Pharmaceutical Professionals Association (美中医药开发协会) was formed in 1991 to foster members' career development and "promote scientific exchange and business cooperation between the US and China." Its 4,000 members belong to chapters in New England, Philadelphia, the SF Bay area, and Shanghai. SAPA makes available "in service to science" a variety of venues to facilitate communication between American and Chinese scientists, policymakers and government officials, while serving as a bridge (that word again) for cooperation.[140]

New York State is host to the Overseas Chinese Physics Association (华人物理学会), a group of some 400 scientists founded in 1990. Although its charter does not mention China specifically, the connection is implied in its first objective "to promote international understanding and mutual awareness of scientific achievements by physicists all over the world"; by its support for "Physics without Borders"; by its co-hosting of events with PRC state entities, such as a 2009 conference with the CAS Institute of Modern Physics in Lanzhou; and by the composition of its membership, which includes scientists at China's Institute of High Energy

Physics, Institute of Condensed Matter Physics, Qinghua and Fudan Universities –along with nuclear facilities at Argonne, Brookhaven, Oak Ridge, Lawrence Livermore, and Los Alamos National Labs.[141]

The Chinese Institute of Engineers, USA (美洲中国工程师学会) grew from a Taiwan-oriented organization with roots that go back to 1917 to a Greater China-affiliated body "with a mission to serve members from all over the United States." Its roster of 5,000 is divided among five regional chapters and one disciplinary chapter,[142] and includes engineers with both PRC and Taiwan backgrounds. The political balance is maintained by hosting major technology exchange events in China (the Sino–American Technology and Engineering Conference) and Taiwan (the Modern Engineering and Technology Seminar) in alternate years.[143]

SATEC meetings, which occur during odd calendar years, are typically sponsored on the China side by the State Economic and Trade Commission, the State Administration of Foreign Experts Affairs, and the China Association for International Exchange of Personnel. At the 2001 event, some 238 topics were proposed by its PRC sponsors, which CIE's leadership *used as a basis for choosing American specialists* to address the conference. The lectures were supplemented by "on-the-spot exchanges" with engineers at Chinese companies.[144] One member of the CIE group reportedly recommended that China buy out insolvent US technology start-ups to "cash in on their research capabilities and talents as a short-cut to meeting global competition."[145]

Finally, there is the Taiwan-oriented Monte Jade Global Science and Technology Association (全球玉山科技協會), which blossomed from a Silicon Valley office in 1989 into a worldwide alliance of 14 chapters, including 11 in the United States. Its "objective is to promote the cooperation and mutual flow of technology and investment" through technical seminars, "high-tech study tours" in Asia, and workshops on overseas investment.[146]

The authors regret that the contributions of other US-based China advocacy groups to China's S&T development cannot be acknowledged here due to lack of space. We also wish to state our belief that these groups do not set out deliberately to subvert the United States. Our claim is that helping China become a competitive power through "transferred" technology entails for these advocacy groups no contradiction, and the implications of their behavior for the larger body of Americans are to them irrelevant. In addition, while declarations of support for China are common, it is hard to find sentiment, not to mention concrete action taken, in favor of their American host.

In the following chapters we examine in detail the circumstances of China's overseas scholars who form the backbone of these groups and the role they play in China's S&T development.

Notes

1   www.gxistc.net/home/kjdt/gjkj/4007.asp.
2   Called the "China International ICT (Information, Communication and Telecom) Innovation Cluster" (国家信息通讯国际创新园) or CIIIC.

3 公使衔科技参赞, literally "S&T counselor at ministerial rank."
4 Yao Shibing (姚诗斌, AKA Bing Yao) founded Jinfonet Software in 1998 and by 2001 had a branch operating in China. An expert in database design, Dr. Yao is former chair of the University of Maryland's computer science department. He is active professionally and socially in the US Chinese community, participating in CAST meetings and serving on the US-based China Foundation.
5 UCTID announced it was sending a delegation to China to gather information and facilitate CIIIC's cooperation with major US telecom firms and "expert personnel in ethnic Chinese companies" in the United States.
6 The project, a joint effort between MOST, the Zhongguancun administrative committee, and the University of Maryland, is designed to further S&T cooperation and promote "transnational resources allocation" (www.cns.hk).
7 The meeting was put together by CAST-USA President Lin Minyue (林民跃), a graduate of Fudan University's physics department employed by the US National Institute of Standards and Technology.
8 Liu Yun (刘云) and Shen Lin (沈林), "海外人才资源开发利用的现状及发展对策" ("The Current Situation and Countermoves on Development and Utilization of Overseas Chinese Experts Intellectual Resources") in 科研管理 (*Science Research Management*) vol. 22.4 (July 2001), pp. 115–125.
9 Ibid.
10 Ibid.
11 Ibid.
12 www.nyconsulate.prchina.org/ch.
13 Ibid. SAFEA recently established a New York office to expedite technology "exchange." In addition to its work with the consulate, the office also supports recruitment efforts by the PRC's UN S&T delegation.
14 www.chinaconsulatechicago.org. According to the consulate's website, the Detroit ACSE "for many years has maintained close relations with the China Association of Automobile Manufacturers and other organizations and actively promoted cooperation and the exchange of information and technology between the Chinese and US auto industries."
15 losangeles.china-consulate.org.
16 Ibid.
17 CAST-USA newsletter, 2008.5.
18 www.chinaconsulatesf.org.
19 www.chinaconsulatesf.org.
20 www.triwayinc.com. Note: the term "S&T" is missing from the site's English language version.
21 Ibid.
22 www.saiep.org. In 2002, SCEA signed a "collaboration contract and formalized a partnership" with the SAIEP office in Silicon Valley "based on mutual benefit" (www.scea.org).
23 www.saiep.org.
24 www.hysta.org.
25 CAS's "100 Persons Program" (百人计划) became a "1,000 Talents Program" (千人计划) and now SAIEP is sponsoring a "10,000 Overseas Scholars Convergence Program." The lack of a single-character morpheme in Chinese meaning "100,000" (百 >千>万 but >十万) may pose a natural constraint to this process, as the magical four-character expression turns into five characters (十万人计划), which is less auspicious. You could omit "person" (人) and go with "100,000 Program" (十万计划), however, which keeps the important canonical format intact.
26 www.saiep.org.
27 www.cast-usa.net.
28 Ibid.
29 Ibid.

30 According to the October 2005 edition of the CAST-USA journal 海外学人 (Over-seas Scholars).
31 www.cast-la.org.
32 www.ise.ncsu.edu/chao/more_info.html.
33 www.castnc.org.
34 castusa-gny.org.
35 www.castct.org.
36 Ibid.
37 Ibid.
38 www.cast-la.org.
39 www.castdc.org.
40 www.sjtu.org/sjtuaa/index.php.
41 www.nuaa-us.org.
42 Ibid.
43 Ibid.
44 www.tsinghua-nc.org.
45 The spelling "Chiao-Tung" is in the original Wade–Giles system, which identifies it as Taiwan-based.
46 Also called the North American International Exchange Center (北美国际交流中心).
47 www.naiec.org, February 2005.
48 www.zzi.net/china/2002NACBECc.shtml.
49 "The first North American New and High Technology Projects and Talented Persons Exchange Conference" (首届北美高新技术项目和人才交流大会) was in fact NAIEC's second such annual meeting.
50 www.scoba.org.
51 www.zzi.net/china/2002NACBECc.shtml.
52 Ibid.
53 www.scoba.org.
54 NAIEC and China's OCAO sponsored these annual events at least through 2007, as a result of which a "large quantity of projects and skilled personnel" were made available to China (news.sina.com.cn/o/2007-01-06/112810937711s.shtml).
55 www.capst.org/events/03172003.htm.
56 www.cast-sd.org/china/InvitationToChina.doc.
57 www.ucapo.org.
58 Ibid. Neither NAIEC nor UCTID, both prominent DC-area S&T transfer organizations, are under UCAPO's umbrella.
59 www.overseas.sh.cn.
60 www.ucapo.org.
61 增进华人与其他族裔的相互理解和相互合作. The English part of UCAPO's website mistranslates the term 其他族裔 as "other minority groups."
62 www.overseas.sh.cn. "Integrate technology resources" means arrange PRC access to US technology. "Market resources" is a euphemism for "venue to commercialize US technology." Stripped of its rhetoric, the phrase simply means "technology developed by experts in the United States is transferred to China for practical application."
63 www.ucapo.org.
64 www.uctid.org/index.asp. Doan claims "intensive management and policy making experiences for many Chinese national R&D projects ." His degrees in thermodynamics and computational fluid dynamics suggest a career spent modeling high-energy physical events, although his China resumé lacks specifics. Doan's direct involvement with the US began in 1978, when he became an international fellow at the Stanford Research Institute.
65 Ibid.
66 Ibid.
67 Ibid.

68 casbi.org.

69 Ibid.

70 Ibid. The politburo members were Zhang Gaoli (张高丽) and Li Yuanchao (李源潮). CASB claims to have gotten two hours of Li's time during the visit.

71 www.overseas.sh.cn. Liu's China credentials can be gauged by his status as the only non-PRC resident appointed to the standing committee of the All-China Youth Federation.

72 www.chinatalents.gov.cn. January 2009.

73 www.cysn.net/zuzhi/000404001.htm.

74 Ibid.

75 During visits to the US by Chinese dignitaries, "NACAST has organized thousands of local Chinese to carry out resolute struggles against international persons involved in Taiwan independence, Tibetan independence and the 'democracy movement', thus creating a good impression on world opinion" (www.overseas.sh.cn).

76 www.capst.org.

77 Ibid.

78 www.chinatalents.gov.cn.

79 A Beijing-based organization formed in 1988 with chapters worldwide. It is run by the CCP Central Committee's United Front Work Department (中共中央统战部).

80 www.chinahouston.org.

81 FACPSU, registered in the state of Georgia, uses the term 国内 (*guonei*, "inside the country") to mean "China." There is a lot going on here psycholinguistically. The assumption is that anyone reading the material understands China to be the country (*guo*) referred to. America, the place where the members reside, is outside "the country."

82 www.facpsu.org.

83 www.acp-atlanta.org.

84 Ibid.

85 www.acse.org/index.

86 Besides Chicago, ACSE has chapters in Atlanta, Boston, Cincinnati, Connecticut, Denver, Indianapolis, Los Angeles, Milwaukee, New Jersey, New York, Phoenix, and Washington, DC. It has professional societies for biotechnology, business administration, chemistry and chemical engineering, computing, finance, industrial and applied mathematics, intelligent transportation systems, law, mechanical engineering, medicine, pharmaceuticals, and telecommunications.

87 www.chinaconsulatechicago.org.

88 www.acse.org/index.

89 Ibid.

90 Ibid.

91 www.scea.org.

92 Northern California Global Trade Assistance Directory, 2000–2001. About 10 percent of SCEA's members are from Taiwan.

93 Bernard P. Wong, *The Chinese in Silicon Valley: Globalization, Social Networks, and Ethnic Identity*, Lanham, MD: Rowman and Littlefield Publishers, 2005, p. 61.

94 www.hxuc.com/qiaotuan/beimeizhou/meiguo/87.htm.

95 http://qwb.sh.gov.cn/shqb/node113/sqxx/node149/userobject1ai7579.html.

96 GSA is a Silicon Valley-based organization founded in 2007 dedicated to helping companies get started with "the global sourcing of IT solutions" (globalsourcinginfo. org).

97 www.scea.org.

98 SCEA news release, May 10, 2004.

99 www.hysta.org.

100 Ibid.

101 Ibid.

102 Ibid.

103 Ibid.
104 www.asvc.org.
105 Ibid. As of June 2009.
106 castaf.org.
107 Ibid.
108 http://big5.fmprc.gov.cn/gate/big5/losangeles.china-consulate.org.
109 www.svsta.org/index.htmls.
110 Ibid.
111 Ibid.
112 gocn.southcn.com/qwxw/200505310028.htm.
113 gocn.southcn.com/qw2index/2006dfqw/2006dfqwsz/200810170067.htm. The article noted that Fan's personal "home in Silicon Valley, USA has become a guest house for entertaining his friends from China. Shenzhen officials visiting the US and technical personnel all gather at his house." The SVSTA website has a photo of a California-style residence with 18 people outside holding a banner which reads, "Strengthen cooperation. Promote Exchange."
114 www.scoba.org.
115 Ibid.
116 Ibid. In 2000 Zhu headed a "high-tech industrial advisory group" of US and Japan-based Chinese experts to China, where the group gave "advisory reports" (咨询报告) and performed technology exchanges at S&T enclaves in Beijing, Tianjin, Xi'an, Suzhou, and Shanghai. Endo Homare credits Zhu with a proposal to the PRC government to set up a "parallel" Silicon Valley in China. His International Society of Information Fusion "has an advisory role for Chinese state policy through overseas specialists in telecommunications." Endo Homare. 中国がシリコンバレーとつながるとき (*When China Links Up with Silicon Valley*). Tokyo: Nikkei BP, 2001, p. 174.
117 www.scoba.org.
118 Endo, *When China Links Up with Silicon Valley*, p. 163.
119 Ibid.
120 Ibid.
121 Ibid., pp. 178–180.
122 Ibid., p. 181. On pp. 198–203, Endo prints schematics showing contacts between SCOBA's members and PRC officials as a means of demonstrating "to what extent these Silicon Valley leaders are linked directly to the Chinese central government and are carrying out a world strategy for China's development."
123 Ibid.
124 Variant names are 美国华裔教授及专家网 and 美国华裔教授与专家人员网.
125 www.scholarsupdate.com.
126 Ibid.
127 Ibid.
128 Ibid. The Chinese phrase is 他们奉献了什么.
129 seis.natsci.csulb.edu/kchan/csa.htm.
130 www.nacsa.com.
131 Ibid.
132 www.svcaca.com.
133 Ibid.
134 Ibid.
135 www.caspa.com. CASPA's claim was recently tempered to read "the most influential."
136 Ibid.
137 www.cina.org.
138 Ibid.
139 www.nsms-caa.org.
140 www.sapaweb.org.
141 www.ocpaweb.org.

142 The Overseas Chinese Environmental Engineers and Scientists Association (海外华人环境保护学会).

143 www.cie-usa.org.

144 www.ctiin.com.cn/gjhz/mzzg.htm, visited October 2001.

145 *China Daily*, October 25, 2001. State Economic and Trade Commission Minister Li Rongrong credited CIE/USA as "instrumental" in helping China solve key technological problems, calling it a "critical venue for absorbing the intellectual resources of overseas Chinese" and an "important forum for supporting the fatherland's economic and technological development."

146 www.montejade.org.

6

CHINA'S FOREIGN STUDENTS IN THE UNITED STATES

Conventional wisdom often cites the large inflows of Chinese graduate students into American hard science university programs and the potential use of those graduate students as conduits for economic and technology espionage. This chapter explores the origins and dynamics of the Chinese postgraduate diaspora in the United States, estimates the scale of the phenomenon, and assesses its potential counter-intelligence implications.

The Chinese student diaspora in the United States

Origins

For well over a century, China has viewed sending students overseas as an indispensable element in its quest for national development and scientific and technological modernization. Reflecting the priority that was attached to these efforts by successive leaders from the Qing Dynasty to the Kuomintang, an estimated 30,000 Chinese students were sent to the United States between 1860 and 1950, while a far greater number studied in Japan.[1] The students focused mainly on engineering and the sciences. Of those studying in the US from 1905 to 1953, for example, more than 40 percent studied engineering and the sciences.[2]

Following the establishment of the PRC in 1949, China continued to send large numbers of students abroad, though the countries to which they were dispatched changed in accordance with China's ideology and Cold War foreign policy orientation. From 1949 to 1966, the Chinese Communist leadership sent 10,600 students to study abroad in more than two dozen countries. The majority of those students were sent to the Soviet Union and Eastern Europe, where most majored in scientific and technical disciplines. About 70 percent of the Chinese who studied in the Soviet Union from 1953 to 1957, for example, studied science and engineering.[3]

At the same time that Beijing was sending students abroad for advanced training, it was also beginning to reap the benefits of the study abroad policies implemented by earlier governments. In the 1950s, several Chinese scientists who had studied in the United States and England returned to China to conduct research in nuclear physics and high-energy physics. Many of these early returned students played key roles in China's atomic bomb and hydrogen bomb development programs.[4] Despite these important successes, however, the Mao-era study abroad program effectively collapsed in the 1960s as the Sino–Soviet split disrupted the educational exchange relationship between China and the Soviet Union and the Cultural Revolution shattered the Chinese educational system.[5]

In all, from 1872 to 1978, China dispatched approximately 130,000 Chinese to study overseas.[6] As China began reforming its economy and opening up to the outside world after 1978, this number – which was accumulated over a period of more than a century, from the final decades of the Qing Dynasty to the end of the era of Mao Zedong – would appear small indeed as the scale and scope of China's study abroad program rapidly expanded.

Returned students in the post-Mao era

According to a Ministry of Education retrospective on China's study abroad policies, related work in the reform and opening era began in 1978, when, after listening to a work report from Qinghua University, Deng Xiaoping said he favored increasing the number of students going abroad for further education.[7] Deng described sending more Chinese to study abroad as one of the most important ways to promote China's development and predicted that the effort would begin to bear fruit within as little as five years. "We should send tens of thousands of students abroad, not just a handful," Deng said enthusiastically. "We should do everything possible to quicken the pace." Deng's comments set the tone for the Chinese government's efforts to rapidly expand the number of Chinese students going abroad for graduate education in the West. Sending students to study in the most advanced countries – particularly the United States – was seen as an essential component of China's plan to build a capable scientific and technological workforce. According to the Ministry of Education retrospective,

> At the same time that Comrade Xiaoping repeatedly stressed the importance of opening to the outside world, he also emphasized that sending students abroad was a powerful means of implementing the opening policy . . . it was only by sending students to study abroad that China could truly study the advanced science and technology of foreign countries.[8]

With the exception of a brief period during the early 1990s, when the number of students receiving approval to go abroad was reduced in the wake of the Tiananmen crackdown, Deng's successors have continued along the same path, adopting policies aimed at "supporting study abroad" (支持留学) and "encouraging students to return to China" (鼓励回国) as part of their effort to increase the pool of highly trained personnel available for China's ongoing economic development and modernization drive. As a result, "sending students to study abroad has become one of China's main channels for cultivating skilled personnel."[9]

Current statistics and trends

According to reports from the official Chinese media, more than 2.24 million Chinese have studied overseas for advanced degrees since the beginning of the economic reform and opening policies between 1978 and 2011, and 818,400, or more than one-third, have returned to China after completing their studies.[10] Among those who had returned, more than half, or 429,300, had done so in just three years from 2009 to 2011.[11] The *China Statistical Yearbook*, which is published by the State Statistics Bureau, provides annual data on the number of students going abroad and the number returning to China for most years since 1978.[12] It confirms that both the number of students studying abroad and the number of returned students have increased markedly in recent years (see Table 6.1). In 2011, nearly 339,700 Chinese students went abroad, more than 10 times the number that left the country to study abroad in 2000 with more than half of them in the United States.

Destinations of overseas Chinese students

Chinese students have studied in more than 100 countries over the past 20 years. The most popular destination has been the United States, which has played a central role in China's reform-era study abroad policies.[19] China sent its first group of 50 students to the United States in late 1978, marking the resumption of US–China educational exchanges. As the implementation of Deng Xiaoping's reform and opening policies progressed, the US quickly emerged as the leading destination for Chinese study abroad students, hosting approximately half of all Chinese students going overseas by the mid-1980s.[20] In the 1983 to 1984 academic year, for example, there were approximately 12,000 Chinese students and visiting scholars in the United States, representing about 2 percent of foreign students in the United States.[21] The number of Chinese students in the US increased rapidly in the 1980s and 1990s, and the Chinese quickly became the largest group of foreign students in the American higher educational system. After many years as the largest group of foreign students in the US, however, the Chinese student contingent fell to second place in 2001 to 2002, eclipsed by students from India. Experts blame the shift

TABLE 6.1 Chinese Students in the United States, 2001–2012 (thousands)[13]

	2001	2002	2003	2004	2005	2006	2007	2008	2009	2010	2011
US	63.2	64.7	61.8	62.5	62.5	67.7	81.1	98.2	127.6	157.6	194
%Δ	15.5	2.4	-4.6	1.2	0.1	8.2	19.8	21.1	29.9	23.5	23.1

on post-9/11 visa restrictions that made it easier for Chinese students to enroll in universities in the UK, Australia, and New Zealand, though experts say the problem pre-dated the terrorist attacks.[22] In 2004, the numbers of Chinese students enrolling in the United States actually declined 4.6 percent, primarily because of concerns about visas.[23] Nonetheless, Chinese students in 2010 accounted for almost 22 percent of the total number of foreign students in the United States, with 158,000 Chinese students enrolled in US universities, a 23 percent increase over 2009 in total and a 43 percent increase at the undergraduate level.[24] Within the United States, the State of California hosted the largest number of foreign students with 93,124, followed by New York with 74,934, and Texas with 58.188.[25]

BOX 6.1 ASYMMETRIC EDUCATION

By contrast, the United States sent only 13,910 students to China in 2009, up only 2 percent on 2008, most of whom studied not hard sciences but social science or language.[26] In August 2009, President Obama announced plans to "dramatically expand" to 100,000 the number of US students who study in China over the next four years, calling such exchanges "a clear commitment to build ties among our people in the steady pursuit of cooperation that will serve our nations, and the world."[27] Yet Washington is trying to fund the effort primarily with benefit concerts with Will.i.am and private sector money, estimating the cost at $68 million.[28] In the 2010/11 academic year, 14,596 US students were studying in China, which was number five on the list of study-abroad destinations, behind the United Kingdom, Italy, Spain and France.[29]

Academic level of Chinese students studying abroad

Since 1978, about 90 percent of the Chinese studying abroad have been graduate students. In more recent years, however, college-age students have reportedly become the fastest growing group of Chinese studying abroad. The Institute of International Education reported that the number of Chinese undergraduates enrolling in US universities increased 6 percent in 2006 and 20 percent in 2007.[30] Following India, China sent the most undergraduate students to the United States in 2007, with 55 percent of universities reporting an increase in Chinese enrollments, more than any other country. By 2008, 60 percent of universities reported an increase in Chinese enrollment, while only 11 percent noted a decline.[31] Undergraduate enrollment reached 26,275, though graduate student enrollment only rose 2 percent, to 57,451.[32]

One troubling trend among Chinese students is the increasing number of allegations of application fraud, including the use of agents to secure admission to US universities. A 2001 *Chronicle of Higher Education* article describes students buying essays, using stand-ins for exams, and obtaining improper access to standardized tests.[33] By the late 2000s, the problems had reportedly gotten worse. Based on interviews with 250 high school applicants in China, one consultant working for US universities estimates that 90 percent of Chinese applicants submit false recommendations, 70 percent get other people to write their personal essays, 50 percent forge their high school transcripts, 30 percent lie on financial aid forms, and 10 percent list academic awards and other achievements they did not earn or receive.[34]

Despite these gains in undergraduate enrollment, the majority of Chinese study abroad students are still pursuing Master's and Doctoral degrees. For example, according to the Institute of International Education in 2010, more than 64 percent of the Chinese students in the US were enrolled in graduate programs,[35] yet this figure was down from 80 percent in 2002.[36] In 2010, Chinese students were awarded 3,735 PhD degrees, the most of any single country of origin and almost twice as many as the next country of origin, India, with 2,140 PhDs.[37] Yet the number of Chinese graduate students in the US has slowed down, while the rate of undergraduate enrollment has accelerated, primarily as a result of universities seeking additional foreign admissions dollars. As a result, it is possible that undergraduate enrollment could surpass graduate enrollment for the first time. In 2008 to 2009, there were 291,439 international undergraduate students, 296,574 graduate students, and 59,233 non-degree students.[38]

Fields of concentration of Chinese students studying abroad

The most popular fields of study for Chinese students going overseas have been engineering and the sciences. From 1978 to 1984, the vast majority of government-sponsored students in the US studied physical sciences (31%), life sciences (8%), engineering (23%), and mathematics (7%), and a smaller number studied computer science (4%).[39] Relatively few Chinese students – whether government-sponsored or in the US with private support – were studying business, humanities, or social sciences.[40]

Chinese doctoral students in the US have continued to concentrate heavily on the sciences. In 1995, slightly more than half of all Chinese PhD students in the United States were studying natural sciences, according to the US Department of Education,[41] and from 1988 to 1996, more than 16,500 out of the approximately 17,900 Chinese who received doctorates in the US were in scientific and technical disciplines.[42] The fields of study with the largest numbers of Chinese doctoral recipients were engineering, physical sciences, biological sciences, and mathematics. Reflecting perhaps the maturation of the US–China trade relationship and the Chinese economy, the majority of Chinese students in the 2011 school year were enrolled in business management (28.7%) followed by engineering (19.6%) math/computer science (11.2%) and physical/life sciences (9.9%).[43]

Trends in sponsorship

Of the approximately 320,000 students China sent abroad between 1978 and 1998, more than 150,000 went abroad at their own expense, while roughly 90,000 relied on support from various work units and approximately 47,000 received scholarships from the government.[44] The number of students paying their own expenses to study abroad was initially small, but increased dramatically beginning in the late 1980s and early 1990s.[45] Nearly half (47%) of Chinese undergraduates, and 29 percent of all foreign undergraduates, received some discounts on their tuition based on their academic record in 2009.[46]

Chinese student associations and the Beijing government

Most major universities in the United States have a Chinese student association, many of them a branch of the China Students and Scholars Association (CSSA),[47] including top universities like MIT,[48] Harvard,[49] Stanford,[50] Cornell,[51] Duke,[52] UCLA,[53] and Penn.[54] Nationwide, we can find 196 branches of CSSA, listed in Table 6.2.

TABLE 6.2 Number of CSSA Branches, by State, 2011

State	# Branches	Universities
Alabama	3	Auburn University, Troy University, University of Alabama
Alaska	1	University of Alaska at Fairbanks
Arizona	2	Arizona State University, Northern Arizona University
Arkansas	2	Arkansas Tech University, University of Arkansas
California	18	University of California at Berkeley, Caltech, California State University, San Diego State University, San Francisco State University, San Jose State University, Stanford, University of Southern California, UCLA, University of California at Davis, University of California at Irvine, University of California at San Diego, University of California at Riverside, University of California at Santa Barbara, University of California at Santa Cruz, University of California at San Francisco
Colorado	6	Colorado School of Mines, Colorado State University, Metropolitan State College of Denver, University of Colorado at Boulder, University of Denver, University of Northern Colorado
Connecticut	3	University of Connecticut, Western Connecticut State University, Yale University
District of Columbia	4	American University, Catholic University of America, George Washington University, Georgetown University
Delaware	1	University of Delaware
Florida	10	Florida Atlantic University, Florida Institute of Technology, Florida International University, Florida State University, NOVA Southeastern University, University of Central Florida, University of Florida, University of Miami, University of South Florida

TABLE 6.2 (Continued)

State	# Branches	Universities
Georgia	3	Emory University, Georgia State University, Georgia Tech
Hawaii	1	University of Hawaii
Idaho	2	Idaho State University, University of Idaho
Illinois	10	DePaul University, Eastern Illinois University, Illinois Institute of Technology, Illinois State University, Loyola University, Northern Illinois University, Northwestern University, Southern Illinois University, University of Chicago, University of Illinois at Chicago, University of Illinois at Urbana
Indiana	6	Indiana State University, Indiana University, Indiana University – Purdue University Indianapolis, Notre Dame, Purdue University, Valparaiso University
Iowa	3	Iowa State University, University of Iowa, University of Northern Iowa
Kansas	6	Emporia State University, Fort Hays State University, Kansas State University, Pittsburg State University, University of Kansas, Wichita State University
Kentucky	3	Murray State University, University of Kentucky, University of Louisville
Louisiana	4	Louisiana State University, Louisiana Tech University, Tulane University, University of New Orleans
Maryland	2	Johns Hopkins University, University of Maryland
Massachusetts	12	Babson College, Boston College, Boston University, Brandeis University, Harvard University, MIT, Northeastern University, Suffolk University, Tufts University, University of Massachusetts Amherst, University of Massachusetts, Worcester Polytechnic University
Michigan	5	Central Michigan University, Lawrence Technological University, Michigan State University, Michigan Technological University, University of Michigan
Minnesota	2	St. Cloud University, University of Minnesota
Missouri	3	Saint Louis University, University of Missouri, Washington University in St. Louis
Montana	2	Montana State University, University of Montana Missoula
Nebraska	3	Creighton University, University of Nebraska-Lincoln, University of Nebraska-Omaha
Nevada	1	University of Nevada-Las Vegas
New Hampshire	1	University of New Hampshire
New Jersey	5	New Jersey Institute of Technology, Princeton University, Rutgers University, Seton Hall University, Stevens Institute of Technology
New Mexico	2	New Mexico Institute of Mining and Technology, University of New Mexico

New York	17	City University of New York, Columbia University Medical Center, Columbia University, Cornell University Medical College, Cornell University, Fordham University, Long Island University, New York University, Rensselaer Polytechnic Institute, Rochester Institute of Technology, SUNY Binghamton, SUNY Stony Brook, SUNY Postdam, Syracuse University, University of Albany, University of Buffalo, University of Rochester
North Carolina	4	Duke University, North Carolina State University, University of North Carolina, Wake Forest University
North Dakota	1	University of North Dakota
Ohio	9	Bowling Green University, Case Western Reserve University, Cleveland State University, Kent State University, Ohio State University, Ohio University, University of Akron, University of Cincinnati, University of Dayton
Oklahoma	1	Oklahoma State University
Oregon	3	Oregon State University, Portland State University, University of Oregon
Pennsylvania	8	Carnegie Mellon University, Drexel University, Lehigh University, Penn State University, Temple University, University of Pennsylvania, University of Pittsburgh, Villanova University
Rhode Island	2	Brown University, University of Rhode Island
South Carolina	1	Clemson University
South Dakota	2	South Dakota School of Mines and Technology, University of South Dakota
Tennessee	3	Middle Tennessee State University, University of Tennessee, Vanderbilt University
Texas	7	Baylor University, Rice University, Texas A&M University, Texas Tech University, University of North Texas, University of Texas at Austin, University of Texas
Utah	1	University of Utah
Vermont	1	University of Vermont
Virginia	5	George Mason University, Old Dominion University, University of Virginia, Virginia Commonwealth University, Virginia Tech University
Washington	2	University of Washington, Washington State University
West Virginia	1	West Virginia University
Wisconsin	1	University of Wisconsin-Madison
Wyoming	1	University of Wyoming
TOTAL	196	

These organizations serve primarily as a social outlet for Chinese students, organizing dances and sports activities, but they also provide orientation assistance for recent arrivals to the United States.

From a counter-intelligence perspective, the main concern about these student associations is the extent of their relationships with the Chinese government, either as a mechanism for monitoring the activities of Chinese students abroad, tasking students with particular actions, or facilitating access of Chinese government personnel to university resources. The official Chinese government liaison organization for these associations are the education sections of the Chinese embassy in Washington, DC,[55] and consulates in New York,[56] San Francisco,[57] Los Angeles,[58] Houston,[59] and Chicago.[60] The Chinese Embassy Education Section webpage succinctly describes the full range of their mission, including the need to "provide services and guidance for Chinese students and scholars in the USA."[61] The Houston consulate education section website even includes links to the China Students and Scholars Associations in the states that fall under its purview.

Concerns about potential Chinese government influence over these associations have been raised again in the past few years, as the groups appeared to be systematically mobilized to protest the disruptions of the Olympic torch in the run-up to the 2008 Beijing Olympics and the visit of the Dalai Lama to the White House in February 2010. After disruptions of the torch relay in London and Paris by Tibetan independence activists and Falungong adherents, large numbers of pro-China supporters turned out for the torch run through San Francisco, including contingents of local CSSA branches.

Prior to the Dalai Lama's April 2008 visit to Seattle to receive an honorary degree from the University of Washington, the local chapter of the CSSA sent two letters to the university leadership protesting the visit, declaring:

> As Chinese citizens, we want to reaffirm that Tibet was, is and will always be part of the People's Republic of China. . . . We are against any kind of violence. We believe that every country in the world should show respect to the others' own domestic issues. Therefore, we hope the University of Washington will make sure that Dalai Lama's upcoming visit has no political agenda, and that his speech will be focused on non-political issues only.[62]

Similarly, the CSSA branch of the University of Northern Iowa issued the following statement prior to the Dalai Lama's May 2010 visit:

> [T]he recent overwhelming PR efforts on the Dalai Lama's visit to UNI have reinforced the negative image of China in the minds of the American students, faculty, and staff as well as the local community. . . . If this is an educational event, the Chinese Students and Scholars Association (CSSA) of UNI does not deem it appropriate for the University of Northern Iowa, as a state university, to endorse Dalai Lama's political agenda on UNI's official Web site or any public occasion during the event.[63]

When a film on Tibet was shown at Cornell University in April 2008, Chinese students allegedly made death threats on the school's CSSA website against the organizers.[64] More troubling, a Chinese student at Duke University was reportedly threatened on an email list run by the school's CSSA branch for attending a pro-Tibet demonstration, publishing her contact information and the names and addresses of her family members in China for possible retaliation,[65] though the association formally condemned the action in an open letter to the Duke University community.[66]

After graduation, where do they go?

The early waves of Chinese graduate students decided overwhelmingly to stay in the United States after graduation. According to a National Science Foundation report, for example, between 1988 and 1996, more than 85 percent of the 16,550 Chinese students who received doctoral degrees in science and engineering in the US planned to remain in the US after graduation for employment or postdoctoral appointments.[67] A survey by the *Wall Street Journal* in 2007 found that an astonishing 92 percent of Chinese doctoral candidates who received their degrees in 2002 were still in the United States,[68] which was the same level as a 1995 Department of Education survey.[69] For purposes of comparison, only 81 percent of Indian graduates and 55 percent of Canadian graduates stayed behind over the same period.[70]

More recent statistics reveal that Chinese graduate students are still staying in the United States in large numbers following graduation (see Table 6.3), though the numbers have declined almost 10 percent since 2006.

Why do they stay?

US government policies encouraging Chinese students in the US

Permissive US immigration policies are one reason for the popularity of the United States as a destination for Chinese students. Most Chinese students come to the United States on a non-immigrant visa, either a J-1 (cultural exchange) or an F-1 (foreign student). The J-1 visa was created in 1948 to promote educational and cultural exchange activities between the United States and other countries. It is designed for those engaged full-time in study at a college or university usually for some limited period of time with the support of either a US government agency or the student's own government. Intended in large part to build bridges between the United States and the sending countries, J-1 visas restrict employment to that directly related to the student's academic training and usually stipulate that the recipient return to his country of origin for two full years following the completion of his or her course of study.

TABLE 6.3 Numbers and Percentages of Chinese Doctoral Students Staying in the United States After Graduation, 2002–2011[71]

	2002	2003	2004	2005	2006	2007	2008	2009	2010	2011
#	2290	2483	2995	3588	4441	4714	4526			
%	91.7	90.6	89.5	89.4	89.9	89.6	87.7	88.3	82.1	82.0

J-1 visas are partly governed by international agreements with the dispatching country. Section 212e of the J-1 visa prohibits the holder from changing his or her status and remaining in the United States until he or she has returned to his or her country of origin and met the residency requirement. This requirement becomes applicable if either the student has received funding from his or her own government or he or she possesses certain skills that are included on his or her country's exchange visitor skills list. J-1 visas were the most common visas issued to Chinese students in the 1970s and early 1980s. China includes most skills on its skills list and in the past was notorious for providing minimal amounts of funding, such as the bus fare to the airport, in order to force students to return.[72]

Waivers of the two-year return requirement are not readily granted, but there is anecdotal evidence that Chinese students frequently tried to have these restrictions waived.[73] They are sometimes able to obtain waivers on the grounds that a US government agency is interested in having them remain. Chinese students most often received these waivers through their universities that can act as sponsors under this category of waiver if the research the student is involved in rises to the level of national interest.[74]

As China opened up more to the outside world and its economy began to grow, increasing numbers of Chinese students opted to travel to study in the United States without Chinese government funding. These students were able to obtain F-1 visas, commonly referred to as student visas. To qualify for an F-1 visa, however, applicants have to prove that they have sufficient funds available to cover their first year of study and that they have identified additional funds for each year of study thereafter.[75] By the early 1980s, some Chinese students could rely on their families for tuition and living expenses. Others tapped into their networks of friends, relatives, and acquaintances who helped them identify and obtain scholarships from US universities.[76] According to one source, by 1985 over half of Chinese students traveling to the United States had obtained assistance from US universities.[77]

While it is fairly difficult for Chinese students on J-1 visas to change their status while still in the United States, the same cannot be said of those on F-1 visas.[78] According to both observers of and participants in the process, it is relatively easy to obtain a degree and get practical training while on a student visa, then to find a job and eventually qualify for permanent residence status or even citizenship. A significant proportion of those admitted on F-1 and other non-immigrant visas do just that.[79] By the late 1980s, it had become clear that only a relatively small percentage of Chinese students were returning to the country after completing their degrees overseas, sparking concern among Chinese leaders that encouraging students to go abroad was resulting in a "brain drain."

The Chinese government crackdown on student protesters in Tiananmen Square on June 4, 1989 created an opportunity for the tens of thousands of Chinese students in the United States at the time. Within hours of the crackdown, President George Bush ordered the Attorney General to take action to allow students and other Chinese nationals who so desired to remain in the United States for up to one year even if their visa status expired. In addition, Chinese researchers who had grants or other support from the National Science Foundation (NSF) were invited to apply for supplemental funding to cover an extension of their stay as a result of this delay in departure.[80]

Shortly thereafter, citing concerns about reprisals against the pro-democracy movement in China, both the House and the Senate introduced bills designed to allow all mainland Chinese students residing in the country on June 5, 1989 to apply for a change of visa status. Under the bill, those who applied would be granted employment authorization. The Emergency Chinese Immigration Relief Act of 1989 passed the Senate 97–0 in July 1989. A similar bill sponsored by Congresswoman Nancy Pelosi of California passed the House of Representatives 403–0. Despite the unanimous show of support for this action in both Houses of Congress, in late November 1989 President Bush vetoed the bill, citing the potential damage it could do to exchange programs and diplomatic relations between the United States and China.[81]

In its stead, Bush expanded the measures he had initially taken so that they would provide the same level of protection for Chinese nationals in the United States as would have been accorded by the vetoed bill. His Executive Order included: (1) an irrevocable waiver of the two-year home country residence requirement until January 1, 1994; (2) assurance of continued lawful immigration status for those who were legally in the United States on June 5, 1989; (3) authorization for employment of Chinese nationals present in the United States on June 5, 1989; and (4) notice of expiration of non-immigrant status, rather than institution of deportation proceedings, for individuals eligible for deferral of enforced departure whose non-immigrant status had expired.[82]

Nonetheless, Chinese students through the newly formed Independent Federation of Chinese Students and Scholars (IFCSS) continued to lobby Congress for a blanket amnesty bill. The Bush Administration's delayed departure program was viewed as insufficient because it required Chinese students to go on record as saying they did not want to return to their homeland. After what has been described by some as a "sophisticated lobbying campaign" led by the IFCSS with assistance from a prominent Washington law firm, the Chinese Student Protection Act (CSPA) passed Congress in 1992 and was signed into law by President Bush in October of that year.[83] The CSPA authorized the Department of Justice to grant permanent residence status (PRS) to nationals of the People's Republic of China who were in the United States after June 4, 1989 and before April 11, 1990.

Estimates of the numbers of students who benefited from the general amnesty vary from 40,000 to 80,000.[84] Statistics collected by the Immigration and Naturalization Service show that the number of students adjusting their status from student to permanent resident increased by 55,000 between 1993 and 1994. This increase has been attributed largely to the Chinese Student Protection Act that came into effect in 1993.[85]

This one-time change in US immigration policy in the wake of the suppression of the Tiananmen pro-democracy movement in 1989, combined with a booming US high-tech economy, and an increase in Chinese students who held the more flexible F-1 visas, resulted in even fewer students considering returning to China.[86]

Since Tiananmen, the biggest institutional obstacles to Chinese students coming to the United States were the changes in the visa system following 9/11, which caused huge disruptions in educational applications. By the late 2000s, however, the 9/11 visa problems had largely gone away. Speaking in 2008, Peggy Blumenthal, the chief operating officer of the Institute for International Education, told the *Associated Press*:

> The misperceptions have finally been laid to rest – that it's impossible to get a visa, Students choosing schools are looking strictly at academic issues, because there's no reason to believe they'll have any more trouble getting to the States than getting to Australia.[87]

Chinese students who stay to work in US companies

Chinese students in the United States have overwhelmingly gravitated toward degrees in the hard sciences and engineering. In recent years this has meant semiconductors and information technologies including software design and development. It is perhaps unremarkable, therefore, to discover that given the opportunity to remain in the United States for employment after obtaining their degrees, Chinese students have been drawn to the same clusters of knowledge-based industries that have attracted their American-born colleagues. One geographic region has exerted a particular pull – the Silicon Valley of Northern California. The booming high-tech industry of the late 1980s and early 1990s attracted many of the Chinese students who benefited from the post-Tiananmen amnesty. According to estimates, the San Francisco Bay area in 2000 was home to approximately 20,700 professional workers in the high-technology sectors who were born in greater China (Mainland, Hong Kong, and Taiwan).[88]

Returned students: reversal of fortune?

Despite the historically low rate of return of Chinese students who have gone abroad for higher education, a steady increase in the number of students returning to China since the late 1990s has led some to proclaim that China's "brain drain" is becoming a "brain gain." Recent state-run media reports highlight the growing number of students returning to China in recent years,[89] and official documents assert that the combination of an increasingly attractive economic environment, government incentives, and patriotism is motivating large numbers of students to return to China.[90] Some official media articles are even proclaiming that the country is now enjoying the benefits of a "reverse brain drain"[91]; however, others highlight the continued exodus of China's top university graduates, continuing to warn of the potential social and economic consequences of a prolonged "brain drain."[92]

Factors motivating a decision to return to China

In a large-scale 2002 survey of Chinese and Indian immigrant engineers conducted by Anna Lee Saxenian, a professor of regional development at the University of California, Berkeley,[93] respondents were asked to rank the importance of five factors that might influence their decisions to return to China: (1) professional opportunities in China; (2) culture and lifestyle in China; (3) favorable government treatment of returnees in China; (4) limits on professional advancement in the United States; and (5) desire to contribute to the economic development of China. Favorable government treatment of returnees was viewed as a significant factor. About 11 percent of the respondents ranked it as an extremely important consideration in their decision to return. But it ranked third in importance behind professional opportunity and culture and lifestyle. Professional opportunity was the factor cited most often as "extremely important" (29%), outranking the second most important factor, culture and lifestyle (17%), by a wide margin. The survey did not attempt to directly gauge patriotism as a motivating factor, but to some extent it is possible to see a desire to contribute to the economic development of China as a proxy for that. This factor ranked fourth in overall importance behind professional opportunity, culture and lifestyle, and government incentives.

According to an official PRC Ministry of Personnel document, economic development and scientific and technological progress in China present Chinese students who are studying overseas with an array of new opportunities to return to China to seek employment after completing their studies.[94] Returned students are leaders in many scientific and technical fields in China and have won numerous awards for their research. Others have launched successful businesses in China. According to Chinese government statistics, as of April 2002, returned students had established about 4,000 enterprises in China. In addition, many hold important positions with universities, research institutes, and government departments at all levels in the Chinese political system. For example, at the prestigious Chinese Academy of Sciences, 80 percent of the faculty studied abroad, as did more than half of those at the Chinese Academy of Engineering.[95]

Rapid economic development in China is highlighted in official media reports as the primary factor that is drawing students back to China. In the words of a representative *China Daily* article, "China's booming market is reversing the brain drain."[96] Major multinational corporations increasingly view China as one of the world's most dynamic emerging markets. According to Chinese government statistics, in the first ten months of 2002, China attracted $46.4 billion in actual FDI and $76.5 billion in contracted FDI, increases of 20 percent and 35 percent over the same period the previous year. By late 2008, official Chinese media reported that 483 of the world's top 500 firms had developed business in China, establishing 365 corporate headquarters in the country and managing more than 4,100 subsidiary companies.[97]

In addition to the increase in attractive economic opportunities available in cities like Shanghai and Beijing, another factor that makes returning to China an appealing option for many Chinese students is the ongoing recession in the United States. Some returned students have specifically cited the contrast between the global economic slowdown and the continued vibrancy of the Chinese economy as the reason for their decision to return to China to seek employment.

The relatively high social status accorded to returnees that derives from the various incentives the Chinese government has used to entice students to return also serves as a lure. Government connections continue to be perceived as essential to success in business in China and potential returnees recognize that their status opens doors for them that are unavailable to their counterparts in China. One Silicon Valley entrepreneur who frequently travels to China commented on the access that accrues to him because of his status as an overseas student: "It's easier for me to meet with local mayors than it is for Chinese CEOs."[98]

Chinese government policies encouraging students to return

Since the late 1990s, central government and local officials have promulgated a series of policy measures aimed at encouraging Chinese students overseas to return to China, either on a long-term or temporary basis. These policies reflect the Chinese government's renewed emphasis on tapping the expanding pool of foreign-educated Chinese students and businessmen. At a late December 2001 meeting, for example, Vice-Premier Li Lanqing described overseas Chinese students as "a precious resource of the nation." Li said that "the need for talent is urgent," especially in the wake of China's accession to the World Trade Organization, and urged officials to "work hard to create the conditions to attract these talented people to come back." As part of this program, Chinese leaders have set ambitious goals. In November 2011, Ministry of Personnel officials said they intended to attract back to China 2,000 "talents" to work for the central government and 10,000 overseas Chinese students per year to work in provinces and large cities.[99] The students would be encouraged to work in financial services – especially in banking, insurance, and securities – as well as for high-tech companies and large state-owned enterprises. The incentives designed to achieve these targets include providing funding to overseas Chinese students and scholars for advanced research as well as financial support for businesses established in China by returned Chinese students.

The first part of this subsection addresses central government policies that are aimed at increasing the number of overseas Chinese students and scholars returning to China. The second part provides an overview of preferential policies offered by several local governments. The final part of the subsection discusses government incentives that are designed to take advantage of the skills and expertise of members of the overseas Chinese community by encouraging them to return to China for short-term service (短期回国服务).

Central government policies

Central government incentive programs designed to attract overseas Chinese students, scholars, and entrepreneurs back to the mainland involve several organizations, including the Ministry of Education, Ministry of Personnel, Ministry of Science and Technology, and Ministry of Public Security.[100] Although the range of incentives offered is wide, they can be divided into three broad groups: (1) policies aimed at promoting the involvement of overseas students and scholars in science and education; (2) incentives designed to entice overseas students and entrepreneurs to establish companies in China; and (3) general preferential policies offered to all returned students and professionals.

Many of the central government's preferential policies for returned students are aimed specifically at getting more of the students who have earned advanced degrees in the sciences and engineering at universities in the US and other Western countries to return to China. The Ministry of Personnel supervises many of the incentive programs, including several that provide financial assistance to students participating in major research projects.[101] The level of funding allocated for these programs is impressive. The Ministry of Personnel has spent more than RMB200 million on programs designed to attract returned students to engage in scientific research over the past 15 years,[102] and the government has reportedly dedicated RMB600 million for programs that are intended to recruit several hundred overseas Chinese scholars to return to the mainland.[103] Among the programs sponsored and managed by the central government are the following:

- *Ministry of Education "Yangtze Scholar Award Plan."* Established in 1998 by the Ministry of Education and Hong Kong businessman Li Ka-hsing, the program will provide funding to create several hundred special positions for professors in important fields of study within three to five years. It also provides annual monetary rewards to several scholars for outstanding achievements.
- *Chinese Academy of Sciences "100 Person Plan."* Initiated in 1994, the CAS "100 Person Plan"(百人计划) offers appointments to overseas Chinese aged 45 and younger who have received doctorates and have an outstanding record of achievement in scientific research.
- *Ministry of Education Returned Student Scientific Research Start-up Fund.* This fund provides financial assistance to Chinese students who received doctorates or engaged in post-doctoral research overseas to return to China to work for educational institutions or scientific research organizations.
- *Chinese Academy of Sciences Return to China Work Fund.* This CAS program provides start-up research funds to Chinese students and visiting scholars younger than age 50 who have studied overseas.
- *Ministry of Personnel Financial Assistance Programs.* These programs provide assistance to Chinese students returning to China to work in areas outside of the educational system.
- *National Post-Doctoral Science Fund.* This fund provides financial assistance to post-doctoral students who return to China.

- *National Outstanding Youth Science Fund.* This program encourages overseas scholars to return to work in China and to become leaders in their fields, and to conduct basic and applied research in the natural sciences in China.

Other central government programs focus on bringing overseas students back to the mainland to start new businesses, especially in the high-tech sector. One of the major parts of this effort has been the establishment of specially designated science and technology business parks for returned students. Officials have opened dozens of "pioneer parks" for returned students throughout the country.[104] Many of the parks are established jointly by the Ministry of Personnel and local governments, and are administered by local officials. Specially designated returned students venture parks receive support from the Ministry of Personnel, Ministry of Science and Technology, and Ministry of Education. Other incentives for high-tech are discussed in more detail in Chapter 3.

In addition to policies that are tailored specifically to students with science backgrounds and business experience, the central government has crafted a variety of more general incentives that promise to ease the transition of a return to China:

- The government offers to help find employment for the family members of returned students.
- In 2000, the Ministry of Public Security issued a circular concerning preferential policies that are intended to simplify entry and exit procedures for returned students and make it easier for them to acquire residence permits. The preferential policies detailed in the MPS circular are aimed specifically at "high-tech talents and investors."[105]
- Many returned students who hold foreign passports are also eligible for simplified entry and exit procedures under policies adopted by the Ministry of Education and Ministry of Public Security.[106]
- The Ministry of Personnel has also established a service center for overseas Chinese students and scholars, along with some 20 consulting and service centers in cities throughout China.
- The government has also established the "China Talents" website (www.chinatalents.gov.cn), which provides information on many of these incentives and preferential policies, and is intended to serve as a convenient source of information for overseas Chinese students. The website features an online guide for students who are considering returning to China.[107]
- For returned students, after-tax income can be converted into foreign currency and remitted abroad.

The Chinese government is also trying to attract Chinese students studying overseas to return to work in Western provinces as part of its drive to increase the pace of economic development in the western regions. Targeted cities include Xi'an, Chengdu, and Chongqing, where the government has established numerous high-tech industrial parks and is offering a variety of financial incentives to entice overseas students to consider a journey to the west instead of working in the more economically developed and dynamic coastal provinces.[108] To promote these efforts, the Ministry of Personnel has organized tours for overseas students considering establishing enterprises in the western provinces.

In addition to implementing the policies listed above, the central government has also assisted local governments in their efforts to encourage Chinese students residing abroad to return to China, especially to work in the high-tech sector and to invest in high-tech companies. According to an official document, the central government supports local governments and departments in their efforts "to create excellent work and living conditions" for returned students and encourages economic and high-tech development zones and returned students' industrial parks to use preferential policies (优惠政策), including land use and tax incentives, visa assistance,[109] and reduced bureaucracy, to attract students to return from overseas.[110] In addition, protecting the intellectual property rights of returned students is seen as another way to make returning to China a more attractive option, though China clearly still has a long way to go in this regard.

Local government incentives

While the central government is concerned primarily with increasing the overall number of returned students, and channeling some into less-developed regions as part of its effort to develop the Western provinces, the interests of local governments are somewhat different in that they are competing with each other to attract the best overseas Chinese talent. Among the preferential policies established by provincial governments to attract returned students are tax reductions, and in some cases tax exemptions for firms founded by returned students, special funds set aside for returned students, and the establishment of special zones that offer investment incentives to returned students' companies. Local governments throughout China have founded more than 40 high-tech parks that are intended to attract investments from Chinese students returning from overseas study.[111] Among the municipalities and provinces that have established returned students' business parks are Beijing, Shanghai, Tianjin, Heilongjiang, Jilin, Liaoning, Shaanxi, Guangdong, Shandong, Henan, Zhejiang, Fujian, Hunan, Guangxi, and Gansu. Free office space (usually for one year), seed funds, and low-interest loans are provided to returning students establishing businesses in the high-tech office parks. Representatives from these high-tech parks, along with local officials, hold frequent recruiting events in the United States. The seminars they arrange in Silicon Valley have been drawing large crowds as a result of the US economic downturn. Among the cities offering the most comprehensive packages of incentives to attract returned students are Shanghai, Beijing, and Hangzhou.

While most local government incentive programs are aimed at enticing Chinese students to return for commercial opportunities, some provincial governments are attempting to recruit returned students to fill provincial and city government positions. For example, in Liaoning Province, officials from the provincial personnel bureau have reserved more than 50 government posts for Chinese returning from foreign study.[112] Another city that has looked abroad to fill key government positions is Shenzhen, where city officials in late 2001 opened several posts at the deputy director level to overseas Chinese candidates.[113]

Short-term returnees and overseas Chinese helping from abroad

Many of the incentives and preferential policies discussed above are intended to attract overseas Chinese students to return to China on a long-term basis, but the Chinese government also offers incentives to students and scholars interested in returning to China only temporarily, and even to those who may be able to contribute their expertise while remaining abroad. These incentive programs reflect Beijing's recognition that it is possible for overseas Chinese students, scholars, and entrepreneurs to "serve the motherland" in a variety of ways without returning permanently to China. As a Qinghua University administrator put it, "It doesn't matter where they live. They are all Chinese and will be able to serve the country."[114] Indeed, according to an official document issued jointly by the Ministry of Personnel, Ministry of Education, Ministry of Science and Technology, Ministry of Public Security, and Ministry of Finance, for example, Chinese students studying abroad do not need to return to China to serve the country:

> Chinese students overseas have strong patriotic feelings (强烈的爱国热情) and a fervent desire to serve their country. Some have returned to China, where they have taken the lead in improving education and science and technology. At the same time, many students who remain overseas or work abroad after completing their studies can employ their advanced science and technology know-how and firm grasp of management techniques to serve China and contribute to its economic and social development. The ways in which they can do so include holding a concurrent post or part-time position in China; carrying out cooperative research projects with scientists or institutes in China; traveling to China to give lectures; participating in academic and technical exchanges; establishing companies in China; providing consulting services; acting as an intermediary; and engaging in other pursuits that contribute to the development of the Chinese economy and advancement of Chinese society.[115]

Some of the associated incentive programs are intended to attract overseas Chinese scholars and technicians to accept concurrent or part-time appointments and advisory or honorary positions with higher education institutions, scientific research institutes, national key laboratories (国家重点实验室), technology research centers, and enterprises. Other incentives are intended to encourage Chinese who have gone overseas for graduate study to engage in cooperative research with scholars and scientists at Chinese universities, research institutes, and enterprises. The overseas scholars can conduct the research in the countries in which they reside or by returning to work in China on a short-term basis. Chinese who have studied overseas are also encouraged to invest in Chinese companies or establish their own companies in China; to help Chinese enterprises train and educate their employees; to provide technology, consulting services, and financial support to promote the development of the Western provinces; to establish intermediary organizations (中介机构) to bring foreign investment and technology to China; and to contact foreign experts to invite them to engage in academic exchanges in China and with Chinese academic and technical delegations traveling overseas.[116]

The following programs, all of which are advertised on the website of the Chinese Consulate in San Francisco,[117] are among those specifically intended to attract students and scholars to return to China for short-term service (短期回国服务):

- *"Spring Sunshine" Plan* (春晖计划). Initiated by the Ministry of Education in 1997, the "Spring Sunshine" Plan provides financial assistance to overseas Chinese students to return to China on a short-term basis to participate in academic conferences; take part in scientific research and academic exchanges; help improve technology at large and medium-sized state-owned enterprises; and introduce technology into impoverished areas.[118] Under the auspices of this program, more than 600 Chinese studying abroad have received funding to travel to China to attend academic conferences and participate in a host of cooperative research projects and joint educational endeavors.
- *"Spring Sunshine" Plan Academic Vacations* (春晖计划学术休假). This plan provides funding for students studying or performing research abroad to return to China for three- to nine-month sabbatical leaves to teach in China (see www.1000plan.org/qrjh/article/7527).
- *National Outstanding Youth Science Fund Type B Financial Assistance.* Administered by the National Natural Sciences Fund Committee (国家自然科学基金会), the program funds outstanding young scholars and recipients of doctoral degrees who are willing to return to China for two or more months per year for several years to work on research projects.
- *Chinese Academy of Sciences High-level Visiting Scholar Plan.* This program pays for housing and living expenses for overseas Chinese scholars with PhD degrees and five or more years' research experience to serve as visiting scholars at the Chinese Academy of Sciences for a period of six months to one year.
- *National Natural Sciences Fund Committee Short-term Return Fund.* This fund is used to provide financial assistance to overseas Chinese who hold doctoral degrees and who are willing to travel to China to attend conferences, give lectures, and conduct research in the natural sciences.
- *Ministry of Personnel Short-term Return Financial Assistance Program.* Administered by the Ministry of Personnel, this program gives funding to Chinese students studying abroad to travel to China to attend conferences, give lectures, engage in cooperative research, and participate in national, ministry/commission, province, or city-level scientific research projects. Among the program goals

are facilitating technology transfer (技术转让) and technological exchanges (技术交流).

- *Chinese Academy of Sciences (CAS) Academic Meetings Financial Aid Program.* Managed by CAS, this program provides funding to encourage exchanges and contacts between young scholars in China and Chinese students studying abroad to conduct research at CAS or universities in China for at least two months of the year.
- *Wang Kuancheng Scientific Research Prize.* Established by CAS and the Hong Kong-based Wang Kuancheng Education Foundation, the prize funds international conference travel for Chinese students who have received doctorates abroad and return to China.

Continuing problems for returning scholars

Despite significant government resources and energy devoted to attracting returned scholars, there are still substantial complaints and obstacles. According to a survey of returnees conducted by the Central Organization Department in the first half of 2011, scholars complained that many domestic researchers still prefer to spend time on cultivating relationships with officials or appraisers rather than concentrating on research projects.[119] They called for a system of fairly allocating government funds, replacing the current system that relies heavily on these cultivated connections.[120] Other returnees complained about the failure on the part of hiring departments to deliver on schedule what they had promised and the cumbersome administrative red tape on the resident status for their family members who hold foreign passports.[121] Other concerns include China's notoriously terrible air and water quality, food safety, social security, health insurance coverage, and sky-high apartment prices in major cities.[122] At the same time, some scholars have decried the rampant epidemic of academic plagiarism in China, which undermines public confidence in their credentials.[123] Taken together, all these factors presented a demonstrable disincentive to leave Western lifestyles and academic standards to return to China.

Implications

The final section of this chapter examines the technology transfer and counter-intelligence implications of China's study abroad and returned students policies. It is clear from open sources that the Chinese government regards some Chinese students and scientists traveling to or residing in the United States as potential facilitators of overt and covert transfer of technology and technological know-how.

Overt transfer of technology and technological know-how

The Chinese government views overseas Chinese scientists as a potential conduit for the transfer of foreign technology and technological expertise. This is reflected in several recent articles in Chinese science and technology journals, which have advocated expanding the role of Chinese scientists living overseas in conducting research on behalf of Chinese research institutes and facilitating technology transfer.[124]

Covert transfer of technology and technological know-how

Chinese scholars and scientists in the United States and other countries are also potential targets for China's intelligence services, especially when they travel to China to attend conferences, according to a former FBI counter-intelligence official.[125] In some cases, the MSS has approached Chinese students preparing to study in the United States before their departure to establish a clandestine relationship.[126] In addition, Chinese scientists and scholars who have studied in or visited the United States (and presumably other countries) are sometimes debriefed after returning to China, and the MSS recruits and co-opts some Chinese who are traveling overseas as part of educational exchange programs or as members of scientific delegations, tasking them with acquiring information or performing other operational activities.[127]

Notes

1 For an overview of US–China educational exchanges from the 1800s to the founding of the PRC, see D.M. Lampton, *A Relationship Restored*, Washington, DC: National Academies Press, 1986, pp. 16–20.
2 Ibid., pp. 182–183. As remains the case today, this distribution was a function of both Chinese government priorities and the availability of foreign funding.
3 For a concise overview of Sino–Soviet educational exchanges, see ibid., pp. 20–23.
4 "Returned Students and HEP Research in China," Institute of High Energy Physics, October 10, 2002, www.ihep.ac.cn/english/r.s.&hep/index.htm. According to the Institute for High Energy Physics, "It can be said that the development of high energy physics in China is inseparable from the returned students." For an in-depth look at another returned student, Qian Xuesen, who became a key figure in China's missile development program, see Iris Chang, *Thread of the Silkworm*, New York: Basic Books, 1995.
5 Educational exchanges between China and the Soviet Union were resumed at a more modest level only in the 1980s.
6 "New Policies to be Issued to Lure Overseas Students Home," *People's Daily*, July 29, 2000.
7 Wei Yu (韦钰), 出国留学工作二十年: 纪念邓小平同志关于扩大派遣留学人员讲话二十周年 ("20 Years of Study Abroad Work: Commemorating the 20th Anniversary of Comrade Deng Xiaoping's Speech on the Expansion of Sending Personnel to Study Abroad"), *China Education Daily*, June 23, 1998, p. 3.
8 Wei Yu, "20 Years of Study Abroad Work."
9 Wei Yu, "20 Years of Study Abroad Work."
10 www.wantchinatimes.com/news-subclass-cnt.aspx?id=20111127000017&cid=1701.
11 "Fewer China Overseas Students Staying Abroad," *China Daily*, 24 January 2013.
12 National Bureau of Statistics, *China Statistical Yearbook 2002*, Beijing: China Statistics Press, 2002, p. 675.
13 The data presented in the *China Statistical Yearbook* also suggest that the number of

returned students frequently provided by official media sources may be too high. The most recent edition does not provide a total number of students studying abroad or returning to China since 1978, but based on the annual data it provides for the years 1978, 1980, and 1985 to 2001, it seems that the actual total number of returned students is perhaps closer to 90,000 to 100,000 than it is to the higher numbers frequently cited in official media reports. It should be noted that the definitions of the key terms are somewhat unclear: none of the sources we reviewed offers a full definition of the terms "returned students" (学成回国留学人员) or "students studying abroad" (出国留学人员). This lack of a standardized definition suggests one possible explanation for the apparent discrepancies between various sources: official media reports may be using broader and thus more inclusive definitions of the key terms than does the *China Statistical Yearbook*. Some media reports, it seems, may be counting non-students, such as Chinese who have studied overseas as visiting scholars and returned to China, as "students studying abroad" and as "returned students." It is also possible, of course, that some sources are deliberately exaggerating the number of Chinese students who have returned to China after completing their studies overseas.

14 www.skyscrapercity.com/showthread.php?t=603811.

15 www.china.org.cn/china/news/2009-03/26/content_17502548.htm.

16 http://helinjiangliuxue.blog.sohu.com/146503590.html.

17 http://helinjiangliuxue.blog.sohu.com/146503590.html.

18 http://edu.sina.com.cn/a/2012-02-16/1633212392.shtml.

19 The US, moreover, has played a central role in China's educational exchange policies since the late Qing Dynasty period. In all, according to the Ministry of Personnel and Ministry of Education, as of June 2002, some 460,000 Chinese had studied overseas, and by far the largest number – more than 150,000 of the total –have studied in the United States. See "Chinese Studying Abroad Top the World," *People's Daily*, June 18, 2002.

20 Lampton, *A Relationship Restored*, p. 2.

21 Ibid.

22 Beth McMurtrie, "No Welcome Mat for the Chinese? US Visas Seem Harder to Get," *The Chronicle of Higher Education*, September 24, 1999.

23 Remarks of Donald M. Bishop, Minister-Counselor for Press and Cultural Affairs, American Embassy Beijing, speaking at the American Center for Educational Exchange on January 26, 2005. See www.iienetwork.org/?p=56814.

24 www.iie.org/Who-We-Are/News-and-Events/Press-Center/Press-Releases/2011/2011-11-14-Open-Doors-International-Students; and http://chronicle.com/article/International-Enrollments-at/129747/.

25 Tamar Lewin, "China Is Sending More Students to US," *New York Times*, November 16, 2009.

26 www.iie.org/Who-We-Are/News-and-Events/Press-Center/Press-Releases/2011/2011-11-14-Open-Doors-Study-Abroad.

27 Mary Beth Marklein, "Chinese College Students Flocking to US Campuses," *USA Today*, December 8, 2009, http://usatoday30.usatoday.com/news/education/2009-12-08-1Achinesestudents08_CV_N.htm.

28 www.state.gov/p/eap/rls/2011/156504.htm; www.state.gov/r/pa/prs/ps/2012/02/184614.htm; and www.state.gov/p/eap/regional/100000_strong/index.htm.

29 See Institute for International Education, *Open Doors 2012*, accessed at www.iie.org/Research-and-Publications/Open-Doors/Data/US-Study-Abroad/Leading-Destinations/2009-11

30 "Chinese Students Pursuing US Education," *Associated Press*, November 17, 2008.

31 Tamar Lewin, "China Is Sending More Students to US," *New York Times*, November 16, 2009.

32 Marklein, "Chinese College Students Flocking to US Campuses."

33 Daniel Walfish, "Chinese Applicants to US Universities Often Resort to Shortcuts or Dishonesty," *Chronicle of Higher Education*, January 5, 2001.

34 Ian Wilhelm, "Falsified Applications Are Common Among Chinese Students Seeking to Go Abroad, Consultant Says," *Associated Press,* June 14, 2010.
35 Beth McMurtie, "International Enrollments at US Colleges Grow but Still Rely on China," *Chronicle of Higher Education,* November 14, 2011, http://chronicle.com/article/International-Enrollments-at/129747/.
36 Institute for International Education, *Open Doors 2002,* Table 2, Foreign Students by Academic Level and Place of Origin 2001/2002.
37 www.nsf.gov/statistics/sed/pdf/tab25.pdf.
38 www.iie.org/Who-We-Are/News-and-Events/Press-Center/Press-Releases/2011/2011-11-14-Open-Doors-Study-Abroad.
39 Ibid.
40 Lampton, *A Relationship Restored,* pp. 2–3.
41 National Center for Education Statistics, US Department of Education, "Degrees Earned by Foreign Graduate Students: Fields of Study and Plans After Graduation," November 1997, p. 1.
42 National Science Foundation, Division of Science Resource Studies, Statistical Profiles of Foreign Doctoral Recipients in Science and Engineering: Plans to Stay in the United States, November 1998, NSF 99-304.
43 Institute of International Education (2012). "Fields of Study of Students from Selected Places of Origin 2011/12." *Open Doors Report on International Educational Exchange.* Retrieved from www.iie.org/opendoors.
44 Wei Yu, "20 Years of Abroad Study Work."
45 This trend may have worrisome implications for China as government-sponsored students are far more likely to return to China.
46 Marklein, "Chinese College Students Flocking to US Campuses."
47 After the Tiananmen Square turmoil in 1989, an "opposition" student organization, known as the Independent Federation of Chinese Students and Scholars, was established, with over 1,000 student representatives from 200 universities attending its first congress in August 1989. According to its bylaws, the mission of IFCSS is to (1) disseminate information and educate the public regarding the democratic movement in China, (2) represent the wishes of Chinese students and scholars in the United States and protect their interests; promote freedom, democracy, the rule of law, human rights in China as well as China's scientific, cultural, and economic development, and (3) participate in and support activities to protect the interests of Chinese students and scholars in the United States, and promote China's democratic movement. See http://research.nianet.org/~luo/IFCSS/Archives/Constitution/IFCSS_bylaws_94.PDF.
48 http://cssa.mit.edu/.
49 www.hcssa.org/.
50 http://acsss.stanford.edu/cgi-bin/entry/.
51 www.cornellcssa.com/.
52 http://dukechina.org/blog/.
53 http://sites.google.com/site/cssaucla2009/.
54 http://cssap.org/.
55 www.sino-education.org/english/index.htm.
56 www.nyconsulate.prchina.org/chn/jysw/.
57 www.chinaconsulatesf.org/chn/jy/default.htm.
58 http://losangeles.china-consulate.org/eng/hzjl/edu/.
59 http://houston.china-consulate.org/chn/jy/. The Houston education section covers Chinese student affairs in Texas, Oklahoma, Arkansas, Louisiana, Alabama, Mississippi, Georgia, Florida, and Puerto Rico.
60 www.chinaconsulatechicago.org/eng/ywzn/jy/.
61 www.sino-education.org/english/index.htm.
62 http://blog.seattlepi.com/schoolzone/archives/136186.asp.
63 http://wcfcourier.com/news/local/29b9f862-605d-11df-a484-001cc4c002e0.html.

64 Michael Stratford, "E-mails Target Professor For Showing Tibet Film," *Cornell Sun*, April 16, 2008.
65 Paul Mooney, "Chinese Student at Duke U. Hit With Online Attacks for Alleged Sympathy for Tibet," *Chronicle of Higher Education*, April 14, 2008.
66 http://dukechina.org/blog/archives/2812.
67 National Science Foundation, Division of Science Resource Studies, *Statistical Profiles of Foreign Doctoral Recipients in Science and Engineering: Plans to Stay in the United States*, November 1998, NSF 99-304, pp. 4–5; see also Jean M. Johnson and Mark C. Regets, "International Mobility of Scientists and Engineers to the United States – Brain Drain or Brain Circulation?," *National Science Foundation Issue Brief*, November 10, 1998 (revised).
68 www.wantchinatimes.com/news-subclass-cnt.aspx?id=20111127000017 &cid=1701.
69 National Center for Education Statistics, US Department of Education, "Degrees Earned by Foreign Graduate Students: Fields of Study and Plans after Graduation," November 1997, p. 2.
70 www.wantchinatimes.com/news-subclass-cnt.aspx?id=20111127000017 &cid=1701.
71 "Doctorate Recipients from US Universities: Summary Report 2007–08," Washington, DC: National Science Foundation, NSF 10-309, December 2009.
72 Interview with Veronica Jeffers, immigration attorney, December 6, 2002. Chinese students made use of the internet to share tips on successful strategies by setting up their own websites. Immigration attorneys also maintain websites which provide information on what is permissible under current law.
73 Ibid.
74 Work on the Human Genome Project or HIV-related research would fall into this category.
75 "Tips for US Visas: Foreign Students," US Department of State, Bureau of Consular Affairs. This information is posted on the US State Department website at: http://travel.state.gov/visa/foreignstuden.html.
76 Interviews, December 2002, Silicon Valley.
77 This statistic is from a book by Qian Ning (钱宁) on his impressions of life as a student in the United States entitled *Studying in America* (留学美国), excerpts of which are quoted in a February 1997 report from the US Embassy in Beijing, "Vice Premier Qian's Son Writes Book on the Experiences of Chinese Students in the United States," available at: www.usembassy-china.org.cn/english/sandt/webqiann.htm.
78 Although student visas for Great Britain, Australia, and Canada are somewhat easier to obtain, it is reportedly more difficult to move from student to employee status in those countries than it is in the United States.
79 David S. North, "Some Thoughts on Nonimmigrant Student and Worker Programs" in *Temporary Migrants in the United States*, ed. B. Lindsay Lowell, US Commission on Immigration Reform, 1996, p. 67. Available at: www.utexas.edu.lib/uscir/respapers/tm-96.pdf.
80 "Chinese Researchers in the US Who Receive Support from the NSF," *What's News*, June 30, 1989.
81 George Bush, "Memorandum of Disapproval for the Bill Providing Emergency Chinese Immigration Relief," November 30, 1989, http://bushlibrary.tamu.edu/papers/1989/89113002.html.
82 Ibid.
83 Norman Matloff, "A Fax On Both of Your Houses," summer 1993. This article is available at: www.uwsa.com/issues/imigratn/imig001.html.
84 Accurate figures for the numbers of non-immigrant visa holders in the US at any one time are difficult to obtain. Media reports quoted estimates of between 40,000 and 70,000 Chinese students in the country at the time. In his November 30, 1989 veto memo President Bush used the number 80,000 to refer to the cumulative number of Chinese students who had studied in the United States under student and scholar exchange programs up until 1989. This figure was subsequently picked up by

the media and others to reflect the number of students who would benefit from the amnesty. This number is clearly erroneous.

85 North, "Some Thoughts on Nonimmigrant Student and Worker Programs," p. 68.
86 For a survey of the views of Chinese students in the United States during this period of time, see David Zweig and Chen Changgui, *China's Brain Drain to the United States: Views of Overseas Chinese Students and Scholars in the 1990s*, University of California, Berkeley, 1995.
87 "Chinese Students Pursuing US Education," *Associated Press*, November 17, 2008.
88 Cited in Anna Lee Saxenian, *Local and Global Networks of Immigrant Professionals in Silicon Valley*, Public Policy Institute of California, April 2002. Includes information on how these figures were estimated.
89 See, for example, "Shandong Province Welcomes Returned Students," *Xinhua*, February 3, 2002.
90 人事部,教育部, 科技部, 公安部,财政部关于引发"关于鼓励海外留学人员以多种形式为国服务"的若干意见 (Ministry of Personnel, Ministry of Education, Ministry of Science and Technology, Ministry of Public Security, and Ministry of Finance Notice Regarding "Several Suggestions Concerning Encouraging Personnel Studying Overseas to Serve the Country in a Variety of Ways"), May 14, 2001, Ministry of Personnel Document No. 49. Posted on the website of the Ministry of Education, www.moe.edu.cn/guoji/chuguo/cgzhengce/01.htm. See, for example, "Students Coming Home to Serve," *China Daily*, December 9, 2002.
91 Among the many articles that report a "reverse brain drain" or "brain gain," some of the most illuminating put the issue in a comparative perspective, examining not only China, but also India and other countries. See, for example, Leslie Pappas, Monika Halan, and Daniel Heft, "Brain Gain," *The Industry Standard*, August 7, 2000.
92 See, for example, Ray Cheung, "Talented Workers Stream Overseas," *South China Morning Post*, July 29, 2002; and Ray Cheung, "Brain-Drain Fears Deepen as Graduates Join Foreign Exodus," *South China Morning Post*, April 2, 2002. According to an official Xinhua news service report cited in the latter article, for example, about 30 percent of Beijing University's 2001 graduating class left China to pursue graduate studies abroad.
93 Saxenian, *Local and Global Networks of Immigrant Professionals in Silicon Valley*.
94 "Several Suggestions Concerning Encouraging Personnel Studying Overseas to Serve the Country in a Variety of Ways."
95 http://articles.latimes.com/2009/feb/24/business/fi-china24.
96 "Students Coming Home to Serve," *China Daily*, December 9, 2002.
97 "82% of world's top 500 in China found trade unions," *People's Daily*, October 13, 2008, http://english.people.com.cn/90001/90776/90882/6514202.html.
98 Interview with Hong Chen, Silicon Valley, December 2002.
99 "China lures back overseas talent to help steer national development," *Want China Times*, November 27, 2011, www.wantchinatimes.com/news-subclass-cnt.aspx?id=20111127000017&cid=1701.
100 This makes for a rather crowded bureaucratic landscape and complicates analysis of the policies.
101 "New Policies to be Issued to Lure Overseas Students Home," *People's Daily*, July 29, 2000.
102 "China Allotted 200 Million Yuan for Students Returned from Overseas," *People's Daily*, January 22, 2002. The funds have been awarded to 4,000 students who returned to China permanently and 3,000 who came back on a short-term basis.
103 Jasper Becker, "Research Revamp Aids IT Catch-Up," *South China Morning Post*, January 11, 2002.
104 Han Rongliang, "China Opens a Wider Sphere for Returned Students from Overseas to Make Careers," *People's Daily*, February 4, 2002.
105 "Returned Overseas Chinese, Relatives Encouraged to Develop High-Tech Industries," *Chinese Education and Research Network News*, April 2001.

106 Liu Wanyong, "PRC Simplifies Procedures for Returned Students to Work in China," *Zhongguo Qingnian Bao (China Youth Daily)*, March 1, 2002, in FBIS, March 1, 2002.

107 中国留学人材信息网--回国指南 (Chinese Study Abroad Talent Information Network – Return to China Guide), www.chinatalents.gov.cn/hgzn/index02.htm.

108 "Western China: Where Returned Students Become Successful Businessmen," *People's Daily*, July 5, 2001. According to this article, "Many students returning from overseas universities have become successful business people in western China and their high-tech businesses are prosperous."

109 For example, Chinese personnel who need to enter China multiple times on a temporary basis are eligible to receive multiple-entry "F" visas that remain effective for up to five years, and those who will reside in China are eligible for foreign resident permits that remain valid for up to five years along with multiple-entry and exit "Z" visas.

110 "Several Suggestions Concerning Encouraging Personnel Studying Overseas."

111 "China Acts to Attract Returned Students," *Xinhua*, September 4, 2001.

112 "Liaoning Recruits Government Officials among Returned Students," *People's Daily*, July 8, 2001.

113 Clara Li, "Shenzhen Looks Abroad for Talent," *South China Morning Post*, December 17, 2001. The article cites a *Shenzhen Economic Daily* report that officials were seeking overseas candidates for positions in the Shenzhen High-tech Industrial Zone Executive Office and the Shenzhen Information Technology Office.

114 Quoted in Cheung, "Brain-Drain Fears Deepen as Graduates Join Foreign Exodus."

115 "Several Suggestions Concerning Encouraging Personnel Studying Overseas."

116 Ibid.

117 The information on these incentive programs is drawn from the website of the Education Division of the Chinese Consulate in San Francisco (the information is only available in Chinese): http://sf.chinaconsulatesf.org/Education/0815/p8-ch-7.htm.

118 The program description notes that it is intended primarily for students who have received a doctorate and have an outstanding record of academic achievement in their fields.

119 "China lures back overseas talent to help steer national development," *Want China Times*.

120 Ibid.

121 Ibid.

122 Ibid.

123 Louisa Lim, "Plagiarism Plague Hinders China's Scientific Ambition," *National Public Radio*, August 3, 2011: www.npr.org/2011/08/03/138937778/plagiarism-plague-hinders-chinas-scientific-ambition.

124 See "China: Journals Urge Use of Overseas Scientists for Technology Transfer," FBIS Report, December 6, 2001, which cites articles from *Keyan Guanli*, a journal of the Chinese Academy of Sciences, and *Keji Guanli Yanjiu*, a science and technology policy journal published by the Guangdong provincial government.

125 The official is quoted in Vernon Loeb, "Espionage Stir Alienating Foreign Scientists in US," *Washington Post*, November 25, 1999.

126 See Nicholas Eftimiades, *Chinese Intelligence Operations*, Annapolis, MD: Naval Institute Press, 1994, pp. 61–65.

127 Ibid., esp. pp. 27–32.

7

BRINGING TECHNOLOGY "BACK" TO CHINA

Sending students abroad provided no guarantee that China would benefit from their skills. As discussed in the previous chapter, most Chinese who studied abroad – the overseas Chinese scholars or OCS (留学人员) – did not return. Those who did return faced sparse technical and financial resources, were cut off from their international peers, or had difficulty reintegrating into Chinese society. Promises made to returnees evaporated locally, where the foreign-educated experts ran into the age-old problems of bureaucracy, discrimination, lax standards, and a culture hostile to innovation.

By the same token, there is ample evidence that expectations were frustrated at both ends. Chinese scientists willing to return to these sub-par conditions were not always of the caliber sought by Beijing. Thus while PRC ministries and outreach organizations continued appealing to overseas scholars to return and "render service to the fatherland," a counter-current of caveats, requirements, and calls for specific skill sets may also be seen in the policy declarations of these same organizations. Meanwhile, China promoted an alternative strategy of "serving in place" that allows Chinese scholars to stay abroad and transfer foreign technology remotely and continuously – a fee-for-service approach that reduces the exposure of both parties.

A final step to ensure foreign technology flows to China was the creation of more than 150 "OCS pioneering parks" (留学人员创业园) in the hearts of 54 "National New and High Technology Development Zones" (国家高新技术开发区). These ultra-modern facilities were designed for returning specialists to "incubate" (find commercial or military applications for) technologies acquired overseas and to support short-term visits by Chinese employed in high-tech sectors abroad, including labs funded with foreign tax money. These returnee parks are home to some 8,000 companies founded entirely on technologies created abroad.

Policy support for OCS recruitment

China has relied on overseas scholars to transfer foreign technology for over a century. While Japan and Russia at times were the preferred venues, the United States is first choice for Chinese students today. According to a study posted by the University of Southern California, 229,300 Chinese students went abroad in 2009 to 2010, 128,000 of whom came to the US. That number is growing, absolutely and relative to the number of foreign students in America.[1] Although the ratio of students returning to China is rising, this is less of an issue to Chinese policy-makers than before, since the PRC is now able to exploit OCS who remain abroad, go back to China, or return "for short periods."

Our task here is to show how China positioned itself to use OCS "talent" more fully to obtain and transfer foreign technology. In the previous chapter we listed factors responsible for the large number of Chinese students abroad, and gave specifics on the subjects studied, state incentives, motivation, career choices, and counter-intelligence implications for host countries. In this chapter we offer an insider's view of the role that China's diaspora scholars – PRC students abroad and co-opted participants born outside China – play in the transfer process, as seen through PRC ministry sources and Chinese academic studies.

A key document defining Beijing's goals vis-à-vis overseas Chinese scholars is Ministry of Personnel (MOP) No. 75, "Plan for Working with Overseas Scholars in the Personnel System during the Ninth Five-Year Plan" ("九五"期间人事系统留学人员工作规划), released in 1996. This document – the foundation for China's current approach to OCS management – begins by acknowledging the mission's importance:

> Working with overseas Chinese scholars is an important component of China's reform and development. Overseas scholars are a precious source of human talent. Completing this work with overseas scholars is an important task for our country's total development and use of talent resources.

The document notes that from 1977 to 1995 China sent a quarter of a million students abroad, 170,000 of whom failed to return. Both groups – the returnees and those still overseas – are important resources, given their "grasp of the world's advanced science and technology." Accordingly, the document goes on, China enacted a series of regulations guiding efforts to attract OCS back to China, who made outstanding contributions on all "battlefronts." Their numbers along with those still abroad "serving China by multiple means" keep increasing.

These successes aside, the "tasks ahead are still formidable." China must "build a scientific system[2] for working with overseas Chinese scholars consistent with our socialist market economy," nurture a collection of overseas scholars of all types who understand the world's advanced sciences and technologies, form a "cadre of people to work with them" (留学人员工作队伍) and encourage them to serve China by multiple means. In particular, we must:

Perfect the system for working with overseas scholars and associated policies, laws, and regulations; train a cadre of cross-century overseas scholars; build an information market for their intellectual skills; support the creation and development of high-tech entrepreneurial parks for their use; support the creation and development of multi-channel, capital-intensive funding for their activities; and support and guide developmental activities of overseas scholar associations and academic organizations.

In plain terms, the PRC government is announcing its creation of a comprehensive technology transfer program based on overseas Chinese experts – those living abroad and those who return permanently or periodically – to include a dedicated corps of S&T transfer specialists distinct from the technical experts themselves, whose task is to identify overseas experts and find use for whatever information they have. The MOP plan goes on to outline specific tasks within these categories, highlights of which include:

- To create an operational system (工作制度) for scholars abroad to serve China by multiple means. Understand and get a grasp on the circumstances of top notch Chinese scholars abroad and adopt measures to encourage and draw them into serving China by returning for short periods to lecture, cooperate, and develop technological and intellectual exchanges.
- To create a system for exchanging at regular intervals information with China's embassies and consulates abroad on operations with OCS.
- To release information at regular intervals on supply of and demand for overseas scholars' intellectual skills at home and abroad. This information needs to be systematized and online nationwide by 2000.

"Bases" (基地) will be offered to returning Chinese scholars for R&D work, productization, and business investment. These entrepreneurial parks (described later in this chapter) will be used "to introduce knowledge they acquire abroad, the technologies they master, and their accumulated experience and research results."

Beyond laying the groundwork for transferring overseas Chinese "talent" – and confirming what we noted earlier about the role played by Chinese diplomatic missions abroad in this process – the MOP document lays to rest any notion the outside world may have had about the independence of China's overseas support groups, such as the foreign-based S&T advocacy groups discussed in Chapter 5, and Chinese student associations treated in Chapter 6. Specifically, the plan calls for:

- Creating multiple types of overseas scholar friendship associations and academic groups as a means of organizing their academic and technical exchange activities.
- Increasing contact with overseas scholar and student associations abroad and "endeavoring to broaden their channels of contact with the fatherland."
- Making these friendship associations into "a bridge and bond that links overseas scholars to the [PRC] government and all aspects of society."

The document cautions that exploiting foreign-trained talent is a long-term strategic task. Ministry departments on all levels must fully understand the importance of this work, use the advantages their offices provide, and work systematically to make the project a success. Reiterating a point made earlier about the need for specialized handlers, the document calls for a cadre of "overseas study management personnel" (留学管理人员) trained in S&T, law, computers, and foreign languages to interact with overseas scholars.

Five years after MOP 75's release, a remarkably prescient article appeared in the July 2001 issue of a leading Chinese science policy journal summarizing efforts made by the MOP and other ministries to harness foreign technologies acquired by diaspora Chinese and proposing additional steps needed to take full advantage of ethnic scholars abroad.[3] Entitled "Current Situation and Measures to Develop and Utilize Overseas Chinese Talent Resources," authors Liu Yun and Shen Lin base their study on the following premise:

> Although overseas Chinese scholars and ethnic Chinese specialists are living abroad, their hearts belong to their families and country. They are concerned constantly with the development of their ancestral country . . . and are willing to use what they learned in the service of China. . . . How to more effectively develop and utilize this precious intellectual resource and encourage them to contribute to China's scientific development and economic construction by various means will affect whether China can play an active strategic role in the fierce international competition.[4]

Liu and Shen spend several pages describing work done by China's ministries of Personnel, Education, Science and Technology, the Chinese Academy of Sciences, the Natural Science Foundation of China, and the State Administration of Foreign Experts Affairs in locating overseas Chinese talent and channeling it to China's service. Notwithstanding these efforts, they argue, the following problems remain:

1. The increased mobility of overseas scholars has made it difficult for the PRC government to keep track and make use of them.
2. The various government departments are tripping over each other in their individual efforts to attract overseas scholars. There is insufficient coordination.
3. Financial inducements to return for long- and short-term work are inadequate. Some programs are limited to PRC citizens abroad and "are not useful for attracting the larger range of foreign scholars of Chinese ethnicity" (华裔华人学者).
4. Not enough effort is being made to meet the individual needs of those recruited. More multifaceted (多元化) approaches are necessary.
5. Most attention is paid to ethnic Chinese overseas scholars in universities and research institutes with insufficient efforts directed at Chinese personnel in foreign companies.
6. Policy, organizational, and administrative mechanisms need improvement.[5]

Liu and Shen's proposed solutions to these problems were all, in one form or another, put into practice. Accordingly, we believe the article's purpose was to convey state decisions already taken and to build a consensus for their implementation, while avoiding embarrassment to the government over the aggressive nature of the proposals.[6] Their recommendations merit a detailed accounting.

The article urges that an "OCS data center" be established to share overseas talent more fully and that "intermediate service and information networks" be strengthened. Databases supporting these networks will host information on overseas Chinese experts provided by the education and science offices of China's foreign embassies and consulates, NGOs abroad (presumably front organizations like CAIEP and COEA), and the "broad connections of overseas Chinese S&T organizations" (the foreign S&T advocacy groups described in Chapter 5). Intermediary organizations "run by civilians with help from the government" (民办政助) should be set up in areas of high-ethnic Chinese concentration overseas as a bridge for domestic recruitment.[7]

Using the martial metaphors characteristic of official prose, the article advocates building an "overseas S&T corps" (海外科技兵团) that unites expatriate Chinese scientists and engineers within a broad network. There are limits to what can be done with 140,000 OCS in the United States relying solely on existing overseas organizations. We need "something on the order of a Chinese S&T development overseas advisory committee (咨询委员会) established in the important advanced countries" and provided with fixed support by the Chinese government. The advisory committee will control different "expert committees" (专业委员会) staffed by exemplary overseas scholars, whose responsibility will be to "contact and organize ethnic Chinese experts and scholars" and invite them to contribute to China's S&T enterprise by "enacting S&T plans, giving advice and evaluation, and at the same time promoting China's foreign S&T cooperation and exchange."[8]

Meanwhile, China should make full use of the overseas Chinese S&T organizations and set up multi-regional overseas expert advisory committees. The overseas groups will support "discussion forums" in China for foreign experts to share information on the latest science and technology; deliver reports on "special topics" to relevant organizations in China; offer background information for talks between the Chinese government and foreign entities on S&T cooperation and exchange; conduct liaison between the PRC and foreign governments, universities, companies, and research institutes; "help China introduce technology"; give advice and counsel on important national S&T projects; evaluate Chinese state S&T projects; "arrange for direct exchanges between overseas experts and their counterpart units in China"; and "invite responsible persons from influential foreign science and technology organizations back to China for exchange visits, lectures, consultations, and participation through suitable means in S&T cooperation with their counterpart units."[9]

The article advocates nothing less than PRC state control and manipulation of foreign-based ethnic Chinese scientists; or to put a neutral spin on it, the merger of the PRC and diaspora Chinese S&T expert communities in support of China's development. Proposals made here expand the 1996 MOP plan, while plugging gaps that surfaced during its implementation. Other passages in the article are simply mind-boggling – or would be had they not played out in practice.

For example, on page 123 we learn that China must expand its financial subsidies (资助) to OCS to "rapidly transfer overseas research work to China or bring back [*sic*] to China important technological inventions and patents already completed for commercialization." By the same token:

> When conditions permit, we can identify certain fields critical for China's development and set up R&D facilities abroad to subsidize by means of planned projects the research of top overseas scholars and the reversion (归属) of their research results to China.

Recognizing that it is not always advantageous or possible to persuade OCS to return to China, Liu and Shen argue the need to create more channels for ethnic Chinese experts abroad to "serve the fatherland." Domestic PRC companies should be encouraged to establish R&D facilities and subsidiaries abroad to "induce overseas Chinese scholars and ethnic Chinese specialists to join the alliance" (加盟). China must also "use the 'two bases' formula to promote an organic synthesis between the work of overseas scholars and R&D work done in China."[10] In lay terms, this means that "research" in China should be informed wholly or in part by parallel projects run in foreign laboratories, whose results are passed to China, cost-free, by diaspora scholars working the foreign project.

This "two bases" approach to Chinese tech transfer is treated in detail later. Meanwhile, we conclude our presentation of the Liu and Shen piece, as do they, with an admonition that needs no interpretation on our part:

> To protect the personal interests of overseas persons of talent, China should adopt a "do more, talk less" (多做少说) or "do it but don't talk about it" (只做不说) policy on recruitment and foreign S&T cooperation, especially in sensitive fields, and avoid by all means propagandizing on a large scale in domestic and foreign newspaper reports successes in our cooperation and recruitment, to avoid making them vulnerable (授人以柄) and putting these overseas persons of talent in an embarrassing situation.[11]

Tweaking the OCS strategy

In February 2003, shortly after these proposals were aired, a report was issued by the PRC ministries of Personnel, Education, Science and Technology, Finance, Foreign Affairs, Public Security, Foreign Trade and Cooperation, the State Planning Commission, State Economic and Trade Commission, Bank of China, Chinese Academy of Sciences, and State Administration of Foreign Experts Affairs announcing the establishment under MOP auspices of a "Joint Working Committee for OCS to Return and Serve the Country" (留学人员回国服务工作部际联

席会议)[12] to "study and implement the Party's and State Council's policies" on the utilization of OCS. The group was mandated to convene semi-annually to examine new circumstances and issues pertaining to OCS; discuss measures for linking up with them; report on their situation; and propose means to carry out relevant work. Addressing Liu and Shen's second point (above), each member organization was required to work within its own area of responsibility.

Then, in 2006, on the tenth anniversary of its 1996 edict, the MOP issued a second major directive entitled "Notice on Printing and Promulgating the Eleventh Five-Year Plan Regulations on Working for the Return of OCS" (关于印发留学人员回国工作 "十一五" 规划的通知) that expanded the scope of the project still further. The document began by pointing out that due to the pace of worldwide technology development, China's efforts to utilize diaspora experts were *still* inadequate. Accordingly, the ministry promised:

> We will unceasingly build new mechanisms for OCS to render service to China, encourage them and their groups to return and build bases from which to serve China, and support their linking up with special development projects needed in key domestic regions and industries.

The document called for the number of OCS parks at all levels throughout the country to reach 150 over the next five years (the goal was overachieved), 40 or 50 of which would be built by the MOP jointly with local governments, to host up to 10,000 returnees (they doubled their quota). At the same time, China would aim for 200,000 person-instances of OCS rendering service to China by a variety of appropriate means "without asking where they are, only that they be useful" (不求所在但求所用). OCS personnel and groups would be drawn from broader categories, wider regions, and higher levels to act as a bridge and conveyor belt (桥梁和纽带) to foreign technology by means such as "dual appointments, cooperative research, returning to lecture, carrying out academic and technological exchanges, consultant activities and on-the-spot investigations, and intermediary services." The document also stipulated a system of "fixed period exchanges" and stepping up "macro guidance" for short-term returnees.

The MOP vowed to make full use of OCS organizations and social bodies within China and abroad to positively affect these cooperative outcomes, share resources and cooperative services, expand OCS information networks and databases, "build an integrated nationwide talented overseas persons information system," and continuously create service projects that match the needs and special characteristics of the OCS, mediated by consulting hotlines (咨询热线), networking platforms, instruction manuals, and media dissemination.

Importantly, the document also called for attention to the quality of information and skills brought "back" by co-optees. New emphasis would be placed on attracting high-level OCS as the "cornerstone for building an innovative country" and to allow China to "leap over" stages other countries went through in their development. Dubbed the "Green Channel" (绿色通道), the new policy called for "fewer but better" and for "flexible and diversified" means of inducing OCS support.

Ministry-level edicts from about 2005 on stressed this new goal of seeking top-level overseas scholars. Whereas the earlier mission had been merely to catch up with worldwide scientific developments, the newer strategy called for surpassing other countries in key S&T sectors by recruiting world-class talent. For example, a 2005 MOP policy notice promised preferential arrangements (从优安排) to overseas scientists with "exceptional expertise in areas where China badly needs support."[13] The Ministry offered a schedule of salaries based on academic background and performance, with additional compensation for those with critical skills.

Another document issued by the MOP that same year raised the bar for OCS targeted via the Green Channel, seeking only:

- scientists known for contributions they have made as innovators in their fields;
- academics at famous universities who have attained the rank of associate professor or higher;
- high-level managers at Fortune 500 companies, famous MNCs, or financial institutes;
- managers at mid- or top-level positions in foreign governments or famous NGOs;
- experts and academics who have made important contributions to their specialties or fields, published influential articles in famous journals or received awards of international scope, whose accomplishments are at the forefront of their fields;
- experts, scholars, and technical persons who have led large, international scale R&D or engineering projects and have rich experience in scientific research and engineering technology;
- people who have important technological inventions and patents or specialized technology;
- talented persons who possess a particular specialized skill urgently needed by China.[14]

This same definition of "high-level OCS" appeared in a document issued subsequently by MOP and 15 other members of the Joint Working Committee on March 29, 2007, indicating its acceptance as state policy.[15] The importance of top-level OCS in China's scheme for development was captured in a scripted "question-and-answer" session appended to the joint announcement, which noted that an astonishing 81 percent of the Science Academy members had studied abroad, *as had 21 of the 23 people* awarded for their work on China's "atomic bomb, ballistic missile and earth satellite" (两弹一星) projects. Almost the entire upper echelon of scientists responsible for China's strategic weapons programs learned their skills abroad.

A final notice released by the PRC Ministry of Education also in 2007, titled "Opinions on Further Strengthening Our Work to Bring in Outstanding Overseas-educated Talent Abroad," rounds out our understanding of the breadth of

China's effort to manipulate overseas scholars and the extent to which these efforts permeate (or spawn) diaspora scholarly organizations.[16] According to the document, the MOE issues information on China's needs for particular skills through "multiple formats and channels," including "overseas embassies and consulates, the Chinese Service Center for Scholarly Exchange,[17] the China Scholarship Council,[18] Chinese Scholars Abroad,[19] and other organizations." The ministry also sponsors "online exchanges" and "two-way interactive chat rooms" to promote ties between domestic employers and OCS.

In the 2007 document, the MOE promised to strengthen leadership over OCS organizations abroad, make full use of the "bridging effect" with these OCS bodies, and offer "information on demand" to PRC employers obtained from the overseas advocacy groups. The ministry would also "perfect the system for managing OCS information used by the education offices at Chinese embassies and consulates abroad," build a database of skilled OCS assessed as candidates for support (what intelligence services would call "developmentals"), and make recommendations for recruiting leading OCS who work in areas of urgent demand (i.e., targeting leads). We are reminded in the document that China's education attaches "vigorously provide information and other support to PRC employers with particular needs."[20]

The ministry signaled its intent to move beyond reactive talent spotting and to try to forecast demand for OCS skills by canvassing the needs of "all categories of domestic work units." It now advertises this information to the overseas talent pool through web-based portals and "trade talk working groups" (洽谈工作团组) made up of HR personnel from PRC companies, who travel to countries where OCS are concentrated to negotiate their return. Like MOP and the Ministry of Science, MOE sponsors face-to-face technology exchanges, returnee subsidy programs, OCS innovation parks for diaspora experts who "have in hand contemporary S&T achievements,"[21] and to that extent sheds much of the innocence one is predisposed to grant the coordinator of China's academic programs.

Contributing to China from "two bases"

Besides encouraging OCS to return, China also seeks diaspora Chinese willing to "serve in place," i.e., service China's technology needs while living abroad. Born of the fact that most Chinese who study abroad do not return, the rationale for pursuing this "two bases" (两个基地) option has long since changed from making the most of a bad situation to a goal pursued cynically in its own right. Get past the metaphors and into specifics, and there is little to distinguish the policy from state-supported espionage.

"Two bases" simply means being abroad all or most of the time doing research at a host country facility and passing on the knowledge one obtains – in the form of know-how, data, or physical samples – to China, either gratis or in exchange for compensation. The Chinese literature dealing with this subject does not dwell on subtleties that host countries obsess over such as whether the technology is owned by the OCS researcher or is merely accessible.

Rather, the focus of the two bases documents we have examined is on transfer venues and their sustainability – how to get the information "back" to China and how to keep it coming back. While the formula has a benign aspect – students "gradually transfer the core of their overseas research work to China and ultimately effect a 'soft landing' to return and serve China" – its usual expression, as Liu and Shen describe it,

> means having one end abroad and the other end in China, providing a more stable "foothold" in China and foundation for cooperative research, so that the service rendered by overseas scholars to China can develop in a "deeply layered, sustainable, easily managed, and effective" direction.[22]

The origin of the two bases policy can be traced to China's National Natural Science Foundation, which from August 1992 "had in effect specialized funding programs aimed at subsidizing the return of OCS to China for short periods of time to work and lecture."[23] These programs were seen as "enormously successful." A decade later NNSF was still promoting the technique, resolving to "continuously improve and develop the two bases formula." By raising subsidies and through "spirited organization and guidance" the foundation hoped more OCS would "tighten the connections between the work they do abroad and in China, and link up with important domestic research projects."[24]

Two years after NNSF had codified the concept, China's MOP in 1994 issued a document that expanded the idea beyond "two bases" and science to "returning for short periods" and to China's development in general. Entitled "MOP Notice on 'Implementing Temporary Measures for Subsidizing Overseas Chinese Scholars to Return to China for Short Periods to Work in Areas Outside the Educational System'" (关于下发《资助留学人员短期回国到非教育系统工作暂行办法》的通知), the measure promised subsidies to OCS volunteers who have:

- outstanding academic achievements, received an influential award in the natural or social sciences, or published a high-level academic paper in an influential journal;
- important inventions or received a patent;
- access to advanced technology urgently needed by China and who intend to return and carry out cooperative research or developmental exchanges.

Returning for short periods entails having a regular job at a second, overseas "base." The MOP further defined eligibility as a willingness to:

- tackle key problems in scientific research at the state, committee, provincial, or municipal level;
- help work units in China solve critically important R&D issues;
- return for cooperative research, lecturing, training, project development, technology transfer, and technology exchange;

- participate in and give specialized reports at important international conferences held in China or important nationwide academic conferences;
- engage in other academic and technological exchange activities recognized by the MOP.

Interested OCS were encouraged to apply to the MOP through a sponsoring organization in China, or work through the education office in a Chinese embassy or consulate abroad. Alternatively, a company in China with a technological problem could apply to the MOP, which "will work through the education office and other offices in Chinese embassies and consulates overseas to contact the needed personnel." It is hard to find a clearer statement than this about the role of China's overseas diplomatic corps in brokering informal tech transfers.

A closer look at how the system operates in practice is provided by Japanese researcher Endo Homare, who has had privileged access to the inner workings of China's tech transfer organizations. Endo described a gathering in Xi'an of "short-term" OCS visitors, who were hosted by the municipal S&T committee. The session began with a speech by the organizer flattering the guests, who responded by describing in detail the technologies and patents they brought "back" and in what forms they could be made available. The committee then listed the city's own needs, whereupon both sides delved more deeply into specifics. Endo noted that the technologies were medical and biological but he was reluctant to describe them, because "although not exactly secret" they were negotiated "deep inside China's interior."[25]

By the turn of the century "two bases" had broadened into "serve the country by multiple means" (以多种形式为国服务). The new, extended formula was defined in a communiqué issued jointly by the ministries of Personnel, Education, Science and Technology, Public Security, and Finance in 2001 entitled "Circular on the Release of Opinions on Encouraging Overseas Chinese Scholars to Serve the Country by Multiple Means" (关于印发关于鼓励海外留学人员以多种形式为国服务的若干意见的通知) as:

> Chinese studying or working in foreign countries and their professional teams shall carry out various activities for the purpose of promoting the social and economic development of China through holding concurrent posts in China, conducting cooperative research at home or abroad *as assigned by domestic entities*, returning to lecture, carrying out academic and technology exchanges, founding businesses in China, doing consultancy work, on-site evaluations, and performing intermediary services [emphasis added].

Examples given of venues were "holding concurrent and honorary posts, or working as consultants in PRC universities, research institutes, state key laboratories and engineering centers, companies and non-industrial organizations." More to the point:

> Overseas Chinese scholars are encouraged to cooperate in research with domestic universities, colleges, scientific research institutes, and industrial enterprises by taking advantage of advanced technologies, facilities and financial support in the countries where they are located. . . . Research may be done in foreign countries and then shifted back home for a short or long term. OCS are encouraged to establish R&D bases at home and abroad through cooperation with domestic organizations.

Compensation for services to the fatherland was also addressed: "The government offers financial support to OCS for introducing world class and internationally competitive cooperative R&D projects." In addition, "OCS engaged in national priority research projects or returning home for short periods to render service will have their expenses paid by the national or local government and employing unit." The document also encourages them "to transfer the results of their scientific research" at Pioneering Parks for Overseas Chinese Scholars (海外留学人员创业园), which we discuss below.

A MOP spokesperson provided more specific points at the scripted "public" session that typically follows these ministry announcements:

> "Joint positions" include higher education, R&D labs, state key labs, engineering technology research centers as well as various kinds of jointly held company and business, advisory, and honorary posts. "Cooperative research" can be done in schools, research labs or companies or involve setting up cooperative R&D bases in China or abroad. "Commissioned research" involves China commissioning OCS to do R&D abroad.
>
> OCS can convert intellectual property or scientific research results into products or businesses in China, or use the technical skills and information [obtained while abroad] to set up specialized consultancy companies. They can also help train PRC specialists; perform intermediary services that bring capital, technology and projects to China; and build relationships between Chinese and foreign academic and technical organizations.

They can do all this without leaving their host country or by traveling to China for short periods only. The spokesperson continued, "Of course, rendering service to China is not limited to the above-mentioned methods. We encourage OCS in practice to create other appropriate methods to better serve China." The session ended with a reminder that China's policy is to "borrow knowledge" (借智) and "borrow brains" (借脑), so please oblige us.

Science towns and OCS parks

In 1994, the same year in which MOP adopted the "two bases" formula, China established its first dedicated returnee park – the Jinling Overseas Chinese Scholar S&T Park (金陵海外学子科技园) – in Nanjing, a joint venture of the city's office of personnel and the "Nanjing New and High Technology Industry Development Zone." The Jinling OCS Park, the method by which it was established, and its location at the center of one of China's designated zones for "indigenous" high-tech development became a model repeated more than 150 times as China created a national S&T infrastructure based largely on information provided by overseas returnees. We know of no other country with a structure that is remotely similar.

In this section we discuss the legislative basis for these returnee centers and in the subsequent section provide examples of their organization, layout, and functioning. Our first task, however, is to make sense of the confusing layers of administration that link OCS parks with the facilities hosting them. The largest of these super-ordinate organizations in which the OCS parks are embedded are the "National New and High Technology Development Zones" (国家高新技术开发区), which are distributed among all the major Chinese cities (some cities have two or more such science towns, 科学城). There are also at least 130 national-level "Innovation Service Centers for New and High Technology" (高新技术创业服务中心), to productize technology brought "back" by returnees or acquired by other means (see box below).

As the importance of returnees in China's development scheme grew, the taxonomy distinguishing these units began to break down. "Pioneering Parks for Overseas Chinese Scholars" (海外留学人员创业园) were originally created *within* innovation service centers, or within the New and High-tech Development Zones directly (which hosted the service centers), but in time they became coterminous with either or both superordinate bodies. For example, the website for the Guangzhou Innovation Service Center sports a second masthead today for the OCS Park (留学人员广州创业园) – the two are one organization.[26] In Wuxi one nameplate carries both the Innovation Service Center's and OCS Park's logos,[27] and so on through most of the 150 or so cases we studied. Examples with three logos are not uncommon.

The following is typical: Jiading National OCS Pioneering Park (国家留学人员嘉定创业园), also called Shanghai Jiading OCS Pioneering Park (上海嘉定留学人员创业园), was set up in 1996 within the Shanghai Jiading High-tech Park District (上海嘉定高科技园区).[28] The latter began life in 1994 as one of six sectors in the Shanghai Zhangjiang Hi-tech Park Zone (上海张江高科技园区). That, in turn, is one of China's science towns, established in July 1992 in the central area of Shanghai's Pudong District.

According to a description on the OCS Park Alliance website, Jiading was one of the first national OCS parks ordained by MOST, MOP, and MOE, and "uses the two labels–one set of teams formula (两块牌子--套班子) for managing the commercialization of enterprises," i.e., the OCS Park and Jiading Hi-tech Park operations are integrated, and may even be the same thing.[29] This is the norm for returnee parks today and speaks volumes about their importance in China's S&T development. The association of the OCS Park with the science town itself is also acknowledged on the Jiading website: "Thanks to the cumulative effect of the national science town's and OCS park's two trademarks, the park area has become an important vehicle for guiding companies' autonomous innovation and bringing the incubator function into play."[30] In other words, returnees support the science town's "innovation."

INNOVATION SERVICE CENTERS FOR NEW AND HIGH TECHNOLOGY (高新技术创业服务中心)

China began planning business incubators (企业孵化器)[31] in the mid-1980s as part of its Torch Program (火炬计划), approved by the Central Committee and State Council in August 1988. The first example of an "S&T innovation service center" – the name for a major class of "incubator" – appeared in Wuhan in 1987.[32] Hence they pre-date high-tech zones and OCS parks by one and seven years, respectively, although it has become a distinction without a difference. By 2001, there were 250 incubators operating in China hosting 7,693 enterprises. MOST predicted that 1,000 of them would exist by 2005.[33]

In December 2006, MOST provided the legal basis for certifying locally financed incubators as national enterprises in a document entitled "Means for Accrediting and Managing S&T Commercial Incubators (Innovation Service Centers for New and High Technology)."[34] The purpose of the "innovation" centers was defined up front as "converting S&T achievements," which would seem contradictory in a non-Chinese context. The remainder of the document laid out the requirements for national accreditation, which entitles occupants to a broad range of policy and financial incentives. In particular, the centers:

> support small and medium-sized tech companies by providing a location and shared facilities for research and development, trial production, operation and management along with policy, legal, fiscal, financing, market promotion and training services to lower innovation risk and capital, and raise survivability and success rates.

Underscoring our point about the interconnectedness of China's tech transfer facilities, MOST requires that companies "under incubation make full use of opportunities for research, experimentation, measurement and production available through nearby R&D institutes, universities, companies and enterprise service mechanisms."[35] Today nearly all National Innovation Service Centers are co-located with – or identical to – an OCS Pioneering Park.[36]

In 2001 about 10 percent of the OCS parks were co-designated "incubators" and that percentage rose over the years. The relevant point, however, is not what a unit nominally does (their goals and starting points are shared in any case) but whether one or more ministries subsidize a facility by accrediting it, for example, as a "national-level OCS park." Bearing in mind their overlapping functions and the impossibility of distinguishing these organizations in any practical sense, let us look at the documents that supported the creation of China's science towns and the OCS parks within them.

On March 6, 1991 China's State Council issued a "Circular on the Approval of National Development Zones for New and High Technology Industries and the Relevant Policies and Provisions" (国务院关于批准国家高新技术产业开发区和有关政策规定的通知), which along with a co-published Annex recognized 26 development zones that had been operating locally since 1988. Thus were born China's "science towns." The zones were to be managed jointly by the city or province where they were located and by the Science Ministry, which defined their physical boundaries. In 1992, 25 zones were added, the total eventually stabilizing at 54.[37]

The Circular also defined some 11 technical disciplines, corresponding to areas targeted for development in the Five-year Plan, as within the zones' purview. The science towns, from their outset, were not built to *create* new technologies but "to accelerate the commercialization and industrialization of achievements in high technology" – an entirely different mission that depends on access to outside "talent" and the ideas of others. While administration of the zones was to be a government function, the Circular was clear about who ran them, namely:

> The persons in charge of the enterprises shall be the scientists who are familiar with the research, development, production and sale of the products in their enterprises, and shall be the full time personnel of the enterprises.[38]

Documents issued jointly by the Central Committee and State Council in 1999,[39] and by MOST in 1999[40] and in 2002,[41] continued to push the basic theme of using the science towns to "transform high and new technology achievements," as opposed to accomplishing the achievement. "Innovation" was consistently understood in the narrower sense of adapting breakthroughs done elsewhere to products that directly supported China's industrialization and international competitiveness. Experimenting "for its own sake" was discouraged in favor of a "practical and realistic" approach that adapted ideas brought in from abroad.[42]

The adapting could be done in China's science towns, or it could be done through Chinese proxies overseas. According to a third MOST document on high-tech zones issued in 2002,

> The role of China's science and technology institutions in foreign countries shall be brought into full play to help the enterprises in the National New and High-tech Zones introduce the advanced technologies from abroad, which shall be assimilated and innovated.[43]

Indicative of the Science Ministry's thinking is a cogently argued study entitled "Leading Innovation and Imitative Innovation" that appeared in a PRC S&T policy journal in 2001.[44] The article bears citing because it describes so well the direction Chinese science followed as recently as a decade ago and even today. According to its authors, there are two types of innovation: "leading innovation" (率先创新) and "imitative innovation" (模仿创新). People ignore the latter, when in fact it is a key element in expanding the economy. Whereas leading innovation, where fruitful, may improve a company's finances, its effect on the country as a whole, they argue, is "infinitesimally small" (微于其微).[45]

The authors give compelling reasons for China to concentrate its resources on imitative innovation – the argument itself being an adaptation of the "early adopter" theory that posits success not to the innovator but to the first user. Risk is minimized. It is easier to make practical products. Return on investment is faster. It is more suitable to later developing countries (such as China), which typically are weaker in human capital, have an inadequate technology base, and "lack an ability to create things themselves" (自创能力差). Since no one copies a bad innovation, the technical level of society as a whole is raised.[46]

Although imitation risks IPR violations, the article claims that this is not a necessary outcome with a proper legal framework and correct assessment of the trade-offs inherent in buying and licensing. One obvious problem with imitation as a strategy, the authors note, is that the owners of new technology may not want it "diffused" (扩散). But that problem can be overcome by focusing not on the "monopoly protection characteristics" of technology but on its open and transferable aspects along with opportunities for "forced transfer" (强制转让).[47] Taking this into account, the emphasis on creativity is misplaced. China "should not blindly pursue leading innovation." Doing so is a waste of resources and opportunities.[48]

The Science Ministry, meanwhile, has continued to emphasize right up until the present the need to "internationalize" technology innovation. Here are some planks from MOST's 2006 to 2010 plan for development of the high-tech zones:

- China must "expand international cooperation and exchange" and "seize opportunities to transfer international industries and R&D."
- Gathering information on international technology and transferring that technology is part of our task to create high-tech industries during the eleventh Five-year Plan.
- "Make full use of the S&T resources of multinational corporations in China and encourage their technological cooperation with domestic firms through multiple means."
- We must concentrate on international "S&T information work" as the basis for developing China's high-tech industry and "help domestic companies utilize by multiple means foreign innovation resources."[49]

MOST's plan also calls for setting up a "Chinese innovation network" (中国创新网络) that links up China's high-tech zones, technology incubators, technology transfer organizations, and "international innovation relay centers" (国际创新驿站机构) worldwide to promote tech transfer. The network will further blur the already fuzzy distinctions between these units, although the centrality of overseas Chinese scholars to the operation – those who return to China and those who transit back and forth – is evident in official statistics.

According to MOST, some 22,000 OCS were attracted to the New and High Technology Development Zones as of 2006.[50] This number is up from 9,700 occupants claimed by the ministry for 2000,[51] and close enough to the 20,000 figure given by the OCS Park Alliance in 2009[52] for the occupancy of OCS facilities inside the zones to conclude that most returnees to science towns end up in OCS parks, that OCS parks for all intents have merged with them, or that the parks themselves are defined by concentrations of returnees.

These "OCS Pioneering Parks" first appeared in 1994 under municipal or provincial sponsorship and were referenced in the MOP's 1996 "Plan for Working with Overseas Scholars in the Personnel System during the Ninth Five-Year Plan."[53] They achieved national status in 2000 in a tri-ministry document entitled "Notice on Trial Work to Organize and Develop the Model Construction of National OCS Pioneering Parks," which stated:

> Some 300,000 Chinese have studied abroad since the country was opened up and more than 100,000 have returned, constituting an important resource for China's development of new and high technology enterprises. To implement General Secretary Jiang Zemin's instruction at the 15th Party Congress to "encourage overseas Chinese scholars to return to China to work or serve their ancestral country through various means" the Ministries of Science, Personnel and Education adopted various practices over the years to bring them home to found businesses and serve China. Meanwhile, local organizations made use of National New and High Technology Development Zones and Innovation Service Centers for New and High Technology to establish more than 30 OCS pioneering parks, creating an excellent environment and conditions for them to return and found businesses.
>
> Under these new conditions, to accelerate the building of OCS pioneering parks, MOST, MOP and MOE have joined to ratify the creation of the first batch of national base model Overseas Chinese Scholar Pioneering Parks on the foundation of existing parks and to guide their development nationally, to build more favorable conditions for OCS to return and found businesses.
>
> 1. Ten or so of the better OCS parks will be chosen for the first batch of trials and as experience accumulates, they will serve as models for developing OCS entrepreneurial parks throughout the entire country.
> 2. Existing parks will apply for model status and be selected by the three ministries with recommendations from provincial or local government authorities.[54]

The document served notice that the PRC national government, through the three ministries charged with managing OCS "talent," was putting its weight and money behind the returnee park project. Locally built OCS parks that showed promise were selected in batches for state funding and promotion. MOST had more to say about OCS parks the following year in a July 2001 paper on technology "incubators."

> Under the new plan priority will be given to promoting the construction of Pioneering Parks for Overseas Chinese Scholars in cooperation with MOP, MOE and SAFEA to attract even more OCS back to China. We will also move ahead with pioneering parks for dual military–civilian technology conversion.[55]

The July paper recognized the State Administration of Foreign Experts Affairs' role in the program. It also included a rare reference to the use of returnees for military projects. Direct involvement by China's Education Ministry, for its part, was signaled in a document released by MOE a few years later, which stated:

> The MOE is building OCS innovation parks and perfecting their incubator function to attract groups of OCS who have in hand contemporary S&T achievements and their own IPR and modern management skills to facilitate their cooperation with domestic employers and promote effective integration of advanced foreign technology with domestic resources.[56]

As part of its consolidation effort and as an indication of the program's maturity, MOST, MOE, and the Ministry of Human Resources and Social Security (successor to MOP) in 2008 formed a "Returned Scholars Venture Park Alliance of the China Association of Technology Entrepreneurs" (中国技术创业协会留学人员创业园联盟) from 44 of the returnee parks.[57] Its purpose was:

> To support the development of returnee enterprises; accelerate the conversion of their S&T achievements; promote interaction with the government, commercial, academic and research sectors; improve their ability to provide internationalized services; and attract high-level skilled persons to China.[58]

Organizationally, the Alliance acts as a platform to connect member parks with government offices at the national and local levels. It also aims at "strengthening cooperation between returnees and domestic events" such as the Guangzhou Convention of Overseas Scholars in S&T and the Overseas Chinese Scholars Business Founding Week (see Chapter 5), i.e., to encourage returnees who already made the transition to pitch those still sitting on the edge.[59]

Some insight into the Alliance's day-to-day operations may be gleaned from its emphasis on databases. These include a "database of S&T accomplishments"

(科技成果库), a database for difficult (难题) technological problems, and a "common service platform for transferring S&T accomplishments." Another database holds information on returnees with businesses in China in order to "integrate the enterprises and personnel resources of member units with society." As of 2010, the Alliance was fielding a system to "disseminate information about the needs and availability of technologies" to member park stakeholders.[60]

A small but critical change in the Alliance's structure came from a 2010 decision to allow "organizations for returned scholars" to become members of the park alliance, eliminating the need for a physical presence on site. OCS associations and NGOs brokering returnee skills – including support from diaspora Chinese back for short periods – now have a role in park policy decisions.[61] Headed by the secretary of MOST's Torch Program Incubator Management Office (火炬中心孵化器管理处), the Alliance will ensure that the parks develop in ways that are supportive of national S&T planning.[62]

Central role of OCS parks

Returnee parks are not isolated islands within China's science towns but are embedded within their organizational hierarchies, integrated with surrounding components, and are the towns' most prominent and persistent components. An example is Zhongguancun (ZGC, 中关村), a science town with seven subdivisions in the northwestern part of Beijing and host to 16 OCS parks, some of which are administered as "companies."

The Beijing ZGC International Incubator Co., Ltd. (北京中关村国际孵化器有限公司) is recognized by MOST as a National Innovation Service Center for New and High Technology (国家高新技术创业服务中心), a New and High-tech Commercial Incubation Base (高新技术产业孵化基地), and a sponsor of Beijing OCS Pioneering Park (北京留学人员创业园). The firm was established in December 2000 from several pre-existing organizations, including three government bodies, four state-owned companies, and the original Beijing OCS Park, which was the basis for the new organization. It is focused entirely on returnees.[63]

Similarly, The ZGC Software Park Incubation Service Center Co., Ltd. (中关村软件园孵化服务有限公司) was founded in November 2001 from the pre-existing ZGC Software Park OCS Pioneering Park (中关村软件园留学人员创业园) and ZGC Software Park Incubator (中关村软件园孵化器). It was recognized by the Beijing Municipal S&T Committee in 2002 as a New and High-tech Commercial Incubation Base; in January 2004 the ZGC Science Town formally named it an OCS Pioneering Park; and in December 2006 MOST recognized it as a National Innovation Service Center for New and High Technology. Each of these five names appears on the website's masthead today.[64] In 2007 the Beijing Personnel Office and the city's S&T Committee also recognized it as a Beijing OCS Pioneering Park, one of 27 (!) returnee parks in the capitol area alone.[65]

Another OCS park in the ZGC complex is CUTM Returned Student Pioneer Park (中国矿业大学留学人员创业园), established in 2007 jointly by ZGC

Science Town and the Chinese University of Mining and Technology. Its website also sports two logos, including one for the Zhongguancun Energy and Safety Science Park (中国村能源与安全科技园).[66]

One more example in Zhongguancun is CASIA Incubator Park, run by the Chinese Academy of Sciences.[67] The park began in April 2004 as the CAS Automation S&T Commercial Incubator Co., Ltd. (中自科技产业孵化器有限公司) established by CAS and the same Beijing ZGC International Incubator Co. identified with Beijing OCS Pioneering Park (above). It acquired its present name and status as an OCS park in 2005.[68] The park teams up with the Beijing National Technology Transfer Center (北京国家技术转移中心) to "offer specialized services to returning OCS, such as conversion of R&D results, integration of S&T resources, international S&T exchanges, and linkups with large-scale company projects."[69] If the park does any "pioneering" at all, it is not apparent in its description.

Besides the Jiading National OCS Pioneering Park described above, Shanghai has at least six more OCS parks. An example is Caohejing OCS Park (上海留学人员漕河泾创业园区) established in 1996 by Shanghai's Caohejing New Technology Open Economic Zone and the Shanghai Office of Personnel. It is "three units in one" (三位一体): an OCS Pioneering Park, National Innovation Service Center for New and High Technology, and an International Company Incubator set up to support PRC firms "commercializing S&T achievements." The park had 95 OCS businesses "under incubation" in 2011. Half originated in the US.[70]

No better illustration of the importance of returnee parks in China's scheme for high-tech development can be found than Guangzhou's Entrepark (留学人员广州创业园, "Guangzhou OCS Pioneering Park"). Established in August 1999 by the ministries of Science, Education, and the "Guangzhou Development District" (the science town), Entrepark is allied with 30 local universities and research facilities to support commercialization of returnees' technical skills. Many of these labs and colleges have centers at the park to facilitate interaction. The park also brokers "multifaceted alliances" between OCS and PRC companies.[71]

English names for the six joined "parks" that make up the main complex are: Science Town Consolidated R&D Incubation Zone, Guangzhou International Incubator for Technological Enterprises, Science Town Information Building, Guangzhou Development District Western Zone, Guangzhou Software Science Park, and Guangzhou Technology Innovation Base. These six parks are not simply affiliated with the OCS park; they were "established" (建成) by it for the benefit of returnees, who to date have incubated some 455 high-tech companies.

Nearby Shenzhen, with its own science town (Shenzhen Hi-tech Industrial Park), is host to the co-located Shenzhen Overseas Chinese High-Tech Venture Park (深圳留学生创业园). The facility started out in 2001 as Longgang OCS Park, was certified in its present incarnation by MOP in 2004, and was named an Innovation Service Center for New and High Technology by MOST in 2008, growing in the process from 25,000 square feet to 720,000 square feet.

A useful exercise for readers with more specialized interests might be to plot the intersection (geophysical, organizational, personnel) of OCS parks with large centers of defense research at, for example, Mianyang, Xi'an and Hefei. For us, our goal is simply to show the centrality of OCS parks and of returnees in general to China's S&T development.

This concludes our survey of PRC policy support and domestic infrastructure for converting technology that Chinese scholars acquire abroad into weapons and competitive products. The Chapter complements material presented in the preceding chapter on PRC students abroad, and closes the loop on the question of what Beijing actually does with its foreign-trained talent. In the next chapter we examine the role that traditional espionage plays in China's technology transfer process.

Notes

1 Vivian Lin, "Chinese Students Pour into the United States," *US-China Today*, November 18, 2010, www.uschina.usc.edu/w_usct/showarticle.aspx?articleID=16091.
2 Note the nuance: not a system to do science, but a "scientific system" to make use of overseas scientists.
3 Liu Yun (刘云) and Shen Lin (沈林), "海外人才资源开发利用的现状及发展对策" ("The Current Situation and Countermoves on Development and Utilization of Overseas Chinese Experts Intellectual Resources") in 科研管理 (*Science Research Management*), vol. 22.4 (July 2001), pp. 115–125.
4 Ibid., p. 115.
5 Ibid., p. 121.
6 The likelihood of this being a quasi-official communiqué is strengthened by the appearance a few months later in a second major Chinese language S&T policy journal, *Keji Guanli Yanjiu* (科技管理研究), of a similar proposal to step up exploitation of OCS. The article recommended subsidizing the "recruitment and utilization of overseas S&T personnel" and sponsoring activities with overseas Chinese S&T associations. Mirroring Liu and Shen's proposal, it also endorsed building an "international S&T personal information database, an overseas Chinese experts database, and supporting systems for information networks and decisions." Zeng Lu (曾路), "机遇与挑战--广东省对外科技合作的环境与对策" ("Opportunity and Challenge: International S&T Cooperation Environment and Measures for Guangdong Province"), in *Keji Guanli Yanjiu* (科技管理研究), 2001.5, October 2001.
7 Ibid., p. 122.
8 Ibid.
9 Ibid.
10 Ibid., p. 123.
11 Ibid., pp. 124–125.
12 By 2006 its membership had increased to 16 with the addition of the State Council's Overseas Chinese Affairs Office, the General Administration of Customs, the State Administration of Taxation, and the National Development and Reform Commission. By 2011 the roster of participants stood at 22.
13 关于回国(来华)定居工作专家有关政策 (Policies Relating to Experts Returning (or Coming) to China to Reside Permanently and Work), MOP, 2005.
14 关于在留学人才引进工作中界定海外高层次留学人才的指导意见 (Guiding Opinions for Defining High-level Talent in Our Work to Bring in Overseas-educated Talent), MOP, 2005.
15 关于建立海外高层次留学人才回国工作绿色通道的意见 (Opinions on Building a Green Channel for the Return to China of High-level Overseas-educated Talent Abroad), MOP, 2007.
16 关于进一步加强引进海外优秀留学人才工作的意见 (Opinions on Further Strengthening Our Work to Bring in Outstanding Overseas-educated Talent Abroad), MOE, 2007.

17 中国留学网 www.cscse.edu.cn.
18 国家留学网 www.csc.edu.cn.
19 神州学人 www.chisa.edu.cn.
20 关于进一步加强引进海外优秀留学人才工作的意见 (Opinions on Further Strengthening Our Work to Bring in Outstanding Overseas-educated Talent Abroad), MOE, 2007.
21 Ibid.
22 Liu Yun and Shen Lin, "The Current Situation and Countermoves on Development and Utilization of Overseas Chinese Experts Intellectual Resources," p 123.
23 资助海外留学人员短期回国工作讲学 (Subsidizing OCS to Return for Short Periods to Work and Lecture). CAS, Institute of Mechanics, undated article posted to www.imech.ac.cn, viewed March 2010. The programs were the "Special Fund to Subsidize OCS to Return to China for Short Periods to Work and Lecture" (资助留学人员短期回国工作讲学专项基金), and the "Overseas Scholars Cooperative Research Fund" (海外学者合作研究基金).
24 Ibid.
25 Endo Homare, 中国がシリコンバレーとつながるとき (*When China Links Up with Silicon Valley)*. Tokyo: Nikkei BP, 2001, pp. 266–270.
26 www.entrepark.com/WEB/gzstip/index.htm.
27 www.wxsp.gov.cn.
28 Also known as the Shanghai Zhangjiang New and High-tech Industrial Development Zone – Jiading Park (上海张江高新技术产业开发区嘉定园 or simply 上海张江高新区嘉定园).
29 www.rcsp.com.cn. Item number 28, viewed October 25, 2010.
30 www.jdhitech.com.
31 Also called "Incubators for Technological Enterprises" (科技企业孵化器).
32 高新技术创业服务中心概论 (Introduction to Innovation Service Centers for New and High Technology). Yuan Huan (袁环), Huang Cuiqin (黄翠琴), Zhang Lili (张莉莉), and Zhang Li (张力), October 1995.
33 关于"十五"期间大力推进科技企业孵化器建设的意见 (Opinions on Construction of Incubators for Technological Enterprises During the Tenth Five Year Plan), MOST, July 9, 2001.
34 科技企业孵化器（高新技术创业服务中心）认定和管理办法 (Means for Accrediting and Managing S&T Commercial Incubators (Innovation Service Centers for New and High Technology)), MOST, December 7, 2006.
35 Ibid.
36 www.kscyy.com.cn.
37 By early 2013, the number of designated "science towns" in China had surpassed 80.
38 国家高新技术产业开发区高新技术企业认定条件和办法 (Conditions and Measures for the Designation of High and New Technology Enterprises in National High Technology and New Technology Industry Development Zones), Section 3, March 6, 1991.
39 中共中央、国务院关于加强技术创新，发展高科技，实现产业化的决定 (Decision of the Chinese Communist Party Central Committee and the State Council on Strengthening Technical Innovation, Developing High Technology and Realizing Industrialization), August 22, 1999.
40 关于加速国家高新技术产业开发区发展的若干意见 (Various Opinions on Speeding up the Development of National New and High Technology Development Zones), MOST, August 11, 1999.
41 关于国家高新技术产业开发区十年发展情况的报告 (Report on the Status of Ten Years of Development of National New and High Technology Development Zones), MOST, March 15, 2002.
42 关于国家高新技术产业开发区管理体制改革与创新的若干意见 (Various Opinions on the Reform and Innovation of the Administration System of the National New and High Technology Development Zones), MOST, March 8, 2002.
43 关于进一步支持国家高新技术产业开发区发展的决定 (Decision on Further

Supporting the National New and High Technology Development Zones), MOST, January 31, 2002.

44 吴瓊 (Wu Qiong), 郎錫君 (Lang Xijun), 吴海西 (Wu Haixi), "率先创新与模仿创新" ("Leading Innovation and Imitative Innovation"). In 科技・人才・市场 ("Scientec, Talent, Market"), April 2001.

45 Ibid., p. 8.

46 Ibid., pp. 9–10.

47 Ibid., p. 11.

48 Ibid., p. 9.

49 关于印发国家高新技术产业化及其环境建设（火炬）十一五发展纲要和国家高新技术产业开发区十一五发展规划纲要的通知 (Notice on Promulgating the Eleventh Five-year Development Program for National New and High Technology Commercialization and Its Infrastructure (Torch) and the Eleventh Five-year Developmental Planning Program for National New and High Technology Development Zones), MOST, April 4, 2007.

50 2006 年国家高新区发展态势, (Developmental Status of National New and High-tech Zones for 2006), MOST, June 28, 2007.

51 国家高新技术产业开发区"十五"和2010年发展规划纲要 (National New and High Technology Development Zones Tenth Five-year and 2010 Developmental Planning Program), MOST, September 12, 2001.

52 bbs.533.com/viewthread.php?tid=109549.

53 "九五"期间人事系统留学人员工作规划 (Plan for Working with Overseas Scholars in the Personnel System during the Ninth Five-year Plan), MOP, 1996.

54 关于组织开展国家留学人员创业园示范建设试点工作的通知 (Notice on Trial Work to Organize and Develop the Model Construction of National OCS Pioneering Parks), MOST, MOP, MOE, June 21, 2000.

55 关于"十五"期间大力推进科技企业孵化器建设的意见 (Opinions on Construction of Incubators for Technological Enterprises During the "Tenth Five-year Plan"), MOST, July 9, 2001.

56 关于进一步加强引进海外优秀留学人才工作的意见 (Opinions on Further Strengthening Our Work to Bring in Talented OCS), MOE, February 2, 2007.

57 By the end of 2009, 61 of 149 OCS parks had joined the alliance, constituting 76 percent of the national-level returnee parks.

58 "Introduction" from the Alliance website, www.rcsp.com.cn, dated October 25, 2010.

59 Ibid.

60 Ibid.

61 Alliance website <www.rcsp.com.cn>. Information dated October 8, 2010.

62 Ibid.

63 www.incubase.net.

64 www.zgcspi.com.

65 北京留学人员创业园达27家 (Beijing's OCS Pioneering Parks Reach 27 Units), December 18, 2008, www.chinaqw.com/lxs/cytd/200812/18/142735.shtml.

66 www.zgces.com.

67 The English name does not capture the term "OCS Pioneering Park" present in its actual Chinese name (中科院中自留学人员创业园).

68 www.rcsp.com.cn.

69 Ibid.

70 www.cscse.edu.cn/publish/portal0/tab888/info5888.htm and www.chinatalents.gov.cn/lxcyyq/shanghai.htm.

71 www.entrepark.com.

8

TRADITIONAL CHINESE ESPIONAGE

Foreknowledge comes from the minds of men, not divination.

– Sun Zi

The value of any PowerPoint briefing on China is inversely proportional to the number of Sun Zi quotes in the briefing.

– Mulvenon's Third Law

While previous chapters have detailed China's non-traditional approaches to collecting and exploiting foreign science and technology information, this chapter examines the role of the PRC's traditional intelligence services, including the Ministry of State Security (MSS), the PLA's Military Intelligence Department (aka Second Department or 2PLA), and the PLA's SIGINT organization (Third Department or 3PLA). The chapter will first outline the scope and threat posed by Chinese intelligence operations in the United States, as described by senior US counter-intelligence and policy officials. Because much of the literature on Chinese intelligence is either outdated or fatally weakened by mythology and misinformation, the chapter will then proceed to critically examine some of the prevailing views of Chinese intelligence tradecraft. This new framework will then be applied specifically to the large and growing set of China technology espionage cases, identifying commonalities and differences among them.

Scope and scale of the problem

Over the past decade, American government officials have consistently warned of a serious and growing threat from China's intelligence services, particularly economic and technology espionage. As early as 2005, Dave Szady, then assistant director of the FBI's counter-intelligence division, told the *Wall Street Journal* that

"China is the biggest [espionage] threat to the US today."[1] In the wake of the Chi Mak case in 2008, FBI spokesman William Carter declared:

> The intelligence services of the People's Republic of China pose a significant threat both to the national security and to the compromise of US critical national assets. . . . The PRC will remain a significant threat for a long time as they attempt to develop their military capabilities and to develop their economy in order to compete in today's world economy.[2]

This view was corroborated by current and former officials in an August 2010 *60 Minutes* story, in which former Director of the Office of the National Counterintelligence Executive, Michelle Van Cleave, told the interviewer:

> The Chinese are the biggest problem we have with respect to the level of effort that they're devoting against us, versus the level of attention we are giving to them. . . . Virtually every technology that is on the US control [sic] technology list has been targeted at one time or another by the Chinese. . . . Sensors and optics . . . biological and chemical processes . . . all the things we have identified as having inherent military application . . . I think we are a real candy store for the Chinese and for others.[3]

Her successor at NCIX, Joel Brenner, also publicly seconded her remarks:

> The Chinese are putting on a full-court press in this area. . . . They are trying to flatten out the world as fast as possible. . . . One of the ways they accelerate that process is economic espionage. If you can steal something rather than figure it out yourself, you save years. You gain an advantage.[4]

While Brenner and others acknowledge that technology thieving is "the norm" among industrial nations, China does stand out as among the most active nations.[5]

While quantifying the threat is difficult, given the problem of non-reporting, credible estimates of the scale of the problem and its growth over time are available from government sources. In 2007, the then head of the FBI's counterintelligence division, Bruce Carlson, told *USA Today* that "about one-third of all economic espionage investigations are linked to Chinese government agencies, research institutes or businesses,"[6] and that between 2000 and 2005, "the total number of [economic espionage] charges [against Chinese] has grown by around 15% annually."[7] In response, the FBI increased the number of agents working on Chinese counter-intelligence issues from 150 in 2001 to 350 in 2007.[8]

The increasingly predominant position of Chinese intelligence operations is not limited to the United States. A leaked MI-5 report in 2010 asserted that China "represents one of the most significant espionage threats to the UK."[9] The head of domestic intelligence for the southwestern German state of

Baden-Württemberg, Johannes Schmalzl, said: "Sixty percent of our alleged cases [of economic espionage] are related to China."[10] The then director of the Canadian Security Intelligence Service (CSIS), Jim Judd, told a Senate committee meeting in May 2007 that "China accounts for close to 50 percent of our counterintelligence program."[11]

The apparent global success of Chinese intelligence demands that we closely examine the tactics, techniques, and procedures of Beijing's operations. At first glance, the Chinese intelligence apparatus appears to have a deep cultural affinity for intelligence affairs, a long and storied history of successful operations, and, as we shall see in Chapter 9, an impressive ability to exploit new methods of collection such as cyber-espionage. Our understanding of PRC methods and goals, however, has been impeded by a long-standing set of misconceptions, misperceptions, and myths about Chinese intelligence operations, perpetuated by an extensive English-language literature on the subject. The following section will examine each of these concepts in turn, assessing them in the light of known empirical evidence from over 50 years of cases.

Truth or myth, or outdated? Assessing some common beliefs about Chinese espionage

The public discourse on PRC espionage has long been dominated by a set of core beliefs (hereafter described as the "Old School") about the tactics, techniques, and procedures used by the Chinese intelligence services to collect secrets in the United States. As Mattis argues, these Old School principles have become predominant through articles and op-eds written by former FBI counter-intelligence analyst Paul Moore and "media interviews with retired US officials," such as David Szady, Joel Brenner, Rudy Guerin, Bruce Carlson, and Michelle Van Cleave.[12] At their core, the Old School argues that the Chinese services practice a fundamentally different approach to intelligence collection, especially when compared with the more "classic" approach of the United States and Russian services.[13] The main tenets of the Old School are that Chinese intelligence:

- Prefers to use large numbers of amateur collectors (also known as the "thousand grains of sand") rather than conduct formal operations with established agents.
- Abjures buying stolen secrets in favor of inducing people to give them away.
- Prefers to recruit ethnic Chinese agents.
- Prefers to recruit "good people" rather than exploiting flawed or vulnerable personalities.
- Does not use traditional tradecraft, such as dead drops and covert communications.

In fact, all of these accepted principles are open to close examination and even empirical refutation. This chapter will examine each in turn, and then offer a new framework of "layered" collection and analysis to explain current operational behavior, especially with respect to science and technology collection.

Thousand grains of sand

In the Chinese intelligence literature, the most common shorthand for China's approach to intelligence operations is known as the "thousand grains of sand," also described as the "mosaic,"[14] "legion," "human wave," or "vacuum-cleaner" approach.[15] The classic story narrative of the "thousand grains of sand" methodology, particularly in contrast to traditional intelligence behavior, is provided by Paul Moore:

> If the composition of the sand on a certain beach were identified as an intelligence target by the nations of the world, some countries would solve the challenged by dispatching a submarine to sit offshore from the beach. In the dark of night, a commando team would emerge from the submarine, paddle in a rubber raft to the beach, scoop up a bucket or two of sand, and beat a retreat back to the submarine. Analysis of the buckets of sand would produce a great deal of data. Other countries would task their satellites flying overhead to turn their sophisticated infrared and spectrographic scanners on the beach, and this would produce a wealth of data. China, however, would approach the problem by allowing ten thousand of its citizens to spend a day at the beach. At sunset they would all go home and simply shake out their towels; and the Chinese would end up with more sand – and more data – than other nations.[16]

Former Army counter-intelligence officer and China defense attaché Larry Wortzel concurs, arguing that China "sends out thousands of people with limited tasking, flooding the target country."[17] In this view, "anyone and everyone is a potential intelligence asset."[18] Using large numbers of amateur collectors means that intelligence gains take a long time and operations do not create large counter-intelligence signatures. As Moore argues, "To the extent we suffer losses against China, typically we suffer them day in and day out on a modest scale of operation."[19]

But is this model effective? How does it work in practice? In his 2011 "Studies in Intelligence" article, former government analyst Peter Mattis summarizes the mechanics of the "thousand grains of sand" approach:

> Chinese intelligence builds a cohesive intelligence picture out of disparate, seemingly unrelated or insignificant data . . . Chinese intelligence services collect "small pieces of intelligence" to assemble later into a more comprehensive picture. The implication is Chinese intelligence has a very low threshold for collection, sucking up information without respect to being classified or unclassified.[20]

For counter-intelligence professionals like Moore, this behavior is "unusual, unprofessional and suspect."[21] He explains his criticism further:

> Chinese collection effort often enough appears to be extremely inefficient in terms of the numbers of people involved, the relative lack of security brought about by the lack of central direction or control, the redundant activities of many of the participations and the inherent awkwardness of having a large group of people collect small bits of information. In my opinion, the effort appears to be inefficient because it indeed is inefficient, and that inefficiency is brought on by the reliance on *guanxi* as the vehicle through which to accomplish collection.[22]

For Moore, "*guanxi* networks are a deeply flawed intelligence mechanism" that have been "'borrowed' to do intelligence work." The process only succeeds when you bring enough people to bear on the problem. In his article "Actuarial Intelligence," Moore concludes that if you work with "large enough numbers [of people], you don't have to supervise the activities of individuals, for 'actuarial' principles will take over."[23] The contrast with the highly controlled Western model of intelligence collection could not be more striking. As Moore pithily puts it, "China has a planned economy but a market-driven intelligence program. . . .We have just the opposite."[24]

While the "thousand grains of sand" view has been dominant for decades, Mattis and other New School analysts have become increasingly critical of this central shibboleth of the Chinese intelligence canon. They do not deny that Beijing uses large numbers of untrained collectors, but question the core assumptions of the analysis. Arguing against "human wave" tactics, Mattis asserts:

> The supposed Chinese intelligence reliance on amateur "human wave" collection tactics probably is the least credible of all the conventional propositions. The very definition of a permanent intelligence bureaucracy includes professionalism, even if the performance is not up to an arbitrary standard. This [thousand grains of sand] proposition logically leads to the statement that China's intelligence services are largely irrelevant to Beijing's intelligence requirements. . . . Furthermore, amateur hordes scooping up every grain of sand imply the Chinese services do not collect intelligence with deliberate intent.

In fact, the empirical record repeatedly reveals a clear connection between expertise, requirements, and tasking. In the Chi Mak case, for example, the government introduced two key pieces of evidence found in his home, including one machine-printed document in Chinese urging him to join professional associations and attend more seminars on advanced research ("special subject matters"), and a list of technologies of interest, including torpedoes, "aircraft carrier electronic systems" and "submarine propulsion technology," and a "space-launched magnetic levitational platform."[25] Both notes had been shredded and thrown in the garbage.[26] In similar fashion, Rockwell and Boeing engineer Dongfang Chung was tasked by Chinese agents to supply documents and to give lectures in China on space technology and military systems.[27] According to the indictment,

> The documents taken by defendant Chung from Rockwell and Boeing matched requests for specific types of technology contained in letters and tasking lists sent to defendant Chung in the past by officials of the PRC. Defendant Chung took the documents with the intent to benefit the government of the PRC by providing the information in the documents to the government of the PRC.[28]

Mattis also criticizes another aspect of the "vacuum-cleaner" approach, assessing that it wrongly assumes the Chinese system is capable of horizontal integration:

> The "vacuum cleaner" proposition assumes a robust processing and analytic capability to produce insight from volumes of low-quality data. And the "thousand grains of sand" concept arrived before the widespread use of networked computers. Yet we have no evidence of a strong analytic capability – and impressionistic evidence to the contrary. Second, analysts did not evaluate the structure of the Chinese system, which militates against an open information environment. . . . The documented existence of provincial MSS departments and at least some municipal-level bureaus suggests the MSS is not immune from these problems.[29]

Indeed, Mattis' analysis of Chinese bureaucratic dysfunction and the inability of the Chinese system to effectively integrate horizontally or vertically rests on a robust and unchallenged Sinological literature, as exemplified in the works of Lieberthal, Oksenberg, and others.[30] These experts highlight a core structural breakdown between vertical lines of authority within hierarchies and the horizontal relationships with logical interagency organizations, leading to problems with coordination, information sharing, and, as a result, suboptimal policy-making. According to Lieberthal, "one key rule of the Chinese system is that units of the same rank cannot issue binding orders to each other."[31] In other words, Chinese government bureaucracies should not be viewed as a monolith. Within the intelligence apparatus, for example, this means that the Ministry of State Security and its constituent elements from the national to the local level have no structural imperative or incentive to coordinate their activities or share information with their military counterparts in 2PLA (military intelligence). This dominant model of Chinese bureaucratic behavior, confirmed through many respected studies, interview projects, and Chinese scholars' own descriptions of the dysfunction in their system, fatally undermines the "thousand grains of sand" model, which would be difficult if not impossible to coordinate and execute in such an environment.

Instead, it is likely more accurate to say that Chinese intelligence and scientific organizations do employ many different types of collectors gathering small pieces of information, but the fruits of this collection are likely stove-piped and fragmented at the other end, preventing their re-assembly for maximal exploitation and gain.

Stealing secrets vs. inducing people to give them away

The traditional China intelligence literature also has an unorthodox view of why individuals provide information to Beijing, arguing that Beijing does not "steal secrets" as much as it "induces" people to give them away for a variety of reasons, ranging from ethnic identity to a transnational scientific interest in human progress. Again, Paul Moore carries the standard:

> In almost all of its collections operations, China is not so much looking at opportunities for stealing things . . . as devising all sorts of opportunities for you to come to the conclusion that you would be willing to give at least some of these things. . . . It's the mundane, day-to-day contacts that are killing us, not the exotic spy operations.[32]

To achieve this, the Chinese services are willing to wait years for the opportune time to pitch a target for a sliver of useful information, bypassing a formal recruitment altogether. According to this view, the target may not even know he's been "developed."[33] According to James Lilley, a former CIA station chief and US ambassador to China, the Chinese services prefer "a rather blurred line between 'cooperator' and 'undercover agent.' "[34]

Most often, the approaches for this "cooperation" occur on trips to the PRC, where Chinese interlocutors (usually a scientific colleague or "friend") can leverage jet lag, soporific banquets, alcohol, and the reciprocal demands of hospitality to elicit information.[35] Moore argues:

> What the Chinese are after is an indiscretion. . . . It doesn't have to be classified, it just has to be helpful, and they want it to be more than what they would normally get, more than what they are entitled to get. That's the way they play the game: They want "X-plus." I call it espionage by indiscretion.[36]

In these situations, Godfrey highlights the use of passive techniques, letting the cooperator come to their own conclusion about whether to help:

> When they do make an approach, it's usually a subtle pressure, with references to relatives in China and possible business opportunities. . . . They tend to allow people to draw their own line. It's like fishing. They hit everybody, and some people bite.[37]

In addition, Moore and others claim that "China seldom pays its agents for the intelligence they produce."[38] When they do pay, the Old School argues that the currency is rarely cash. As Godfrey argues:

> the Chinese form of payment is a lot more subtle too. . . . Instead of a lump sum cleared through a dead drop, they will offer legitimate business opportunities. All those things make Chinese cases harder to prosecute.[39]

The empirical case record certainly has many supporting examples of US citizens, usually scientists, giving away classified or sensitive information to Chinese officials and their scientific peers seemingly for free. Peter Lee, a Chinese-American nuclear scientist, admitted that he was approached in a Beijing hotel room in January 1985, where Chen Nengkuan of the Chinese Academy of Engineering Physics asked for his help, emphasizing that China was a "poor country."[40] Lee told the FBI, according to court records, that he told his interlocutors about his research on using inertial confinement fusion to simulate nuclear detonations because he wanted to bring China's scientific capabilities "closer to the United States."[41] On a later trip in 1995, Lee told a different group of scientists at the Institute for Applied Physics and Computational Mathematics about his research on submarine tracking technology.[42] While Lee admitted receiving compensation for travel and accommodation expenses in both cases, the government prosecutor in 1997 conceded that money was not the primary motive for Lee's behavior.[43]

Many other examples illustrate this Chinese intelligence collection methodology. Wen Ho Lee and his wife Sylvia were invited in both 1986 and 1988 to conferences in China at the Institute for Applied Physics and Computational Mathematics, which is roughly analogous in function and personnel to one of the US nuclear weapons labs. He later admitted that he had been approached in his hotel room by Chinese nuclear weapons designer Hu Side and another top weapons scientist in 1988 and asked for classified information about the designs of US thermonuclear weapons.[44] Similarly, Greg Dongfan Chung was invited in June 1985 to "give lectures on aircraft and spacecraft technology at government-controlled universities and aircraft manufacturers in the PRC."[45] The topics of his lectures include "Space Shuttle Heat Resistant Tiles, Brief Introduction and Stress Analysis," "General Aircraft Design and Fatigue Life," and "F-15 Jet Fighters," providing PRC scientists with extended periods of time to ask questions and probe him for information.[46] He received additional follow-up questions from Nanchang Aircraft Company a month after returning to the United States, and informed Nanchang's chief engineer via mail in December 1985 that he had begun collecting 27 manuals on the B-1 bomber and other military aircraft, which he subsequently passed through the Education Consul at the PRC Consulate in San Francisco.[47] Chung later traveled to the PRC in April 2001, where he gave additional lectures on the Space Shuttle program, and made subsequent trips in 2003 and 2006.[48]

The net result of this approach is that China is able to conduct "espionage without evidence," wherein even sources may be unaware that they are providing valuable data.[49] For example, Moore and others couldn't conceive of Chinese spymasters asking Peter Lee or any other scientist, Chinese or not, to download classified documents and deliver them to Beijing, as it would entail too much risk.[50] Instead, Chinese intelligence officers "want what's between their ears, not what's in the briefcase."[51] According to counter-intelligence officials and Federal prosecutors, this strategy makes Chinese intelligence operations "bulletproof" to US counter-espionage personnel and prosecutors:[52]

> It's nice to think, but it's not true, that where there's espionage there inevitably is evidence of espionage. . . . The Chinese have found a way to commit espionage against the United States which does not leave sufficient evidence behind for there to be successful investigations and successful prosecutions.[53]

But is it true that Chinese intelligence primarily induces people to give secrets away, rather than paying them for secrets? In fact, there is also strong empirical evidence of the latter. Larry Wu-Tai Chin was paid "about a million dollars" by Chinese intelligence.[54] [55] Noshir Gowadia was paid $110K for his consulting services, either in cash, or money transfers to a bank in Switzerland.[56] [57]After twice failing the Foreign Service exam required for State Department employment, Glenn Duffie Shriver was still paid $30,000 by the Chinese, and in 2007, after applying for a position in the CIA National Clandestine Service, he received an additional $40,000.[58] [59] Katrina Leung told the FBI she was paid $100,000 by Chinese intelligence because Yang Shangkun "liked her."[60] When the FBI searched Katrina Leung's home, they found three classified documents. One related to an FBI investigation of Peter Lee, a scientist convicted in 1998 of providing the Chinese with information that may have helped them develop their nuclear program. The second was an intercepted conversation between two Chinese agents "Luo" and "Mao" discussing "issues relevant to national security." The third was described as a secret FBI electronic communication.[61] [62] [63] [64]

In the case of Greg Bergersen, a Defense Security Cooperation Agency employee convicted of spying for China, his handler, Kuo Taishen, was paid $50,000 to pass the materials to his Chinese contact through e-mails and telephone calls to Beijing.[65] In a now infamous FBI surveillance video inside Bergersen's car, Kuo is seen shoving a wad of bills into his asset's shirt pocket.[66] Kuo also paid for Bergersen's meals at restaurants, gambling in Las Vegas, and shows.[67] In return, Kuo asked him for classified material related to the DoD's Global Information Grid "roadmap" and future arms sales to Taiwan. In response to the first request, Bergersen gave Kuo the following documents: (1) Implementing the Global Information Grid; (2) GIG Tactical Edge Networks Engineering White Paper Version 0.4 (dated August 26, 2005, "For Official Use Only, Draft"); (3) Evolving to the GIG and NNEC; (4) Information Operations Roadmap (dated October 30, 2003, and marked "Secret"; this document was declassified in January 2006; the strikeout was added when the document was declassified); and (5) GIG Enterprise-Wide Systems Engineering

Update (dated May 16, 2007, and marked "Pre-Decisional – Distribution Limited to SSEB," which is an acronym that refers to the Source Selection Evaluation Board).[68] In response to the second request, Bergersen allowed Kuo to take notes from the Taiwan section of the 2007 Javits Report, which is classified SECRET and "lists in spreadsheet format the potential military and direct commercial sales of military equipment from the United States to foreign nations."[69] Kuo's other asset, James Fondren, sold "opinion papers" for between $350 and $800 apiece through Fondren's home-based consulting business.[70]

In sum, it appears true that Chinese intelligence has been successful in inducing people, mainly scientists, into giving away classified or sensitive information in informal settings for free, but it is clear that Chinese intelligence also understands the importance of financially compensating its assets for their intelligence activities, in some cases quite handsomely.

China prefers to recruit ethnic Chinese

The most controversial tenet of the Old School view is that China prefers to recruit ethnic Chinese agents to the exclusion of non-ethnics:

> Over the years, China has displayed a very strong preference for collecting as much intelligence as possible from individuals of ethnic Chinese heritage, and when it recruits agents, it almost invariably recruits ethnic Chinese.[71]

According to the 2004 *Intelligence Threat Handbook*, published by Interagency OPSEC Support Staff (IOSS), the Chinese-American community is the target of an estimated 98 percent of recruitment efforts by the MSS.[72] By contrast, no more than a quarter of Soviet HUMINT efforts targeted recruitment of ethnic Russian agents.[73]

The proposition that Beijing only recruits from among ethnic Chinese is usually explained in a number of ways, ranging from efficiency to culture- or nationalism-based reasons. The efficiency argument is summarized by Paul Moore:

> There is no evidence that the PRC considers Chinese Americans to be more vulnerable to approach than any other group. It is likely the PRC has adopted its distinctive ethnic targeting intelligence strategy because it is much more capable of mounting effective approaches against individuals of ethnic Chinese ancestry than those of any other background.[74]

Another efficiency argument points to the disproportionate numbers of ethnic Chinese working in valuable science and technology sectors. For example, one source claims that Chinese-Americans make up only 1 percent of the population but comprise more than 15 percent of the R&D community.[75] The second explanation is cultural-exceptionalist in orientation, arguing that Beijing is "more comfortable going after individuals with whom there is a shared culture, language and history."[76] The third rationale centers on exploiting a sense of patriotic or nationalist obligation in the target:

the selling point in a normal PRC recruitment operation is not an appeal to ethnicity per se, but to whatever feelings of obligation the targeted individual may have towards China, family members in China, old friends in China, etc. . . . The crux of the PRC's approach is not to try to exploit a perceived vulnerability but to appeal to an individual's desire to help China out in some way. Whatever the reason, ethnic targeting to arouse feelings of obligation is the single most distinctive feature of PRC intelligence operations.[77]

This approach is described as a "soft recruitment" over a long period of time to become a "friend of China," rather than the hard recruitment tactic to become a formal asset of the Chinese intelligence services.[78] As one analyst puts it, Beijing's "major effort is to try and develop relations with Chinese-Americans, as many of them as possible, in the hopes that the relations will turn out to be profitable – someday, somehow, somewhere."[79] While the "appeal to patriotism" may be positive in orientation, the references to extended family may in some cases be perceived as a threat, creating the impression that Beijing may use its authoritarian security apparatus to "apply pressure to a potential agent's family."[80]

Detractors of this view accuse its proponents of engaging in ethnic profiling or outright racism.[81] Old School proponents counter that Beijing is actually doing the ethnic profiling. According to Harry Brandon, a former head of FBI counter-intelligence who retired in 1995:

> critics say our government is racist because the government is targeting Chinese-Americans because they are Chinese. . . . And the answer is, Yes, we are targeting them, because they are targets (of Beijing). . . . The only people racially biased in this case is the Chinese intelligence service, which continues to target Chinese-Americans for the only reason that they are ethnic Chinese . . . [But] probably 99.99 percent of Chinese-Americans wouldn't have anything to do with [Chinese intelligence approaches].[82]

Even some critics of the proposition acknowledge that Beijing's methods may make them vulnerable to suspicion and accusation, but they say that the FBI needs to have better tools to distinguish loyal Chinese-Americans from traitors.

When one looks at the empirical records of cases, there is a great deal of evidence to support the idea that Beijing prefers to recruit ethnic Chinese. One could list dozens of examples of Chinese-Americans who have aided Beijing's intelligence collection, ranging from passive scientific assistance to full-blown asset recruitment. Reading through the cases of Larry Wu-Tai Chin,[83] Peter Lee,[84] or Chi Mak, there are consistent threads of appeals to culture, nationalism, or "fairness" in the distribution of global scientific knowledge. In the Dongfang "Greg" Chung case, the US government introduced illustrative pieces of correspondence between Chung and his China-based interlocutors. In 1978, Chung wrote to Ku Chenlung at Harbin Institute of Technology, an elite technical university in China with close ties to the Chinese military and defense-industrial base:

I don't know what I can do for the country. Having been a Chinese compatriot for over 30 years and being proud of the people's efforts for the motherland, I am regretful for not contributing anything . . . I would like to make an effort to contribute to the Four Modernizations of China.[85]

Ku wrote back to Chung on September 9, 1979:

We are all moved by your patriotism. You have spent so much time to reorganize the notes from several years ago; copying and finding the information that could be needed by us, and you have actively put in your efforts towards the Four Modernizations of the Motherland. Your spirit is an encouragement and driving force to us. We'd like to join our hands together with the overseas compatriots in the endeavor for the construction of our great socialist motherland.[86]

Within this topic, the most controversial case is that of Wen Ho Lee, who claims that the government targeted him because of his ethnicity.[87] In his book, Lee declares emphatically: "Had I not been Chinese, I never would have been accused of espionage and threatened with execution."[88] Lee's claims were supported by Robert Vrooman, chief counter-intelligence officer at Los Alamos National Laboratory from 1987 to 1998, and Charles Washington, both of whom gave sworn statements asserting that he was "singled out for investigation as an espionage subject because of [his] ethnicity."[89] Yet the Bellows Report, a review conducted by the Attorney General's office of the handling of the investigation, concludes that there was "no exclusive targeting of Chinese Americans."[90] Of the list of 12 suspects, then Attorney General Janet Reno testified that only half had Asian-American surnames.[91] Notra Trulock and his supporters point out that Lee was a suspect owing to multiple counter-intelligence threat factors, including his professional and personal travel to China, his admitted failure to report contacts with Chinese nuclear scientists, and his 1982 contact with another scientist who was under investigation.[92] These same advocates insist that the Wen Ho Lee case fell apart not because of the weakness of the evidence, but because of the serial bungling of the FBI and prosecutors in the case, which made conviction impossible.

Regardless of Lee's actual innocence or guilt, he is now the poster child for ethnic profiling of Chinese-Americans by the US counter-intelligence apparatus, and the perceived injustice of the case now acts as a cautionary tale for every subsequent investigation of possible traitorous behavior by ethnic Chinese-Americans. Fair or not, his case is now paired with a case of genuine injustice involving missile scientist Qian Xuesen, who was driven out of the American defense research establishment in the 1950s by McCarthyist excesses and ended up establishing a missile program in China, the products of which now target the United States.[93]

Recent writings on Chinese intelligence operations, however, offer a revisionist perspective on the issue of ethnic targeting. First, Mattis makes a powerful argument that ethnic Chinese targeting may not be deliberate strategy and shows how this belief may actually undermine US counter-intelligence efforts:

> Even if every Chinese agent we identified was ethnically Chinese, this only means Chinese case officers have been successful in recruiting ethnic Chinese agents – not that they are the focus. Should we really be surprised that a group of case officers growing up behind the "bamboo curtain" with little, if any, exposure to foreigners would be more successful in recruiting agents with shared cultural understanding? This logical fallacy has created no end of grief for US counterintelligence. The conventional rebuttal – that Chinese intelligence profiled first – to adverse reactions from the Asian-American community only heightens suspicions. In the fields of counterintelligence and counterterrorism, authorities often need the support of local communities to identify people dangerous to national security. Civic trust should not be jeopardized for a lack of clear thinking. Unless the empirical record tells us something radically different, we should strike this third proposition from future discussions of Chinese intelligence operations and focus on how China matches potential sources to intelligence requirements.[94]

Second, even Old School analysts admit that the ethnic targeting strategy doesn't always work, undermining their earlier efficiency arguments. Moore asserts that the Chinese seek to "make as many friends as possible" and be content with a "minuscule positive response." Moreover, they will "approach even previously unhelpful friends over and over, since their requests are modest and nonthreatening."[95] Mattis adds that "focusing on ethnic Chinese at home and abroad sharply limits the kind of information Chinese intelligence officers can collect."[96] On the other hand,

> There are however certain kinds of missions that targeting ethnic Chinese becomes a necessity, e.g., tracking dissidents, Taiwan, and monitoring the Chinese Diaspora. All of these missions relate to protecting the power of the Chinese Communist Party, which – according to press and defector information going back almost thirty years – is the highest priority for Chinese intelligence.[97]

Finally, there is circularity to the standard argument, suggesting that insufficient data have led some observers to emphasis correlation over causation. For example, Moore argues:

> So the reason that it is always ethnic Chinese who seem to be involved in Chinese intelligence matters is that they typically are the only ones China asks for assistance. It's just that simple.[98]

One must ask: How would the theory explain Chinese intelligence recruitments of non-ethnics?

In fact, while there is a clear historical pattern of the Chinese intelligence services recruiting ethnic Chinese assets, more recent cases strongly suggest that Beijing is moving beyond its traditional preference.[99] Gregg Bergersen and James Fondren, both Caucasian, were recruited in a "false flag" operation to acquire political and military information related to US–Taiwan defense relations. [100] [101] They were clearly approached because their positions at the Defense Security Cooperation Agency and US Pacific Command, respectively, gave them access to the intelligence that Beijing wanted, despite the fact that there are Chinese- and Taiwanese-Americans working at those organizations and related units with access to the same information. The most interesting recent case involves Glenn Duffie Shriver, the young Caucasian man from Michigan who was recruited and paid by Chinese intelligence to become an agent-in-place at either the State Department or Central Intelligence Agency.[102] [103] While the Shriver operation was an embarrassing failure for Beijing, it should perhaps be seen as an operational response to US counterintelligence's assumption about ethnic Chinese targeting, believing perhaps that Caucasian applicants are subject to less scrutiny than their ethnic counterparts.

In sum, while Chinese intelligence does have a historically strong track record of attempting to recruit ethnic Chinese, primarily because of cultural and language affinity, more recent cases suggest that they have broadened their tradecraft to recruit non-ethnic assets as well, perhaps as a way of complicating US counterintelligence efforts.

Lack of traditional tradecraft

Another commonly held belief about Chinese intelligence operations is that they do not use the traditional spy tradecraft associated with American and Soviet agents during the Cold War. As Paul Moore puts it, the Chinese "do not spy the way God intended."[104] Specifically, the Old School view claims that Chinese intelligence officers rarely use diplomatic cover, and when they do use cover they do not recruit or run agents. In addition, they argue that Chinese intelligence personnel do not use dead drops, avoid clandestine contacts of any kind between agents and handlers on US or even their own soil,[105] and rarely even ask a source for a classified document.[106] Instead, Moore and others argue that the Chinese services prefer to use their own scientists to elicit "small bits and pieces of information" from their American counterparts during conferences and private conversations.[107]

In fact, the empirical record is filled with rich counter-examples. With respect to the use of diplomatic cover for intelligence operations, assistant military attaché Hou Desheng and consular officer Zhang Weichu left the United States in late 1987 after being caught engaged in "activities incompatible with their diplomatic status."[108] While they were not declared *persona non grata*, Hou and Zhang were "caught with their hands in the cookie jar," accepting what they believed was a classified NSA document from an undercover FBI agent.[109]

Chinese agents have also been caught employing technical exfiltration methods, as well as using technical counter-surveillance technologies like encryption and other covert communications methods. Larry Wu-Tai Chin "provided his intelligence on rolls of 35mm undeveloped film of documents that he smuggled out of his workplace."[110] Babur Maihesuti, 62, was convicted for handing information about the health, travel patterns, and political leanings of other Uighurs to a journalist and diplomat who was, in fact, a Chinese intelligence officer.[111] Maihesuti had infiltrated a political body for Uighurs in exile – the World Uighur Congress – and would secretly pass information to his contact with the help of "a special system for dialing telephones."[112] Noshir Gowadia used covert e-mail addresses to communicate with his handlers.[113] Chi Mak and his family utilized advanced encryption to obfuscate their activities. During the trial, the prosecutor explained to the jury:

> It's not an encryption program that you can go to Fry's or Office Depot
> and buy. It was a custom-made encryption program and its author was a
> Chinese man.[114]

He alleged that American investigators would have been unable to break the encryption if a search of the home of Mr. Mak's brother hadn't turned up a 113-letter key[115] to the code.[116] According to court documents, the Maks encrypted the disks to avoid detection and used coded words to arrange a drop-off of the disks to a Chinese intelligence operative. In one phone conversation, the brother, Tai Wang Mak, intimated that he would be traveling with his wife and a third companion he described as his "assistant" – a reference, prosecutors said, to the disks, hidden in his luggage.[117] In the Bergersen and Fondren cases, Kuo wrote encrypted e-mail messages to an individual described in the court documents as "PRC Official A," using the commercial public key cryptography program, Pretty Good Privacy (PGP), and transmitted the messages to PRC Official A, Kang Yuxin, and Bergersen via three different ISPs.[118] The same Chinese official communicated with Kuo via Yahoo! and Hotmail accounts registered under false names, and maintained five different phone numbers.[119]

Other Chinese assets have used traditional counter-surveillance techniques in their dealings with their Chinese intelligence handlers. Katrina Leung began using an alias ("Luo") to communicate with her PRC handler, who chose the nom de guerre "Mao."[120] Leung also told a Chinese official from the PRC consulate in San Francisco to call her from a public telephone because she had something urgent to convey that she did not want anyone to hear and was likely aware that the FBI had the consulate under FISA surveillance.[121] In the 1980s, convicted spy Chi Mak first served as courier for another Chinese intelligence asset, Greg Dongfan Chung, acting as a cut-out for the delivery of his material to Beijing. In the Bergersen and Fondren cases, Kuo used Kang Yuxin, a PRC citizen and a Lawful Permanent Resident Alien in the US,[122] as a cut-out to interact with their two assets and deliver their products to "PRC Official A."[123] Kuo told PRC Official A that they needed to be careful because the United States is watching "China's spy action."[124] Kang was well aware of her role, because Kuo told her on at least one occasion that PRC Official A was paying Kuo for the work he performs, and that Kuo in turn was using that money to support her. In the most bizarre case of the PRC's use of cut-outs,

Chinese intelligence provided Larry Wu-Tai Chin with an emergency contact, Mark Cheung, who was an illegal operating in the United States as a legitimately ordained Catholic priest, though he was also married with a wife in China![125]

Perhaps the most important element of Chinese counter-surveillance tradecraft is their preference for meeting with assets outside of the United States, usually in China or an affiliated locale like Hong Kong or Macau. As one US official told the *Los Angeles Times* in 1988, "the Chinese prefer to do their actual recruiting in China for obvious security reasons."[126] Examples abound, but a few are illustrative of the consistent dynamic. In a letter of May 2, 1987, AVIC official Gu Weihao asked Greg Dongfang Chung to come to Guangzhou, where Gu could arrange a meeting in a place that was "safe." The letter suggested "cover stories" for travel to the PRC, including an invitation from an art institute to defendant Chung's wife, an artist, to visit the PRC. Gu also suggested that passing information through another engineer in the United States, Chi Mak, was "faster and safer." When Noshir Gowadia would visit China to transfer information during his consulting work, his PRC handlers added an additional layer of travel security, altering the stamps in his passport or moving him through passport control without stamping the passport at all.[127] Larry Wu-Tai Chin made frequent trips to Hong Kong to meet his handler, Ou Qiming,[128] and later met with handlers in Toronto, Hong Kong, Macau, and Beijing.[129] One of the secondary purposes of his trips was to hide his financial gains from espionage, depositing more than $192,000 in gold and in American and Hong Kong currency in Hong Kong bank accounts from December 1978 through June 1983.[130] Chi Mak's brother, Tai Mak, traveled to China to deliver encrypted disks of information, meeting with his handler, Pu Peiliang, in Guangzhou, where the latter worked as an operations researcher at Zhongshan University's 2PLA-funded Chinese Center for Asia Pacific Studies.[131] Kuo regularly traveled to Beijing and maintained an office in Beijing.[132] "PRC Official A" met with Kuo during each of his trips to Beijing, leading Kuo to conclude that the "[CCP] Central Committee has assigned him to take care of me."[133]

In sum, Chinese intelligence operations for decades exhibit significant evidence of tradecraft, both on the part of case officers and their assets, strongly suggesting that the Old School view is wrong.

China only collects intelligence from good people

Within the Chinese intelligence literature there is a common belief that the PRC services don't recruit people motivated by revenge, financial problems, emotional issues, or other vulnerabilities, but only collect intelligence from "good people." Paul Moore puts it succinctly: "China never looks for or approaches individuals with personal or financial problems who are the staple of other nations' intelligence efforts against the US."[134]

Again, the fact record suggests the opposite.

The best examples involve China's deft use of honey traps, often exploiting the adulterous desires of married, usually male targets in long-term affairs to acquire intelligence. The award for the most bizarre case involves French diplomat Bernard Boursicot and his long-time relationship with a Chinese opera performer and intelligence asset named Shi Peipu, later dramatized in the play *M. Butterfly*. Boursicot maintained an active and what he believed was a heterosexual relationship with Shi, who claimed he had borne a child for Boursicot but was actually a man.[135] In May 2004, a 46-year-old Japanese code clerk working in Tokyo's Shanghai consulate committed suicide after Japanese weekly magazine *Shukan Bunshun* revealed that he was being blackmailed by Chinese intelligence over his affair with a bar worker. In his suicide note, the diplomat said he would rather die than give in to blackmail: "I can't sell out my country." He was pressured to provide names and other information about diplomats and the flight numbers used to take encrypted classified documents to Japan.[136]

Other successful Chinese honey traps are one-night stands or similarly brief rendezvous. In 2008, an aide to UK Prime Minister Gordon Brown had his BlackBerry phone stolen after being picked up by a Chinese woman who had approached him in a Shanghai hotel disco.[137] Later that year, Deputy Mayor of London Ian Clement was allegedly drugged by an attractive woman who he met at a party in Beijing.[138] After he passed out, she reportedly went through his room, collecting information from his briefcase about London's operations and business dealings, and downloading material from his BlackBerry. Nothing was taken from his wallet.[139]

Chinese intelligence handlers have also shown a penchant for recruiting assets with other moral problems. Kuo regularly took Gregg Bergersen to Las Vegas, where he was observed providing him with piles of casino chips for gambling.[140] Larry Wu-Tai Chin allegedly "had multiple girlfriends, a penchant for sex toys, gambled tens of thousands of dollars in Las Vegas."[141] He was charged with assault for allegedly fondling a teenage girl in the laundry room of his apartment building, but the charges were later dropped.[142] He reportedly engaged in regular phone sex with a "niece" in New York, who sometimes met him for rendezvous.[143] Because of these marital problems, he asked his handler for $150,000 to pay off his wife and get a divorce, but Beijing declined.[144]

In contrast to the Old School view, the evidence suggests that the Chinese intelligence services have no problem recruiting assets with substantial moral deficiencies and, like their counterparts around the world, exploit those vulnerabilities for their own gain.

China has 3,000 front companies in the US

One of the most persistent urban legends about Chinese intelligence operations is the accusation that Beijing controls 3,000 front companies in the United States. This allegation first appeared in public in media reporting on the Cox Commission in the late 1990s. Despite the efforts of researchers on both sides of the political spectrum to convince the Commission otherwise, the final draft of the Cox Report made the following claim:

[I]n Senate testimony on the same day in 1997, the [Defense] Department said it could identify only two PLA companies that were doing business in the United States, while the AFL-CIO identified at least 12, and a Washington-based think-tank identified 20 to 30 such companies. The Select Committee has determined that all three figures are far below the true figure.

The Select Committee has concluded that there are more than 3,000 PRC corporations in the United States, some with links to the PLA, a State intelligence service, or with technology targeting and acquisition roles.[145]

The committee defined "front companies" as any affiliated with the Chinese government, its security services, or the People's Liberation Army, its military arm, that were set up to acquire Western technology, give cover to spies, launder or raise money, or influence the US government.

The Washington-based think-tank cited by the Cox Report was the RAND Corporation, and the individual testifying was James Mulvenon, who had written a book on the Chinese military's international business empire[146] as well as several internal studies on the subject for RAND's government customers.[147] In his 1998 testimony, Mulvenon highlighted at least 14 companies that could be definitively linked to the Chinese military, such as PTK International, Inc., Poly USA, Inc., Dynasty Holding Company, JF&D International, H&D International, Novell International, and various subsidiaries of Xinxing, all of which were dissolved after indictments and bad press in the mid-1990s or PLA divestiture in 1998.[148] Similarly, Mulvenon exposed 12 subsidiaries of NORINCO, then China's defense ordnance production company, many of which were producing chemicals, optics, lighting fixtures, sport guns, and auto parts for Walmart and other major chains.[149] The AFL-CIO representative was Jeffrey L. Fiedler, the then president of the Food and Allied Trades Department, a unit that had campaigned for years against allowing affiliates of the People's Liberation Army to do business in the US. In the 1990s, the department sponsored a website entitled "Kick the PLA Out of the USA," which contained links to testimony and reports about the PLA and to proposed legislation barring such enterprises from operating in the US. Despite very different agendas, Mulvenon and Fiedler, who had worked closely together for years, roughly agreed on the scale of Chinese front companies, and told members of the Commission they were vastly overstating the number of Chinese front companies operating in the United States.[150]

Shortly after publication, the *Los Angeles Times* carried an article investigating this allegation, concluding that the number "could only be reached by lumping together civilian, military and defense-industrial companies incorporated in the US – and that there is little chance that all could be equally under the thumb of Chinese military or espionage agencies."[151] The article pointed out that the Cox Report did not produce a list of the 3,000 "fronts" or explain how it reached that figure.[152] In the article, numerous China and trade experts refuted the claim. "The idea that most of these companies are set up by the [state security agency] is absolute nonsense," said Nick Lardy, now a senior Fellow at the Peterson Institute for International Economics.

Despite consistent repetition of the figure by senior US government officials, there is no evidence that the Chinese government operates "3,000 front companies" in the United States, and this urban legend has served mainly to distract the national debate about Chinese espionage from more serious threats to national security and technological competitiveness that include the informal relationships which mostly legitimate companies in the US have with elements of the Chinese government, as opposed to being established by them.

Science and technology espionage

While the preceding pages have called into question the applicability of the "Old School" view for China's current intelligence operations, many of the principles continue to be dispositive for Beijing's efforts to acquire sensitive science and technology information. According to the 2004 *Intelligence Threat Handbook*, PRC operations against S&T targets are generally "not directed and controlled by PRC intelligence services."[153] Although USG sources acknowledge that "there are specific MSS components charged with running technology collection operations," it is striking that "the MSS does not appear to be notably active in organizing covert operations to collect US technology."[154] Instead, the "consumers" of S&T intelligence such as institutes or factories define collection requirements, design the collection strategy, and carry out the collection. For example,

> In some instances, a delegation will visit a PRC consulate in the United States and identify the company that produces the technology or information the delegation is interested in. Intelligence officials will give the delegation members the names of company employees with whom the officials have established ties, and the delegation will appeal to them for covert assistance in obtaining a restricted item. If successful the delegation may ask the consulate to use the diplomatic pouch to mail it back to China.[155]

In other cases, the scientists and engineers in the delegations act as spotters:

> when delegations and PRC students or researchers have contact with US laboratories or advanced research facilities, they as a rule do not attempt to steal or covertly acquire restricted information; they simply identify what they need and invite knowledgeable individuals to make reciprocal visits to the PRC. While there, the Chinese hosts will attempt to persuade the American guests to make unauthorized disclosures. The PRC students or delegation members thus become vectors, not for theft of information, but for convincing US experts that they give their technical knowledge away.[156]

TABLE 8.1 Technology Espionage Cases Involving China, 2007–2011[157]

Date of Conviction	Type of Case	Perpetrators	Technologies
October 2011	Export Control	Li Li, Xian Hongwei	Radiation-hardened microchips for satellites
March 2011	Export Control	Lian Yang	Radiation-hardened microchips for satellites
March 2011	Export Control	Sixing Liu	Precision navigation devices
February 2011	Trade Secrets	Wenchyu Liu	Elastomeric polymer
January 2011	Export Control, Communicating National Defense Information	Noshir Gowadia	Low-signature cruise missile exhaust system, lock-on range for infrared missiles against the B-2 bomber
January 2011	Export Control	Yuefeng Wei, Zhenzhou Wu, Bo Li	Phased-array radar, electronic warfare missile guidance, and military satellite communications components
October 2010	Export Control	York Yuan Chang, Leping Huang	Analog-to-digital converters
September 2010	Export Control	Chi Tong Kuok	Military encryption, communications and global positioning system equipment
September 2010	Export Control	Phillip Andro Jamison	Combat-grade night vision devices, riflescopes, and laser aiming devices
August 2010	Trade Secrets	Kexue Huang	Biotechnology
May 2010	Export Controls	Sam Ching Sheng Lee	Thermal imaging cameras
March 2010	Export Control	Hok Shek Chan, Wong Fook Loy, and Ngo Tek Chai	Indicators servo tachometers for C-130 military flight simulators
February 2010	Economic Espionage	Dongfang "Greg" Chung	Information related to the Space Shuttle, Delta IV rocket
October 2009	Export Control	Jianwei Ding (Singapore), Kok Tong Lim (Singapore), Ping Cheng (USA)	Carbon-fiber material with applications in aircraft, rockets, spacecraft, and uranium enrichment
August 2009	Export Control	William Chai-Wai Tsu	Integrated circuits for use in military radar systems

TABLE 8.1 Continued

Date of Conviction	Type of Case	Perpetrators	Technologies
July 2009	Export Control	Zhiyong Guo	Thermal-imaging cameras
July 2009	Export Control	John Reece Roth	Plasma stealth for UAVs
July 2009	Export Control	Bing Xu (PRC)	Night-vision technology
May 2009	Export Control	Joseph Piquet	High-power amplifiers for early warning radars and missile target acquisition systems
April 2009	Trade Secrets	Yan Zhu	Environmental software
April 2009	Export Control	Fu-Tian Lu	Microwave amplifier
April 2009	Export Control	Quansheng Shu	Space launch technical data and cryogenic fueling systems
March 2009	Export Control	Yaming Nina Qi Hanson, Harold Dewitt Hanson	Unmanned Aerial Vehicle (UAV) autopilots
January 2009	Export Control	Michael Ming Zhang	Counterfeit Cisco components and tank-related electronics
December 2008	Economic espionage	Hanjuan Jin	Military-related technology data from Motorola
November 2008	Trade Secrets	Fei Ye and Ming Zhong	Semiconductor technology
September 2008	Export Control	Qing Li	Military-grade accelerometers
August 2008	Export Control	Desmond Dinesh Frank	C-130 military aircraft training equipment
June 2008	Export Control	Xiaodong Sheldon Meng	Military source code for training fighter pilots
March 2008	Export Control	Chi Mak	Navy warship technology, including Quiet Electric Drive
December 2007	Export Control	Ding Zhengxing, Su Yang, and Peter Zhu	Amplifiers for digital radios and wireless area networks
December 2007	Export Control	Philip Cheng	Night vision camera
August 2007	Export Control	Fung Yung	Microwave integrated circuits

These cases illustrate the fact that Chinese universities, research institutes, and factories are frequently aided by what might be termed "espionage entrepreneurs" on the US side, or what Paul Moore and others call the "cottage industry." These individuals are often naturalized Chinese or Taiwanese citizens who operate small, mom-and-pop businesses, usually from their residences. They are actively trawling for access to technologies or components sought by mainland customers, and then seek to exploit the vagaries of US export control laws to illegally ship them to China. As early as 1998, China was already the primary target for US Customs agents in about 50 percent of all illegal technology transfer cases on the west coast.[158] While these technologies are sometimes cutting-edge, more often than not they are less advanced items that are nonetheless essential to specific Chinese programs. According to a former export control enforcement official: "The Chinese aren't going for the cutting-edge stuff – laser killer-satellite technology and so forth. They are primarily after mid-range and dual-use technology that has both civilian and military applications – a computer that drives an auto production plant, for example."[159] They are also not directed agents of the Chinese state, and are motivated almost entirely by money. As former FBI Assistant Director for Counterintelligence Bruce Carlson puts it: "The basis for the whole program is money. People [in the US] are looking to make a buck. China has money to spend."[160]

If we step back and look at all the cases of Chinese technology espionage over the past 40 years as an analytical whole, it is helpful to systematically categorize different modes of economic and technology espionage. Mattis identifies at least five forms involving varying degrees of government or intelligence service involvement:

1. Intelligence service collection of economic secrets for state-supported industrial development.
2. Intelligence service collection of technology for military intelligence and planning as well as strategic economic intelligence.
3. Government-sponsored, non-intelligence service collection for state-supported industry.
4. Economic actors stealing competitors' secrets for the actor's own benefit.
5. Entrepreneurial individuals stealing economic secrets to sell to any of the above actors and/or go into business for themselves.[161]

If we apply this framework to the cases in the Appendix, it is clear that "cases conclusively linked to mainland China demonstrate all five modes of economic espionage and technology transfer."[162] First, in 1993, Wu Bin and two other Chinese nationals were prosecuted for smuggling export-controlled equipment to China at the direction of the MSS.[163] In the second category, two accredited Chinese diplomats – one an assistant military attaché reporting to 2PLA – in the United States were expelled in 1987 after attempting to purchase cryptographic materials in an FBI sting operation.[164] Third, the Chinese military owns or owned several import–export companies to facilitate the purchase of foreign dual-use technologies, such as poly technologies.[165] Combining the fourth and fifth categories, two Silicon Valley engineers, Ye Fei and Zhong Ming, were indicted in 2002 for the attempted theft of technical schematics from Sun Microsystems and Transmeta. Ye and Zhong wanted to start their own company in China. They also sought state funding through the national technical modernization program, the 863 Program, according to court documents.[166] Finally, in late 2005, Bill Moo was arrested prior to exporting General Electric's newest engine for the F-16. Moo reportedly stood to make a profit of a million dollars for selling the engine to the Chinese military.[167]

Conclusion

For too long, the literature on Chinese intelligence operations has relied on a set of outdated proverbs and shibboleths. As Mattis argues persuasively in his recent publications, "each of these propositions has serious flaws in its internal logic, foolhardy assumptions, or dangerous implications that should be addressed before comparing the conventional view to the record."[168] After systematically assessing the Old School tenets with the empirical record, the result is (not surprisingly) a mixed bag. Some hoary chestnuts, such as the belief that China doesn't pay for secrets or doesn't use traditional tradecraft or only recruits "good people," seem to be completely at variance with the facts. Others, particularly the focus on recruitment of ethnic Chinese, appear to be less ironclad than in the past, but should also be viewed in a much more nuanced light lest they lead to mindless ethnic profiling. A few of the more high-profile concepts, such as the infamous "thousand grains of sand," have been exposed for their faulty internal logic and mischaracterization of Chinese bureaucratic behavior, suggesting that they may have arisen from attempts to reduce our own cognitive dissonance in the face of key missing data. In addition, some of the core tenets of the Old School, such as the Chinese focus on convincing scientists to give away sensitive information in informal settings, appear to be alive and well.

In the end, the evidence on Chinese intelligence operations supports Mattis' notion of a "layered approach to intelligence collection," ranging from traditional service-driven operations with modern tradecraft to the "amateur espionage" (业余间谍) entrepreneurs operating out of their homes. Yet this multi-level approach is clearly even more challenging for US counter-intelligence than the traditional model where intelligence services maintain exclusive control over operations. As former FBI official Dave Szady asserts, China "can work on so many levels that [they] may prove more difficult to contain than the Russian threat."[169] Moreover, as we shall see in the next chapter, traditional Chinese intelligence collection operations are being quickly overtaken by the ease, deniability, and stunning effectiveness of cyber-intelligence collection.

Notes

1 Jay Solomon, "FBI Sees Big Threat from Chinese Spies," *Wall Street Journal*, August 10, 2005, p. A1.
2 Joby Warrick and Carrie Johnson, "Chinese Spy 'Slept' in US for Two Decades," *Washington Post*, April 3, 2008, www.washingtonpost.com/wp-dyn/content/article/2008/04/02/AR2008040203952.html.
3 Michelle Van Cleave on *60 Minutes*. See also "Caught on Tape," *CBS News*, August 30, 2010, www.cbsnews.com/8301-18560_162-6242498.html.
4 David Lynch, "Law Enforcement Struggles to Combat Chinese Spying," *USA Today*, July 23, 2007, www.usatoday.com/money/world/2007-07-22-china-spy-1_N.htm.
5 Ibid.
6 Ibid.
7 Solomon, "FBI Sees Big Threat from Chinese Spies."
8 Lynch, "Law Enforcement Struggles to Combat Chinese Spying."
9 David Leppard, "China Bugs and Burgles Britain," *The Sunday Times*, January 31, 2010.
10 "Merkel's China Visit Marred by Hacking Allegations," *Spiegel Online International*, August 27, 2007.
11 J. Michael Cole, "Friendship is No Bar to Espionage," *Taipei Times*, November 1, 2009, www.taipeitimes.com/News/editorials/archives/2009/11/01/2003457356.
12 Peter Mattis, "Beyond Spy vs. Spy: The Analytic Challenge of Understanding Chinese Intelligence Services," *Studies in Intelligence* 56, no. 3, September 2012, www.cia.gov/library/center-for-the-study-of-intelligence/csi-publications/csi-studies/studies/vol.-56-no.-3/pdfs/Mattis-Understanding%20Chinese%20Intel.pdf. See also Peter Mattis, "Chinese Intelligence Operations Revisited: Toward a New Baseline," MA Thesis, Georgetown University, 2011.
13 Paul Moore, "Spies of a Different Stripe," *Washington Post*, May 31, 1999, p. A23.
14 For examples of the "mosaic" view, see Paul Moore, "How China Plays the Ethnic Card: Beijing's Strategy of Targeting Chinese Americans is Hard to Counter With US Security Defense" *Los Angeles Times*, June 24, 1999; Stein, "Espionage without Evidence: Is It Racism or Realism to Look at Chinese-Americans When Trying to Figure Out Who's Spying for China?"
15 "Special Report: Espionage with Chinese Characteristics," StratFor Global Intelligence Report, 24 March 2010; Paul Moore, "How China Plays the Ethnic Card"; Paul Moore, "Chinese Culture and the Practice of 'Actuarial' Intelligence," in Douglas Daye, *A Law Enforcement Sourcebook of Asian Crime and Cultures: Tactics and Mindsets*, Boca Raton, FL: CRC Press, 1997, pp. 377–382; Neil Lewis, "Chinese Espionage Cases Raising Concerns in Washington," *New York Times*, July 10, 2008.
16 Moore, "Chinese Culture and the Practice of 'Actuarial' Intelligence."
17 Mark Magnier, "China's Style of Espionage in Spotlight," *Los Angeles Times*, July 17, 2005, reprinted in *Seattle Times*, http://seattletimes.nwsource.com/html/nationworld/2002386112_chinaspy17.html.
18 Simon Cooper, "How China Steals US Military Secrets," *Popular Mechanics*, August 2009, www.popularmechanics.com/technology/military/3319656.
19 Peter Grier, "Spy Case Patterns the Chinese Style of Espionage," *Christian Science Monitor*, November 30, 2005, www.csmonitor.com/2005/1130/p01s01-usfp.html.
20 Mattis, "Beyond Spy vs. Spy." See also Mattis, "Chinese Intelligence Operations Revisited."
21 Moore, "Chinese Culture and the Practice of 'Actuarial' Intelligence."
22 Ibid.
23 Ibid.
24 Josh Gerstein, "Prosecutors Reverse Course in China Spy Case," *New York Sun*, April 12, 2007.

25 Lynch, "Law Enforcement Struggles to Combat Chinese Spying," and Grier, "Spy Case Patterns the Chinese Style of Espionage."
26 Warrick and Johnson, "Chinese Spy 'Slept' in US for Two Decades."
27 United States v. Dongfan "Greg" Chung, SA CR 08-00024, United States District Court, Central District of California, February 6, 2008.
28 United States v. Dongfan "Greg" Chung.
29 "State Security Department Set Up in Fujian," *BBC Summary of World Broadcasts*, October 17, 1983; "Anhui Sets Up State Security Department," *BBC Summary of World Broadcasts*, June 5, 1995; "Sichuan Arrests Falun Gong Follower for State Secrets Leak," *BBC Summary of World Broadcasts*, November 5, 1999; Erik Eckholm, "Researcher for *The Times* in China Is Detained," *New York Times*, September 24, 2004; "China Releases Last of Four Japanese Charged With Military Zone Intrusion," *Xinhua News*, October 9, 2010.
30 Kenneth Lieberthal, *Governing China: From Revolution through Reform*, New York: W.W. Norton and Company, 1995, pp. 169–170.
31 Kenneth Lieberthal, "China's Governing System and its Impact on Environmental Policy Implementation," Wilson Center China Environment Series 1, 1997, p.3, www.wilsoncenter.org/sites/default/files/ACF4CF.PDF.
32 Solomon, "FBI Sees Big Threat from Chinese Spies."
33 Jeff Stein, "Espionage without Evidence: Is It Racism or Realism to Look at Chinese-Americans When Trying to Figure Out Who's Spying for China?" *Salon.com*, August 26, 1999: www.salon.com/news/feature/1999/08/26/china/index.html.
34 Mark Magnier, "China's Style of Espionage in Spotlight," *Los Angeles Times*, July 17, 2005, reprinted in *Seattle Times*, http://seattletimes.nwsource.com/html/nationworld/2002386112_chinaspy.html.
35 Dan Stober and Ian Hoffman, *A Convenient Spy: Wen Ho Lee and the Politics of Nuclear Espionage*, New York: Simon and Schuster, 2002, p.77.
36 Stein, "Espionage without Evidence."
37 William Overend, "China Seen Using Close US Ties for Espionage: California Activity Includes Theft of Technology and Surpasses That of Soviets, Experts Believe," *Los Angeles Times*, November 20, 1988, http://articles.latimes.com/1988-11-20/news/mn-463_1_chinese-espionage.
38 Moore, "How China Plays the Ethnic Card."
39 Overend, "China Seen Using Close US Ties for Espionage."
40 David Wise, *Tiger Trap: America's Secret Spy War with China*, Boston, MA: Houghton Mifflin Harcourt, 2011, p. 158.
41 Jeff Gerth and James Risen, "Reports Show Scientist Gave US Radar Secrets to China," *New York Times*, May 10, 1999.
42 Wise, *Tiger Trap*, p. 155.
43 William Claiborne, "Taiwan-Born Scientist Passed Defense Data: Ex-Los Alamos Worker Gave Secrets to China," *Washington Post*, December 12, 1997.
44 Lee denied giving them classified information and "passed" a subsequent polygraph exam. See Wen Ho Lee, with Helen Zia, *My Country Versus Me: The First-Hand Account by the Los Alamos Scientist Who Was Falsely Accused of Being a Spy*, New York: Hyperion, 2001.
45 United States v. Dongfan "Greg" Chung.
46 Ibid.
47 Ibid.
48 Ibid.
49 Stein, "Espionage without Evidence."
50 Ibid.
51 Ibid.
52 Ibid.
53 Ibid.
54 Wise, *Tiger Trap*, p. 202.

55 In the Case of United States v. Larry Wu-tai Chin. United States of America, Plaintiff-appellee, v. Cathy Chin, Defendant-appellant (United States Court of Appeals, Fourth Circuit. – 848 F.2d 55, Argued Nov. 6, 1987. Decided May 27, 1988)

56 Noshir Gowadia Convicted of Providing Defense Information and Services to People's Republic of China (DOJ press release, 9 August 2010)

57 Hawaii Man Sentenced to 32 Years in Prison for Providing Defense Information and Services to People's Republic of China" (DOJ press release, 25 Jan 2011)

58 Bill Gertz, "Spy's Arrest Underscores Beijing's Bid for Agents," *Washington Times*, October 25, 2010, www.washingtontimes.com/news/2010/oct/25/spys-arrest-underscores-beijings-bid-for-agents/.

59 In the Case of United States v. Glenn Duffie Shriver (United States District Court for the Eastern District of Virginia, Case 1:10-cr-00402-LO).

60 Wise, *Tiger Trap*, p. 149. As a double or triple agent, Leung was actually making money from both ends. Leung received $1.7 million as an operational FBI asset, including $951,000 after the FBI learned in 1991 that she was passing information to the MSS. Of this, $1.2 million were reimbursements for expenses, and $521,000 for passing information.

61 "They Let Her Clean the China," *The Economist*, May 15, 2003.

62 Statement of the US Attorney on the Guilty Please Entered by Katrina Leung (DOJ, 16 Dec 2005)

63 A Review of the FBI's Handling and Oversight of FBI Asset Katrina Leung, Special Report (DOJ/IG, 24 May 2006)

64 Former Defense Department Official Sentenced to 57 Months in Prison for Espionage Violation (DOJ Press Release, 11 July 2008)

65 Jerry Markon, "Man Gave Military Secrets To China," *Washington Post*, May 14, 2008.

66 "Caught on Tape," *CBS News*.

67 United States v. Tai Shen Kuo, Gregg William Bergersen, and Yu Xin Kang, "Affidavit in Support of Criminal Complaint, Three Arrest Warrants and Three Search Warrants," United States District Court for the Eastern District of Virginia, Alexandria Division.

68 United States v. Tai Shen Kuo, Gregg William Bergersen, and Yu Xin Kang.

69 Ibid.

70 "Defense Department Official Charged with Espionage Conspiracy," Department of Justice Press Release, May 13, 2009, www.justice.gov/opa/pr/2009/May/09-nsd-469.html.

71 Moore, "How China Plays the Ethnic Card."

72 Centre for Counterintelligence and Security Studies, *Intelligence Threat Handbook*, 2004, p. 21. This book was prepared for and published under the auspices of the former Interagency OPSEC Support Staff (IOSS) as an UNCLASSIFIED//FOUO document. A copy may be accessed at www.fas.org/irp/threat/handbook.

73 Centre for Counterintelligence and Security Studies, p. 21.

74 Ibid.

75 Paul Moore, "How China Plays the Ethnic Card: Beijing's Strategy of Targeting Chinese Americans is Hard to Counter With US Security Defense," *Los Angeles Times*, June 24, 1999, www.articles.latimes.com/1999/jun/24/local/me-49832.

76 Moore, "How China Plays the Ethnic Card."

77 Centre for Counterintelligence and Security Studies, p. 21.

78 Moore, "How China Plays the Ethnic Card."

79 Stein, "Espionage without Evidence."

80 Moore, "How China Plays the Ethnic Card"; Paul Moore, "Spies of a Different Stripe," *Washington Post*, May 31, 1999, p. A23; "Special Report: Espionage with Chinese Characteristics," StratFor: p. 5; *2009 Annual Report to Congress*, USCC, pp. 149–150; Eftimiades, *Chinese Intelligence Operations*, pp. 60–61.

81 For the Asian-American reaction, see Wang Ling-chi, "Spy Hysteria," *Asian Week* 20

(March 25, 1999); Helen Zia, "I am not a Spy – Are You?" *Asian Week* 20 (June 10, 1999); Emil Amok, "The Everyman Spy: The New Yellow Peril," *Asian Week*, August 19, 2005; George Koo, "FBI's Ongoing Racial Profiling Hurts National Interest," *FinalCall.com News*, August 29, 2005; George Koo, "Warning to Chinese Americans: FBI Still Obsessed with Chinese-American 'Spies,'" *New America Media*, May 17, 2007.

82 Stein, "Espionage without Evidence."

83 Wise, *Tiger Trap*, pp. 202–213.

84 Wise, *Tiger Trap*, pp. 154–166.

85 United States v. Dongfan "Greg" Chung.

86 Ibid.

87 Lee, *My Country Versus Me.*

88 Ibid., p. 327.

89 Ibid., p. 288.

90 Bellows Report, p. 385.

91 Reno testimony, pp. 7, 15.

92 Notra Trulock, *Code Name Kindred Spirit: Inside the Chinese Nuclear Espionage Scandal*, San Francisco: Encounter Books, 2003, pp.178–179.

93 Perla Ni, "Author Denounces Cox Report: Iris Chang tells conventioneers that her research was misused," *Asiaweek*, June 3, 1999, www.asianweek.com/060399/news_irishchang.html.

94 Mattis, "Beyond Spy vs. Spy." See also Mattis, "Chinese Intelligence Operations Revisited."

95 Moore, "How China Plays the Ethnic Card."

96 Mattis, "Beyond Spy vs. Spy." See also Mattis, "Chinese Intelligence Operations Revisited."

97 Ibid.

98 Moore, "How China Plays the Ethnic Card."

99 The Ron Montaperto case is a tough one. On the one hand, Montaperto apparently violated security rules by keeping documents judged to be classified in his home and not reporting contacts with Chinese military officers and intelligence personnel. On the other hand, Montaperto had been instructed to liaise with Chinese military officers and intelligence personnel at one point in the US–China relationship, and was punished for maintaining those relationships after the policy had shifted. Similarly, some of the documents in his possession at home appear to have been retroactively classified. These dilemmas are common for cleared government and contractor personnel who regularly travel to China and interact with PLA personnel for official or government contractual reasons, but are forced to engage in complex mental compartmentation and then naturally worry that they will be scrutinized by their own counter-intelligence personnel who view all interactions with Chinese military personnel as suspicious. Finally, critics of the Montaperto case believe that the NCIS ruse that led to his polygraph confessions smells of entrapment, especially given Montaperto's well-known penchant for emotionalism and Catholic guilt, both of which are fatal qualities for the poly. Like the Don Keyser case, there is little argument about the mishandling of classified documents, but intense disagreement about whether either man was a recruited spy for a foreign intelligence service.

100 Jury Convicts Defense Department Official James W. Fondren Jr. of Unlawful Communication of Classified Information and Making False Statements (DOJ Press Release, 25 September 2009)

101 Defense Department Official Pleads Guilty to Espionage Charge Involving China (DOJ Press Release, 31 March 08)

102 Gertz, "Spy's Arrest Underscores Beijing's Bid for Agents."

103 In the Case of United States v. Glenn Duffie Shriver (United States District Court for the Eastern District of Virignia, Case 1:10-cr-00402-LO)

104 Bill Gertz, "Chinese Espionage Handbook Details Ease of Swiping Secrets," *Washington Times*, December 26, 2000.
105 Stein, "Espionage without Evidence."
106 Ibid.
107 Ibid.
108 James Mann and Ronald Ostrow, "US Ousts Two Chinese Envoys for Espionage," *Los Angeles Times*, December 31, 1987, www.articles.latimes.com/1987-12-31/news/mn-7581_1.
109 Mann and Ostrow, "US Ousts Two Chinese Envoys for Espionage."
110 Centre for Counterintelligence and Security Studies, *Intelligence Threat Handbook*, 2004, p. 21.
111 "Sweden Jails Uighur Chinese Man for Spying," *Reuters*, March 8, 2010, www.reuters.com/article/idUSTRE6274U620100308.
112 "Sweden Jails Uighur Chinese Man for Spying."
113 United States v. Noshir Gowadia, United States District Court for the District of Hawaii, CR 05-00486 HG-KSC, October 25, 2007.
114 Josh Gerstein, "Prosecution: Spy Case Shows China's Effort to Steal US Secrets."
115 Josh Gerstein, "Prosecutors Reverse Course in China Spy Case," *New York Sun*, April 12, 2007.
116 Gerstein, "Prosecution: Spy Case Shows China's Effort to Steal US Secrets," *New York Sun*, March 29, 2007, www.nysun.com/national/prosecution-spy-case-shows-chinas-effort-to-steal/51450/.
117 Warrick and Johnson, "Chinese Spy 'Slept' in US for Two Decades."
118 United States v. Tai Shen Kuo, Gregg William Bergersen, and Yu Xin Kang.
119 Ibid.
120 "A Review of the FBI's Handling and Oversight of FBI Asset Katrina Leung," Department of Justice Office of the Inspector General, May 2006, www.justice.gov/oig/special/s0605/final.pdf.
121 "A Review of the FBI's Handling and Oversight of FBI Asset Katrina Leung."
122 "Defense Department Official and Two Others Arrested on Espionage Charges Involving China," Department of Justice Press Release, February 11, 2008, www.justice.gov/opa/pr/2008/February/08_nsd_105.html; and United States v. Tai Shen Kuo, Gregg William Bergersen, and Yu Xin Kang.
123 United States v. Tai Shen Kuo, Gregg William Bergersen, and Yu Xin Kang.
124 Ibid.
125 Wise, *Tiger Trap*, p. 206.
126 Overend, "China Seen Using Close US Ties for Espionage."
127 United States v. Noshir Gowadia.
128 Wise, *Tiger Trap*, p. 202.
129 Ibid.
130 Ronald Ostrow, "Accused Spy Chin Faces New Charges," *Los Angeles Times*, January 3, 1986, http://articles.latimes.com/1986-01-03/news/mn-23858_1_foreign-broadcast-information-service.
131 Lynch, "Law Enforcement Struggles to Combat Chinese Spying."
132 United States v. Tai Shen Kuo, Gregg William Bergersen, and Yu Xin Kang.
133 Ibid.
134 Moore, "How China Plays the Ethnic Card."
135 Joyce Wadler, "The True Story of M. Butterfly – The Spy Who Fell in Love with a Shadow," *The New York Times Magazine*, August 15, 1999, www.nytimes.com/1993/08/15/magazine/the-true-story-of-m-butterfly-the-spy-who-fell-in-love-with-a-shadow.html?pagewanted=all.
136 Justin McCurry, "Japan Says Diplomat's Suicide Followed Blackmail by China," *Guardian*, December 20, 2005, www.guardian.co.uk/world/2005/dec/29/japan.china.

137 David Leppard, "China Bugs and Burgles Britain," *The Times of London (Online)*, January 31, 2010, www.timesonline.co.uk/tol/news/uk/crime/article7009749.ece.

138 Kate Mansey, "Boris Johnson's deputy: 'I had sex with a Chinese spy'," *Sunday Mirror*, November 29, 2009, www.mirror.co.uk/news/top-stories/2009/11/29/boris-johnson-s-deputy-i-had-sex-with-a-chinese-spy-115875-21858098/.

139 Ibid.

140 Wise, *Tiger Trap*, p. 222.

141 Ibid., p. 202.

142 Ibid., p. 206.

143 Ibid., p. 209.

144 Ibid., p. 206.

145 *Report of the Select Committee on US National Security and Military/Commercial Concerns with the People's Republic Of China* (Cox Commission Report), Washington, DC: Government Printing Office, 1999, p. 34.

146 James Mulvenon, *Soldiers of Fortune: The Rise and Fall of the Chinese Military-Business Complex, 1978–98*, Armonk, NY: M.E. Sharpe, 2001.

147 James Mulvenon, *Chinese Military Commerce and US National Security*, Santa Monica, CA: RAND, 1997, MR-907.0-CAPP.

148 Mulvenon, *Chinese Military Commerce and US National Security*.

149 Ibid.

150 James Mulvenon, Testimony before the Select Committee on US National Security and Military/Commercial Concerns with the People's Republic of China, October 15, 1998.

151 Hael A. Hiltzik and Lee Romney, "Report's Claim on China 'Front' Firms Disputed," *Los Angeles Times*, May 27, 1999.

152 Ibid.

153 Centre for Counterintelligence and Security Studies, *Intelligence Threat Handbook*, 2004, p.18.

154 "Report to Congress on Chinese Espionage Activities against the United States by the Director of Central Intelligence and the Director of the Federal Bureau of Investigation," December 12, 1999.

155 Centre for Counterintelligence and Security Studies, p.18.

156 Ibid.

157 These case summaries were provided by the FBI. See www.justice.gov/nsd/docs/summary-eaca.pdf.

158 William Overend, "China Seen Using Close US Ties for Espionage: California Activity Includes Theft of Technology and Surpasses That of Soviets, Experts Believe," *Los Angeles Times*, November 20, 1988, http://articles.latimes.com/1988-11-20/news/mn-463_1_chinese-espionage.

159 Overend, "China Seen Using Close US Ties for Espionage."

160 Lynch, "Law Enforcement Struggles to Combat Chinese Spying."

161 Mattis, "Beyond Spy vs. Spy." See also Mattis, "Chinese Intelligence Operations Revisited."

162 Ibid.

163 Cox Commission Report, pp. 69–70.

164 Eftimiades, *Chinese Intelligence Operations*, pp. 37, 93–94; Mann and Ostrow, "US Ousts Two Chinese Envoys for Espionage."

165 Kan Zhongguo, "Intelligence Agencies Exist in Great Numbers, Spies Are Present Everywhere; China's Major Intelligence Departments Fully Exposed." *Chien Shao* (Hong Kong), January 1, 2006, p. 27; Cox Commission Report, p. 65. It is unclear to what extent the forced military divestiture of commercial enterprises affected those companies used by the Chinese military to acquire technology. See Michael Chase and James Mulvenon, "The Decommercialization of China's Ministry of State Security," *International Journal of Intelligence and Counterintelligence* 15, No. 4, November 2002, pp. 481–495; and Mulvenon, *Soldiers of Fortune*.

166 Terence Jeffrey, "Two Silicon Valley Engineers Indicted for Economic Espionage Aiding China," *Human Events*, January 13, 2003, pp. 1, 8.

167 Simon Cooper, "How China Steals US Military Secrets," *Popular Mechanics*, August 2006, www.popularmechanics.com/technology/military/3319656.

168 Mattis, "Beyond Spy vs. Spy." See also Mattis, "Chinese Intelligence Operations Revisited."

169 Solomon, "FBI Sees Big Threat from Chinese Spies", p.A1.

9

CHINESE CYBER ESPIONAGE

The scale of the problem

Cyber espionage is the latest and perhaps most devastating form of Chinese espionage, striking at the heart of American military advantage and technological competitiveness. Without mentioning China, General Keith Alexander, NSA Director and Commander of USCYBERCOM, told an audience at the Aspen Security Forum on July 26, 2012 that cyber espionage represents the "greatest transfer of wealth in history." Other government agencies are less circumspect about calling out Beijing for its cyber theft.[1] The Office of the National Counterintelligence Executive's 2011 report *Foreign Spies Stealing US Economic Secrets in Cyberspace* boldly asserts: "Chinese actors are the world's most active and persistent perpetrators of economic espionage."[2] While the media began reporting rumors of large-scale intrusions in 2005,[3] US officials did not publicly acknowledge exfiltrations of data until August 2006, when the Pentagon asserted that hostile civilian cyber units operating inside China had launched attacks against the NIPRNET and downloaded up to 20 terabytes of data.[4] In March 2007, the then Vice-Chairman of the Joint Chiefs General Cartwright told the US-China Economic and Security Review Commission that China was engaged in cyber reconnaissance, probing computer networks of US agencies and corporations.[5] This view was seconded in the 2007 *China Military Power Report*, an annual Pentagon assessment mandated by the National Defense Authorization Act, which claimed that "numerous computer networks around the world, including those owned by the US government, were subject to intrusions that appear to have originated within" the People's Republic of China.[6] Former White House and DHS cyber official Paul Kurtz told *Business Week* that the Chinese activity was "espionage on a massive scale."[7] A 2009 study by Northrup Grumman for the US-China Economic and Security Review Commission concluded: "Chinese espionage in the United States now comprises the single greatest threat to US technology . . . and has the potential to erode the United States' long-term position as a world leader in S&T [science and technology] innovation and competitiveness."[8] The problem appeared to be getting worse over time. Robert Jamison, the top cyber-security official at DHS, told reporters at a March 2008 briefing, "We're concerned that the intrusions are more frequent, and they're more targeted, and they're more sophisticated."[9] After the Operation Aurora intrusions against Google and other Silicon Valley companies in 2009 and 2010, officials became worried that China was escalating its intrusions. Whereas before the activities were targeted at government and military networks, threatening US military advantage and government policies, the new intrusions went beyond state-on-state espionage to threaten American technological competitiveness and economic prosperity.

Because the underlying evidence was classified, government and military officials could not provide detailed evidence of these allegations against the Chinese government and military, which naturally led to scrutiny of the specific attribution to China. In his confirmation testimony questions, current CYBERCOM Commander General Alexander agreed that "attribution can be very difficult."[10] Former senior DHS cyber-security official Greg Garcia told the *New York Times* in March 2009 that "attribution is a hall of mirrors."[11] With respect to China, Amit Yoran, the first director of DHS's National Cyber Security Division, cautioned, "I think it's a little bit naive to suggest that everything that says it comes from China comes from China."[12] Yet other officials were more confident in the assessment of Chinese responsibility. The then director of the DNI National Counterintelligence Executive, Joel Brenner, told the *National Journal* in 2008:

> Some [attacks], we have high confidence, are coming from government-sponsored sites. . . . The Chinese operate both through government agencies, as we do, but they also operate through sponsoring other organizations that are engaging in this kind of international hacking, whether or not under specific direction. It's a kind of cyber-militia. . . . It's coming in volumes that are just staggering.[13]

This view was confirmed by the February 2013 publication of a report by cyber intelligence firm Madiant, detailing highly precise attribution of a major set of network intrusions to a Chinese military intelligence unit in Shanghi.[14]

Strategic context of Chinese cyber espionage: China and cyber as an overt tool of state power

As a rising power, Chinese national interests have logically expanded with the growth in its economic, political, diplomatic, and military power. Yet its rise has occurred within a world system still dominated by American unilateral authority. Because of these imbalances, China has naturally sought to find asymmetrical advantages, and cyber space at first glance appears to be a dimension of national power in which the United States is asymmetrically vulnerable owing to its greater dependence on information systems. Moreover, China seems much more comfortable with cyber power as a legitimate, overt tool of state power, especially compared with the United States, which still treats cyber operations as a highly classified, compartmented capability. What do we mean by overt? Countries like China and Russia seem more comfortable with the overt use of cyber conflict, even by non-state proxies acting on their behalf, as we saw in numerous Chinese "patriotic hacker" events in the late 1990s and the Russian cyber conflicts in Estonia in 2007 and Georgia in 2008. When confronted with their potential involvement in these incidents, both Beijing and Moscow appeared to believe that the plausible deniability of the network was a sufficient fig-leaf to cover their barely veiled affiliations and common cause with the attacks. By contrast, Washington does not even have a vocabulary for discussing these capabilities in public, as seen in the incoherence of official US comments about possible computer network exploit activities against Milosevic during ALLIED FORCE and the Stuxnet industrial control systems hack in 2011.

Why cyber espionage?

Within the rubric of the Chinese government's view of cyber as a tool of national power, it is clear that this new dimension offers Beijing certain key strategic advantages, particularly with respect to intelligence collection, technological competitiveness, intelligence preparation of the battlefield, and strategic intelligence to policy-makers.

Intelligence collection advantages

Cyber espionage is now a favored mode of tradecraft for China, principally because of its logistical advantages and the promise of plausible deniability. On the first issue, Joel Brenner highlights the relative ease of cyber versus other traditional forms of espionage: "Cyber-networks are the new frontier of counterintelligence. . . . If you can steal information or disrupt an organization by attacking its networks remotely, why go to the trouble of running a spy?"[15] Take the case of Greg Dongfan Chung, discussed in Chapter 8, as an example. Managing Chung required significant institutional resources, including case officers, covert communications, money transfers, and travel arrangements. In the end, Chung was caught, and his "perp walk" and public trial proved to be an embarrassment to the Chinese government. Now imagine a scenario in which the same volume of information can be exfiltrated out of Boeing or Rockwell's computer networks in a single evening via an exquisite computer network exploitation operation, covered by the plausible deniability of network intrusions. Given the choice between the two modes, it is only natural that intelligence services would increasingly pick the less risky, cheaper, and faster way of doing business.

Technological competitiveness advantages

After more than 30 years of serving as the world's assembly point and export processing zone, the Beijing government has clearly made the decision to transform Chinese economic development by encouraging "indigenous innovation."[16] Since 2006, James McGregor and others have highlighted "Chinese policies and initiatives aimed at building 'national champion' companies through subsidies and preferential policies while using China's market power to appropriate foreign technology, tweak it and create Chinese 'indigenous innovations' that will come back at us globally."[17] In the information technology sector, McGregor notes: "Chinese government mandate to replace core foreign technology in critical infrastructure – such as chips, software and communications hardware – with Chinese technology within a decade." Among the tools being actively used to achieve these goals are:

> a foreign-focused anti-monopoly law, mandatory technology transfers, compulsory technology licensing, rigged Chinese standards and testing rules, local content requirements, mandates to reveal encryption codes, excessive disclosure for scientific permits and technology patents, discriminatory government procurement policies, and the continued failure to adequately protect intellectual property rights.[18]

Missing from this excellent list, however, are traditional technical espionage and technical cyber espionage, which many companies believe are already eroding their technical advantage. The logic for these latter approaches is clearly outlined by David Szady, former head of the FBI's Counterintelligence Unit: "If they can steal it and do it in five years, why [take longer] to develop it?"[19] Rather than destroying US competitiveness through "cyber war," former DNI McConnell argues that Chinese entities "are exploiting our systems for information advantage – looking for the characteristics of a weapons system by a defense contractor or academic research on plasma physics, for example – not in order to destroy data and do damage."[20]

Examples of Chinese cyber espionage to obtain science and technology can be divided into two broad categories: external and insider. The 2011 NCIX report offers three illustrative examples of insider cyber threats:

> David Yen Lee, a chemist with Valspar Corporation, used his access to internal computer networks between 2008 and 2009 to download approximately 160 secret formulas for paints and coatings to removable storage media. He intended to parlay this proprietary information to obtain a new job with Nippon Paint in Shanghai, China. Lee was arrested in March 2009, pleaded guilty to one count of theft of trade secrets, and was sentenced in December 2010 to 15 months in prison.
>
> Meng Hong, a DuPont research chemist, downloaded proprietary

information on organic light-emitting diodes (OLED) in mid-2009 to his personal e-mail account and thumb drive. He intended to transfer this information to Peking University, where he had accepted a faculty position, and sought Chinese government funding to commercialize OLED research. Hong was arrested in October 2009, pleaded guilty to one count of theft of trade secrets, and was sentenced in October 2010 to 14 months in prison.

Xiangdong Yu (aka Mike Yu), a product engineer with Ford Motor Company, copied approximately 4,000 Ford documents onto an external hard drive to help obtain a job with a Chinese automotive company. He was arrested in October 2009, pleaded guilty to two counts of theft of trade secrets, and was sentenced in April 2011 to 70 months in prison.[21]

External cyber threats to scientific and industrial data, believed to originate in China, have been well documented in reports by outside vendors. Some examples include:

In its *Night Dragon* report, McAfee documented "coordinated covert and targeted cyberattacks have been conducted against global oil, energy, and petrochemical companies," "targeting and harvesting sensitive competitive proprietary operations and project-financing information with regard to oil and gas field bids and operations."[22]

In his *Shady Rat* report, McAfee's Dmitry Alperovitch identified 71 compromised organizations in one set of intrusions, including 13 defense contractors, 13 information technology companies, and six manufacturing companies.[23]

In January 2010, Google reported a "highly sophisticated and targeted attack on our corporate infrastructure originating from China that resulted in the theft of intellectual property," including source code.[24] Google claimed that the intrusion also targeted "at least twenty other large companies from a wide range of businesses – including the Internet, finance, technology, media and chemical sectors," and was corroborated in separate admissions by Adobe.[25]

In its *GhostNet* report, researchers at Information Warfare Monitor found 1,295 infected computers in 103 countries, including a range of political, diplomatic and economic target organizations such as Deloitte and Touche's New York office.[26] The follow-on report, *Shadows in the Cloud*, identified additional targets, including Honeywell.[27]

Each of these reported intrusions were traced to IP addresses in China, and almost certainly represent only a fraction of the known hacks, given the reluctance of companies to report data breaches.

Intelligence preparation of the battlefield (IPB)

It is also important to contextualize China's interest in cyber espionage within Beijing's threat perceptions of potential scenarios for military conflict. In the minds of the Chinese leadership, the available evidence suggests that the most important political-military challenges and the most likely flashpoints for Sino–US conflict involve Taiwan or the South China Sea. Since the late 1990s, the PLA has been hard at work bolstering the hedging options of the leadership, developing advanced campaign doctrines, testing the concepts in increasingly complex training and exercises, and integrating new indigenous and imported weapons systems.

Yet cyber operations are also expected to play an important role in these scenarios, necessitating intelligence preparation of the cyber battlefield. At the strategic level, the writings of Chinese military authors suggest that there are two main centers of gravity in a Taiwan scenario, both of which can be attacked with computer network operations in concert with other kinetic and non-kinetic capabilities. The first of these is the will of the Taiwanese people, which they hope to undermine through exercises, cyber attacks against critical infrastructure, missile attacks, SOF operations, and other operations that have a psychological operations focus. Based on assessments from the 1995 to 1996 exercises, as well as public opinion polling in Taiwan, China appears to have concluded that the Taiwanese people do not have the stomach for conflict and will therefore sue for peace after suffering only a small amount of pain. The second center of gravity is the will and capability of the United States to intervene decisively in a cross-strait conflict. In a strategic sense, China has traditionally believed that its ICBM inventory, which is capable of striking CONUS, will serve as a deterrent to US intervention or at least a brake on escalation.[28]

Closer to its borders, the PLA has been engaged in an active program of equipment modernization, purchasing niche "counter-intervention" capabilities such as anti-ship ballistic missiles, long-range cruise missiles and submarines to shape the operational calculus of the American carrier strike group commander on station.[29] According to the predictable cadre of "true believers," both of the centers of gravity identified above can be attacked using computer network operations. In the first case, the Chinese IO community believes that CNO will play a useful psychological role in undermining the will of the Taiwanese people by attacking infrastructure and economic vitality. In the second case, the Chinese IO community envisions computer network attacks against unclassified NIPRNET and its automated logistics systems as an effective way to deter or delay US intervention into a military contingency and thereby permit Beijing to achieve its political objectives with a minimum of fighting. In both cases, China must conduct substantial computer network exploitation (the military term for cyber espionage) for intelligence preparation of this battlefield, and the alleged intrusion set into NIPRNET computer systems would appear to fulfill this military requirement.

Why does the Chinese military believe that the deployment phase of US military operations, particularly the use of the unclassified NIPRNET for logistics deployments, is the primary focus of vulnerability? Since DESERT STORM in the early 1990s, the PLA has expended significant resources analyzing the operations of what it often and euphemistically terms "the high-tech enemy."[30] When Chinese strategists contemplate how to affect US deployments, they confront the limitations of their current conventional force, which does not have sufficient range to interdict US facilities or assets beyond the Japanese home islands.[31] Nuclear options, while theoretically available, are nonetheless far too escalatory to be used so early in the conflict.[32] Theater missile systems, which are possibly moving to a mixture of conventional and nuclear warheads, could be used against Japan or Guam, but uncertainties about the nature of a given warhead would likely generate responses similar to the nuclear scenario.[33] Instead, PLA analysts of US military operations presciently concluded that the key vulnerability was the mechanics of deployment itself. Specifically, Chinese authors highlight DoD's need to use civilian backbone and unclassified computer networks (known as the NIPRNET), which is a function of the requirements of global power projection, as an "Achilles Heel." There is also recognition of the fact that operations in the Pacific are especially reliant on precisely coordinated transportation, communications, and logistics networks, given what PACOM calls the "tyranny of distance"[34] in the theater. PLA strategists believe that a disruptive computer network attack against these systems or affiliated civilian systems could potentially delay or degrade US force deployment to the region while allowing the PRC to maintain a degree of plausible deniability.

The Chinese are right to highlight the NIPRNET as an attractive *and* accessible target, unlike its classified counterparts. It is attractive because it contains and transmits critical deployment information in the all-important time-phased force deployment list (known as the "tip-fiddle"), which is valuable for both intelligence gathering about US military operations but also a lucrative target for disruptive attacks. In terms of accessibility, it was relatively easy to gather data about the NIRPNET from open sources, at least before 9/11. Moreover, the very nature of the system is the source of its vulnerabilities, since the needs of global power project a mandate that it has to be unclassified and connected to the greater global network, albeit through protected gateways.[35]

DoD's classified networks, on the other hand, are an attractive but less accessible target for the Chinese. On the one hand, these networks would be an intelligence gold mine, and is likely a priority computer network exploit target. On the other hand, they are less attractive as a computer network attack target, thanks to the difficulty of penetrating its high defenses. Any overall Chinese military strategy predicated on a high degree of success in penetrating these networks during crisis or war is a high-risk venture, and increases the chances of failure of the overall effort to an unacceptable level.

Chinese CNE or CNA operations against logistics networks could have a detrimental impact on US logistics support to operations. PRC computer network exploitation activities directed against US military logistics networks could reveal force deployment information, such as the names of ships deployed, readiness status of various units, timing and destination of deployments, and rendezvous schedules. This is especially important for the Chinese in times of crisis, since the PRC in peacetime utilizes US military websites and newspapers as a principal source for deployment information. An article in October 2001 in *People's Daily*, for example, explicitly cited US Navy websites for information about the origins, destination, and purpose of two carrier battle groups exercising in the South China Sea.[36] Since the quantity and quality of deployment information on open websites were dramatically reduced after 9/11, the intelligence benefits (necessity?) of exploiting the NIPRNET have become even more paramount.[37] Computer network attack could also delay resupply to the theater by misdirecting stores, fuel, and munitions, corrupting or deleting inventory files, and thereby hindering mission capability.

The advantages to this strategy are numerous: (1) it is available to the PLA in the near-term; (2) it does not require the PLA to be able to attack/invade Taiwan with air/sea assets; (3) it has a reasonable level of deniability, provided that the attack is sophisticated enough to prevent tracing; (4) it exploits perceived US casualty aversion, over-attention to force protection, the tyranny of distance in the Pacific, and US dependence on information systems; and (5) it could achieve the desired operational and psychological effects: deterrence of US response or degrading of deployments. Looking back over more than ten years of China-origin intrusions into the very NIPRNET systems identified by PLA analysts as a high-priority network attack target as early as 1995, the logic of the intrusion sets becomes much clearer.

Strategic intelligence

An additional motivation for cyber espionage is strategic intelligence about the policies and intentions of civilian and military officials as well as the internal debates within the US government and political parties:

1   In June 2006, the State Department was victimized by a series of intrusions at its foreign posts and headquarters in Washington. According to the *Associated Press*, "hackers stole sensitive information and passwords, and implanted 'back doors' in unclassified computers to allow them to return." Employees told the *AP* that State's East Asian and Pacific Affairs Bureau was particularly hard hit by the intrusion, suggesting that the intruders had a special interest in Asia-related information.[38] Two reporters from *Business Week* relate the story of what happened:

> The attack began in May, 2006, when an unwitting employee in the State Dept.'s East Asia Pacific region clicked on an attachment in a seemingly authentic e-mail. Malicious code was embedded in the Word document, a congressional speech, and opened a Trojan "back door" for the code's creators to peer inside the State Dept.'s

innermost networks. Soon, cyber security engineers began spotting more intrusions in State Dept. computers across the globe. The malware took advantage of previously unknown vulnerabilities in the Microsoft operating system. Unable to develop a patch quickly enough, engineers watched helplessly as streams of State Dept. data slipped through the back door and into the Internet ether. Although they were unable to fix the vulnerability, specialists came up with a temporary scheme to block further infections. They also yanked connections to the Internet. One member of the emergency team summoned to the scene recalls that each time cyber security professionals thought they had eliminated the source of a "beacon" reporting back to its master, another popped up. He compared the effort to the arcade game Whack-A-Mole. The State Dept. says it eradicated the infection, but only after sanitizing scores of infected computers and servers and changing passwords.[39]

2   In 2007, intruders broke into the e-mail system for Defense Secretary Robert Gates' office, and the Pentagon shut down about 1,500 computers for more than a week while the attacks continued. Officials told the *Financial Times*: "an internal investigation has revealed that the incursion came from the People's Liberation Army. One senior US official said the Pentagon had pinpointed the exact origins of the attack. Another person familiar with the event said there was a 'very high level of confidence. . . . trending towards total certainty' that the PLA was responsible."[40]

3   In the summer of 2008, the FBI informed both the Obama and McCain presidential campaigns that their computer systems had been infiltrated. *Newsweek* quoted an FBI agent as telling both teams: "You have a problem way bigger than what you understand. . . . You have been compromised, and a serious amount of files have been loaded off your system."[41] The *Financial Times* later cited that investigators "had determined that the attacks originated from China, but cautioned that they had not ascertained whether they were government-sponsored, or just unaffiliated hackers."[42] In a cyber-security policy speech early in his presidency, Obama referred to the incident:

> I know how it feels to have privacy violated because it has happened to me and the people around me. It's no secret that my presidential campaign harnessed the Internet and technology to transform our politics. What isn't widely known is that during the general election hackers managed to penetrate our computer systems. To all of you who donated to our campaign, I want you to all rest assured, our fundraising website was untouched. So your confidential personal and financial information was protected. But between August and October, hackers gained access to emails and a range of campaign files, from policy

position papers to travel plans. And we worked closely with the CIA – with the FBI and the Secret Service and hired security consultants to restore the security of our systems.[43]

These three sample cases show that Beijing clearly views cyber as a collection modality for obtaining strategic intelligence at the highest levels of the US government.

Chinese government denials

> The lady doth protest too much, methinks.
> – *Shakespeare, Macbeth*

In counter-intelligence offices in Washington, one often sees the following sign: "Admit Nothing, Deny Everything, Make Vigorous Counter-Accusations." This philosophy is also a deeply held conviction of the Chinese side when it comes to discussing their possible role in cyber intrusions. First, they admit nothing and deny everything. When asked about the China-origin intrusions into German Chancellor Angela Merkel's office network, for example, "the Chinese Embassy in Berlin described the accusation of state-controlled hacking as "irresponsible speculation without a shred of evidence."[44] In perhaps its most Kafka-esque move to date, the Chinese government responded to the highly detailed Mandiat report in 2013 by denying that the designated military 91638 Unit involved in cyber espionage even existed, despite the fact that the report contained photographs, maps and other clear evidence proving it did.[45] Chinese officials also point to Chinese laws as an ironclad defense of its own lack of involvement. Reacting to accusations that Chinese hackers were responsible for the intrusions revealed by Google in January 2010, Foreign Ministry spokeswoman Jiang Yu countered that "Chinese law proscribes any form of hacking activity."[46] After the release of the Office of the National Counterintelligence Executive's 2011 "Report to Congress on Foreign Economic Collection and Industrial Espionage," Chinese officials denigrated the quality of the analysis, asserting that "identifying the attackers without carrying out a comprehensive investigation and making inferences about the attackers is both unprofessional and irresponsible."[47] Then, the Chinese government impugns the motives of the accusers, making its own counter-accusations. In his response to questions about GhostNet, Foreign Ministry spokesman Qin Gang accused foreigners of having a "Cold War mentality":

> The problem now is that some people abroad are keen to fabricate the rumor of the so-called "Chinese cyber spy network." The allegation is utterly groundless. . . . There is a ghost called Cold War and a virus called China's threat theory overseas. Some people, possessed by this ghost and infected with this virus, fall ill from time to time. Their attempts of using rumors to disgrace China will never succeed. We should rightly expose these ghosts and viruses.[48]

Wang Baodong, a spokesman for the Chinese government at its embassy in Washington, darkly hinted that "anti-China forces" are behind the allegations.[49] After the US-China Economic and Security Review Commission's release of a Northrup-Grumman report on Chinese cyber espionage, Qin Gang railed:

> The report takes no regard of the true situation. . . . It is full of prejudice, and out of ulterior motive. We urge the so-called commission not to see China through colored lens and not to do things that interfere with China's internal affairs and undermine China–US relations.[50]

Finally, the Chinese government describes itself as the victim of cyber intrusions. After a detailed exposé of Chinese cyber espionage appeared in *Business Week*, Wang Baodong e-mailed the magazine's editors, claiming that China is "frequently intruded and attacked by hackers from certain countries."[51] When asked in early 2010 about Google's complaint that it had been hacked from China, Foreign Ministry spokesman Ma Zhaoxu said Chinese companies have also been hacked, adding that China resolutely opposes the practice.[52] Other officials have cited the fact that most of the world's botnets are controlled from servers in the United States, insinuating that Washington needed to get its own cybersecurity in order before accusing other countries of hacking. Finally, the Chinese government tried to paint itself as the patron of global cyber security, in contrast to the "militarized" US approach to cyber: "China is ready to build, together with other countries, a peaceful, secure and open cyberspace order."[53] While Beijing's style of strategic communications is not limited to cyber espionage, as seen in its rhetoric during crises (Belgrade Embassy bombing in 1999, EP-3A hostage crisis in 2001, etc.), the reaction of its officials has the unintended consequence of increasing suspicion.

How good are they? Or does it matter?

Measuring Chinese cyber espionage capability also involves the assessment of a group or country's ability to generate new attack tools or exploits. Outside analysts, many of whom are programmers themselves, tend to reify countries like Russia that abound with highly talented programmers, and look down upon countries or individuals that simply use off-the-shelf "script kiddie" tools or exploit known vulnerabilities, preferring to admire more advanced cyber operators who can discover their own "zero-day" vulnerabilities.[54] Indeed, analysts who have examined Chinese intrusions in detail often comment on their relative lack of sophistication and especially their sloppy tradecraft,[55] leaving behind clear evidence of the intrusion and sometimes even attribution-related information. For example, analysts who examined possible Chinese intrusions into energy companies concluded that Chinese hackers were "incredibly sloppy," "very unsophisticated," "made mistakes and left lots of evidence."[56] Perhaps the Chinese cyber operators are so convinced of the plausible deniability afforded by the current global network architecture that they do not see the need to hide more effectively, or perhaps they believe that their communications are secure because they are using Chinese language. Both are true to some extent, especially the latter, as many Chinese correctly perceive that their difficult language is actually the country's first line of defense, its first layer of cryptography, and there are actually few foreigners with the skills or bandwidth to penetrate the veil. Most important, however, the Chinese probably perceive that they do not need to "up their game" because their relatively primitive and sloppy efforts have thus far been wildly successful and therefore they see no need to change. In fact, one could argue that China's cyber espionage successes to date are more a function of the vulnerability of US systems than any inherent capability on the Chinese side. As time passes, however, one would expect Chinese capability to improve, particularly as information about China-origin intrusions becomes more widespread and victims begin to take concrete measures to protect themselves. This view is endorsed by former counterintelligence chief Joel Brenner, who told the *National Journal* in 2008 that Chinese hackers are "very good and getting better all the time."[57]

Notes

1 "General Warns of Dramatic Increase of Cyber-Attacks on US Firms," *Los Angeles Times*, July 27, 2012.
2 Office of the National Counterintelligence Executive, *Foreign Spies Stealing US Economic Secrets in Cyberspace: Report to Congress on Foreign Economic Collection and Industrial Espionage, 2009–2011*, October 2011, www.dni.gov/reports/20111103_report_fecie.pdf.
3 Tom Espiner, "Chinese Hackers Breach US Military Defenses," *Silicon.com*, November 2005; and Bradley Graham, "Hackers Attack Via Chinese Web Sites," *The Washington Post*, August 2005.
4 Dawn Onley and Patience Wait, "Red Storm Rising: DoD's Efforts to Stave Off Nation-State Cyber Attacks Begin with China," *Government Computer News*, August 2006.
5 See General James E. Cartwright, in hearing, *China's Military Modernization and Its Impact on the United States and the Asia-Pacific*, US-China Economic and Security Review Commission, 110th Congress, 1st Sess., March 29–30, 2007, p. 90, at www.uscc.gov/hearings/2007hearings/transcripts/mar_29_30/mar_29_30_07_trans.pdf.
6 Shane Harris, "China's Cyber Militia," *National Journal*, May 31, 2008.
7 Brian Grow, Keith Epstein and Chi-Chu Tschang, "The New E-spionage Threat," *Business Week*, April 21, 2008, pp. 32–41.
8 Bryan Krekel, *Capability of the People's Republic of China to Conduct Cyber Warfare and Computer Network Exploitation*, published by the US-China Economic and Security Review Commission, October 9, 2009.
9 Harris, "China's Cyber Militia."
10 "Advance Questions for Lieutenant General Keith Alexander USA, Nominee for Commander, United States Cyber Command," published by Senate Armed Services Committee, accessed at http://armed-services.senate.gov/statemnt/2010/04%20April/Alexander%2004-15-10.pdf.
11 Shaun Waterman, "Chinese Cyberspy Network Pervasive," *Washington Times*, March 30, 2009.
12 Harris, "China's Cyber Militia."
13 Ibid.
14 See http://intelreport.mandiant.com/ For a range of views on the attribution issue, see Krekel, *Capability of the People's Republic of China to Conduct Cyber Warfare and Computer*

Network Exploitation; McAfee® Foundstone® Professional Services and McAfee Labs™, *Global Energy Cyberattacks: 'Night Dragon'*, February 10, 2011; Shishir Nagaraja and Ross Anderson, "The Snooping Dragon: Social-Malware Surveillance of the Tibetan Movement," UCAM-CL-TR-746, University of Cambridge Computer Laboratory Technical Report 746, March 2009; Dmitri Alperovitch, *Revealed: Operation Shady RAT*, McAfee, August 2011; and Information Warfare Monitor, *Tracking GhostNet: Investigating a Cyber Espionage Network*, Toronto: SecDev and Citizen Lab, March 29, 2009.

15 Harris, "China's Cyber Militia."
16 James McGregor, *China's Drive for Indigenous Innovation: A Web of Industrial Policies*, Washington, DC: US Chamber of Commerce, July 2010.
17 James McGregor, "Time to rethink US–China trade relations," *Washington Post*, May 19, 2010. See also McGregor, *China's Drive for Indigenous Innovation*.
18 Ibid.
19 Nathan Thornburgh, "The Invasion of the Chinese Cyberspies (and the Man Who Tried to Stop Them," *Time*, August 29, 2005.
20 Nathan Gardels, "China is Aiming at America's Soft Underbelly: The Internet," *The Christian Science Monitor*, February 5, 2010, accessed at www.csmonitor.com/ Commentary/Global-Viewpoint/2010/0205/China-is-aiming-at-America-s-soft-underbelly-the-Internet.
21 Office of the National Counterintelligence Executive, *Foreign Spies Stealing US Economic Secrets in Cyberspace*.
22 McAfee, *Night Dragon*.
23 Alperovitch, *Operation Shady RAT*.
24 http://googleblog.blogspot.com/2010/01/new-approach-to-china.html.
25 http://blogs.adobe.com/conversations/2010/01/adobe_investigates_corporate_ n.html.
26 Information Warfare Monitor, *Tracking GhostNet: Investigating a Cyber Espionage Network*, Toronto: SecDev and Citizen Lab, March 29, 2009, accessed at www.scribd. com/doc/13731776/Tracking-GhostNet-Investigating-a-Cyber-Espionage-Network.
27 Information Warfare Monitor and Shadowserver, *Shadows in the Cloud: Investigating Cyber Espionage 2.0*, Toronto: SecDec and Citizen Lab, April 6, 2010, found at www.shadows-in-the-cloud.net.
28 Office of the Secretary of Defense, *Annual Report to Congress: Military and Security Developments Involving the People's Republic of China 2011*, p. 3.
29 Ibid., pp. 2–4, 28–29.
30 Ibid., p. 22.
31 Ibid., p. 31.
32 Ibid., p. 34.
33 Ibid., pp. 29,78.
34 For a PACOM/J4 perspective on the issue, see www.navsup.navy.mil/scnewsletter/ 2009/jan-feb/cover1.
35 For an unclassified summary, see www.disa.mil/Services/Network-Services/Data/ SBU-IP.
36 "Whom, If Not China, Is US Aircraft Carriers' Moving onto South China Sea Directed Against?" *Renmin Ribao*, August 24, 2001.
37 The Department of Defense's revised website administration guidance, which may be found here (www.defenselink.mil/webmasters/policy/dod_web_policy_ 12071998_with_amendments_and_corrections.html), specifically prohibits the following: "3.5.3.2. Reference to unclassified information that would reveal sensitive movements of military assets or the location of units, installations, or personnel where uncertainty regarding location is an element of a military plan or program."
38 "Computer Hackers Attack State Dept.," *Associated Press*, July 12, 2006.
39 Grow, Epstein and Tschang, "The New E-spionage Threat."
40 Sevastopluo, Demetri, "Chinese Hacked into Pentagon," *FT.com*, September 3, 2007.

41 Evan Thomas, "Center Stage," *Newsweek*, November 6, 2008; David Byers, Tom Baldwin and Tim Reid, "Obama computers 'hacked during election campaign'," *Times Online*, November 7, 2008.
42 *Financial Times*, November 2008.
43 "Remarks by the President on Securing our Nation's Cyber Infrastructure," Office of the Press Secretary, The White House, May 29, 2009.
44 "Merkel's China Visit Marred by Hacking Allegations," *Spiegel Online International*, August 27, 2007.
45 "Former Defense Official Denies Chinese Hacking," *Xinhua*, 3 March 2013.
46 Miguel Helft and John Markoff, "Google Alerted Activists of Attacks," *New York Times*, January 15, 2010.
47 "China Rebuts US Accusation of Hacker Attacks," *China Daily*, October 31, 2011.
48 "China Denies Allegations on 'Cyber Spy Network'."
49 Grow, Epstein and Tschang, "The New E-spionage Threat."
50 Mark Clayton, "Google cyber attack: the evidence against China," *Christian Science Monitor*, January 13, 2010.
51 Grow, Epstein and Tschang, "The New E-spionage Threat."
52 "China Says Google, Foreign Firms Must Respect Laws," *CIOL*, January 19, 2010.
53 "China Rebuts US Accusation of Hacker Attacks," *China Daily*, October 31, 2011.
54 http://en.wikipedia.org/wiki/Zero-day_attack
55 Keizer, Gregg, "Chinese Hackers Called Sloppy but Persistent," *Computerworld*, February 12, 2011.
56 Ibid.
57 Harris, "China's Cyber Militia."

10

CHINESE INDUSTRIAL ESPIONAGE IN CONTEXT

China's programs to transfer foreign technology do not exist in isolation; they are a collage of interacting components. For descriptive purposes we have had to portray this integrated system as a set of discrete elements in chapters on early history, the use of open source, foreign R&D in China, PRC-based transfer organizations, US-based facilitators, the role of overseas students and scholars, PRC policy initiatives, clandestine support for technology transfer, and China's abuse of cyber space. The distinctions are a convenience, as the composite picture is more complex.

By the same token, these chapters provide only a glimpse of the transfer practices China uses. Our major challenge has been to reduce the enormous amount of openly available material to a manageable size. In some cases we discarded recent examples from open sources that replicate information which others might treat as sensitive. Hence the materials given here should be regarded as pieces of a much larger picture. How these elements interact, how foreign technologies are targeted for acquisition, and how they move from design to implementation are issues we have barely touched. We hope this study inspires broader research, both inside and outside government.

By way of conclusion, we shall mention a few transfer ploys not yet discussed, and correct any misconception we may have given our readers that the United States is the only country on earth targeted by China for informal transfers. The problem affects all industrialized nations. We will also attempt in this final chapter to account for this behavior. China's use of proxies as a short cut to development is as much a product of culture and mindset as it is the outcome of necessity or design. Naming the causes of this endemic "borrowing" is essential to breaking the pattern.

While moving beyond these parasitic practices makes sense from a Westerner's perspective, there are reasons why China may retain its present pattern – if it can do so without penalty. We assume in the West that radical creation is the touchstone to success when a good case can be made for China's approach of hanging back and "taking the fisherman's profit" (渔翁得利). Thus it is likely that recent calls by PRC policy-makers for innovation will be misunderstood outside of China as a move toward sharing and creativity across the entire society, when the plan, at least in the near term, is to continue with business as usual, using foreign technology while diverting a growing portion of China's own assets to original work where the regime has identified a stake.

Other transfer techniques

Earlier we touched on the role of US-based Chinese companies in transferring technology to China. Chinese firms enter the United States with a range of motivations that include market expansion, technology spotting, and "informal" technology acquisition. One category, which includes some companies associated with the defense industrial base (e.g., NORINCO) and the military (e.g., Poly, USA), serve primarily as commercial outlets for Chinese civilian goods to retail chains like Walmart and are not known to be involved in transfers to China. A second category of companies such as Huawei USA/Futurewei and Haier are opening their doors in the United States to reduce the stigma of their Chinese origin and achieve greater success in penetrating the American market to build their global brand.

Finally, there are companies such as UTI whose technology transfer activities are cataloged in the book's Appendix. These firms – transplanted from China or started by Chinese nationals who began here as students – focus to a greater or lesser degree on acquiring technology for transfer "back" to China. We do not claim that most or even many of them operate illegally. Our argument is that the legality of their operations is irrelevant, as China has ways – countless ways – to work the middle ground. It makes no sense to debate how many "front companies" China runs in the US, since the concept is immaterial. Allegiance and business practices are what matter.

A new concern is the growth of knowledge-based companies with ties to the PRC government, focused on new and emerging technology areas that insinuate themselves into the innovation fabric of the US. These include "hybrid" companies of two varieties that are technically private but which enjoy substantial support from the Chinese government in the form of loans, tax breaks, or political support.

Some of these companies are started up in China, often by returnees, and use government subsidies to buy their way into specific industries by creating a unique capability.[1] One such company is Beijing Genomics Institute which now houses the largest gene sequencing capacity in the world, funded by Chinese state loans.[2] It publishes a paper in a major Western scientific journal almost weekly[3] and has more potential for access to genomic data than anywhere else in the world.[4]

Our research suggests that the preferred method of establishing a research beachhead in the Unites States is through the formation of a joint research center with a prominent US university. One illustrative example is the China–US Joint Research Center for Ecosystem and Environmental Change at the University of Tennessee, Knoxville.[5] Launched in 2006, researchers from the University of Tennessee and the DOE-funded Oak Ridge National Laboratory partnered with the Chinese Academy of Sciences to address "the combined effects of climate change and human activities on regional and global ecosystems and explore technologies for restoration of degraded environments."

The Center's research focuses on science at the heart of the "green technology" revolution, which is one of Beijing's major national industrial policy objectives. Its website lays out three goals that match neatly with a tech transfer agenda: (1) organize and implement international scientific and engineering research; (2) *serve as a center for scientific information exchange*; and (3) provide international education and technical training.[6] The website goes on to outline cooperative mechanisms to achieve these goals, including joint research projects, academic exchange, student education, and "*technical transfer and training* [emphasis added]."[7] This dynamic differs fundamentally from the mission of Western research facilities abroad, which is to adapt technology already in their portfolios to sell product in foreign markets. A PRC study on the benefits of overseas "research" to obtain foreign technology put it this way: "How can you get the tiger if you don't go into the tiger's den?" (不入虎穴, 焉得虎).[8]

Another way to get the tiger is to circumvent the developmental process altogether by stealing the product. While not technology transfer per se, counterfeiting is so common in China that it has the same practical effect. Schemes range from the subtle to the blatant: benchmarking against ISO standards;[9] patent research where a design is modified slightly, if at all, re-patented in China and "legally" produced with government protection;[10] reverse engineering;[11] "imitative innovation" (模仿创新)[12] with or without the innovation (also called "imitative remanufacturing" 模仿改造);[13] and finally marketing the pirated product either without or with its original logo.[14] The 2006 Hanxin (chip) scandal is the poster boy example. The reader can fill in examples of PRC counterfeiting from the thousands available.

What is puzzling amidst China's official promises – and some genuine efforts – to clean up its IPR problem is the counter-current of sophistry in otherwise responsible PRC journals justifying this behavior. A 1996 article in the Science Ministry's official newspaper *Keji Ribao* (科技日报, S&T Daily) argued that the West forced on China an "inequitable distribution of the benefits of science and technology" depriving China of its "legal rights."[15] To other people's patents? A 1998 *China Trade Journal* (中国贸易报) piece declared matter-of-factly "industrial espionage" to be within China's moral purview.[16] Other published arguments equate China's loose IPR regime to the West's appropriation of gunpowder, the compass,[17] and old Chinese novels.[18]

In the same vein, *Science and Technology Management Research* (科技管理研究, a high-level S&T policy journal) argued that China must determine beforehand the costs of IPR enforcement in terms of its effects on consumer prices and economic development.[19] Compliance is a matter of convenience. Another mainstream policy journal (*Science Research Management*, 科究管理) blamed "strategic technology alliances" led by the United States for monopolizing "the world's scientific and technological knowledge" and controlling its distribution.[20] Patents and IPR are contrived by the West to keep "the world's" technology out of developing countries', especially China's, hands. Hence the need for work-arounds. A third S&T policy journal (*Science & Technology Progress and Policy*, 科技进步与对策) attacked the US by name for "using S&T as a tool to carry out struggles with non-Western ideologies."[21] The journal went on to claim:

> The owners of technology in the developed countries increasingly are setting up among themselves strategic alliance networks and the IPR systems in each of these countries are constantly being perfected. As a result, the tendency toward technology monopolies is strengthened.[22]

These and similar comments in responsible PRC media suggest that many in China resent the West's insistence on IPR and patents protection.

Other "donor" nations

China's appetite for foreign technology and its network for informal technology acquisition extend well beyond the United States. Personal bias has caused us to dwell on the challenges America faces from these backdoor tactics to piggyback on our creative resources, but the problem confronts all advanced nations, beginning with China's own neighbors.

Everything we have written about PRC technology transfer practices directed at the United States applies equally to Japan. Here is a list of some S&T "cooperative" ventures China has arranged with Japan, according to MOST's China S&T Exchange Center.

> Since 1982 we have signed S&T exchange agreements with such representative Japanese multinational corporations as Mitsubishi (33 companies), Sumitomo (22 companies), Sanwa (72 companies), Mitsui & Co., Hitachi and Soni. At the same time, in order to promote the development of S&T exchanges with the Japanese people, we have established permanent S&T exchange relationships with a large number of non-governmental organizations such as Japan's Keidanren, Japanese Federation of Employers Associations, Japan International Trade Society, Japan International Technology Service Industry Association (JISA), the Asia-Japanese Society for Cooperation on Science and Technology, Japan Skilled Volunteers Association, Japan S&T Society, Sino-Japanese S&T Association, etc.

This continues down to provincial and city levels.[23] Bearing in mind the disparity between the two countries' technical capabilities, one wonders exactly how, from a technological standpoint, Japan benefits from these "exchanges." A description by MOST's Sino–Japanese Technology Cooperation Center (part of its S&T Exchange Center) of "Sino–Japanese intergovernmental cooperation" sheds no light on advantages that accrue to Japan, while providing the following outline of how things work from the Chinese side:

> Through the cooperation, we have introduced many advanced and practical technologies and processes from Japan, and implemented a number of effective projects in China. With Japanese technology and funding, we have established and expanded a range of high-level institutions for the research and promotion of practical technologies. These, in turn, have become a platform for broader Sino–Japanese cooperation in science and technology.[24]

The above relates to official and non-official S&T relationships. There is also an off-the-books unofficial component represented by more than a dozen Sino-Japanese S&T advocacy groups, both general and technology specific, dedicated to China's growth and their members' personal enrichment, as well as the expected Chinese student associations at Japanese universities, whose role in the technology exchange process is ad hoc and varied.[25] Data posted to Sino-Japanese S&T advocacy sites are uncannily similar to material posted by their counterparts in the United States, which suggests some measure of coordination – or that there are only so many ways to bend over.

The following is a gist of the Introduction to one such S-J advocacy group, the All-Japan Federation of Overseas Chinese Professionals (中国留日同学总会):[26]

> Many thousands of Chinese students who study in Japan stay after graduating and enter Japanese companies, universities and research labs. In addition, China has undergone reform and there are "new taskings for overseas Chinese scholars to serve the country. To adapt to the new situation, strengthen connections between OCS employed in Japan, better promote their work in service to China, and encourage friendly Sino–Japanese exchange activities, the All-Japan Federation of Overseas Chinese Professionals was stood up on Feb. 1, 1998."[27]

The Federation's Charter is equally illuminating. We learn that the purpose of the organization is to:

> bring into play the advantages and intellectual talent of OCS, organize and encourage them to return to China and render service or serve China through multiple means, participate actively in building up the native country, and promote friendly Sino-Japanese exchanges.[28]

As a condition of membership one must "fervently love China and the Chinese people" (热爱祖国, 热爱中华民族). Apparently one need not love Japan.

Does any of this sound familiar? The Federation acknowledges the powerful support (大力支持) and comprehensive leadership (全面的指导) provided by China's diplomatic representation in Japan, by the PRC ministries of Education and Personnel, the United Front Work Department of the Chinese Communist Party Central Committee, sundry PRC youth groups, and the Western Returned Scholars Association (see Chapter 5).[29]

The Association of Chinese Scientists and Engineers in Japan (在日中国科学技术者联盟) is another such organization run for the benefit of China and for its members' well-being. ACSEJ was established on May 15, 1993 – five years before the Federation – and claims a membership of 1,300, "90 percent of whom have PhDs."[30] That is a serious concentration of brainpower. Over the years, ACSEJ has repeatedly:

> helped the Chinese government and non-official S-J friendship organizations manage various kinds of S&T expos and returnee trips to found businesses in China, and perform on-site inspections and engage in exchange activities in service to China. Imbued with the spirit of 'service' the ACSEJ has done much work as a 'go between' for its members to return to China on inspection tours, work there for short periods of time, and do joint research. These activities have earned the association unanimous praise from China's Ministry of Science and Technology, Ministry of Personnel, State Economic and Trade Commission, the State Council's Overseas Chinese Affairs Office, the All-China Federation of Returned Overseas Chinese, the Natural Science Foundation of China, Chinese Academy of Science, and government and academic organizations at all levels.[31]

These are the same PRC organizations that plug into the US-based China S&T advocacy groups described in Chapter 5. A third Sino-Japanese S&T group – the Chinese Association of Scientists and Engineers in Japan (全日本中国人博士协会) – was founded in 1996 to contribute to China's scientific and technical development and to "build bridges for academic exchanges between China and Japan." Its bylaws state the ways these goals are to be met, including "helping form China's S&T policy and supporting China's development of new high technology," sponsoring academic exchanges, helping members find dual appointments at PRC research institutes, and arranging joint research projects.[32]

CASEJ has its own "Foreign Relations Department" and "China Affairs Office." The group responds to tasking from the PRC embassy in Japan for participation in technology exchange projects sponsored by the State Council's Overseas Chinese Affairs Office, MOST, and MOP.[33] Although they are separate organizations, CASEJ and ACSEJ jointly attend PRC-sponsored events in both China and Japan, including celebrations of Chinese holidays hosted by the embassy, which as in the US-based examples serve as venues to mobilize patriotic sentiment and renew face-to-face commitments to transfer technology. In terms of their structure, goals, and activities, there is little to distinguish Japan's China advocacy groups from those in the United States.

The pattern repeats itself in Australia, Canada, Great Britain, continental Europe, South Korea, Singapore, and Russia. A glance at the European network will round out our survey of non-US "donors" to China's S&T development. Leading the Sino-European S&T advocacy groups is an umbrella organization called the Federation of Chinese Professional Associations in Europe (全欧华人专业协会联合会), founded in Frankfurt in 2001 by "ten or so" Sino-European Chinese professional organizations as "a cross-discipline body of intellectuals who will do their part for China's reform and development."[34] Member organizations today are found in: Austria 1, Belgium 3, Denmark 1, England 4, France 6, Germany 13, Netherlands 3, Portugal 1, Sweden 1, Switzerland 3; there is also a Europe-wide group for IT experts – 37 organizations in all, which is comparable to the number of major Chinese S&T advocacy groups in the United States.

The Federation is not shy about its goals: item one under "Purpose" is simply "to serve China" (为国服务). That's the whole of it, right there. The charter explains:

> Long periods of life overseas have caused us to deeply appreciate that without the strength and greatness of our ancestral country there's no talking about individual dignity. Whether we return to China and render service, or render service in place, we are making our contribution to China.[35]

Assimilation is apparently not an option nor an avenue to self-respect. The Federation vows to continuously repay its debt of service and "find new and better ways of doing things for China" (为国献计献策).[36] Not by coincidence, in 2001 – the same year the Federation was set up – MOST's China S&T Exchange Center created a China–EU Science and Technology Cooperation Promotion Office (中国-欧盟科技合作促进办公室) to manage the growing Sino–European S&T relationship and encourage Chinese participation in the EU's Framework Program for Research and Technological Development.[37]

Typical of these EU member organizations is the Association des Scientifiques et des Ingénieurs Chinois en France (全法中国科技工作者协会). Established in 1992, its "main duties" are to "unite the Chinese S&T workers in France, organize S&T exchange activities and, while bringing into full play its conveyor belt and bridging function, promote Sino–French cooperation in education and technology."[38]

The Association claims that many of its members are "famous university professors, researchers at national R&D centers, entrepreneurs and top-ranked engineers." Several received funds under China's Changjiang Scholar program (长江计划, essentially a stipend to return to China for short periods and to be debriefed) . The Association itself reportedly enjoys support from the Education

Office within the PRC embassy in France and receives funding under the MOE's "Spring Light" program (春晖计划) for technical support to PRC projects.[39]

Pathology or shrewd strategy?

Since the mid-nineteenth century – some 150 years or more – China's worldwide role in science and technology has been that of a taker, not a giver. This fact is unquestioned even inside China. The picture we present of a country hell-bent on acquiring "existing" (other people's) technology and applying it practically, instead of creating ideas of its own to share with the world community, is unlikely to be debated by anyone with insight into the real state of affairs, least of all Chinese policy-makers themselves. The evidence is too overwhelming.

Whether China will become an S&T powerhouse 10, 50, or 100 years from now is unknown and probably unknowable. We have queried Chinese, Japanese, European, and American experts in and out of government – including science attachés, scientists with hands-on experience in China, professional study groups, patents specialists, law enforcement officials, and Nobel Prize-winning experts – and the replies vary from wildly optimistic to "no way" pessimistic, both between and within groups. Clearly the money is there, leadership intent is mostly a given, and the brainpower is huge, but moving beyond creativity in niche areas to developing an innovative society, which includes most Chinese universities and businesses, will be a huge undertaking.

Part of the confusion, we assert, is definitional: What exactly is "China" in this context? And what does "innovative" really mean? Although assessments of China's potential for indigenous S&T achievements are mixed, few would disparage the creative skills of expatriate Chinese scientists – graduate students and post-docs – in American and European labs. But is this China? In a sense, yes. As we have been at pains to show, work done by overseas Chinese scholars is often funneled "back" to China through a complex web of transfer mechanisms designed to erase the distinction between work done at home and abroad. By the same token, does the output of PRC companies and labs staffed or directed by Western personnel count as "Chinese" science?

Our point is that it is impossible, with matters as they stand, to use statistics on S&T output to measure "Chinese" scientific progress. The distinction between China's achievements and what it takes from abroad is too blurred and the connections are too interwoven. While this matters little from the standpoint of *realpolitik*, it matters a lot when one tries to assess the quality of science inside the People's Republic and propose explanations for that country's fixation on foreign "borrowing." It is the same with innovation. Science in China has been – and largely *still* is – focused on incremental changes to basic ideas imported from elsewhere.

Key here as well is considering what are China's goals in its calls for innovation, which include things that are new to the world, things new to China, as well as things brought to China and then "tweaked." We should not confuse niche areas of creativity aimed at meeting strategic goals with building an unstratified educational system and society. Recent reforms and attempts at injecting rigor into research have boosted the quantitative statistics but say very little about the difference China is actually making, especially given persistent scandals of academic plagiarism.[40]

True, most of the world's science is built in the same way "a brick at a time," and flashes of creative genius are uncommon in any culture. But deep-seated cognitive preferences by the Han Chinese for stability and concrete action, enforced ("triggered" in sociobiological terms) by traditional culture, bias China to creativity of the deductive type that builds on elements in a known framework, instead of the paradigm-breaking creativity based on induction that involves bisociating abstract patterns from different cognitive domains.[41] Achievements of this "type-2" creative sort are not impossible in selected domains, as China has increasingly demonstrated, although scaling these gains to the entire society at large will prove difficult.

This is a strong statement to make in today's intellectual climate but 3,000 years of history[42] demonstrate that Chinese *in China* have not been creative in the radical sense and have not distinguished themselves in the sphere of abstract science either. The statistics are hard to refute. Charles Murray of "Bell Curve" fame, in a carefully documented study on accomplishment in the arts and sciences, identified over 3,000 "significant figures" who left their marks on the world from −800 to 1950. If you tally Murray's choices of pioneers by nation and region, the contrast between them is striking (Table 10.1).[43]

One could argue that Murray's data reflect a Western author's bias, but that argument is difficult to sustain in the face of figures provided by him showing comparable performance by East Asia in art and literature.

But let us look anyway at a scholar whose China-friendly credentials are beyond reproach: Joseph Needham, the historian of Chinese science, who spent a lifetime documenting hundreds of clever Chinese inventions. His passion notwithstanding,

TABLE 10.1 Pioneers by Nation and Region

	*West**	*China*	*Japan*
Astronomy	120	1	0
Biology	193	0	0
Chemistry	203	0	1
Earth sciences	85	0	0
Physics	210	0	2
Mathematics	182	3	0
Medicine	154	0	2
Technology	236	2	0
Art	479	111	81
Literature	835	83	85

Note: *Europe, Russia, United States[44]

Needham puzzled over "the lack of theoretical science in China" despite the "high level of technological progress achieved there."[45] In the end, Needham was forced to distinguish between the "*practical*" (emphasis added) science done in China and the "modern" science done in the West, which he characterized as:

> the application of mathematical hypotheses to nature, the full understanding and use of the experimental method, the distinction between primary and secondary qualities, the geometrisation of space, and the acceptance of the mechanical model of reality.[46]

All of this went missing in the Middle Kingdom. Needham's findings complement those of physicist and intellectual historian Qian Wenyuan, whose honest concern for his country led him to this conclusion: "China's incapability of developing modern science has been so conspicuous that, even with conscious and official importation, the state of non-development nevertheless dragged on and on."[47] Qian's insensitive scholarship is ignored by academics, but there is no escaping the truth of his observation. Hajime Nakamura, another historian of Asian thought, also ran into trouble with establishment colleagues for his low opinion of Chinese science, which he regarded as "practical" and not theory-based.[48]

Nakamura, moreover, had the temerity to ascribe China's failure to develop abstract science to a preference for concrete thought, claiming famously that Chinese "dwell reluctantly on that which is beyond the immediately perceived."[49] The common thread among these scholars – and many others – is that progress in Chinese science is frustrated by its practitioners' unwillingness to move past practical utility and think abstractly about the nature of the work itself.[50] China's bias for, and extraordinary ability to achieve, incremental progress in S&T is the result of a particular mindset that values concrete and devalues abstract achievement. Whether this is the result of a country always in catch-up mode remains to be seen.

How far-reaching are these differences? Psychologist Richard Nisbett demonstrated through controlled testing a dichotomy of cognitive preferences between Eastern and Western subjects that he characterized as continuity vs. discreteness, field vs. object, relationships vs. categories, dialectics vs. logic, experienced-based knowledge vs. abstract analysis, interdependence vs. independence, and communal vs. individualistic, which he boiled down later to "holistic" vs. "analytic" thought, validating generalizations made on both sides of the Pacific for a century.[51]

It gets more interesting. Citing Nisbett's work, neuroscientists Joan Y. Chiao and Katherine D. Blizinsky in a much-quoted article "Culture-gene coevolution of individualism-collectivism and the serotonin transporter gene" proposed a tidy sociobiological explanation for the coevolution of collectivist behavior and the dominance in East Asian populations of a genetic variant that codes for the psychotropic drug serotonin, which impacts emotion and cognitive bias. In their words:

we speculate that S [East Asian] and L [most European] allele carriers of the serotonin transporter gene may possess at least two kinds of information processing biases in the mind and brain that enhance their ability to store and transmit collectivistic and individualistic cultural norms, respectively.[52]

Chiao and Blizinsky correlate the distribution of the 5-HTTLPR S allele with the greater ability of East Asians to resist "psychopathology" such as anxiety and depression (without noting that, stripped of the value judgment, both psychological states are associated strongly with type-2 creativity in the sciences). They go on to acknowledge that:

> S allele carriers may be more likely to demonstrate negative cognitive biases, such as engage in narrow thinking and cognitive focus, which facilitate maintenance to collectivistic cultural norms of social conformity and interdependence, whereas L allele carriers may exhibit positive cognitive biases, such as open, creative thinking and greater willingness to take risks, which promote individualistic cultural norms of self-expression and autonomy.[53]

It has long been clear that individualism supports radical creativity, which by definition entails a rupture from the collective wisdom and, usually, negative affect from peers. Or put the other way: "There is no doubt that salient factors of extrinisic constraint in the social environment can have a consistently negative impact on the intrinsic motivation and creativity of most people most of the time" (Hennessey and Amabile).[54] Other factors cited in the creativity literature as inhibiting novel discovery are conformist education, lack of privacy and political centralism,[55] ethnic homogeneity,[56] and isolation from "diverse sociocultural environments"[57] (such as Internet restrictions). To us, this sounds a lot like China.

Another impediment to Chinese creativity is the character writing system. Unlike Western alphabets that force learners to parse naturally occurring syllables into abstract phonemes and make other types of analytic judgments, *hanzi* (Chinese characters) map directly onto syllables, depriving children of an early, life-changing opportunity to move beyond the concrete artifacts served up by nature to an abstract representation of one's surroundings. Nor does the writing identify words – another abstract construct with no counterpart in raw speech. The characters, which are mostly opaque and identify vague units of meaning, are run together without relief.

This is not to say that Chinese writing doesn't work. It can express language like any orthography, but with a two orders-of-magnitude greater investment in mind-sapping memorization, without the cues that help trigger analytic thought. A microcosm of China itself, the system substitutes complexity for abstractness. The cost of neglecting abstraction – for this or any other reason – is its negative impact on creative thinking, which depends critically on one's ability to work a few levels up from "the immediately perceived."[58] Although it is hard to know where the causality began, it is evident there is little in China to facilitate creativity and much to prevent it.

Does any of this matter? Probably not. We included Japan in Murray's data (above) in part to illustrate our belief that radical creativity, which that country was not famous for either, unless backed by a serious IPR regime with penalties for cheating, has no necessary link to a nation's prosperity. Countries can prosper without it and those with it may not succeed economically. What matters more is the ability to adapt creations, wherever they are made, to real-life problems. *It's not risk takers who prevail but early adapters of proven innovations.* China's genius, as it were, is in putting together a system that capitalizes on its practical skill at adapting ideas to national projects, while compensating for its inability to create those ideas by importing them quickly at little or no cost. By outsourcing its creativity, China keeps dissent in check and can focus on expanding its economic and political spheres.

Of course, the dynamite combination is a culture that can build practical applications for what the world creates in the abstract, while focusing parts of its diaspora network and emerging indigenous capability on selected science and engineering areas where breakthroughs will have radical game-changing consequences. This is the course China is following today and the piece that we find most troubling.

China's aggressive policy is threatening what few advantages the US has long enjoyed as a scientifically creative nation. Meanwhile, recent trends point to a decline in US students getting advanced degrees in science and technology, R&D funds that have shrunk and will probably be cut further, as well as a hollowing out of our manufacturing base.[59] Pair this up with a more scientifically competent China that is also using the discoveries of others, and future US competitiveness comes into question. China has for several decades made S&T development a priority and appears to have the political will to see it through. This is demonstrated by the R&D funding programs it has put in place, the investment in core scientific infrastructure that is in some cases unparalleled anywhere else in the world, and a national, scientifically oriented industrial policy.[60]

Good science does not occur in a vacuum and the world-class facilities China is building will be a kind of "bait" for the international scientific community. China sees these facilities as an important part of its rise in the global community and something that will facilitate a shift in the global center of gravity for scientific research toward China. This impacts US competitiveness as we can no longer assume an endless stream of the world's smart people coming through our doors. Just as China argues for the importance of a multipolar world in foreign affairs,[61] it wants to be the destination of the world's great minds. There are already some indications of this shift, perhaps best demonstrated by China's assistance to Germany during its 2011 public health crisis with the *E. Coli* outbreak. A technically sophisticated Western nation reached out to China for help instead of to the US. What other proof is needed?

We seem to have forgotten how we got to the top technologically, that what is learned along the way feeds the next generation of discovery and trains the next generation of experts. A country becomes good by doing things. Skills and infrastructure cannot be built overnight, and those who are doing the work are the ones who will eventually make the innovations. If you are not in the game – and we would argue that ceding entire areas of manufacturing and technology means just that – you cannot make the incremental changes or innovations, and you will certainly not be able to make the big jumps in capabilities but instead will simply stagnate.

Notes

1 Huiyao Wang, , David Zweig, and Xiaohua Lin, "Returnee Entrepreneurs: impact on China's globalization process," *Journal of Contemporary China* 20, no. 40 (May 2011): 413–431; Wenxian Zhang, Huiyao Wang, and Ilan Alon (eds), *Entrepreneurial and Business Elites of China: The Chinese Returnees Who Have Shaped Modern China*, Bingley, UK: Emerald Group Publishing, 2011.
2 For an illustrative example of the state sources of BGI's funding, including the 863 Program, see www.plosbiology.org/article/info:doi/10.1371/journal.pbio.1000533.
3 BGI's impressive list of publications may be found at: http://en.genomics.cn/navigation/show_navigation.action?navigation.id=97.
4 The holdings of BGI's database may be found at: http://en.genomics.cn/navigation/show_navigation.action?navigation.id=99.
5 http://jrceec.utk.edu/.
6 http://jrceec.utk.edu/about.html.
7 Ibid.
8 Zhou Wei (周伟), "我国企业对外直接投资战略分析" ("Analysis of China's strategy for corporate foreign direct investment"), 科技进步与对策 (*Science & Technology Progress and Policy*), 2004.11, p. 56.
9 We are grateful to Robert Skebo Sr. (personal communication) for pointing this out.
10 Zeng Zhaozhi (曾昭智), Niu Zhengming (牛争鸣), and Zhang Lin (张林), "利用专利文献促进科技创新" ("Using patent resources to promote scientific and technological innovation"), 技术与创新管理 (*Technology and Innovation Management*), 2004.6, pp. 46–48.
11 Cai Meide (蔡美德), Du Haidong (杜海东), and Hu Guosheng (胡国胜), "反求工程原理在高职课程体系创新中的应用" ("Using the principle of reverse engineering for innovation in high-level knowledge processes and systems"), 科技管理研究 (*Science and Technology Management Research*), 2005.7.
12 Peng Can (彭灿), "基于国际战略联盟的模仿创新" ("Imitative innovation based on international strategic alliances"), 科研管理 (*Science Research Management*), 2005.2, pp. 23–27.
13 Zhang Ying (张莹) and Chen Guohong (陈国宏), "跨国公司在中国的技术转移问题及对策分析" ("Analysis of the problem of technology transfer of multinational corporations in China and measures for dealing with it"), 科技进步与对策 (*Science & Technology Progress and Policy*), 2001.3, p. 134.
14 See e.g., Brett Kingstone, *The Real War Against America*, Specialty Publishing/Max King, LLC, 2005.
15 "International S&T cooperation and the sharing of intellectual property," *Keji Ribao*, May 13, 1996.
16 "The international economic intelligence war," *Zhongguo Maoyi Bao*, November 19, 1998.
17 Hong Kong AFP dispatch. June 3, 1996.
18 Zhou Zhu (周竺) and Huang Ruihua (黄瑞华), "知识产权保护的全球化, 中国面临的挑战及对策" ("The globalization of IPR protection: challenges facing China and their countermeasures"), 科技管理研究 (*Science and Technology Management Research*), 2004.3, p. 67.
19 Ibid., pp. 66–68.

20 Bao Sheng (宝胜), "论经济全球化背景下企业间的策略性技术联盟" ("On strategic technical alliances by corporations against the background of economic globalization"), in 科研管理 (*Science Research Management*), 2002.9.

21 Peng Yixin (彭宜新), Wu Xinwen (吴新文), and Zou Shangang (邹珊刚), "国际技术保护主义与我国高技术产业发展" ("International technology protectionism and the development of China's high-tech industry"), 科技进步与对策 (*Science & Technology Progress and Policy*), 2001.8, p. 59.

22 Ibid., p. 58.

23 www.cstec.org.cn.

24 Ibid.

25 An abbreviated list with hotlinks to association websites is available at www.acskp.org/link/acs.html.

26 The All-Japan Federation of Overseas Chinese Professionals (中国留日同学总会) underwent a name change on October 22, 2000 from its original 全日本在职中国留学人员联谊会, which more closely matches the English.

27 www.obsc.jp.

28 Ibid.

29 Ibid.

30 www.come.or.jp/acsej.

31 Ibid.

32 www.casej.jp/newpage.

33 Ibid.

34 www.fcpae.com.

35 Ibid.

36 Ibid.

37 www.ceco.org.cn.

38 www.asicef.org.

39 Ibid.

40 Louisa Lim, "Plagiarism Plague Hinders China's Scientific Ambition," *National Public Radio*, August 3, 2011, www.npr.org/2011/08/03/138937778/plagiarism-plague-hinders-chinas-scientific-ambition.

41 In Brick's (1997) schema: "intrarepresentational" and "interrepresentational," respectively.

42 Hannas' Law of Chinese historiography predicts that every 20 years, 1,000 more are added to "Chinese history." The count is now at 5,000 years and rising. This formulation complements Mulvenon's Third Law on Sunzi quotations proposed earlier.

43 We include Murray's statistics on Japan, which was not known historically for breakthrough science either and by many accounts struggles even today to overcome a "creativity problem." William C. Hannas, *The Writing on the Wall: How Asian Orthography Curbs Creativity*, Philadelphia: University of Pennsylvania Press, 2003, pp. 8–33, 91–97.

44 Adapted from Charles Murray, *Human Accomplishment: The Pursuit of Excellence in the Arts and Sciences, 800 B.C. to 1950*, New York: Harper, 2003, pp. 515–573.

45 Joseph Needham, *Science and Civilisation in China: History of Scientific Thought*, New York: Cambridge University Press, 1956, p. 11.

46 Joseph Needham, *The Grand Titration: Science and Society in East and West*, London: George Allen & Unwin, 1969, p. 15.

47 Wen-yuan Qian, *The Great Inertia: Scientific Stagnation in Traditional China*, London: Croom Helm, 1985, p. 50.

48 Hajime Nakamura, *Ways of Thinking of Eastern Peoples: India, China, Tibet, Japan*, Honolulu: University of Hawaii Press, 1964. pp. 189–190.

49 Ibid., p. 180.

50 Richard Baum (ed.), *China's Four Modernizations: The New Technological Revolution*, Boulder, CO: Westview Press, 1980, p. 1170; Richard Suttmeier, "Science, Technology, and China's Political Future – a Framework for Analysis", in Simon and Goldman (eds),

Science and Technology in post-Mao China, Cambridge, MA: Harvard University Press, 1989, p. 379; Robert K. Logan, *The Alphabet Effect*, New York: Morrow, 1986, p. 49.

51 Richard E. Nisbett, Kaiping Peng, Incheol Choi, and Ara Norenzayan, "Culture and Systems of Thought: Holistic Versus Analytic Cognition," *Psychological Review* 108. 2 (April 2001), pp. 291–310, pp. 193–194, and Richard E. Nisbett, *The Geography of Thought: How Asians and Westerners think differently . . . and why*, New York: The Free Press, 2003. pp. 56, 88.

52 Joan Y. Chiao and Katherine D. Blizinsky, "Culture-gene coevolution of individualism-collectivism and the serotonin transporter gene (5-HTTLPR)," *Proceedings of the Royal Society B: Biological Sciences* 277, no. 1681, 2010, pp. 529–537.

53 Ibid.

54 Beth A. Hennessey and Teresa M. Amabile, "The conditions of creativity," in Robert J. Sternberg (ed.), *The Nature of Creativity*, New York: Cambridge University Press, 1988, pp. 11–38, p. 34.

55 Dean Keith Simonton, "Creativity, leadership, and chance," in Robert J. Sternberg (ed.), *The Nature of Creativity*, New York: Cambridge University Press, 1988, pp. 386–428, pp. 404–415.

56 Kevin Dunbar, "How Scientists Really Reason: Scientific Reasoning in Real-World Laboratories," in Robert J. Sternberg and Janet Davidson (eds), *The Nature of Insight*, Cambridge, MA, MIT Press, 1995, pp. 384–385.

57 Scott C. Findlay and Charles J. Lumsden, "The Creative Mind: Toward an Evolutionary Theory of Discovery and Innovation," *Journal of Social and Biological Structures* 11, no. 1, January 1998, pp. 3–55, p. 17.

58 Hannas, *The Writing on the Wall*.

59 World Economic Forum, "US Competitiveness Ranking Continues to Fall; Emerging Markets Are Closing the Gap," September 7, 2011, www.weforum.org/news/us-competitiveness-ranking-continues-fall-emerging-markets-are-closing-gap.

60 Ibid.

61 See most recently Richard Haas, "The Age of Nonpolarity," *Foreign Affairs* 87, no. 3, May–June 2008, pp. 44–56; Kishore Mahhuhani, "The Case against the West," *Foreign Affairs*, 87, no. 3, May–June 2008, pp. 111–124; Fareed Zakaria, *The Post-American World*, New York: W.W. Norton, 2008.

CONCLUSION

Countries that embrace risk and innovation must protect their investments and advantages from attempts by other countries to access them at no cost, and from people within their own borders who profit at the expense of the commonwealth. We offer a few suggestions on how this may be done.

Managing "cheaters" in a global society

We can recover our competitiveness by manufacturing what we invent and rebuild the scientific foundation on which our competitive edge depends. But unless we deal with non-reciprocators who bypass the costs of innovation that the rest of us bear, our efforts at national reconstruction will be wasted. As we have shown, our current defense of intellectual property has not been effective in refuting appropriation by China, by all accounts the world's worst offender. It makes no sense to rebuild our scientific base – however much we need to do so – when our advantages are sapped from under us.

To address this problem we need to take a hard look at its causes. On the one hand, we should investigate – formally and in greater depth – how a foreign state with dubious intent was able to access our technology and use it to push US manufacturers out of the marketplace. That done, measures should be taken to insure that the interests of the United States are not sacrificed to narrow constituencies who benefit from these one-sided transactions. On the other hand, we must recognize that the root cause of the problem is nothing less than our own individualism and find ways as a nation to take collective action against the common threat, because the same trait that makes us good at creating things makes it hard for us to defend our national interests.

It is ironic that we do so badly as a nation what humans are wired from birth to perform, namely to work with other members of society to thwart "cheaters" who benefit at the expense of society. This innate talent, an adaptation for group survival, is documented in evolutionary psychology and executed by the laws a country makes to protect itself. A successful group expects members to act altruistically on its behalf. In an individualistic society such as ours, however, altruism can be trumped by short-term goals. What do I gain personally by shunning cheap goods built with stolen technology? Don't we benefit through lower prices? Read Brett Kingstone's account of how China looted his firm and ask yourself honestly if you really care.[1]

Recognizing that arguing for national interests in the United States is an uphill battle, we propose a few points for consideration.

First, we need a better understanding of the benefits and costs of admitting large numbers of foreign students to our academies. We have already given many reasons why the presence of nearly 194,000 PRC students on US campuses is not an unqualified blessing. We all know the justifications: American students don't study science. University departments cannot stay open without them. PRC students are brilliant lab workers who give as much as they take. They return to China spreading goodwill and democracy. Their presence here gives us an insight into what is happening there, and so on.

Each of these arguments is overstated and, in the "empty chair" case, tends to perpetuate the problem that immigrant students are supposed to solve. Moreover, there are two glaring policy problems related to PRC students in the United States – separate from the fact that US taxpayers are funding their training – neither of which is easy to solve. The first is simply knowing who is here and where they are studying, should the need arise to investigate their activities. The current system, known as the Student and Exchange Visitor Information System (SEVIS),[2] is designed "to track and monitor schools and programs, students, exchange visitors and their dependants while approved to participate in the US education system." SEVIS collects data on surnames and first names, addresses, date and country of birth, information on dependants, nationality/citizenship, funding, school, program name, date of study commencement, education degree level, and authorization for on-campus employment.[3]

The good news is that the FBI has access to all of the student data contained in SEVIS, and no longer needs the permission of DHS to initiate investigations of foreign students.[4] The bad news is that the laws, regulations, and directives governing SEVIS do not require some additional critical pieces of information, which are nonetheless perceived to be important in order to manage the program. According to GAO,

- The non-immigrant visa number, expiration date, and issuing post are optional and only captured if entered into the system by the school or exchange visitor program.
- The non-immigrant driver's license number and issuing state were imposed by the interagency working group and support investigative efforts.
- The non-immigrant passport number, passport expiration date, and passport

issuing country are optional and are only captured if entered into the system by the school or exchange visitor program.[5]

It is difficult to ascertain from open sources whether these problems have been fixed, but the non-mandatory data are key investigative input that would be critical for Federal law enforcement seeking to assess possible illicit technology transfers by students.

The second major policy problem involves PRC student access to controlled technology under the deemed export system. According to the Commerce Department, a deemed export is defined as follows: "An export of technology or source code (except encryption source code) is 'deemed' to take place when it is released to a foreign national within the United States."[6] Under these rules, a university or research lab does not "need a license or authorization for the mere presence of a foreign graduate student," but does need a deemed export license if they "plan to transfer controlled technology to a foreign national and the export of that technology is restricted to the foreign national's home country."

Following from recommendations in a 2004 US Department of Commerce Office of Inspector General (OIG) Report entitled "Deemed Export Controls May Not Stop the Transfer of Sensitive Technology to Foreign Nationals in the US," Commerce published an "Advance Notice of Proposed Rulemaking: Revision and Clarification of Deemed Export Related Regulatory Requirements" (ANPR) in the *Federal Register* on March 28, 2005.[7] Following an avalanche of largely negative public comments, primarily from universities and research labs, Commerce withdrew the ANPR and issued "Revisions and Clarification of Deemed Export Related Regulatory Requirements" (RIN 0694-AD29) on May 31, 2006, which reiterates that the "current BIS licensing policy related to deemed exports is appropriate and confirms that the existing definition of 'use' adequately reflects the underlying export controls policy rationale in the Export Administration Regulations (EAR)."[8] Yet the continued sieve of controlled technology to the PRC and the findings of GAO studies on the problems of university oversight[9] strongly suggest that the 2004 OIG recommendations should be re-examined, as our research shows that the flow of technology "back" to China has continued unabated.

Second, S&T collaboration with China isn't just a feel-good part of the Sino–US relationship, but is something that is important to Beijing and something that they want, as it helps them build capabilities they still need help with. It would seem that US advantages here could be employed to good effect.

Third, given its well-documented weaknesses, gaps, and implementation problems in the post-Cold War era, another way to restore the balance would be to reform the export control system. In 2009, President Obama "directed a broad-based interagency reform of the US export control system with the goal of strengthening national security and the competitiveness of key US manufacturing and technology sectors by focusing on current threats and adapting to the changing economic and technological landscape."[10] In simple terms, the White House seeks "fundamental reform in all four areas of our current system – in what we control, how we control it, how we enforce those controls, and how we manage our controls."[11] Specifically, the

> Export Control Reform Initiative aims to build higher fences around a core set of items whose misuse can pose a national security threat to the United States. By facilitating trade to close partners and allies, the Commerce Department can better focus its resources ensuring the most sensitive items do not end up where they should not.[12]

In concrete terms, the reform initiative is synchronizing the two existing control lists, the Munitions List and the Commerce Control List, so that they:

- are "tiered" to distinguish the types of items that should be subject to stricter or more permissive levels of control for different destinations, end uses, and end users;
- create a "bright line" between the two current control lists to clarify which list an item is controlled on, and reduce government and industry uncertainty about whether particular items are subject to the control of the State Department or the Commerce Department;
- are structurally aligned so that they can potentially be combined into a single list of controlled items.[13]

Moreover, the lists will be transformed into a "positive list" that describes controlled items using objective criteria (e.g., technical parameters such as horsepower or microns) rather than broad, open-ended, subjective, generic, or design intent-based criteria.[14] After applying these criteria, the list will be divided into three tiers:

1. Items in the highest tier are those that provide a critical military or intelligence advantage to the United States and are available almost exclusively from the United States, or are weapons of mass destruction or related items.
2. Items in the middle tier are those that provide a substantial military or intelligence advantage to the United States and are available almost exclusively from our multilateral partners and allies.
3. Items in the lowest tier are those that provide a significant military or intelligence advantage to the United States but are available more broadly.[15]

The designers hope that this system will "permit the government to adjust controls in a timely manner over a product's life cycle in order to keep lists targeted and current based on the maturity and sensitivity of an item."[16] Once a controlled item is placed into a tier, a corresponding licensing policy will be assigned to it to focus agency reviews on the most sensitive items. The Administration has developed an initial set of proposed licensing policies for dual-use items:

- A license will generally be required for items in the highest tier to all destinations. Many of the items in the second tier will be authorized for export to multilateral partners and allies under license exemptions or general authorizations. For less sensitive items, a license will be required for some, but not all, destinations.
- For items authorized to be exported without licenses, there will be new limitations imposed on the re-export of those items to prevent their diversion to unauthorized destinations.[17]

On the one hand, these reforms could greatly improve the efficiency of the export control bureaucracy, preventing fewer technologies from slipping between the cracks and finding their way to China. They could also make the system and its control lists more flexible and better able to keep pace with technological change, which had been a major problem with the old system, particularly with regard to fast-moving information technologies. On the other hand, the reforms appear to loosen controls over dual-use technologies, which China has a long and successful track record of integrating into advanced systems, and which can form the core of new innovations, since much of the cutting-edge research is not yet controlled while it is still in the lab.

Fourth, as defined by a 2010 General Accounting Office report, the Committee on Foreign Investment in the United States (CFIUS) is an interagency committee that serves the President in overseeing the national security implications of foreign investment in the economy.[18] As China's economy and financial weight has grown, CFIUS has reviewed an increasing number of proposed acquisitions of American companies and infrastructure by Chinese entities. Many of these proposed mergers have received high levels of media and Congressional attention, and most of the high-profile cases have ended in rejection or strong discouragement leading to abandonment of the deal:

- The decision by the China National Offshore Oil Company (CNOOC) to drop its proposed acquisition of Unocal oil company in 2005 was partly due to concerns about an impending CFIUS investigation of the transaction.[19]
- In February 2008, Bain Capital and Huawei Technologies withdrew its offer to acquire the network and software firm, 3Com, for $2.2 billion, due to an inability to successfully negotiate a mitigation agreement with members of CFIUS. Bain Capital is a privately held asset management and investment firm, and Huawei Technologies is the largest networking and telecommunications equipment supplier in China. 3Com is a publicly held company that specializes in networking equipment and in the Tipping Point network intrusion prevention software, which is used to protect some DoD networks. Bain Capital and Huawei reportedly withdrew their proposal after they failed to agree to terms with CFIUS over a mitigation agreement and stated that they would restructure the deal and resubmit it at a later date in 2008.[20]

- In December 2009, the Chinese firm Northwest Nonferrous International Investment Corp., a subsidiary of China's largest aluminum producer, attempted to acquire US-based Firstgold, but failed due to objections by the US Department of the Treasury that Firstgold had properties near sensitive military bases.[21]
- In June 2010, China's Tangshan Caofeidian Investment Corporation withdrew its proposed acquisition of Emcore, which makes components for fiber optics and solar panels, due to "regulatory concerns."[22]
- In May 2010, Huawei bought the bankrupt intellectual property of 3Leaf server technology company for $2 million, but did not file with CFIUS until November of that year.[23] By February 2011, Huawei said it would back away from the deal, bowing to pressure that it should divest the assets.

While the CFIUS process may have prevented individual cases of sensitive or illegal technology transfer by scotching these deals, it could also have had the unintended effect of forcing Chinese actors to steal the data through espionage owing to their inability to obtain them through globalized commerce.

Fifth, a final channel for restoring the balance might be the bilateral Sino–US dialogues, including the Strategic and Economic Dialogue (S&ED) and the Strategic Security Dialogue (SSD). The origins and purpose of the dialogues are summarized by Glaser and Freeman:

> The US–China Strategic and Economic Dialogue (S&ED) was established by President Barack Obama and President Hu Jintao during their first meeting in April 2009 and represents the highest-level bilateral forum to discuss a broad range of bilateral, regional, and global issues between the two nations. The upgraded mechanism replaced the earlier Senior Dialogue and Strategic Economic Dialogue, which were initiated under the George W. Bush administration. By merging the economic and security tracks, the Obama administration seeks to break down the barriers inside both the US and Chinese governments to more effectively tackle cross-cutting issues such as climate change, development, and energy security.[24]

Issues related to technology security and trade are actually ideal for the S&ED, as well as one of its new components, the SSD – a joint civilian–military dialogue. Of course, there are significant obstacles. First, the Chinese side will strongly resist discussing technology espionage at the bilateral level, denying the content of the accusations and condemning them as arising from a "Cold War mentality." Second, even if the Chinese were willing to discuss it, American companies are reluctant to go public with the details of their losses and their unwillingness to credibly threaten to back out of the China market. In a sense, only Google could leave China, because its business model does not require a bricks-and-mortar presence and retail distribution relationships. The Ciscos and Microsofts of the world do not have the same luxury, undermining any threats made in a bilateral economic dialogue.

Some China shibboleths

This completes our study of China's "informal" technology transfer practices. Aware that our thesis is contentious, and taking a cue from the "Communist Party that does not fear criticism,"[25] we conclude with a catechism of replies to anticipated complaints.

1 It's normal business practice

China has gained enormous traction in the world by calling itself a "special case," and we are inclined to agree here. No other country approaches China's efforts and success at raiding foreign sources of technology. It is neither "normal" nor "business" but a state-sponsored assault on foreign invention that includes every dodge and malpractice up to and including espionage – then goes beyond espionage through a Gulag of "transfer centers" that ensure the pillage goes into products.

2 There is no evidence China makes use of "informally" transferred foreign technology.

This is precisely the function of China's National Technology Transfer Centers (NTTCs, 国家技术转移中心) or National Technology Transfer Demonstration Organizations (国家技术转移模范机构), introduced in September 2001 and established in policy in December 2007 through the "National Technology Transfer Promotion Implementation Action Plan" (国家技术转移促进行动实施办法). Examples of NTTCs are provided in Chapter 4. Some 202 "demonstration" centers exist today, built up in three "batches" of 76, 58, and 68. Bear in mind that these centers are *models* for emulation by other transfer facilities; we have no figures on their true number. Their charters explicitly name "domestic and foreign technology" as targets for "commercialization."

3 China is changing into a creative nation; or conversely, China is not creative at all

It is hard to assess China's creative output given the ambiguity in what China manufactures, borrows, and steals. More fundamentally, traditional assessments of China's output – numbers of patents and publications – do not take into account the degree of novelty. Tweaks to foreign patents and expansions of paradigms conceived outside China should be weighed differently than native creation. In addition, whereas China's S&T leadership accepts innovation in principle, until recently it has caveated its acceptance with reminders of the need for practical results. It is unclear what the impact of this approach will be as China moves in some areas to change its educational system and culture in the lab. Assuming China's efforts succeed – which is likely for some areas – it becomes more important to protect ourselves from a peer competitor who makes its own rules.

4 The book is yet another example of Western "racism" toward China

Our focus is national practices. Is it "racism" when the Japanese complain about the same thing? Nonetheless, there will be groups in the US, such as the Committee of 100, that decry our work in the same way they did the Cox Report and the Wen Ho Lee case, where they likened the US government to a third world dictatorship.[26] One cannot help but be amused by the irony here. While we do not fear criticism from these parties, we challenge them – given the information presented in this book and their stated charter of fostering constructive relationships – to demonstrate their objectivity by being *as forceful with the Chinese government as they have been with their own* in addressing this issue and in using their influence to protect US competitiveness and, dare we say, US interests.

5 The bilateral relationship and hundreds of billions in bilateral trade are "more important"

Some analysts who approach US–China relations from a predominantly realist perspective argue that the pure calculation of the United States' self-interest demands less confrontation and more cooperation between the two countries. Proponents of this laissez-faire view point to the (present) differentials in growth rates and the inevitability of parity as the key determinants of long-term US strategy:

> We must consider the facts. China will continue to grow four to five times faster than the US. In less than 30 years China's GDP will equal that of the US and we will live in a world of two great and equal powers.[27]

In a period of global economic recession these facts become even more dispositive, since strategic tensions may dampen trade flows, hurt American job growth, and reduce national prosperity. These realists would no doubt object to our book on the grounds that it unnecessarily introduces areas of conflict into the relationship and does not see the "big picture." But for us, the big picture is that long-term, dedicated Chinese strategies designed to acquire and exploit science and technology are fundamentally damaging US military advantage, technological competitiveness, and future economic prosperity. In that respect, we believe the realists are too focused on the short term at the expense of the future.

6 Most examples are not espionage, just a consequence of globalization and outdated US technology policies

We must move beyond thinking of espionage in the traditional sense and look at this issue based on its impact on the US. Globalization will work only if we have the same broad view of its benefits. As previous chapters have shown, the PRC government still looks to collaboration as a way to forge ahead, not to share. We recognize the need for collaboration and agree it is part of the scientific endeavor, but argue that "collaboration" without transparency is a one-way street.

7 Chinese scientists and businessmen are like us and work for themselves

China has changed in the past decade and its citizens enjoy more personal freedom than at any other point in time. However, one cannot look at China's appalling human rights record, as documented by the US Department of State,[28] and not wonder what impact this has on a person's free will not to participate in central government programs that are deemed a priority. Chinese students and scientists who study or work abroad are sometimes debriefed – obligatorily – after their return.[29] Team that disconcerting fact with the work of overseas-based advocacy groups that have the stated goal of making China stronger and that is a potent mix.

8 Why anger China unnecessarily?

China has built a cadre of international apologists because it plays hardball and uses its power to its advantage. If you want access to China or even a visa, you must play by China's rules, which means being a "friend" of China and not embarrassing its leaders. This was recently brought to light by academics who had criticized China's human rights policies and were refused visas, by a university that opened a Confucius Institute and saw its activities censored,[30] and by business persons taken to the cleaners who stay quiet because they did not want to make things worse.

9 We need China for our bottom line

This argument is almost an urban legend, as it has been used to justify any and all interaction between US businesses and China, whatever their outcome, as well as the unequal playing field and its negative impact on national security. The claim is that US businesses need China for cheap manufacturing and research talent – a classic case of self-fulfilling prophecy. We then go on to delude ourselves that if we yield on a few minor issues, or transfer more technology, China will surely acquiesce to international business practices. Somehow it never happens, and somehow we *never* learn that these compromises accrue to China's advantage only.

Toward a new relationship

We offer the following challenges to our readers, in particular to those involved with the transfer practices we have described:

We challenge American business persons to think beyond the next quarter and ask yourselves why you are training your future competitors – because when you start cooperative programs with China, and transfer your core technology, that is exactly what you are doing.

We ask our colleagues in defense, intelligence, law enforcement, commerce, and homeland security to look beyond espionage as traditionally defined to this broader and more pervasive threat. The world is not as clear as it used to be. Deal with it.

To scientists and educators tuned to the big picture, please appreciate that many countries do not – and never will – share your high view of international society, and that politics, not wishful thinking, will continue to govern the behavior of successful nations.[31]

Finally, we appeal to the broad masses of Chinese, both in China and abroad, to adopt a more high-minded attitude that will better serve your interests and those of the world. *You have come a long way* and earned the world's respect. Now make this final transition.

Notes

1   Brett Kingstone, *The Real War Against America*, Max King LLC, 2005.
2   General Accounting Office, "Homeland Security: Performance of Information System to Monitor Foreign Students and Exchange Visitors Has Improved, but Issues Remain," GAO-04-69, June 2004, accessed at: www.gao.gov/new.items/d04690.pdf. SEVIS was mandated by the Illegal Immigration Reform and Immigrant Responsibility Act (IIRIRA) of 1996 and augmented by the USA Patriot Act of 2001, Enhanced Border Security and Visa Entry Reform Act of 2002, the Cyber Security Research and Development Act of 2002.
3   www.ice.gov/doclib/sevis/pdf/quarterly_rpt_mar2011.pdf.
4   Matthew Gruchow, "FBI Gets Access to SEVIS," *Minnesota Daily*, accessed at: www.mndaily.com/nuevo/2004/09/22/fbi-gets-access-sevis.
5   General Accounting Office, "Homeland Security: Performance of Information System to Monitor Foreign Students and Exchange Visitors Has Improved, but Issues Remain," GAO-04-69, June 2004, accessed at: www.gao.gov/new.items/d04690.pdf.
6   For the authoritative FAQ on deemed exports, see www.bis.doc.gov/deemedexports/deemedexportsfaqs.html.
7   US Department of Commerce Office of Inspector General (OIG) Report entitled "Deemed Export Controls May Not Stop the Transfer of Sensitive Technology to Foreign Nationals in the US," (Final Inspection Report No. IPE–16176 – March 2004).
8   http://edocket.access.gpo.gov/2006/pdf/E6-8370.pdf.
9   General Accounting Office, "Export Controls: Agencies Should Assess Vulnerabilities and Improve Guidance for Protecting Export-Controlled Information at Universities," GAO-07-70, accessed at: www.gao.gov/new.items/d0770.pdf.
10 www.bis.doc.gov/news/2011/bis_press06162011.htm.
11 White House Office of the Press Secretary, "President Obama Announces First Steps Toward Implementation of New US Export Control System," December 9, 2010, accessed at: www.whitehouse.gov/the-press-office/2010/12/09/president-obama-announces-first-steps-toward-implementation-new-us-export.
12 www.bis.doc.gov/news/2011/bis_press06162011.htm.
13 White House Office of the Press Secretary, "President Obama Announces First Steps Toward Implementation of New US Export Control System."
14 Ibid.
15 Ibid.
16 Ibid.
17 Ibid.

18 James K. Jackson, "The Committee on Foreign Investment in the United States," CRS Report RL33388, July 29, 2010, Congressional Research Service, Washington, D.C., available at www.fas.org/sgp/crs/natsec/RL33388.pdf (accessed June 13, 2011).

19 Jackson, "The Committee on Foreign Investment in the United States."

20 Ibid.

21 Ibid.

22 Stephanie Kirchgaessner, "US Blocks China Fibre Optics Deal Over Security," *Financial Times*, June 30, 2010.

23 Sinead Carew and Jessica Wohl, "Huawei Backs Away From 3Leaf Acquisition," *Reuters*, February 19, 2011, accessed at: www.reuters.com/article/2011/02/19/us-huawei-3leaf-idUSTRE71I38920110219.

24 Charles Freeman and Bonnie Glaser, "The US–China Strategic and Economic Dialogue," May 11, 2011, accessed at: http://csis.org/publication/us-china-strategic-and-economic-dialogue-0.

25 党不怕批评.

26 October 13, 2000 by George Koo Member, Committee of 100 Remarks before the China Institute, New York, from Committee of 100 website.

27 William Owens, "America Must Start Treating China as a Friend," *Financial Times*, November 17, 2009.

28 According to the US Department of State, China 2010 Human Rights Report, "A negative trend in key areas of the country's human rights record continued, as the government took additional steps to rein in civil society, particularly organizations and individuals involved in rights advocacy and public interest issues, and increased attempts to limit freedom of speech and to control the press, the Internet, and Internet access."

29 See Nicholas Eftimiades, *Chinese Intelligence Operations*, Naval Institute Press, 1994, pp. 61–65.

30 The censorship is now inserted up front in the contract that establishes the institute.

31 We note with wry amusement the prominent place in Chinese bookstores these days of the early Republican-era Machiavellian classic *Hou Hei Xue* (后黑学 lit. "the science of thick [skin] and black [heart]" by Li Zongwu). A few decades ago it was available only on the back shelves of certain bookstores.

APPENDIX 1

Case Histories of Chinese Industrial Espionage[1]

- *Radiation-hardened aerospace technology to China* – On September 30, 2011, defendants Hong Wei Xian, aka "Harry Zan," and Li Li, aka "Lea Li," were sentenced in the Eastern District of Virginia to 24 months in prison for conspiracy to violate the Arms Export Control Act and conspiracy to smuggle goods unlawfully from the United States, in connection with their efforts to export to China radiation-hardened microchips that are used in satellite systems and are classified as defense articles. Both defendants pleaded guilty to the charges on June 1, 2011. The defendants were arrested on September 1, 2010 in Budapest by Hungarian authorities pursuant to a US provisional arrest warrant. On April 4, 2011, they made their initial court appearances in federal court in the Eastern District of Virginia after being extradited from Hungary. According to court documents, Zan and Li operated a company in China called Beijing Starcreates Space Science and Technology Development Company Limited. This firm was allegedly in the business of selling technology to China Aerospace and Technology Corporation, a Chinese government-controlled entity involved in the production and design of missile systems and launch vehicles. According to court documents, from April 2009 to September 1, 2010, the defendants contacted a Virginia company seeking to purchase and export thousands of Programmable Read-Only Microchips (PROMs). The defendants ultimately attempted to purchase 40 PROMs from the Virginia firm and indicated to undercover agents that the PROMs were intended for China Aerospace and Technology Corporation. The investigation was conducted by ICE and DCIS.
- *Radiation-hardened defense and aerospace technology to China* – On March 24, 2011, Lian Yang, a resident of Woodinville, Washington, pleaded guilty to conspiring to violate the Arms Export Control Act by trying to sell radiation-hardened military and aerospace technology to China. Yang was

arrested on December 3, 2010, pursuant to a criminal complaint filed in the Western District of Washington charging him with conspiracy to violate the Arms Export Control Act. According to the complaint, Yang attempted to purchase and export from the United States to China 300 radiation-hardened, programmable semiconductor devices that are used in satellites and are also classified as defense articles under the US Munitions List. The complaint alleges that Yang contemplated creating a shell company in the United States that would appear to be purchasing the parts, concealing the fact that the parts were to be shipped to China. Yang allegedly planned that false purchasing orders would be created, indicating that parts that could be legally exported were being purchased, not restricted parts. Yang and his co-conspirators allegedly wire-transferred $60,000 to undercover agents as partial payment for a sample of five devices. As part of the conspiracy, Yang allegedly negotiated a payment schedule with the undercover agents for the purchase and delivery of the remaining 300 devices in exchange for a total of $620,000. This investigation was conducted by the FBI, ICE, and CBP.

- *Military technical data to China* – On March 8, 2011, Sixing Liu, aka "Steve Liu," of Deerfield, IL, was arrested in Chicago on a criminal complaint filed in the District of New Jersey charging him with one count of exporting defense-related technical data without a license. Liu, a native of China with a doctorate degree in electrical engineering, worked as a senior staff engineer for Space & Navigation, a New Jersey-based division of L-3 Communications, from March 2009 through November 2010. He was part of a team that worked on precision navigation devices and other innovative components for the US Department of Defense. Liu was never issued a company laptop or approved to possess the company's work product outside the firm's New Jersey facility. In November 2010, he traveled to China and, upon his return to the United States later that month, CBP inspectors found him to be in possession of a computer that contained hundreds of documents related to the company's projects, as well as images of Liu making a presentation at a technology conference sponsored by the PRC government. Many of the documents on his computer were marked as containing sensitive proprietary company information and/or export-controlled technical data. The State Department verified that information on Liu's computer was export-controlled technical data that relates to defense items on the US Munitions List. The investigation was conducted by the FBI and ICE.

- *Dow trade secrets to China* – On February 7, 2011, a federal jury in the Middle District of Louisiana convicted Wen Chyu Liu, aka "David W. Liou," a former research scientist, of stealing trade secrets from Dow Chemical Company and selling them to companies in the People's Republic of China. According to the evidence presented in court, Liou came to the United States from China for graduate work. He began working for Dow in 1965 and retired in 1992. Dow is a leading producer of the elastomeric polymer, chlorinated polyethylene (CPE). Dow's Tyrin CPE is used in a number of applications worldwide, such as automotive and industrial hoses, electrical cable jackets, and vinyl siding. While employed at Dow, Liou worked as a research scientist on various aspects of the development and manufacture of Dow elastomers, including Tyrin CPE. The evidence at trial established that Liou conspired with at least four current and former employees of Dow's facilities in Plaquemine, Louisiana, and Stade, Germany, who had worked in Tyrin CPE production, to misappropriate those trade secrets in an effort to develop and market CPE process design packages to Chinese companies. Liou traveled throughout China to market the stolen information, and he paid current and former Dow employees for Dow's CPE-related material and information. In one instance, Liou bribed a then-employee at the Plaquemine facility with $50,000 in cash to provide Dow's process manual and other CPE-related information. The investigation was conducted by the FBI.

- *Stealth missile exhaust designs and military technical data to China* – On January 24, 2011, a federal judge in the District of Hawaii sentenced Noshir Gowadia, 66, of Maui to 32 years in prison for communicating classified national defense information to the People's Republic of China (PRC), illegally exporting military technical data, as well as money laundering, filing false tax returns, and other offenses. On August 9, 2010, a federal jury in the District of Hawaii found Gowadia guilty of 14 criminal violations after six days of deliberation and a 40-day trial. These included five criminal offenses relating to his design for the PRC of a low-signature cruise missile exhaust system capable of rendering a PRC cruise missile resistant to detection by infrared missiles. The jury also convicted Gowadia of three counts of illegally communicating classified information regarding lock-on range for infrared missiles against the US B-2 bomber to persons not authorized to receive such information. Gowadia was also convicted of unlawfully exporting classified information about the B-2, illegally retaining information related to US national defense at his home, money laundering, and filing false tax returns for the years 2001 and 2002. Gowadia was an engineer with Northrop Grumman Corporation from 1968 to 1986, during which time he contributed to the development of the unique propulsion system and low observable capabilities of the B-2 bomber. Gowadia continued to work on classified matters as a contractor with the US government until 1997, when his security clearance was terminated. Evidence at trial revealed that from July 2003 to June 2005, Gowadia took six trips to the PRC to provide defense services in the form of design, test support, and test data analysis of technologies for the purpose of assisting the PRC with its cruise missile system by developing a stealthy exhaust nozzle and was paid at least $110,000 by the PRC. The jury convicted Gowadia of two specific transmissions of classified information: a PowerPoint presentation on the exhaust nozzle of a PRC cruise missile project and an evaluation of the effectiveness of a redesigned nozzle, and a computer file providing his signature prediction of a PRC cruise missile outfitted with his modified exhaust nozzle and associated predictions in relation to a US air-to-air missile. The prosecution also produced evidence which documented Gowadia's use of three foreign entities he controlled, including a Liechtenstein charity purportedly for the benefit of children, to disguise the income he received from foreign countries. This case was investigated by the FBI, the US Air Force Office of Special Investigations, the IRS, US Customs and Border Protection, and ICE.

- *Electronics used in military radar and electronic warfare to China* – On January 27, 2011, Yufeng Wei was sentenced in the District of Massachusetts to 36 months in prison, while on January 26, 2011 her co-defendant, Zhen Zhou Wu, was sentenced to 97 months in prison. Their company, Chitron Electronics, Inc., was fined $15.5 million. Wei, Wu, and Chitron Electronics, Inc. were convicted at trial on May 17, 2010 of conspiring for a period of more than ten years to illegally export to the People's Republic of China military electronics components and sensitive electronics used in military phased array radar, electronic warfare, and missile systems. Several Chinese military entities were among those receiving the exported equipment. Wu and Wei were also both convicted of filing false shipping documents with the US government. As proven at trial, the defendants illegally exported military electronic components to China through Hong Kong. The electronics exported are primarily used in military phased array radar, electronic warfare, military guidance systems, and military satellite communications. The defendants also illegally exported Commerce Department-controlled electronics components to China with military applications such as electronic warfare, military radar, and satellite communications systems. Wu founded and controlled Chitron, with headquarters in Shenzhen, China, and a US office located in Waltham, MA, where defendant Wei served as Manager. Wu and Chitron sold electronics from the US to Chinese military factories and military research institutes, including numerous institutes of the China Electronics Technology Group Corporation, which is responsible for the procurement, development, and manufacture of electronics for the Chinese military. Since as early as 2002, Wu referred to Chinese military entities as Chitron's major customer and employed an engineer at Chitron's Shenzhen office to work with Chinese military customers. By 2007, 25 percent of Chitron's sales were to Chinese military entities. Shenzhen Chitron Electronics Company Limited, Wu's Chinese company through which US electronics were delivered to the Chinese military and other end users, was also indicted. On February 9, 2011, Chitron-Shenzhen received a fine of $1.9 million for refusing to appear for trial. Co-defendant Bo Li, aka "Eric Lee," previously pleaded guilty to making false statements on shipping documents. The case was investigated by the BIS, ICE, FBI, and DCIS.
- *Restricted electronics to China* – On October 11, 2010, York Yuan Chang, known as "David Zhang," and his wife, Leping Huang, were arrested on charges in the Central District of California of conspiring to export restricted electronics technology to the People's Republic of China (PRC) without a

license and making false statements. According to the October 9, 2010 criminal complaint, the defendants are the owners of General Technology Systems Integration, Inc. (GTSI), a California company involved in the export of technology to the PRC. GTSI allegedly entered into contracts with the 24th Research Institute of the China Electronics Technology Corporation Group in China to design and transfer to the PRC technology for the development of two types of high-performance analog-to-digital converters (ADCs). The defendants allegedly hired two engineers to design the technology and provide training to individuals in the PRC. Twice in 2009, US Customs and Border Protection officials stopped the engineers upon their return to the United States and allegedly found computer files and documents indicating illegal technology transfer involving GTSI and China. According to the complaint, Chang and Huang allegedly sought to cover up the project after the authorities contacted the engineers. The ADCs that the defendants allegedly attempted to export to the PRC are subject to export controls for national security and anti-terrorism reasons. This investigation was conducted by the FBI, BIS, ICE, IRS, and DCIS.

- *Sensitive military encryption technology to China* – On September 13, 2010, Chi Tong Kuok, a resident of Macau, China, was sentenced in the Southern District of California to serve 96 months in prison for his efforts to obtain sensitive defense technology used in encrypted US military or government communications and to cause them to be illegally exported to Macau and Hong Kong. On May 11, 2010, Kuok was convicted at trial of conspiracy to export defense articles without a license and to smuggle goods, attempting to export defense articles without a license, and money laundering. Kuok was arrested on June 17, 2009 in Atlanta, GA after he arrived from Paris to catch a connecting flight to Panama in order to meet with undercover federal agents to take possession of controlled US technology. Kuok sought to obtain a variety of encryption, communications and global positioning systems equipment used by the US and NATO militaries. For instance, Kuok negotiated with undercover agents to obtain PRC-148 radios and a KG-175 Taclane Encryptor. The PRC-148 is a multi-band radio originally designed for the US Special Operations Command. The KG-175 Taclane Encryptor was developed by General Dynamics under a contract with the National Security Agency for use by the US military to encrypt Internet Protocol communications. This investigation was conducted by the ICE and DCIS.

- *Stolen US military night vision and optics to China and England* – On September 9, 2010, a grand jury in the Southern District of California returned an indictment charging Phillip Andro Jamison with trafficking in stolen government property, interstate transportation of stolen goods, and exporting defense articles without a license. Jamison, a US Navy employee stationed aboard Naval Amphibious Base in Coronado, California, allegedly stole more than 280 items from the US Navy between October 2008 and September 2009 and then sold these items to customers via eBay, an

Internet auction and shopping website. The indictment further alleges that Jamison illegally exported to Hong Kong and England combat-grade night vision devices, riflescopes and laser aiming devices without first obtaining the required export licenses from the State Department. The investigation was conducted by the ICE and NCIS.

- ***Dow trade secrets to China*** – On August 31, 2010 an indictment was unsealed in the Southern District of Indiana charging Kexue Huang with economic espionage intended to benefit a foreign government and instrumentalities, as well as interstate and foreign transportation of stolen property. Huang was arrested on July 13, 2010 in Massachusetts. The indictment alleges that Huang, a Chinese national and US permanent legal resident, misappropriated and transported trade secrets and property to the People's Republic of China (PRC) while working as a research scientist at Dow AgroSciences LLC (Dow). While he was employed at Dow, Huang directed university researchers in the PRC to further develop the Dow trade secrets. He also allegedly applied for and obtained grant funding that was used to develop the stolen trade secrets. The investigation was conducted by the FBI.

- ***Thermal imaging cameras to China*** – On May 14, 2010, Sam Ching Sheng Lee, part-owner and chief operations manager of Multimillion Business Associate Corporation ("MBA"), pleaded guilty in the Central District of California to conspiracy to violate the International Emergency Economic Powers for illegally exporting national security-controlled thermal imaging cameras to China. His nephew, Charles Yu Hsu Lee, pleaded guilty on the same day to misprision of a felony for the same activity. The Lees were arrested on December 30, 2008 in Hacienda Heights, CA, pursuant to a December 16, 2008 indictment charging them with conspiracy to export and exporting national security-controlled items without a license in violation of the IEEPA. The indictment alleged that the defendants, doing business as MBA, an import/export business located in Hacienda Heights, assisted persons in China to illegally procure export-controlled thermal-imaging cameras. During the period between April 2002 and July 2007, the defendants allegedly exported a total of ten thermal-imaging cameras to China in circumvention of export laws. After being advised of strict export restrictions, Charles Lee allegedly purchased the cameras from US suppliers for approximately $9,500 a piece by withholding the fact that the devices were destined for China. His uncle, Sam Lee, then received the devices and, through his company, arranged for their shipment to Shanghai, China without obtaining proper licenses. One of the recipients is alleged to be an employee of a company in Shanghai engaged in the development of infrared technology. The thermal-imaging cameras are controlled for export to China by the Department of Commerce for national security and regional stability reasons because of their use in a wide variety of military and civilian applications. This investigation was conducted by the EAGLE Task Force in the Central District of California.

- *Military flight simulation technology overseas* – On March 25, 2010 an indictment was unsealed in federal court in the District of Massachusetts charging Hok Shek Chan, Wong Fook Loy, and Ngo Tek Chai with conspiring to and attempting to illegally export munitions without the required licenses. According to the October 2008 indictment, Chan, a Hong Kong citizen, conspired with two Malaysian nationals, Wong Fook Loy and Ngo Tek Chai, and others to cause the export of 10 indicator servo tachometers used in C-130 military flight simulators from the United States without the required license from the State Department. Chan was extradited from Hong Kong to face the charges against him in Boston. The case was investigated by the ICE, BIS, and DCIS.
- *Economic espionage/theft of space shuttle and rocket secrets for China* – On February 11, 2010 former Rockwell and Boeing engineer Dongfan "Greg" Chung was sentenced to 188 months' imprisonment and three years' supervised release following his July 16, 2009 conviction in the Central District of California. Chung was convicted of charges of economic espionage and acting as an illegal agent of the People's Republic of China (PRC), for whom he stole restricted technology and Boeing trade secrets, including information related to the Space Shuttle program and the Delta IV rocket. According to the judge's ruling, Chung served as an illegal agent of China for more than 30 years and kept more than 300,000 pages of documents reflecting Boeing trade secrets stashed in his home as part of his mission to steal aerospace and military trade secrets from Boeing to assist the Chinese government. Chung sent Boeing trade secrets to the PRC via the mail, sea freight, the Chinese consulate in San Francisco, and via a Chinese agent named Chi Mak. On several occasions, Chung also used the trade secrets he misappropriated from Boeing to prepare detailed briefings that he later presented to Chinese officials in the PRC. Chung was originally arrested on February 11, 2008 in Southern California after being indicted on eight counts of economic espionage, one count of conspiracy to commit economic espionage, one count of acting as an unregistered foreign agent, one count of obstruction of justice, and three counts of making false statements to the FBI. The investigation was conducted by the FBI and NASA.
- *Carbon-fiber material with rocket and spacecraft applications to China* – On October 8, 2009, three individuals were sentenced in the District of Minnesota for illegally exporting high-modulus, carbon-fiber material to the China Academy of Space Technology. Jian Wei Ding was sentenced to 46 months in prison. Kok Tong Lim was sentenced to just over one year of confinement because of his cooperation in the case, while Ping Cheng was sentenced to one year's probation due to his cooperation. On March 20, 2009, Ding pleaded guilty to one count of conspiracy to violate the Export Administration Regulations. Cheng entered his plea on February 13, 2009 and Lim entered his plea on March 9, 2009. All three men were indicted on October 28, 2008 for conspiring to illegally export to China controlled

carbon-fiber material with applications in aircraft, rockets, spacecraft, and uranium-enrichment process. The intended destination for some of the materials was the China Academy of Space Technology, which oversees research institutes working on spacecraft systems for the PRC government. For national security, nuclear proliferation, and anti-terrorism reasons, the US government requires a license to export these carbon-fiber materials. Jian Wei Ding was a resident of Singapore and owned or was affiliated with various Singaporean import/export companies, including Jowa Globaltech Pte Ltd, FirmSpace Pte Ltd, and Far Eastron Co. Pte Ltd. Kok Tong Lim was a resident of Singapore and was at one time affiliated with FirmSpace, Pte Ltd. Ping Cheng was a resident of New York and the sole shareholder of Prime Technology Corporation. This investigation was conducted by the ICE and BIS.

- *Restricted integrated circuits with military applications to China* – On August 3, 2009, William Chai-Wai Tsu, an employee of a Beijing-based military contracting company called Dimigit Science & Technology Co. Ltd, and the vice-president of a Hacienda Heights, CA, front company called Cheerway, Inc., was sentenced in the Central District of California to 40 months in prison. Tsu illegally exported more than 400 restricted integrated circuits with applications in military radar systems to China over a 10-month period, according to court documents. These dual-use items are restricted for export for national security reasons. Tsu purchased many of the items from US distributors after falsely telling these US companies that he was not exporting the circuits abroad. According to court documents, Tsu supplied restricted US technology to several customers in China, including the "704 Research Institute," which is known as the "Aerospace Long March Rocket Technology Company" and is affiliated with the state-owned China Aerospace Science & Technology Corporation. Tsu's employer in China, Dimigit, boasted in brochures that its mission was "providing the motherland with safe, reliable and advanced electronic technical support in the revitalization of our national military industry." Tsu was indicted in the Central District of California on February 6, 2009 on charges of violating the International Emergency Economic Powers Act. He later pleaded guilty to two federal counts of the indictment on March 13, 2009. This case was the product of an investigation by the Export and Anti-proliferation Global Law Enforcement (EAGLE) Task Force in the Central District of California, which includes the BIS, ICE, FBI, CBP, Diplomatic Security Service, and the Transportation Security Administration.

- *Restricted thermal imaging technology to China* – On July 27, 2009, Zhi Yong Guo, a resident of Beijing, was sentenced in the Central District of California to 60 months in prison, while Tah Wei Chao, also a resident of Beijing, was sentenced to 20 months in prison. Both were sentenced in connection with a plot to procure and illegally export thermal-imaging cameras to the People's Republic of China without obtaining the required export licenses. Guo and Chao were indicted on federal charges on July 17, 2008. Chao pleaded guilty to three federal counts in July 2008. On February 23, 2009, following a one-week trial, Guo was convicted of two federal counts. The case related to 10 cameras concealed in luggage destined for China in April 2008. The export of these thermal-imaging cameras to China is controlled by the Department of Commerce for national security and regional stability reasons because of their use in a wide variety of civilian and military applications. In March 2008, Chao ordered 10 thermal-imaging cameras from FLIR Systems, Inc. for $53,000. Representatives from FLIR Systems repeatedly warned Chao that the cameras could not be exported without a license. Both Chao and Guo were arrested at Los Angeles International Airport in April 2008 after authorities recovered the 10 cameras that had been hidden in their suitcases. In addition to the 10 cameras intercepted by the federal authorities, Chao admitted that, acting at the behest of Guo, he shipped three cameras to China in October 2007. The evidence at trial showed that Guo, an engineer and a managing director of a technology development company in Beijing, directed Chao to obtain the cameras for Guo's clients, the Chinese Special Police and the Special Armed Police. This case was the product of an investigation by the Export and Anti-proliferation Global Law Enforcement (EAGLE) Task Force in the Central District of California, including the BIS, ICE, FBI, CBP, DSS, and TSA.

- *Military technical data on unmanned aerial vehicles to China* – On July 1, 2009, Dr. John Reece Roth was sentenced in the Eastern District of Tennessee to 48 months in prison, two years supervised release and a $1,700 assessment for illegally exporting sensitive military technical data related to a US Air Force contract. Roth, a former Professor Emeritus at the University of Tennessee, was convicted on September 2, 2008 on 15 counts of violating the Arms Export Control Act, one count of conspiracy, and one count of wire fraud. Roth had illegally exported military technical data relating to plasma technology designed to be deployed on the wings of Unmanned Aerial Vehicles (UAVs) or "drones" operating as weapons or surveillance systems. The illegal exports involved technical data related to an Air Force research contract that Roth provided to foreign nationals from China and Iran. In addition, Roth carried multiple documents containing controlled military data with him on a trip to China and caused other controlled military data to be e-mailed to an individual in China. On August 20, 2008, Atmospheric Glow Technologies, Inc (AGT), a privately held plasma technology company in Tennessee, also pleaded guilty to charges of illegally exporting US military data about drones to a citizen of China in violation of the Arms Export Control Act. AGT was sentenced on February 12, 2010 to a $4,000 assessment and a $25,000 fine. Roth and AGT were first charged on May 20, 2008. In a related case, on April 15, 2008, Daniel Max Sherman, a physicist who formerly worked at AGT, pleaded guilty to information charging him with conspiracy to violate the Arms Export Control Act in connection with this investigation. Sherman was later sentenced to 14 months in prison on August 10, 2009 after cooperating in the investigation. The investigation was conducted by the FBI, ICE, US Air Force Office of Special Investigations, DCIS, and BIS.

- *Military night-vision technology to China* – On July 1, 2009, Bing Xu, of Nanjing, China, was sentenced in the District of New Jersey to 22 months in prison followed by two years of supervised release after pleading guilty on February 24, 2009 to conspiracy to illegally export military-grade night-vision technology to China. Xu, a manager at Everbright Science and Technology, Ltd, a company in Nanjing, China, admitted that he conspired with others at Everbright to purchase certain night-vision technology from a company in the United States, which required a license from the State Department for export. Xu admitted that he and others at Everbright first attempted to obtain the necessary export license for the night-vision equipment. When the license application was denied by the Department of State, Xu agreed with others at Everbright to take steps to export the night-vision optical equipment illegally. Xu has been in custody since his arrest in October 2007 pursuant to a criminal complaint. Xu arrived in New York on October 26, 2007 from China a day after his Chinese employer wire transferred $14,080 to agents as payment for the purchase of the equipment. The investigation was conducted by the ICE and DCIS.
- *Amplifiers and missile target acquisition technology to China* – On May 14, 2009, Joseph Piquet, the owner and President of AlphaTronX, a company in Port St. Lucie, Florida which produces electronic components, was sentenced in the Southern District of Florida to 60 months in prison followed by two years' supervised release. On March 5, 2009 he was convicted of seven counts arising from a conspiracy to purchase military electronic components from Northrop Grumman Corporation, and to ship them to Hong Kong and the People's Republic of China without first obtaining required export licenses under the Arms Export Control Act and the International Emergency Economic Powers Act. Among those items involved in the conspiracy were high-powered amplifiers designed for use by the US military in early warning radar and missile target acquisition systems, as well as low-noise amplifiers that have both commercial and military use. Piquet was first indicted on June 5, 2008, along with his company, AlphaTronX, Inc, as well as Thompson Tam, and Ontime Electronics Technology Limited. Tam is a director of Ontime Electronics, an electronics company in China. On March 2, 2009, the Court ordered the dismissal of the indictment against Alpha-TronX. This investigation was conducted by the BIS and ICE.
- *Trade secrets to China* – On April 10, 2009 Yan Zhu, a Chinese citizen in the US on a work visa, was arrested in the District of New Jersey on charges of theft of trade secrets, conspiracy, wire fraud, and theft of honest services fraud in connection with a plot to steal software from his former US employer and sell a modified version to the Chinese government after he was fired. Zhu was employed as a senior environmental engineer from May 2006 until his termination in July 2008. Zhu worked for a comprehensive multimedia environmental information management portal that developed a proprietary software program for the Chinese market which allows users to manage air

emissions, ambient water quality, and ground water quality. This investigation was conducted by the FBI.

- *Restricted technology to China* – On April 7, 2009, Fu-Tian Lu was arrested in San Francisco pursuant to an April 1, 2009 indictment in the Northern District of California charging him with lying to federal agents and conspiring to illegally export restricted microwave amplifier technology to China. According to the indictment, Lu, and the two companies he founded, Fushine Technology, Inc., of Cupertino, California, and Everjet Science and Technology Corporation, based in China, conspired to export sensitive microwave amplifier technology that was restricted for national security reasons to China without first obtaining a Commerce Department license. On February 17, 2010, a superseding indictment was returned charging Fu-Tian Lu, Fushine Technology, Inc., and Everjet Science and Technology Corporation with conspiracy to violate export regulations and making false statements. This investigation was conducted by the Department of Commerce (BIS), the FBI, ICE, and US Customs and Border Protection.

- *Rocket/space launch technical data to China* – On April 7, 2009, Quansheng Shu, a native of China, naturalized US citizen, and Ph.D. physicist, was sentenced to 51 months in prison for illegally exporting space launch technical data and defense services to the People's Republic of China (PRC) and offering bribes to Chinese government officials. Shu pleaded guilty on November 17, 2008 in the Eastern District of Virginia to a three-count criminal indictment. He was arrested on September 24, 2008. He was President, Secretary, and Treasurer of AMAC International, a high-tech company located in Newport News, VA, and with an office in Beijing, China. Shu provided the PRC with assistance in the design and development of a cryogenic fueling system for space launch vehicles to be used at the heavy payload launch facility located in the southern island province of Hainan, PRC. The Hainan facility will house launch vehicles designed to send space stations and satellites into orbit, as well as provide support for manned space flight and future lunar missions. Shu also illegally exported to the PRC technical data related to the design and manufacture of a Standard 100 M3 Liquid Hydrogen (LH) 2 Tank. In addition, Shu offered approximately $189,300 in bribes to government officials with the PRC's 101 Institute to induce the award of a hydrogen liquefier project to a French company he represented. In January 2007, the $4 million hydrogen liquefier project was awarded to the French company that Shu represented. This investigation was conducted by the FBI, ICE, BIS, and DCIS.

- *Miniature Unmanned Aerial Vehicle components to China* – On March 12, 2009 a federal grand jury in the District of Columbia returned an indictment charging Yaming Nina Qi Hanson, her husband Harold Dewitt Hanson (an employee at Walter Reed Army Medical Center), and a Maryland company, Arc International, LLC, with illegally exporting miniature Unmanned Aerial Vehicle (UAV) autopilots to a company in the People's

Republic of China. The UAV components are controlled for export to China for national security reasons. According to court documents, beginning in 2007, the Hansons began attempting to acquire the autopilots from a Canadian manufacturer in order to re-export them to Xi'an Xiangyu Aviation Technical Group in China. Qi Hanson initially represented that the autopilots would be used for a model airplane civilian flying club in China. When Canadian company officials questioned the utility of autopilots – designed for use on unmanned aircraft – for flying club hobbyists, Qi Hanson claimed that autopilots would be used on US aircraft to record thunderstorm and tornado developments and ice-pack melting rates in the Arctic. On or about August 7, 2008, after having fraudulently taken delivery of 20 of these autopilots (valued at $90,000), Qi Hanson boarded a plane in the United States bound for Shanghai, and hand-delivered the items to Xi'an Xiangyu Aviation Technical Group in China. Both Hansons ultimately pleaded guilty on November 13, 2009 to felony false statement violations. On February 3, 2010 Harold Dewitt Hanson was sentenced to 24 months' imprisonment, while his wife, Yaming Nina Qi Hanson, was sentenced to time served. The investigation was conducted by the BIS and FBI.

- *Restricted electronic components to China* – On January 20, 2009 Michael Ming Zhang and Policarpo Coronado Gamboa were arrested pursuant to indictments in the Central District of California charging them with separate schemes involving the illegal export of controlled US electronic items to China and the illegal trafficking of counterfeit electronic components from China into the United States. Zhang was President of J.J. Electronics, a Rancho Cucamonga, CA business, while Gamboa owned and operated Sereton Technology, Inc., a Foothill Ranch, CA business. Zhang allegedly exported to China dual-use electronic items that have uses in US Army battle tanks. He also allegedly imported and sold in the United States roughly 4,300 Cisco electronic components bearing counterfeit marks from China. Gamboa was charged with conspiring with Zhang to import Sony electronic components with counterfeit marks from China for distribution in the United States. On July 9, 2009 Gamboa pleaded guilty on one count of the indictment and was later sentenced to five years' probation, and was ordered to pay $13,600 restitution to Sony Electronics. On July 6, 2009 Zhang pleaded guilty to count one in each of the indictments. The case was investigated by the FBI, BIS, DCIS, ICE, the US Postal Inspection Service, and the Orange County Sheriff's Department, in conjunction with the EAGLE Task Force in the Central District of California.

- *Trade secrets to China* – On December 9, 2008, in the Northern District of Illinois, Hanjuan Jin was charged in a superseding indictment that added three counts of economic espionage in violation of 18 USC. § 1831. The charges were added to an April 1, 2008 indictment that charged Jin with theft of trade secrets under 18 USC. § 1832. Jin is a former Motorola employee who joined the company in 1998. On February 28, 2007, one day after quitting Motorola, Jin was stopped at O'Hare Airport with over 1,000 Motorola documents in her possession, both in hard copy and electronic format. A review of Motorola computer records showed that Jin accessed a large number of Motorola documents late at night. At the time she was stopped, Jin was traveling on a one-way ticket to China. The section 1831 charges are based on evidence that Jin intended that the trade secrets she stole from Motorola would benefit the Chinese military. Motorola had spent hundreds of millions of dollars on research and development for the proprietary data that Jin allegedly stole. The investigation was conducted by the FBI, with assistance from US Customs and Border Protection.

- *Stolen trade secrets to Chinese nationals* – On November 21, 2008 Fei Ye and Ming Zhong were sentenced in the Northern District of California to one year in prison each, based in part on their cooperation, after pleading guilty on December 14, 2006 to charges of economic espionage for possessing trade secrets stolen from two Silicon Valley technology companies. The pair admitted that their company was to have provided a share of any profits made on sales of the stolen chips to Chinese entities. The case marked the first convictions in the nation for economic espionage. They were first indicted on December 4, 2002. The investigation was conducted by the ICE, FBI, and CBP.

- *Military accelerometers to China* – On September 26, 2008 Qing Li was sentenced in the Southern District of California to 12 months and one day in custody, followed by three years of supervised release, and ordered to pay $7,500 for conspiracy to smuggle military-grade accelerometers from the United States to the People's Republic of China (PRC). Li pleaded guilty on June 9, 2008 to violating Title 18, USC Section 554. She was indicted for the offense on October 18, 2007. According to court papers, Li conspired with an individual in China to locate and procure as many as 30 Endevco 7270A-200K accelerometers for what her co-conspirator described as a "special" scientific agency in China. This accelerometer has military applications in "smart" bombs and missile development, and in calibrating the g-forces of nuclear and chemical explosions. The investigation was conducted by the ICE and DCIS.

- *Military aircraft components to China and Iran* – On August 28, 2008 Desmond Dinesh Frank, a citizen and resident of Malaysia, was sentenced to 23 months in prison after pleading guilty on May 16, 2008 to several felonies in the District of Massachusetts in connection with a plot to illegally export military items to China and Iran. A six-count indictment returned on November 15, 2007 charged Frank, the operator of Asian Sky Support, Sdn., Bhd., in Malaysia, with conspiring to illegally export items to Iran, conspiring to illegally export C-130 military aircraft training equipment to China, illegally exporting defense articles, smuggling, and two counts of money laundering. Frank was arrested in Hawaii on October 8, 2007 by ICE agents. Frank conspired with others to illegally export and cause the re-export of goods, technology, and services to Iran without first obtaining the required authorization from the Treasury Department. He also conspired with others to illegally export 10 indicators, servo-driven tachometers – which are military training components used in C-130 military flight simulators – from the United States to Malaysia and, ultimately, to Hong Kong, China, without the required license from the State Department. This investigation was conducted by the ICE, BIS, and DCIS.

- *US military source code and trade secrets to China* – On June 18, 2008 Xiaodong Sheldon Meng was sentenced in the Northern District of California to 24 months in prison, three years of supervised release, and a $10,000 fine for committing economic espionage and violating the Arms Export Control Act. Meng pleaded guilty in August 2007 to violating the Economic Espionage Act by misappropriating a trade secret used to simulate motion for military training and other purposes, with the intent to benefit China's Navy Research Center in Beijing. He also pleaded guilty to violating the Arms Export Control Act for illegally exporting military source code involving a program used for training military fighter pilots. Meng was the first defendant in the country to be convicted of exporting military source code pursuant to the Arms Export Control Act. He was also the first defendant to be sentenced under the Economic Espionage Act. Meng was charged in a superseding indictment on December 13, 2006. The investigation was conducted by the FBI and ICE.

- *US naval warship data to China* – On March 24, 2008 Chi Mak, a former engineer with a US Navy contractor, was sentenced in the Central District of California to 293 months (more than 24 years) in prison for orchestrating a conspiracy to obtain US naval warship technology and to illegally exporting this material to China. Mak was found guilty at trial in May 2007 of conspiracy, two counts of attempting to violate export control laws, acting as an unregistered agent of the Chinese government, and making false statements. The investigation found that Mak had been given lists from co-conspirators in China that requested US naval research related to nuclear submarines and other information. Mak gathered technical data about the Navy's current and future warship technology and conspired to illegally export these data to China. Mak's four co-defendants (and family members) also pleaded guilty in connection with the case. On April 21, 2008 Chi Mak's brother, Tai Mak, was sentenced to 10 years' imprisonment pursuant to a June 4, 2007 plea agreement in which he pleaded guilty to one count of conspiracy to export defense articles. On October 2, 2008, Chi Mak's wife, Rebecca Chiu, was sentenced to three years in prison for her role in the plot. On October 1, 2008, Fuk Heung Li was sentenced to three years' probation. On September 24, 2007 Yui Mak was sentenced to 11 months' imprisonment. The investigation was conducted by the FBI, NCIS, and ICE.

- *Military amplifiers to China* – On December 19, 2007 Ding Zhengxing, Su Yang, and Peter Zhu were indicted in the Western District of Texas for Arms Export Control Act violations in connection with an alleged plot to purchase and illegally export to China amplifiers that are controlled for military purposes. The amplifiers are used in digital radios and wireless area networks. Ding and Yang were arrested in January 2008 after they traveled to Saipan to take possession of the amplifiers. Peter Zhu, of Shanghai Meuro Electronics Company Ltd in China, remains at large. On July 1, 2009 Ding was sentenced to 46 months' imprisonment. He pleaded guilty on October 17, 2008 to count one of the second superseding indictment. The case was investigated by the ICE.

- *Military night-vision technology to China* – On December 3, 2007 Philip Cheng was sentenced in the Northern District of California to two years in prison and ordered to pay a $50,000 fine for his role in brokering the illegal export of a night-vision camera and its accompanying technology to China in violation of federal laws and regulations. Mr. Cheng pleaded guilty on October 31, 2006 to brokering the illegal export of Panther-series infrared cameras, a device which makes use of "night-vision" technology. He was indicted on June 3, 2004. The technology used in the device was controlled for national security reasons by the United States Department of State. The case was the result of a joint investigation by the ICE, the FBI, the Department of Commerce, and the IRS [Night Vision Technology Corp., a San Jose-based firm that procures infrared technology and other high-tech equipment for overseas buyers, particularly in Taiwan. The company is headed by Martin Shih, 62, a Taiwanese-Canadian executive with wide experience as an electrical engineer, working both in Canada and California with satellite communications company Loral Space & Communications Ltd. Mr. Shih's Taiwanese-American consultant, Philip Cheng, was also charged].

- **Restricted technology to China** – On August 1, 2007 Fung Yang, the President of Excellence Engineering Electronics, Inc., pleaded guilty in the Northern District of California to a charge of illegally exporting controlled microwave integrated circuits to China without the required authorization from the Department of Commerce. Yang was charged by information on July 31, 2007. The investigation was conducted by the BIS and FBI.

Note

1   These case summaries were provided by the FBI. See www.justice.gov/nsd/docs/summary-eaca.pdf.

APPENDIX 2

Protecting against the China Cyber Threat

As difficult as it is to accept, high-tech and other strategic companies now fall into one of two categories: "those that *know they've been compromised* and those that *don't yet know.*"[1] Before a single penny is spent mitigating the damage and risk, however, all personnel from the top to the bottom need to make three key changes in mindset. The first order of business is to admit that they have a cyber-security problem. Denial is *not* just a river in Egypt. The second major shift is philosophical. Companies have to abandon the quaint notion that perimeter cyber defense alone is still effective. In the modern cyber-threat environment it is simply not possible to build a higher wall, dig a deeper moat, or deploy a wider minefield. There are no "magic bullets," either in terms of equipment (firewalls) or software (anti-virus) that will expel the intruders. Instead, companies need to accept that there is very likely advanced persistent threat permanently in their networks, as well as compromised hardware and software. Companies should replace a perimeter defense mindset with a strategy of "active defense" or "defense-in-depth," which focuses on risk mitigation and maintaining operations *despite* APT. The third important shift is financial. The discussion above clearly shows that risk mitigation against cyber threats will not be cheap.

But what are specific "best practices" for companies to follow? Overall, they must adopt a layered approach, combining three rough categories: personnel security, network security, and data security.[2] Personnel security is the most important, because insiders pose the gravest threat to corporate security given their ability to potentially bypass or undermine expensive technical measures.

Personnel security measures should include:

- Mandatory insider security training for the entire staff
- Personnel security and evaluation, including background checks

- Non-disclosure agreements with employees and business partners
- Login "splash pages" and signed employee agreements outlining employee consent to monitoring on corporate machines
- Social networking policies, including rules about use during business hours and guidelines to prevent employee social networking data from being used to refine targeting of corporate networks
- Client machine monitoring software, capturing keystrokes, chat/IM, e-mail, browsing history, and application use
- Foreign travel guidelines for transport of company equipment, including provision of "clean" phones and machines for travel purposes
- Prohibitions and auditing of removable media and thumb drives
- Physical security of network infrastructure, including locks and biometrics
- Separation network administration and security administration roles
- Employee exit procedures.

Network security measures should include:

- Spam and virus firewalls that protect e-mail servers from spam, virus, spoofing, phishing, and spyware attacks
- Advanced intrusion detection/protection systems
- Robust on-site and off-site network archiving and backup for full network restoration after an intrusion
- Multi-factor authentication for servers and clients, such as a combination of biometrics, PINs, and passwords
- A suite of anti-virus programs, since any one program will often fail to recognize the signatures of every malware
- Real-time auditing and monitoring appliances or tools, logging all network activity
- Regular penetration testing by third parties
- Regular testing of backup procedures
- Compartmentation between different domains within the company, restricting access to shared servers in different divisions (especially between headquarters systems and foreign representative offices)
- Network forensics software for analysis of intrusions
- Honeynets to capture intrusion signatures and adversary behavior
- Thin-client systems, permitting control of the application baseline and patching, and sandboxing of proposed additions to the application baseline
- Company-issued mobile phones with additional security layers
- Continuity of operations plans for restoring data and systems.

Data security measures should include:

- Robust public key encryption throughout the network, providing protection for data on servers, whole-disk encryption for client machines, and secure e-mail

- Document management software for classification and metatagging of company proprietary information
- Compartmented access to trade secrets and intellectual property servers.

Despite some or all of these measures, the adversary will likely still get in, but these represent the most robust risk mitigation strategies to deal with an advanced cyber-espionage actor like China.

Notes

1 Dmitri Alperovitch, *Revealed: Operation Shady RAT*, McAfee, August 2011.
2 Some of these suggested measures are taken from the excellent list found in the Office of the National Counterintelligence Executive, *Foreign Spies Stealing US Economic Secrets in Cyberspace: Report to Congress on Foreign Economic Collection and Industrial Espionage, 2009–2011*, October 2011, accessed at: www.dni.gov/reports/20111103_report_fecie.pdf.

BIBLIOGRAPHY

PRC official documents

1956–1967 年科学技术发展远景规划 (*Long-term Plan for the Development of Science and Technology, 1956–1967*). PRC State Science and Technology Commission, December 1956.

1978–1985 年全国科学技术发展规划 (*Regulations on National Science and Technology Development, 1978–1985*). PRC State Science and Technology Commission, 1977.

2006–2010 中长期科技发展规划 (*Medium- and Long-term Plan for S&T Development, 2006–2020*). PRC Ministry of Science and Technology, February 2006.

2006 年国家高新区发展态势 (*Developmental Status of National New and High-tech Zones for 2006*). PRC Ministry of Science and Technology, June 2007.

北京市鼓励留学人员来京创业工作的若干规定 (*Certain Regulations by Beijing Municipality to Encourage Overseas Scholars to Come to Beijing, Found Businesses and Work*). Beijing Department of Personnel, 2000.

关于"十五"期间大力推进科技企业孵化器建设的意见 (*Opinions on Construction of Incubators for Technological Enterprises During the Tenth Five Year Plan*). PRC Ministry of Science and Technology, July 2001.

关于鼓励技术引进和创新，促进转变外贸增长方式的若干意见 (*Various Opinions on Encouraging the Introduction of Technology and Innovation, and Promoting Changes in the Foreign Trade Growth Mode*). PRC Ministry of Science and Technology, July 2006.

关于国家高新技术产业开发区管理体制改革与创新的若干意见 (*Various Opinions on the Reform and Innovation of the Administration System of the National New and High Technology Development Zones*). PRC Ministry of Science and Technology, March 2002.

关于国家高新技术产业开发区十年发展情况的报告 (*Report on the Status of Ten Years of Development of National New and High Technology Development Zones*). PRC Ministry of Science and Technology, March 2002.

关于回国（来华）定居工作专家有关政策 (*Policies Relating to Experts Returning (or Coming) to China to Reside Permanently and Work*). PRC Ministry of Personnel, 2005.

关于加速国家高新技术产业开发区发展的若干意见 (*Various Opinions on Speeding up the Development of National New and High Technology Development Zones*). PRC Ministry of Science and Technology, August 1999.

关于建立海外高层次留学人才回国工作绿色通道的意见 (*Opinions on Building a Green*

Channel for the Return to China of High-level Overseas-educated Talent Abroad). PRC Ministry of Personnel, 2007.

关于进一步加强引进海外优秀留学人才工作的意见 (*Opinions on Further Strengthening Our Work to Bring in Outstanding Overseas-educated Talent Abroad*). PRC Ministry of Personnel, 2007.

关于进一步支持国家高新技术产业开发区发展的决定 (*Decision on Further Supporting the National New and High Technology Development Zones*). PRC Ministry of Science and Technology, January 2002.

关于调整和加强全国科技情报系统文献工作的意见 (*Opinions on Restructuring and Strengthening National S&T Information System Document Work*). PRC State Science and Technology Commission, January 1989.

关于印发国家高新技术产业化及其环境建设(火炬)十一五发展纲要和国家高新技术产业开发区十一五发展规划纲要的通知, (*Notice on Promulgating the Eleventh Five-year Development Program for National New and High Technology Commercialization and Its Infrastructure (Torch) and the Eleventh Five-year Developmental Planning Program for National New and High Technology Development Zones*). PRC Ministry of Science and Technology, April 2007.

关于印发留学人员回国工作"十一五"规划的通知 (*Notice on Printing and Promulgating the Eleventh 5-Year Plan Regulations on Working for the Return of OCS*). PRC Ministry of Personnel, 2006.

关于在留学人才引进工作中界定海外高层次留学人才的指导意见 (*Guiding Opinions for Defining High-level Talent in Our Work to Bring in Overseas-educated Talent*). PRC Ministry of Personnel, 2005.

关于组织开展国家留学人员创业园示范建设试点工作的通知 (*Notice on Trial Work to Organize and Develop the Model Construction of National OCS Pioneering Parks*). PRC Ministry of Science and Technology et al., June 2000.

国防科学技术情报工作条例 (*Regulations on National Defense Science and Technology Information Work*). PRC State Council, July 1984.

国家高新技术产业开发区 "十五" 和2010年发展规划纲要 (*National New and High Technology Development Zones Tenth Five-year and 2010 Developmental Planning Program*). PRC Ministry of Science and Technology, September 2001.

国家高新技术产业开发区高新技术企业认定条件和办法 (*Conditions and Measures for the Designation of High and New Technology Enterprises in National High Technology and New Technology Industry Development Zones*). PRC State Science and Technology Commission, March 1991.

国家科学技术情报发展政策 (*National Science and Technology Information Development Policy*). PRC State Science and Technology Commission, January 1992.

国家自主创新产品认定管理办法 --实行 (*Implementation Plan for the National Indigenous Innovation Products Accreditation Program*). PRC Ministry of Science and Technology et al., November 2009.

教育部关于进一步加强引进海外优秀留学人才工作的若干意见 (*Ministry of Education Views on Further Strengthening the Introduction of Talented Overseas Scholars*). PRC Ministry of Education, March 2007.

"九五"期间人事系统留学人员工作规划 (*Plan for Working with Overseas Scholars in the Personnel System during the Ninth Five-year Plan*). PRC Ministry of Personnel, 1996.

科技企业孵化器(高新技术创业服务中心)认定和管理办法 (*Means for Accrediting and Managing S&T Commercial Incubators (Innovation Service Centers for New and High Technology)*). PRC Ministry of Science and Technology, December 2006.

人事部, 教育部, 科技部,公安部, 财政部关于引发 "关于鼓励海外留学人员以多种形式为国服务" 的若干意见 (*Ministry of Personnel, Ministry of Education, Ministry of Science and Technology, Ministry of Public Security, and Ministry of Finance Notice Regarding*

"Several Suggestions Concerning Encouraging Personnel Studying Overseas to Serve the Country in a Variety of Ways"). PRC Ministry of Personnel et al., May 2001.

中共中央、国务院关于加强技术创新, 发展高科技, 实现产业化的决定 (*Decision of the Chinese Communist Party Central Committee and the State Council on Strengthening Technical Innovation, Developing High Technology and Realizing Industrialization*). CCP Central Committee and PRC State Council, August 1999.

Reports and secondary sources

"Advance Questions for Lieutenant General Keith Alexander USA, Nominee for Commander, United States Cyber Command," published by Senate Armed Services Committee, April 2010.

Alperovitch, Dmitri. *Revealed: Operation Shady RAT*, McAfee, August 2011.

Archibugi, Daniele and Jonathan Michie. "The globalization of technology: a new taxonomy," *Cambridge Journal of Economics* 19, no. 1 (1995): 121–140.

Auerswald, Philip E. and Lewis Branscomb. "Research and Innovation in a Networked World," *Technology in Society* 30 (2008): 339–347.

Bao, Sheng (宝胜). "论经济全球化背景下企业间的策略性技术联盟" ("On strategic technical alliances by corporations against the background of economic globalization"), 科研管理 (*Science Research Management*), 2002.9.

Bartlett, Christopher A. and Sumantra Ghoshal. *Managing Across Borders: The Transnational Solution*, 2nd edn, Boston, MA: Harvard Business School Press, 1998.

Baum, Richard, editor. *China's Four Modernizations: The New Technological Revolution*, Boulder, CO: Westview Press, 1980.

Behrman, Jack N. and William A. Fischer. "Overseas R&D activities of transnational companies," *The International Executive* 22, no. 3 (Fall 1980): 15–17.

Bieler, Stacy. *Patriots or Traitors? A History of American-Educated Chinese Students*, Armonk, NY: M.E. Sharpe, 2004.

Boston Consulting Group (BCG) and Knowledge at Wharton (KW). *China and the New Rules for Global Business*. Report, *Strategy*, May 26, 2004.

Cai, Meide (蔡美德), Du Haidong (杜海东) and Hu Guosheng (胡国胜). "反求工程原理在高职课程体系创新中的应用" ("Using the principle of reverse engineering for innovation in high-level knowledge processes and systems"), 科技管理研究 (*Science and Technology Management Research*), 2005.7.

Cao, Cong, Richard Suttmeier, and Denis Fred Simon. "China's 15-Year Science and Technology Plan," *Physics Today* 59, no. 12 (December 2006): 38–43.

Cartwright, James E. Testimony in Hearing. *China's Military Modernization and Its Impact on the United States and the Asia-Pacific*. US-China Economic and Security Review Commission, 110th Congress, 1st Session, March 29–30, 2007.

Casson, Mark C. "Modelling the Multinational Enterprise: A Research Agenda," *Millennium-Journal of International Studies* 20, no. 2 (1991): pp. 271–285.

Centre for Counterintelligence and Security Studies. *Intelligence Threat Handbook*, 2004.

Chang, Iris. *Thread of the Silkworm*, New York: Basic Books, 1995.

Chase, Michael and James Mulvenon. "The Decommercialization of China's Ministry of State Security," *International Journal of Intelligence and Counterintelligence* 15, no. 4 (November 2002): 481–495.

Chen Jiugeng. "Actual Strength of S&T Information Service System in China," *China Information Review*, no. 10 (2006): 17–22.

Chen, Zeqian (陈则谦) and Bai Xianyang (白献阳). 我国科技信息事业发展的轨迹

("The Locus of Development for China's S&T Information Enterprise"), *Xiandai Qingbao* (现代情报) (December 2007).

Chiao, Joan Y. and Katherine D. Blizinsky. "Culture-gene coevolution of individualism-collectivism and the serotonin transporter gene (5-HTTLPR)," *Proceedings of the Royal Society B: Biological Sciences* 277, no. 1681 (2010): 529–537.

Chu, T.K. "150 years of Chinese Students in America," *Harvard China Review* (Spring 2004): 7–6.

Cooper, Simon. "How China Steals US Military Secrets," *Popular Mechanics*, www.popular-mechanics.com/technology/military/news/3319656, July 10, 2009.

Department of Commerce. "Deemed Export Controls May Not Stop the Transfer of Sensitive Technology to Foreign Nationals in the US," Office of Inspector General Report, No. IPE–16176, March 2004.

Department of Defense. Office of the Secretary of Defense. *Annual Report to Congress: Military and Security Developments Involving the People's Republic of China 2011.*

Department of State. *2010 Human Rights Report*, Country Reports on Human Rights Practices, April 8, 2011.

"Doctorate Recipients from US Universities: Summary Report 2007–08," Washington, DC: National Science Foundation, NSF 10–309, December 2009.

Dunbar, Kevin. "How Scientists Really Reason: Scientific Reasoning in Real-World Laboratories," in *The Nature of Insight*, ed. Robert J. Sternberg and Janet Davidson. Cambridge, MA: MIT Press, 1995.

Eftimiades, Nicholas. *Chinese Intelligence Operations*, Annapolis, MD: Naval Institute Press, 1994.

Endo, Homare. 中国がシリコンバレーとつながるとき (*When China Links Up with Silicon Valley*), Tokyo: Nikkei BP, 2001.

Fairbank, John King. *The United States and China*, 4th edn, Cambridge, MA: Harvard University Press, 1983.

Findlay, C. Scott and Charles J. Lumsden. "The Creative Mind: Toward an Evolutionary Theory of Discovery and Innovation," *Journal of Social and Biological Structures* 11, no. 1 (January 1998): 3–55.

Florida, Richard. "The globalization of R&D: Results of a survey of foreign-affiliated R&D laboratories in the USA," *Research Policy* 26 (1997): 85–103.

Gassmann, Oliver and Max von Zedtwitz. "Organization of industrial R&D on a global scale," *R&D Management* 28, no. 3 (1998): 147–161.

Gassman, Oliver and Zheng Han. "Motivations and Barriers of Foreign R&D Activities in China," *R&D Management* 34, no. 4 (September 2004): 423–437.

General Accounting Office. "Export Controls: Agencies Should Assess Vulnerabilities and Improve Guidance for Protecting Export-Controlled Information at Universities," GAO-07–70, December 2006.

General Accounting Office. "Homeland Security: Performance of Information System to Monitor Foreign Students and Exchange Visitors Has Improved, but Issues Remain," GAO-04–69, June 2004.

Gilboy, George J. "The Myth Behind China's Miracle," *Foreign Affairs* 83, no. 4 (July/August 2004): 33–48.

Gilley, Bruce. "China's Spy Guide: A Chinese Espionage Manual Details the Means by Which Beijing Gathers Technology and Weapons Secrets from the United States," *Far Eastern Economic Review* (December 23, 1999): 14.

Grow, Brian, Keith Epstein and Chi-Chu Tschang. "The New E-spionage Threat," *Business Week* (April 21, 2008): 32–41.

Guan, Jialin (关家麟) and Zhang Chao (张超). 国科技信息事业发展的回顾与展望

("Review and Outlook for Scientific and Technological Information Undertaking of China"), *Qingbao Kexue* (情报科学) 25, no. 1 (January 2007).

Haas, Richard. "The Age of Nonpolarity," *Foreign Affairs* 87, no. 3 (May–June 2008): 44–56.

Hakanson, Lars and Robert Nobel. " Determinants of foreign R&D in Swedish multinationals," *Research Policy* 22, nos 5–6 (November 1993): 397–411.

Hannas, William C. *The Writing on the Wall: How Asian Orthography Curbs Creativity*, Philadelphia: University of Pennsylvania Press, 2003.

Harris, Shane. "China's Cyber Militia," *National Journal* (31 May 2008).

He, Chongling. 青华大学九十年 (*Qinghua University Ninety Years*), Beijing: Tsinghua University Press, 2001.

He, Defang. "As for Indigenous Innovation, Information Should Go Ahead of Rest," *China Information Review*, no. 10 (2006): 12–13.

Hennessey, Beth A. and Teresa M. Amabile. "The conditions of creativity," in *The Nature of Creativity*, ed. Robert J. Sternberg, New York: Cambridge University Press, 1988: 11–38.

Huang, Can, Celeste Amorim Varum, Mark Spinoglio, Borges Gouvela, and Augsto Medina. "Organisation, Programme, and Structure: An Analysis of the Chinese Innovation Policy Framework," *R&D Management* 34, no. 4 (September 2004): 367–387.

Huo, Zhongwen (霍忠文) and Wang Zongxiao (王宗孝). 国防科技情报源及获取技术 (*Sources and Methods of Obtaining National Defense Science and Technology Intelligence*), Beijing: Kexue Jishu Wenxuan Publishing Company, 1991.

Information Warfare Monitor. *Tracking GhostNet: Investigating a Cyber Espionage Network*, Toronto: SecDev and Citizen Lab, March 29, 2009.

Information Warfare Monitor and Shadowserver. *Shadows in the Cloud: Investigating Cyber Espionage 2.0*, Toronto: SecDec and Citizen Lab, April 6, 2010.

"International S&T cooperation and the sharing of intellectual property." *Keji Ribao*, May 13, 1996.

Jackson, James K. "The Committee on Foreign Investment in the United States," CRS Report RL33388, Congressional Research Service, Washington, DC, July 29, 2010.

Jin, Jianmin. "Foreign Companies Accelerating R&D Activity in China," Fujitsu Research Institute, May 13, 2010, http://jp.fujitsu.com/group/fri/en/column/message/2010/2010-05-13.html.

Johnson, Jean M. and Mark C. Rogers. "International Mobility of Scientists and Engineers to the United States – Brain Drain or Brain Circulation?," *National Science Foundation Issue Brief*, November 10, 1998 (revised).

Keizer, Gregg. "Chinese Hackers Called Sloppy but Persistent," *Computerworld* (February 12, 2011).

Kingstone, Brett. *The Real War Against America*, Specialty Publishing/Max King, LLC, 2005.

Krekel, Bryan. *Capability of the People's Republic of China to Conduct Cyber Warfare and Computer Network Exploitation*, US-China Economic and Security Review Commission (October 9, 2009).

Kuang, Ping and Ian Marshall. "Internationalisation of Chinese Higher Education: Application of Knowledge Management to Analysis of Tsinghua University," *Journal of Knowledge Management Practice* 11, no. 1 (2010).

LaFargue, Thomas E. *China's First Hundred: Education Mission Students in the United States, 1872–1881*, Pullman, WA: Washington State University Press, 1987.

Lampton, David M. *A Relationship Restored: Trends in US–China Educational Exchanges, 1978–1984*, Washington, DC: National Academies Press, 1986.

Lee, Wen Ho, with Helen Zia. *My Country Versus Me: The First-Hand Account by the Los Alamos Scientist Who Was Falsely Accused of Being a Spy*, New York: Hyperion, 2001.

Leung, Edwin Pak-Wah. "China's Decision to Send Students West: The Making of a 'Revolutionary' Policy," *Asian Profile* 16 (1988): 391–400.

Lewis, John and Litai Xue. *China Builds the Bomb*, Palo Alto, CA: Stanford University Press, 1991.

Lian, Yanhua (连燕华). "科学研究全球化发展评价" ("An Assessment of the Growth of Scientific Research Globalization"), 科研管理 (*Science Research Management*), July 2000: 1–14.

Liansheng, Meng and Yan Quan Liu. "The present and future of China's National Science and Technology Library: A new paradigm of sci-tech information resource sharing," *New Library World* 106, nos 7/8 (2005): 343–351.

Lieberthal, Kenneth. "China's Governing System and its Impact on Environmental Policy Implementation," *Wilson Center China Environment Series* 1, 1997.

Lieberthal, Kenneth. *Governing China: From Revolution to Reform*, 2nd edn, New York: W.W. Norton, 2003.

Liu, Xielin and Nannan Lundin. "The National Innovation System of China in Transition: From Plan-Based to Market-Driven System," in *The New Asian Innovation Dynamics*, ed. Govindan Parayil and Anthony P. D'Costa, New York: Palgrave Macmillan, 2009.

Liu, Yun (刘云) and Shen Lin (沈林). "海外人才资源开发利用的现状及发展对策" ("The Current Situation and Countermoves on Development and Utilization of Overseas Chinese Experts' Intellectual Resources"), 科研管理 (*Science Research Management*) vol. 22.4 (July 2001): 115–125.

Logan, Robert K. *The Alphabet Effect*, New York: Morrow, 1986.

Lundin, Nannan and Sylvia Schwaag Serger. "Globalization of R&D and China: Empirical Observations and Policy Implications," IFN Working Paper, No. 710, Stockholm: Research Institute of Industrial Economics, 2007.

McAfee Foundstone Professional Services and McAfee Labs. *Global Energy Cyberattacks: Night Dragon*, February 10, 2011.

McGregor, James. "China's Drive for 'Indigenous Innovation': A Web of Industrial Policies," Washington, DC: US Chamber of Commerce (July 2010).

McMurtie, Beth. "No Welcome Mat for the Chinese? US Visas Seem Harder to Get," *Chronicle of Higher Education* 46, no. 5 (September 24, 1999): 59–61.

Mahhuhani, Kishore. "The Case against the West," *Foreign Affairs* 87, no. 3 (May–June 2008): 111–124.

Mao Zedong. "On the People's Democratic Dictatorship," 30 June 1949, *Mao Zedong Xuanji* (Selected Works of Mao Zedong), Beijing: The People's Press, 1965.

Mattis, Peter. "Beyond Spy vs. Spy: The Analytic Challenge of Understanding Chinese Intelligence Services," *Studies in Intelligence* 56, no. 3 (September 2012).

Mattis, Peter. "Chinese Intelligence Operations Revisited: Toward a New Baseline," MA Thesis, Georgetown University, 2011.

Medcof, J.W. "A Taxonomy of Internationally Dispersed Technology Units and Its Application to Management Issues," *R&D Management* 27, no. 4 (1997): 301–318.

Meng, Xin and R.G. Gregory. "The Impact of Interrupted Education on Subsequent Educational Attainment: A Cost of the Chinese Cultural Revolution," *Economic Development and Cultural Change* 50, no. 4 (July 2002): 935–959.

Moore, Paul. "Chinese Culture and the Practice of 'Actuarial' Intelligence," in *A Law Enforcement Sourcebook of Asian Crime and Cultures: Tactics and Mindsets*, ed. Douglas D. Daye, Boca Raton, FL: CRC Press, 1997: 377–382.

Mulvenon, James. *Chinese Military Commerce and US National Security*, Santa Monica, CA: RAND, 1997, MR-907.0-CAPP.

Mulvenon, James. *Soldiers of Fortune: The Rise and Fall of the Chinese Military-Business Complex, 1978–98*, Armonk, NY: M.E. Sharpe, 2001.

Mulvenon, James. Testimony before the Select Committee on US National Security and Military/Commercial Concerns with the People's Republic of China, October 18, 1998.

Murray, Charles. *Human Accomplishment: The Pursuit of Excellence in the Arts and Sciences, 800 B.C. to 1950*, New York: Harper, 2003.

Nagaraja, Shishir and Ross Anderson. "The Snooping Dragon: Social-Malware Surveillance of the Tibetan Movement," University of Cambridge Computer Laboratory Technical Report 746, UCAM-CL-TR-746, March 2009.

Nakamura, Hajime. *Ways of Thinking of Eastern Peoples: India, China, Tibet, Japan*, Honolulu: University of Hawaii Press, 1964.

Narula, Rajneesh and Antonello Zanfei. "Globalization of Innovation: The Role of Multinational Enterprises," in *The Oxford Handbook of Innovation*, ed. Jan Fagerberg, David C. Mowery, and Richard R. Nelson, New York: Oxford University Press, 2005: 18.

National Bureau of Statistics. *China Statistical Yearbook 2002*, Beijing: China Statistics Press, 2002.

National Center for Education Statistics. US Department of Education. "Degrees Earned by Foreign Graduate Students: Fields of Study and Plans After Graduation," November 1997.

National Science Foundation, Division of Science Resource Studies. *Statistical Profiles of Foreign Doctoral Recipients in Science and Engineering: Plans to Stay in the United States*, November 1998, NSF 99–304.

Needham, Joseph. *Science and Civilisation in China: History of Scientific Thought*, New York: Cambridge University Press, 1956.

Needham, Joseph. *The Grand Titration: Science and Society in East and West*, London: George Allen & Unwin, 1969.

Nisbett, Richard E. *The Geography of Thought: How Asians and Westerners Think Differently . . . and Why*, New York: The Free Press, 2003.

Nisbett, Richard E., Kaiping Peng, Incheol Choi, and Ara Norenzayan. "Culture and Systems of Thought: Holistic Versus Analytic Cognition," *Psychological Review* 108, no. 2 (April 2001): 291–310.

Nobel, Robert and Julian Birkinshaw. "Patterns of control and communication in international research and development units," *Strategic Management Journal* 19, no. 5 (1998): 479–498.

North, David S. "Some Thoughts on Nonimmigrant Student and Worker Programs," in *Temporary Migrants in the United States*, ed. B. Lindsay Lowell, US Commission on Immigration Reform, 1996.

Office of the National Counterintelligence Executive. *Foreign Spies Stealing US Economic Secrets in Cyberspace: Report to Congress on Foreign Economic Collection and Industrial Espionage, 2009–2011*, October 2011.

Organisation for Economic Co-operation and Development. *Frascati Manual 2002*, OECD Publishing, 2002.

Orleans, Leo A., ed. *Science in Contemporary China*, Palo Alto, CA: Stanford University Press, 1980.

Osnos, Evan. "Green Giant: Beijing's Crash Program for Clean Energy," *The New Yorker*, December 21, 2009.

Pearce, Robert. "Decentralised R&D and strategic competitiveness: globalized approaches to generation and use of technology in multinational entreprises," *Research Policy* 28, nos 2–3 (March 1999): 157–178.

Pearce, Robert. "The Internationalisation of Research and Development by Multinational Enterprises and the Transfer Sciences," *Empirica* 21, no. 3 (1994): 297–311.

Peng, Can (彭灿). "基于国际战略联盟的模仿创新" ("Imitative innovation based on international strategic alliances"), 科研管理 (*Science Research Management*), 2005.2: 23–27.

Peng, Yixin (彭宜新), Wu Xinwen (吴新文) and Zou Shangang (邹珊刚). "国际技术保护主义与我国高技术产业发展" ("International technology protectionism and the development of China's high-tech industry"), 科技进步与对策 (*Science and Technology Progress and Policy*), 2001.8: 59.

Pillsbury, Michael. "China's Progress in Technological Competitiveness: The Need for a New Assessment," Report prepared for the US-China Economic and Security Review Commission, April 21, 2005.

Qian, Ning (钱宁). 留学美国 (*Studying in America*), Nanjing: Jiangsu Wenyi Chubanshe, 1996.

Qian, Wen-yuan. *The Great Inertia: Scientific Stagnation in Traditional China*, London: Croom Helm, 1985.

Quan, Xiaohong. "MNCs Rush to Set Up R&D Labs in China: What is the Nature?," National University of Singapore East Asia Institute, EAI Background Brief, no. 332 (2007).

Quan, Xiaohong. "MNC R&D Labs in China," Stanford Projects on Regions of Innovation and Entrepreneurship, Presentation, November 29, 2005.

Quan, Xiaohong. *Multinational Research and Development Labs in China: Local and Global Innovation*, unpublished Ph.D. Dissertation, University of California, Berkeley, 2005.

Reddy, Prasada. *Globalization of Corporate R&D: Implications for Innovation in Host Countries*, New York: Routledge, 2000.

Report of the Select Committee on US National Security and Military/Commercial Concerns with the People's Republic Of China. Volume 1, Washington, DC: Government Printing Office, 1999.

"Report to Congress on Chinese Espionage Activities against the United States by the Director of Central Intelligence and the Director of the Federal Bureau of Investigation," December 12, 1999.

Ridley, Charles P. *China's Scientific Policies: Implications for International Cooperation*, Washington, DC: American Enterprise Institute, 1976.

Saxenian, AnnaLee. *Local and Global Networks of Immigrant Professionals in Silicon Valley*, San Francisco: Public Policy Institute of California, April 2002.

Serger, Sylvia Schwaag. "Research and Innovation as a Forward-Looking Policy Response to the Crisis? The Case of Asia," Presentation, June 26, 2009.

Serger, Sylvia Schwaag and Eric Widman. *Competition from China: Opportunities and Challenges for Sweden*, Stockholm: Swedish Institute for Growth Policy Studies, 2005.

Simonton, Dean Keith. "Creativity, leadership, and chance," in *The Nature of Creativity*, ed. Robert J. Sternberg, New York: Cambridge University Press, 1988: 386–428.

Sivin, Nathan. "Science in China's Past," in *Science in Contemporary China*, ed. Leo A. Orleans, Palo Alto, CA: Stanford University Press, 1980.

Spence, Jonathan D. *The Search for Modern China*, New York: Norton, 1999.

Stober, Dan and Ian Hoffman. *A Convenient Spy: Wen Ho Lee and the Politics of Nuclear Espionage*, New York: Simon & Schuster, 2002.

Sun, Lijun (孙理军) and Huang Huaye (黄花叶). "美日技术转移实践及其对我国技术转移中心的启示" ("US and Japanese Technology Transfer Practices and What We Can Learn for Our Country's Technology Transfer Centers"), 科技管理研究 (*Keji Guanli Yanjiu*), 2003.1: 70–72.

Sun, Yifei and Ke Wen. "Country Relational Distance, Organizational Power, and R&D Managers: Understanding Environmental Challenges for Foreign R&D in China," in *Global R&D in China*, ed. Yifei Sun, Maximilian von Zedtwitz, and Denis Fred Simon, London: Routledge, 2009.

Suttmeier, Richard P. "New Directions in Chinese Science and Technology," in *China Briefing*, ed. John Major, Boulder, CO: Westview Press, 1986: 91–102.

Suttmeier, Richard P. *Research and Revolution: Science Policy and Societal Change in China*, Lanham, MD: Lexington Books, 1974.

Thornburgh, Nathan. "The Invasion of the Chinese Cyberspies (and the Man Who Tried to Stop Them," *Time* (August 29, 2005).

Thorpe, Evan. "Bringing R&D to China," *The China Business Review* 35, no. 2 (March/April 2008): 18–20.

Trulock, Notra. *Code Name Kindred Spirit: Inside the Chinese Nuclear Espionage Scandal*, San Francisco: Encounter Books, 2003.

US-China Economic and Security Review Commission. *2009 Report to Congress*, November 2009.

von Zedtwitz, Maximilian. "Managing Foreign R&D Labs in China," *R&D Management* 34, no. 4 (2004): 439–452.

von Zedtwitz, Maximilian. "Managing Foreign R&D in China: Some Lessons," Presentation at the "Asian Rise in ICT R&D Conference," Brussels, February 17, 2011.

Walfish, Daniel. "Chinese Applicants to US Universities Often Resort to Shortcuts or Dishonesty," *The Chronicle of Higher Education*, January 5, 2001.

Walsh, Kathleen. "China R&D: A High-Tech Field of Dreams," in *Global R&D in China*, ed. Yifei Sun, Max von Zedtwitz, and Denis Simon, London: Routledge, 2009.

Wang, Huiyao, David Zweig, and Xiaohua Lin. "Returnee Entrepreneurs: impact on China's globalization process," *Journal of Contemporary China* 20, no. 40 (May 2011): 413–431.

Wang, Jianhua. "On the Relation between Japan and Modernization of Military Education in Late Qing Dynasty," China National Knowledge Infrastructure: SUN: AFSX.0.2004-05-009.

Wang, Xiaochu. "Retrospect of Revelation of the 110-year History of Chinese Returned Students in Japan," China National Knowledge Infrastructure: SUN: XZSB.0.2006-04-000.

Wei, Yu (韦钰). 出国留学工作二十年--纪念邓小平同志关于扩大派遣留学人员讲话二十周年 ("20 Years of Study Abroad Work: Commemorating the 20th Anniversary of Comrade Deng Xiaoping's Speech on the Expansion of Sending Personnel to Study Abroad"), *China Education Daily*, June 23, 1998: 3.

Wise, David. *Tiger Trap: America's Secret Spy War with China*, Boston, MA: Houghton Mifflin Harcourt, 2011.

Wong, Bernard P. *The Chinese in Silicon Valley: Globalization, Social Networks, and Ethnic Identity*, Lanham, MD: Rowman and Littlefield, 2005.

Xia, Chengyu (夏承禹). "科技情报部门领导在新形势下的新角色" ("A New Role for Leaders of S&T Information Departments under the New Circumstances"), 科技进步与对策 (*Science and Technology Progress and Policy*), 2001.1: 104–105.

Xin, Hao and Dennis Normile. "Gunning for the Ivy League," *Science* 319, no. 5860, January 11, 2008.

Yang Dongming and Ji Changhe. "Talking About the Students Studying in Japan and China's Modernization," China National Knowledge Infrastructure: ISSN:1006-1975.0.2005-01-016.

Yao, Linqing, "The Chinese overseas students: An overview of the flows change,"

Australian Population Society Biennial Conference, September 2004, www.apa.org. au/upload/2004-6C_Yao.pdf.

Zakaria, Fareed. *The Post-American World*, New York: W.W. Norton, 2008.

Zander, Ivo. "How do you mean 'global'? An empirical investigation of innovation networks in the multinational corporation," *Research Policy* 28, nos 2–3 (March 1999): 195–213.

Zeng, Zhaozhi (曾昭智), Niu Zhengming (牛争鸣), and Zhang Lin (张林). "利用专利文献促进科技创新" ("Using patent resources to promote scientific and technological innovation"), 技术与创新管理 (*Technology and Innovation Management*), 2004.6: 46–48.

Zhang, Wenxian, Huiyao Wang, and Ilan Alon, eds. *Entrepreneurial and Business Elites of China: The Chinese Returnees Who Have Shaped Modern China*, Bingley, UK: Emerald Group Publishing, 2011.

Zhang, Ying (张莹) and Chen Guohong (陈国宏). "跨国公司在中国的技术转移问题及对策分析" ("Analysis of the problem of technology transfer of multinational corporations in China and measures for dealing with it"), 科技进步与对策 (*Science and Technology Progress and Policy*), 2001.3: 134.

Zhou, Wei (周偉). "我国企业对外直接投资战略分析" ("Analysis of China's strategy for corporate foreign direct investment"), 科技进步与对策 (*Science and Technology Progress and Policy*), 2004.11: 56.

Zhou, Zhu (周竺) and Huang Ruihua (黄瑞华). "知识产权保护的全球化，中国面临的挑战及对策" ("The globalization of IPR protection: challenges facing China and their countermeasures"), 科技管理研究 (*Science and Technology Management Research*), 2004.3: 67.

Zweig, David, Chung Siu Fung, and Donglin Han. "Redefining the Brain Drain: China's 'Diaspora Option'," *Science, Technology & Society* 13, no. 1 (2008): 1–33.

Zweig, David and Chen Changgui. *China's Brain Drain to the United States: Views of Overseas Chinese Students and Scholars in the 1990s*, Berkeley: University of California, 1995.

INDEX

Italic page numbers indicate Tables: with **emboldened numbers** for text boxes; notes are denoted by suffix "n". Abbreviations: OCS = overseas Chinese scholars; S&T = Science and Technology

Lightning Source UK Ltd.
Milton Keynes UK
UKHW01f0058031018
329858UK00006B/93/P